Identification and Character

SUNY Series, Alternatives in Psychology
Michael A. Wallach, editor

Identification and Character

A Book on Psychological Development

Howard Kamler

State University of New York Press

Published by
State University of New York Press, Albany

© 1994 State University of New York

For information, address the State University of New York Press,
State University Plaza, Albany, NY 12246

Library of Congress Cataloging-in-Publication Data

Kamler, Howard.
    Identification and character : a book on psychological development
/ Howard Kamler.
        p.   cm. — (SUNY series, alternatives in psychology)
    Includes bibliographical references.
    ISBN 0-7914-2211-9 (alk. paper). — ISBN 0-7914-2212-7 (pbk. :
alk. paper)
    1. Identification (Psychology) 2. Identity (Psychology)
3. Personality development. 4. Personality change. 5. Character.
6. Self-perception. I. Title. II. Series.
BF175.5.I43K36 1994
155.2—dc20   93-48109
                                                                   CIP

10 9 8 7 6 5 4 3 2 1

To Terence and Rosella, guardians of quality

CONTENTS

ACKNOWLEDGMENTS

This book is the product of many years of interest in the concept of psychological identification. I am convinced that this is the single most important concept for understanding the difference between people as brute animals and people as full-fledged character personalities. The process of identification is central to what makes us come alive as creatures who value the world and find meaning in individual and social activity. A comprehensive understanding of this process requires both a careful analysis of its component elements as they unfold in the psychological development of the individual and a full appreciation of the social impact the process has as it works its way into the life of the culture. The present work is a contribution to the first of these requirements; it is a psychological theory about the role that identification plays in the development of individual character.

I am grateful to the many people with whom I have exchanged ideas about these matters over the years. I would like to give special thanks to Steve Bacckus, Fred Busch, Michael Carlsen-Jones, John Economos, Sharon Feldman, Harry Frankfurt, Sid Gendin, Norman Gordon, Kate Mehuron, Bill Miller, and Al Tucker. I have learned a lot from each of these people and I have appreciated the patience each has shown in helping me talk through many of my confusions. In addition, in arguing and trading insights with them, I am certain that some of their views sometimes became mine—ideas of theirs that I originally might have doubted eventually became ideas of which I took ownership. No doubt there are places in the text where I fail to acknowledge this fact. For that I can only apologize and reiterate my heartfelt thanks for the benefit of my association with these people.

I would also like to thank Nancy Snyder, Kathy Ward, Jill Ferrington, and Sherry Beck for their help with the physical production and proofing of the manuscript.

Finally, I would like to express my gratitude to the people at the State University of New York Press—specifically, to Carola Sautter and her staff, for helpfully ushering me through the publication process, and to Michael Wallach, for his belief in this project and his overall help in bringing it to the light of day.

CHAPTER 1

Introduction: Becoming Someone We Like

Two things seem to matter most in life: finding love and becoming someone we like. Knowing what to say about love has always stumped me, but I do have some thoughts about our becoming someone we like. And that is what I will talk about in this book.

We all have complex images of the kind of person we would like to be, of the ideal kind of character traits we would like to have. Moral prescriptions help us construct parts of that picture. They tell us what we need to do in order to be good people aimed at right action. But alas, there is much more to being someone we like than our just trying to be moral. Indeed, morality aside, some people would also very much like to be charming, perhaps aggressive, maybe even coy, powerful, and humorous. On and on the choices go, and everybody makes them. The fact of the matter is, we all have our own complex character trait images we carry around with us. And they usually take us well beyond the range of mere moral concern. We all line up behind our images in the earnest belief that if we can make them come alive in who we really are with one another, then we truly will be someone we like.

Clearly, though, imagining a character of ideal traits is one thing; actually becoming it is quite another. Life would be eminently wonderful if, with a mere wave of the hand, we could become the ideal likable person we paint in our mind. But there are so many problems. For one thing, we often enough aren't even right about who we think we want to be. From infancy, through childhood, and well into adulthood, many of us go around claiming to be ways that in fact we are not. Self-deception, ambivalence, unconscious interference, and other obstacles make us get it wrong. More times than it is comfortable to admit, we claim to stand for things that in fact we don't; we claim to have a certain kind of character that in fact we don't. Sometimes we are just a little off the mark, sometimes quite a bit. In that regard, life is all about our trying to keep the gap as narrow as possible. It is about getting it right so that we can genuinely own the character we say is us. But while figuring out who we want to be is certainly no picnic, that's not the half of it. Knowing our minds is comparatively easy next to actually doing something about it. Even if we were perfectly clear about what kind of character would make us happy with ourselves, we would still then have to do what it takes to develop ourselves as our ideal character. The truth is that we all have to expend great amounts of effort to ever even come close to matching our images with who we actually become. And as though that weren't difficult enough, then we have to fight the battles of everyday life that would otherwise erode any of our gotten gains in who we've become. And as though *that* weren't difficult enough, when any of us actually want to change parts of who we've become, we have nothing but a struggle ahead of us. Developing as someone we like just is a difficult proposition.

What I propose to do in this book is look at these issues of developing ourselves. They can be cast in terms of three fundamental questions: What do we have to do to make ourselves selves (we like)? What do we have to do to continue being selves (we like) once we have become them? What do we have to do to change them when we find we prefer some better versions? No small moment, these questions. I shall concern myself in this book with the first two and save the vast terrain of the third for another time.[1] I am going to immerse us in an analysis of what I take to be the central concept in understanding everything about becoming and staying a character self. That would be the concept of *psychological identification*. I will be arguing that to the extent that we actually become who we are as characters, we genuinely *identify with* what would otherwise just be our images of how we want to live our lives. In remaining who we would be, we *maintain* our *identifications*. I know that on the face of things there is nothing that sounds extraordinarily revealing in these claims. They seem to be so commonsensical. I am hoping, though, that I can convince the reader that there is more than just common sense here that we can glean from a careful analysis of psychological identification. In talking about this concept, I am going to provide the conceptual framework for understanding various developmental claims about becoming and remaining selves that are made not only in everyday folk psychology but also in psychoanalytic theory. I am going to peel the conceptual onion, as it were, so that psychological identification and its variants are laid bare and assume their proper place in discussions of self development.

My strategy for this first chapter is twofold: It is to introduce the reader to the literature in philosophy and psychoanalysis that my discussion is a part of and then to sketch the thesis about identification for which I will be arguing. Before I begin with any of this, however, I want to do what I can in the first section to make us feel totally at home with the choice I've made to connect talk about identification with talk about self development. I want to get us comfortable with the conceptual melding of the ideas of psychological identification and becoming and staying (that is, being) selves. To do this, I want to share with you some descriptions of a few pictures from my life that I think capture the essence of the essential connections. I would like you to see the kinds of mental representations that take hold of me when I think about identification and developing as a self. What this slice of pictorial autobiography will amount to is a set of narrative paradigms for me about certain universal truths which pertain to my life as an identifying self who becomes and persists. But while my personal picturebook does this job for me, everyone, in fact, carries around their own personally distinct autobiographical album that does the same job. We all have memories of events that are our paradigms of identifying and being a self. Be that as it may, I am still going to favor my own mental pictures here and use them as a dramatic device for getting the ball rolling. I am certain that you will trot out your own appropriate pictures as I show you mine.

I

#1: Here is one of me as a small boy. Dirty smiling face, jeans with grass stains on the knees, baseball glove on the left hand, bat leaning on the right shoulder. Those were the days. I identified with Duke Snider then, center fielder for the Brooklyn Dodgers. He was my hero. Power at the plate, grace in the field—the smooth uppercut swing to send a ball into orbit, the relentless climbing of the fences to snare the impossible fly. These were his forte. These and the omnipotence they represented for me were what I wanted for myself. I practiced his swing; I tried my hand at dramatic fence climbing; I walked around submerged in my share of childhood omnipotence fantasies. All of this activity was about my wanting to become a certain kind of person. Although I understood that no one actually could be just like the Duke, I wanted to come close and give it my own twist. Even at that tender age, I was concerned with making myself special, with creating my own niche. I didn't know it at the time, but this was just part of a much wider life project I had of carving out a self with a full set of traits I wanted. My identification with figures like this baseball hero (and my father, my second grade teacher, and any of a number of others) played a crucial role in the whole business.

There was more than just "hero worship with the aim of building a self" on this hidden agenda, however. For one thing, it is clear that there was something of a self already there to build on. I had already been identifying with being popular, smart, attractive, and aggressive. How's that for a litany of typical childhood arrogancia? Naturally, I wasn't perfectly successful in my project, but I gave it a try because that was my image of who I was to be. And there were still other parts to me, parts I didn't identify with. People have told me, for example, that I was also temperamentally shy and inquisitive. I was honest and doggedly loyal as a friend, and I was a difficult person with my sisters, even though I wasn't aware of these things. And, yes, I was unforgivingly selfish. I am told (thank God for parents and their memories) that I was also energetic, pensive, clever, argumentative, overly sensitive, proud, and bullying. Whether I identified with being these ways or not, they were part of who I was. Clearly I had a complex self long before Duke Snider came on the scene.

There was plenty more identifying to be done after my Duke Snider days. As an adolescent, I would come to identify with my high school, to the point of fighting for its good name. I would come to identify with Robert Redford and the adolescent model of masculine perfection he seemed to embody. But there were other things too, things of more gravity. At a certain point in my adolescence, I began self-consciously wanting to be a person of substance, a person of some moment. I wanted more meaning to my life. While I recognized what had come before as being important qualities of my self—even somewhat meaningful—I now had reached a point where I would engage in such matters with more reflective earnest. And it continues for me now; I continue to develop.

#2: Here is a picture of my wife. See how she has many of what today would be considered politically incorrect identifications. For example, she idolized the glamorous Marilyn Monroe and made herself up in that image. At the same time, she longed for the day when she could begin to rule her own domestic roost in the same homemaker way she was practicing on her dolls. She felt connected with a life of feminine wiles; she thought a girl did best by pursuing her desires through charm. The closer she could come to all these images, the more special she believed she would be.

Of course, she, too, was building all of this onto a self that had long been underway. She, too, had already been identifying with being popular, smart, attractive, and aggressive, realizing these ideals in varying degrees. And she had many more personality traits—things like temperament, emotional tendencies, and so forth—some of which she identified with and some not. And as an adolescent, she, like me, also began in greater earnest carving out a self of more serious substance.

Neither of us was unusual in having this concern for substance. Most evolving adults like to think of themselves as people of serious substance. At least we like to think that we are aimed in that direction. We identify with being solid. For most of us, this means every day making ourselves responsible members of society—identifying with pursuing a career, choosing a mate, rearing a family, developing strong friendships, pursuing our leisure time with gusto, and so on. That is all very meaningful. But then there are also the more abstract "deep" identifications, such as fine-tuning and standing up for our moral commitments or our intellectual pursuits; such as defending our concepts of democracy, egalitarianism, freedom; such as immersing ourselves in our image of being a rebel, perhaps even being an outlaw. Adult identification is the life project of standing for these sorts of things, of solidly driving them home in our personalities. In short, it is to build our character. Building character—that is what all of this activity from early childhood on is all about. As children, we certainly want to be special selves. We flail about in our primitive attempts to get things started. But most of what we do there is just pre-character-building activity. It is just the prelude to the full symphony to come, that being the ultimate adult project of building a "character self." Through identifying with people, things, ideas, institutions, and more, we evolve our slate of images of what a perfect self would be like; and we spend a lifetime reworking the slate, all the while trying to faithfully live out its likeness.

#3: Those two pictures are interesting. But when all is said and done they are just still shots of character-growth activity, an abstract sketch of the general plan about *becoming* a self. Here, though, is an action shot that captures relatively fully formed selves *being* themselves. It is of me as a young man with my fiancee. We are dancing, laughing, and talking with abandon, gazing deeply into one another's eyes. I wonder what we were saying. I wonder what each of us was thinking when the picture was ‑snapped. Although I can't really remember, something else is very clear from just a glance here. This is a photo of two *established* selves. My fiancee and I have a confidence about our actions that selves mostly in process—that is, people first *becoming* selves—don't have. In this picture, we are not tentative with one another. We are characters connecting. In being characters with one another—and not merely human animals causally interacting according to various biological and psychological laws—each of us conveys an air of autonomy, as though each of us has chosen to make this contact and could move away from it if that seemed desirable. Each of us is autonomously pleading a case for how we want life to go. And from the looks of this picture, enjoying ourselves as sexual beings was probably what we both had in mind.

Allow me some poetic license in developing this idea. A person's character is more believable as something essential to who he is when, as in this picture, that person moves about with others in ways that express intention. There is more of a life breathed into the self when we move our bodies through the world on the waves of intention and when we capture one another's concern with our eyes, our touch, our words, our power. We constantly fill each other with our expressions of who we are, of how from one moment to the next we choose to "do" our lives, of the kind of soul we want to take responsibility for in the world of human affairs. We constantly fill one another with expressions of how a given something in life is important to us, expressions of the slant on things we feel life deserves just then. All this expression further legitimizes and consequently more firmly secures the self we have been fashioning. Switching metaphors, we can say we show ourselves to the world as established beacons sending out steady beams of character. We are constantly pulsating with our particular kind of light, unrelentingly filling every pair of eyes in our path with the light of who we are (whether that light is received accurately or not).

In all that we do in the world of character selves, we can't help but be spinners of yarns, tellers of tales, purveyors of meaning, constantly providing the world with the character fodder about which it measures our substance and affirms us as solid identities. So we wash the dishes, take care of our children, and write books, all these activities showing everyone around us what we think the living of life is about. All this intentional action bespeaks the self that is already in place. In being in the world with others, we present one another with solid tablets of meaning—*tabula plena*, as it were. We push against one another with these tablets and know that we are really in the world with other selves who are distinct from us. In part, for example, I know my own calm ways by bouncing off my friend's jangly nerves. I can't avoid his meaning either. Indeed, however meaningless our own self might on occasion feel to us, we can't help but feel the motion of busy meaning swirling about us, sometimes softly touching us, sometimes rolling through us, sometimes becoming an occupying force. There is some, albeit a typically dim, part of consciousness where we persons really can't help but notice, through every expression of the intentional beings who cross our path, the continual supply of meanings flooding the psychological plain. Characters are everywhere. When we interact with them, we take them seriously as fixed meaningful selves to be dealt with through our own character. We are no longer mainly becoming selves here. We are mainly selves of settled structure, of settled *being*. The activity of being ourselves involves our expressing our picture of life to the world.

#4: Although it will not be my focus in this book, I at least want us to take a quick glance at an image of identification *change* in the self. Here is a picture of me as a young man. While I still am significantly the same here as I was in childhood, I can't deny that I have changed some. The stained jeans and bat and glove are gone. But so are parts of my character, having been replaced by some new structures and by some new content to old structures still being articulated. In either case, I don't identify with all the same things anymore. Clearly, this sort of condition is everyone's fate. It is rare to find someone who is absolutely settled in who she is. Some people are more open to change than others, of course. But all of us do some of it over the span of our lifetime. Some even invite it. We try to strike a new pose through various means—sometimes through sheer will, sometimes through new environments, sometimes through psychotherapy, and so on. But whether we so self-consciously invite character change like this or not, what is true about all of us is that at various points in life we face new character images and try them out. Identifications change. We discard some and keep others—always fine-tuning them, always looking for that very special way of presenting them to let others know our unique slant on things. As we find those images that work well for us, though, we are loath to let them go. Change is indeed a part of life, but it does have its boundaries. We are loath to change a self that is in place. Once we identify with being a certain way, we do everything possible to defend it because that identification is part of our self—our most prized possession.

That's enough. I won't show you any more pictures. These make the essential points about identification that I am concerned with our having fixed in our minds. When identifying starts to unfold in the early part of a person's life, the activity of self development begins in earnest. One starts to become a character. When we are character selves in full swing, we are concerned with consolidation and self-maintenance of identifications. And from time to time, we have to deal with the forces of change that would challenge that self-maintenance. In any case, now we have some pictures of these ideas. They and what I've said about them are both the motivation for and general vision of what I think about our becoming and being (and sometimes changing) the person we would hope to be. In the chapters to follow, I am going to flesh out this vision; I am going to clarify the universal truths about identification and becoming and being a self that I think these pictures suggest. Now, however, it's time to lay down some groundwork, to provide some context. I want to introduce you to the literature that my vision of identification fits into. It turns out that there are some important debates about the self going on in both philosophy and psychoanalysis which circle the very issues that interest me. I would like to review them at least briefly here and begin to offer some critical perspective that will be filled in later.

II

I begin with the philosophers. Over the past fifteen years, a new moral-psychology literature concerned with psychological development has sprung up among analytic philosophers. The brightest lights have been Daniel Dennett, Gerald Dworkin, Owen Flanagan, Harry Frankfurt, Jonathan Glover, Thomas Nagel, Amelie Rorty, Richard Rorty, Charles Taylor, Bernard Williams, and David Wong.[2] All of these thinkers want to find a proper analysis for the psychological activity behind a person's becoming and being an adult character self. Taylor claims that the activity we are looking for is moral evaluation, what he calls "strong evaluation." Williams talks about nonmoral valuation. Dworkin speaks of autonomy; Glover, of self-creation. Amelie Rorty and David Wong discuss identification. Frankfurt focuses on reflective evaluation. So much to consider.

It is generally agreed by these people that human selves are essentially different from other animal selves in virtue of their agency. Human selves can take charge of their lives. How so? For starters, humans, as well as other animal species, have desires and other motives. Both Dworkin and Frankfurt see the essence of our autonomous agency in our having reflective desires about these desires and other motives. We have, that is, second-order reflective desires about first-order (presumably causally explainable) psychological states. What is unique about the human self is that many of our decisions about how to act are based on such reflectiveness. Dworkin and Frankfurt diverge from one another at this point. Dworkin defends the idea that second-order reflections about first-order states are precisely a person's identifications,[3] a person's identity or character. Moreover, he argues that identifying with states is the mark of autonomy in us. And although he doesn't go on explicitly to draw this inference, one can't help but conclude from what he says that the essence of the human self is its autonomy and that that autonomy gets expressed through a person's ability reflectively to make decisions about first-order conscious states. Dworkin's focus here is on tying together the ideas of identity (self) and autonomy. Frankfurt takes a different turn in his interest in reflective consciousness. In addition to focusing on autonomy, he is also interested in talking about the evaluational nature of our reflective states and making that the essence of self. He points out that only human selves reflectively evaluate first-order desires. Some of those desires are judged desirable and some undesirable. The ability to do this evaluating is what is unique about the human agent.[4]

Taylor agrees with Frankfurt. He says that "what is distinctly human is the power to evaluate our desires, to regard some as desirable and others as [sic] undesirable"[5] "Our identity is...defined by certain evaluations which are inseparable from ourselves as agents."[6] But Taylor goes on to offer some new distinctions. He points out that there are different kinds of evaluation that people engage in. One is what he calls "strong evaluation." Unfortunately, Taylor's full notion of this concept has been difficult to pin down. Parts of it certainly have changed over the years since he first introduced the idea. As it should be, philosophical exchange about his views has required him to make modifications.[7] However, I don't think we need to trace this evolution. Taylor's final version will suffice, especially since I believe it is the core idea that has been in his writings all along. That idea is that the human agency self as strong evaluator is a being who makes *moral value* choices between first-order desires (and between other first-order states as well—emotions, beliefs, and so on), where these choices are independent of our first-order inclinations and, rather, are based on certain standards of moral judgment. In considering her first-order desires, the human self decides between those which she sees as being right or wrong, based on some standard of right and wrong she is reflecting upon. She morally evaluates the options for how she will live her life from moment to moment and over the long haul.

Taylor distinguishes "strong evaluation" as a kind of reflection on first-order desires from "weak evaluation" of them. The latter idea is that people sometimes evaluate first-order desires as a mere weighing of preferences based on no external standards, that is, a mere weighing of preferences based on relative internal convenience, satisfaction, attractiveness, and so on.[8] Presumably, Frankfurt ran the two kinds of evaluation together; at least, Taylor supposes this. Taylor sees the distinction between strong and weak evaluation as an improvement on Frankfurt's position. I think that, in the final analysis, the distinction certainly can be made, although people like Flanagan have shown that it can't be made so simply. But even giving Taylor this much, the question that must be answered is, What legitimizes Taylor's jumping from the introduction of the idea that there are two kinds of evaluation to the conclusion that strong evaluation is at the heart of what is distinctively human—that it counts and weak evaluation doesn't? We have just seen that he has agreed with Frankfurt that the general "power to evaluate our desires, to regard some as desirable and others as undesirable," in whatever sense of "desirable" or "undesirable" (i.e., "strong" or "weak" evaluation) one is talking about, is "what is distinctively human." For Taylor to go on to make a distinction between two different sorts of reflective evaluation may be interesting, but it doesn't warrant his conclusion that we are to treat *only* "strong evaluation" as what is distinctively human or at least what is at the heart of being a human agency self. Short of further argument to the contrary, Frankfurt's more general position remains the best candidate for what the evaluational analysis of the human self is.[9] But I will have more to say about all of this in chapter 7.

Let me raise a caution here. While I think that Frankfurt's views are closer to the truth in the debate, I don't think finally that he is on the mark either. In fact, I don't believe that evaluation of any kind (either Frankfurt's notion or Taylor's notion) is the crucial element for understanding the essential acts of human self-making (chapter 7). There is an open-question argument underlying my view. If you will allow me the view here at this preliminary juncture—a view I will argue for in the ensuing chapters—that "identifying with a state" has something to do with "choosing to accept that state as being part of who one is," just as we can ask about a person with any first-order state, Does she really *identify with* that state?, so, too, can we ask about a person with any particular reflective evaluation of such a state, Does she really *identify with* that evaluation or not? She might reflectively evaluate, but it is always an open question whether or not she identifies with that reflective evaluation. It is always an open question whether or not that evaluation is part of who she is. If she does identify with such an evaluation, then, and only then, is the evaluation at all involved as an essential part of her self. Even here, though, her evaluation is essential for self making not because it is an evaluation but rather because it is one more identification.

"Identification" is the primitive concept we need to understand if we want to get at the nature of agency in the character self. Interestingly, I believe that this concept fits nicely into Frankfurt's general ideas about first- and second-order psychological states. I think that Frankfurt's general insight that *some* kind of *reflective consciousness* of our first-order states is a key to understanding the uniqueness of human selves is correct; but I think that "identification" rather than "evaluation" is the ticket for understanding what really goes on in this kind of reflective consciousness. I will argue in chapter 7 that what I call "identificatory valuation" is the reflective state we need to understand. We will see that people make daily character-rooted life decisions reflectively based upon identificatory valuations of first-order states and more.

My general line of argument is quite compatible with a point of view Frankfurt has taken in his later writings. He says,

> A person who cares about something is, as it were, invested in it. He identifies himself with what he cares about in the sense that he makes himself vulnerable to losses and susceptible to benefits depending upon whether what he cares about is diminished or enhanced.[10]

All of this, it seems to me, is right on target. It certainly rings true with how I read Heidegger's notion of "care" as an ontological structure of being.[11] It also is the same kind of notion that Williams has in mind when he talks about how our identity is wrapped up in the central "life projects" we identify with.[12] It is the same kind of notion that Flanagan has in mind when he observes that identity is linked "to the strength of one's identifications—to absorption in some end or ends, whatever that end or those ends might be," moral or otherwise.[13] It is the same kind of notion that Dennett has in mind when he talks

about the self as the "center of one's narrative gravity," where by this
he means those motives in life that we care about most.[14] I agree with
these people that a crucial element of a human self is the caring she
does about the things that matter most to her. Indeed, I discuss my
slant on this idea in chapter 8, where I focus on what it is for a person
to take responsibility for being the person she is.

There is one more idea found in the philosophical literature that
I think is crucial to understanding the importance of identification for
being a self. It has to do with something that Richard Rorty talks
about.

Philosophers of self divide into essentialists and nonessentialists.
Taylor thinks moral evaluation is an essential feature of selfhood.
Dworkin favors autonomy. Nonessentialists believe the self is wholly
contingent. In playing his Nietzschean card, Richard Rorty spells out
such a story.[15] All there is to a self is what we create by ourselves,
what we choose to be. We make our choices according to the linguistic descriptions we have chosen to have characterize us. We create
new metaphors—what Rorty calls a "final vocabulary"—to talk about
ourselves as meaningful.[16] Some people are, in Rorty's terms, "ironists" in their understanding of their self. They have "radical and
continuing doubts" about their final vocabularies. The core language
they use to describe their deepest selves (e.g., that they are democratic, egalitarian, decent, etc.) are always open for revision. Moreover,
they know that no one person's vocabulary is better than any other's
at describing some objective reality. Even those who are not ironists
about themselves, but rather are more commonsensical and thus
believe that their words describe the hard truths of the world, have
final vocabularies that ultimately are only contingent. The difference
between the two types is that the ironists are aware of this human
condition while the rest are not. Ironists realize that "the terms in
which they describe themselves are subject to change, [and are]
always aware of the contingency and fragility of their final vocabularies, and thus of their selves."[17] Everyone else has a self that is just
as contingent, but not everyone else is aware of that fact.

We should understand that the contingency Rorty is talking
about is what we might call a "content contingency." He doesn't
believe that we have a human nature of special contents, such as our
being essentially moral, competitive, democratic, and so on. However, it is still possible that there are quite noncontingent *processes*
that all persons universally use to nail down their different content
selves. The reflective consciousness view is certainly a candidate. So

is the view that connects caring about first-order states to selfhood. There is nothing that Rorty says to rule out some noncontingent process idea. In fact, he volunteers a candidate. Along with Glover, he is partial to the process of Nietzschean self-creation. The self is each person's reflexive creation. We choose the traits and actions we would commit our days to. Then we solidify that unfolding self by taking responsibility for it, even though its contents are always open for reformulation—that is, new choices, new responsibilities. These are the essential processes of self making. Such a view, I believe, is quite compatible with talk about identification. The content of two different selves may look radically different—that is, they may have radically different final vocabularies—but those selves come by their particular final vocabularies by identifying with one form of life (as characterized by a given vocabulary) rather than another. And I believe that important components of the identificatory process are, in the broadest terms, right out of the Nietzschean existential mold. I will explore this idea in chapters 5–8. There I will map out the self-creation and responsibility-taking activities involved in identifying our selves into existence.

III

Important psychoanalytic Self theorists have their debates too. For example, some thinkers argue about the timetable for and the quality of the development of the self. So we see "the French School"—including people like Merleau-Ponty, Lacan, and Wallon[18]—claiming that the self doesn't take so long to come on the scene. They believe that a person has a self quite early on and that the solidity of its existence is immediately and forevermore jeopardized by the hard knocks of everyday life. Life, that is, immediately tends to alienate us from our selves. In this view, most of human psychological development is about responding to this alienation. These theorists don't see the life of the self as a many-splendored thing a person works to perfect. Rather, life is a complex activity of, on the one hand, dealing with the self's relative impotence in getting what it wants and, on the other, of dealing with the invasions it feels from other selves. These thinkers believe that in identifying with life projects, the adult does in fact *attempt* to build what we call a "strong healthy self." However, this attempt finally is really nothing more than a papering over of an inconsolable loss of our original state of grace—our original solid self. Indeed, Lacan sees this activity as a sign of our essentially disturbed selves.

In this regard, a person's life is about her responding to an open psychological wound by putting on bandages that are always too small.

On the same general question of timetables, some other theorists argue that we don't gain a self early on (only to then lose it) but, rather, we are born with a self. Some people even claim that we are selves at conception. For both of these kinds of theorists, childhood development isn't the creation of a self but, rather, the learning of how to deal with the losing of the full self that goes on at birth. But the lost self here is different from the alienated self that we just talked about. For these theorists, the trauma of separating from our comfortable symbiosis with the maternal object (mother's body) is dealt with by one's trying to fight off the consequent sense of emptiness and frustrated satisfaction by developing a separate self that undertakes projects such as work, family life, ideologies, and so on. All of these projects are seen as busywork to get us to forget the ultimately solid self—the self of symbiosis—that we are missing out on. In this view, what we come to understand as the individuated autonomous self of later life is really what we learn to settle for. Morris Berman, for example, makes a case for this view.[19]

We won't really get to engage in a careful critique of any of these theorists; I just wanted to point to their existence. My main concern is in moving our attention to a place where I think the most interesting action is going on regarding the self. I'm talking about some discussions that are going on in two of the more mainstream psychoanalytic schools of thought—specifically, in Object Relations Theory and Narcissism Theory. The bright lights in these discussions are too numerous to mention here, but names like Jacobson, Mahler, Meissner, Winnicott, Kohut, and Kernberg[20] are certainly representative. These people are all concerned with drawing a developmental map of the self. Generally speaking, they are interested in understanding the journey we take toward selfhood in the taming of our irrational narcissistic impulses. They want to talk about the self as an ego that tries to bring irrational libidinal impulses under rational control. And they want to talk about when all of this goes on. For these theorists, identification plays a key role in the discussion. It's the final step in the march toward rational ego status. It's the process that unfolds only after the individual has successfully fought the psychologically more primitive wars of being a causally defined object relator and narcissistic satisfaction seeker. With these ideas in mind, what I would like to do now is convey the big picture of the Self issues that the two schools of psychoanalytic thought are interested in.

There's a small language problem both schools have, though, that I want to lay bare first. We can make some allowances for it and then move on. The basic problem is that in describing the developmental phases the infant and child go through in working toward becoming a self, the theorists talk about the infant *self* and child *self* going through those phases. And if we took these references to infant and child *selves* literally, we would be stuck with a circularity that would seem to undercut the very project that motivated all their developmental study in the first place. Theorists need some other term for the infant and child *being*, a term other than "self." It's a difficult point, though, for we are all drawn to making this same mistake. Nevertheless, if these theorists want to make their case, they really should have another locution.

Related to this problem, there is the problem of importing the notion of agency—a notion certainly appropriate when talking about full-fledged (adult) selves—into their talk about the infant or child self. What I mean is this: In talking about where a human being starts her developmental journey toward becoming a full-fledged self, the theorists must have a referent to talk about. Clearly the infant is the thing. And it becomes easy to slide into talk of the "infant self" as though there is already a version of an *agency* in place here, albeit a primitive one. We hear things said among these theorists like, "The infant doesn't let her mother stray too far," "The narcissistic infant or child always insists on satisfying her own desires before anyone elses," "As an object relator, that infant introjects the blanket as a security symbol." It sounds as though the infant acts as an intentional agent on her world. And that's just not so. When all is said and done, this is simply a mistake of adultomorphism. In other words, if we see the world through adult eyes as a place that houses adult agency selves, then where it houses infants it's easy to slide into talking about them as primitive versions of the same general kind of thing we adults are—viz., agencies. The world houses them as "little agency selves," "little people" who eventually grow into more complex adult agencies. In fact, though, what happens on the occasion of a person's becoming a self is that she goes through certain psychological processes that make her something totally different in *kind* from what she's been up until then. She starts out as an infantile nonagent being and eventually ends up as an adult agency self. The model of what goes on in this developmental change is not that of, say, puppies putting on weight and complexity in becoming old dogs. It is more like caterpillars becoming butterflies. Metamorphosis is the order of the day: Agency self status is a whole new world. Even so, the theorists still insist on speaking "puppy talk." We will make allowances, though. We will understand this as loose talk, stand-in language for something like "the locus of mental activity of the body we know of as that *infant* over there"—a mind/body, yes; an agency, no.

Setting these language problems aside, what are these theorists saying? Most seem to agree that the primordial infant (i.e., "the locus of mental activity of the body we know of as *that infant* over there") is more noticeable for the kind of *relations* it is engaged in than for any *being* it might have as an individuated entity with identifiable self properties. Supposedly, it is involved in a *symbiotic* relationship with the primary caretaker. No infant self qua agency, just a locus of mental activity around the central unifying theme of symbiosis. In the infant "mind," there is no self and no parental object. There is a oneness of sorts, a field of mental and bodily activity not distinguishing infant and parent minds and bodies. This symbiosis remains in force so long as the maternal pole (the primary caretaker) of this relationship can do what it takes to keep the infant pole's wants and needs satisfied. Eventually, the maternal pole's work is not satisfying enough. The picture of being alive gets blurred. Still no agency self, the infant begins to do things (in a causal, nonagency fashion) in order to get clarity back. (Certainly it would be easy to slip into infant *self* and *agency* talk here; we'll fight the urge though.) There are parallel tracks of activity that commence, one of them infantile narcissistic, the other infantile object relating.

The very earliest infant narcissistic activity is a project of futility. It involves the infant's "trying" (in a nonagency sense) to hold onto the all-absorbing narcissism she has enjoyed to that point. We will see in chapter 3 that there is a procession of fantasies about the infant's own omnipotence and her mother's place in confirming this power—a power that is placed in the service of trying to keep intact the symbiotic relationship and the all-important satisfaction of the infant's desires. We will see the detail of the central narcissistic activities and of their ultimate abandonment during a later narcissistic phase in favor of the new emerging project of *reflexively creating* the self, an agency aimed at satisfying one's own desires.

Many of the views of Object Relations theorists dovetail nicely with the assumptions of the Narcissism theorists. They too see the infant's primordial situation as anchored in relationship. Supposedly, the infant is related to objects that feed his narcissism and his symbiotic craving. Of course, most literally, he relates to his mother in order to survive (e.g., to get his nourishment, physical comfort, emotional sustenance, and so on). But there are also other interesting objects to talk about. The infant gets his needs met by them well after mother's considerable attention has abated. These are objects that stand in for mother. This is normally all an unconscious affair for the infant. (How would we ever know anyway?) Milk bottle nipples not only provide a way to ingest milk; they also provide a medium for continuing sensual oral gratification with a mother substitute. Stand-in symbiotic satisfactions, qua *symbiosis*, continue on an unconscious level. We will see in chapter 2 the important roles that unconscious psychological mechanisms such as incorporation, introjection, and projection play in maintaining the infant's relationship with the primary object, mother. We will also see how the mechanism of identification is our instrument for overcoming these primitive mechanisms as we mature into agency selves.

Object relating is not only about insuring continuance of narcissistic satisfactions through mother substitutes; it is also about the infant making sense of his world. Some theorists claim that the infant first makes sense of things through the mother medium. When she leaves, the infant gets distressed, not only because his pleasure agent has been lost, but also because his basis for comprehending the world is gone. The substitutes the infant eventually forms in the unconscious are sometimes about these cognitive matters.[21] Whether pleasure-based or cognitive, though, the infant is intent on maintaining substitute psychological object relations at the center of (un)consciousness. In this theory, the infant actually *is* nothing more than these relations. As such, there is necessarily something lacking in the infant being. For it admits to the absence of the desired item, the real symbiotic relation with mother. This is where identification comes into the picture. Both the Narcissism theorist and Object Relations theorist see the infant slowly giving up the ghost and developing his own powers for getting life's goods. (Again we fight the urge to import agency into our meaning here.) He will never get another symbiosis that will work; he will never get his mother back, directly or indirectly, in quite that way. But eventually he can develop his own agency self to get the jobs done that mother and her substitutes had been getting done. He can have a healthy, meaningful, unalienated self that isn't always spinning its wheels because it is inconsolable over the loss of symbiosis. The self I am talking about *simply* accepts these facts of loss and goes on to create something that gets the job done in a different way—viz., a being (a self) with its own agency.

In a transitional movement in this direction, the infant first imitates others who appear to have these kinds of desirable agency powers already. But the infant soon learns that mere imitation doesn't do the trick. He wants to take or borrow qualities of other agents in order to become something *like* them. So, as in the Duke Snider scenario, he now begins to identify with them, the result being an empowered self with some properties similar to those of the admired agents. But here is where the discussion ends for these psychoanalytic theorists. They don't have much more to say about the details of identification. And these details are where the most worthwhile action is.[22] As matters stand now for the analysts, merely to say that identification occurs so that infants eventually become selves is really nothing more than waving a linguistic wand and then producing a "something from nothing," producing an unexplained self in full regalia. Butterflies do come from caterpillars, but we can account for the transition. And that is what we must do about selves that are basically identified into existence. Toward that end, in Part I we will recapitulate the detail of the psychoanalytic perspectives we have just outlined. Then in Part II, we will look at the detail of identification, showing how that discussion fully complements the psychoanalytic perspectives.

IV

That concludes our first pass at the relevant literature. I would like to turn our attention in this section to clearing up more vocabulary matters that could present problems for us if we aren't careful.

For one thing, when philosophers look at something like the photos we looked at earlier, they rightly end up talking about concepts like the "core self," "who a person really is," "what it is about the self that makes life meaningful," "identification," "character," "identity crisis," "the deep issues of the self," and more. Certainly the philosophers I cited in the second section do this. All too often, however, they end up discussing these concepts with the vocabulary of ethics. And that doesn't always serve the cause of conceptual clarification well. I believe that, once in a while, some of these philosophers are unhelpfully saddled with a philosophical tradition that insists that if a person is going to talk about such softheaded notions (and better he doesn't), ethics is the pigeonhole that is closest to appropriately housing them. In fact, though, these concepts really don't appear as an organized body of concepts in any entrenched academic area of philosophy. There is no traditional academic vocabulary that works for them. Rather, they fall between the epistemic cracks. Accordingly, our job will be to peer into the cracks and see what bits of ideas we can find that are useful at all for understanding these notions. Beyond that, what we will do in places is actually construct some of our own vocabulary in order to look at these concepts on their own terms.

Let me move to another point about our vocabulary. Of the concepts listed above, I am considering some as more central than others. You have seen from my pictures that I am most interested in identification as the key process in forming the self, character. "Identification," "self," and "character"—those are operative terms. They are going to saturate the discussion in this book. We would do well, then, at the outset to have some idea of what expressions will be associated with these terms and what expressions won't.

Take "self" for example. What I am interested in with this term is the self of "who I am" connotation—that is, "my real self," "my way of being," "my basic personality," "what I really am like when you get under the surface," "the true me," "what makes me tick," "what makes me unique," "the me I feel at home with," "the everyday me I bring to the world," "the basic me that I carry along through life and that changes only very slowly, if at all." Unhappily, I already have been a bit slippery in this chapter with my talk about this complex sense of self. At different times I have referred to "character self," "ego self," "agency self," "identificatory self," "identity," and "Self," as well as just plain "self," "character," and "ego." Most of these are terribly formal ways of talking about who a person is. So let me do some appropriate linguistic legislating. Since "ego" and "ego self" have both a technical psychoanalytic use and a technical Buddhist meaning, and since both of these have a different focus from the "who I am" sense we are interested in, I will try to steer clear of using them.[23]

We will also have to watch ourselves with "Self." That usually refers to a historical philosophical concept we aren't really so concerned with. From time immemorial, philosophers have asked the question, *What* are persons?, where this has meant something like, What objective features do all people share which make them different from other kinds of beings? The usual answers are that they have minds or souls or moral essence, or that they are uniquely imperceptible material and mental substances, or perhaps that they are but a logical category of the mind.[24] Any of these Selves are selves from a decidedly impersonal perspective. We aren't going to pursue these views except to say that we aren't really interested in the impersonal "what" self, although surely there are better and worse versions of this. We are more concerned with the personal "who" of people. "Who" is clearly different from "what," but how? Again, there is obviously a sense in which there is something profoundly more personal about it. We know, for example, about the individual's psychological history, as in "who I am is someone living at this address, born on such and such a date, parenting this child, loving that kind of music," and so forth. These sorts of things are all unique, unrepeatable, and unanalyzable autobiography. Such information is no doubt important when we want to know who a person is. But it is still not the heart of matters for us. What we really want to know about is "who-ness." What we want to know are the broad categories of questions that a detailed psychological history or autobiography is an answer to. So we want to know things like What kind of person is she?, and What makes that person unique, at least in her own eyes?, and What ideals make that particular person's life meaningful to her? (i.e., What things are most important to her in life?), and What are the particular life choices that person has made?, and What are the sorts of commitments that person takes responsibility for?[25] These and more are the kind of who-ness questions we are interested in looking at. They are not, however, the sort of impersonal thing that philosophers traditionally have had in mind when they ask what the Self is. Accordingly, to the extent that it's possible (and it won't be, completely), we will be staying away from that traditional philosophical concept of the Self and staying close to who-ness.

"Character," "character self," "identity," and even "identificatory self" will finally be my preferred terminology. Add to those the "causal self" and you have the whole family of self terms I will be working with, although we will see that "causal self" plays a very qualified role in the discussion. As for "character" and "character self," I intend no important difference between them. Which one I use will be more a matter of aesthetic taste and literary choice than anything else.[26] Whichever I use, though, it (as well as "identity" and "identificatory self") will be to designate the "who-ness" idea I am interested in.

Quite generally, when we talk about a person's character, we'll mean who a person is in terms of the deeply entrenched traits that in various ways he has voluntarily etched into his personality repertoire over a long period of time. We will see that those traits are the result of the general ways of being that he has chosen above all other considered possibilities. They are his valued ways of being. So someone's character might be made up of traits such as being forgetful, honest, deceitful, dependable, tenacious, lackadaisical, and so on. He chooses to live his life these ways. And there is something about each of them that he values.[27]

Obviously there's much more than this to the idea of character. But this is a good enough rough sketch. We will be filling it in through the ensuing chapters. Before I move on to another term, though, let me caution that there are some ordinary senses of "character" I want us to avoid. One is found in expressions such as "He is a real character," meaning that he is eccentric. Another refers to unreal selves in plays, novels, films, and so forth. And still one more makes "character" synonymous with being moral, as when expressions such as "Now there's a person with a lot of character" are to mean "There goes a very moral person." This one I want to raise a special caution for, because it comes closest to the quite value-laden concept of character that we will be focusing on. However, we will see that my value concept of character is not about moral value.

I want to bring our discussion in this section to a close now by commenting on one last notion. The other who-ness term we will be seeing quite a lot of is "identity." We will come to understand it as a special variation on "character." But right here, I want to make it clear what I *won't* mean by "identity." There is a particular philosophical sense of the term from which we want to keep our distance. That sense is discussed in the age-old debate about the proper criteria for identifying and reidentifying a person over time as the same self he was before, that is, what many philosophers have called "the problem of personal identity." "Identity" in this context is about what logical conditions or criteria need to be met in order to justifiably *recognize* a person as being the same person over the passage of time. That is, identifying refers to a special kind of recognition. The puzzles surrounding this recognition comprise an old chestnut that philosophers like to lay over any of a person's concerns about "who a person is." The truth is, however, this particular logical concern is not what I am centrally interested in here (though what I am centrally interested in does have some important ramifications for it). The kind of identifying I am concerned with, rather, is the psychological process of internalizing features of the world, that internalization process somehow making those features into parts of one's self. That self is the "identity" that we will be talking about.

V

Now that we have reviewed the relevant literature and have been made more aware of some of the do's and don't's of our vocabulary, it's time to say how the main discussion in this book will proceed. As I pointed out earlier, the book will divide into two parts. Part I will be an excursion into the psychoanalytic perspective on psychological identification. Essentially, we will see how theorists understand identification as the crowning achievement of a very long journey people make for self development. We will clarify how the primitive processes of self development outlined in the third section finally lead to identification.

Part II will be about my conceptual analysis of psychological identification. We will see both how that analysis is informed by our Part I psychoanalytic understanding of identification and its developmental precursors and how my analysis, in turn, informs the psychoanalytic project. The main action of Part II, however, will be the analysis itself. We will see that, in general, what I have to say about identification amounts to an existential thesis. It is the view that we persons create ourselves as characters through the process of identification. How?

We autonomously choose who we are to be as character selves. It is fundamentally this choosing that turns us into who we are. As I mentioned in my earlier reference to Richard Rorty's general line of thinking, character selves are not first and foremost entities with inherent, or essential, properties; rather, character properties are chosen. People don't confront one another as entities composed of objective properties shared by all persons. In Sartre's terms, a human being, at its core, is not an *en soi*, but rather a *pour soi* kind of being.[28] We are not inherently, for example, rational beings, moral beings, unchanging mental substances, and so on. Being a self is more the choosing of certain kinds of activities *for* the self—choosing to be rational, choosing to be moral, choosing to be a ballplayer, and so forth.

That is what identification is about. What an adult self is—i.e., its who-ness—is the activity of identifying. The detailed landscape of that activity that varies from person to person is about what things an individual self identifies with. But the central activity itself is all about choosing. It is about a choosing of how to be, a choosing of which traits to exemplify as oneself. A person sees traits in the world—in people, in ideas, in social institutions, and so on—that he would like to have as his own. As an identifier, he chooses them to be part of who he is. And in that special kind of identificatory choosing, he succeeds in actually having those traits constitute his character. In choosing those traits, he takes psychological ownership of them. Obviously, not just any act of choosing will do here. A person can't, for example, simply choose to be the emperor of the universe and seriously expect to have that as a trait of his self. He can't expect to take ownership of it. No, I will argue that the special variety of choosing that makes for identification involves autonomously choosing to ultimately value object traits as one's ideal standards for experiencing and evaluating one's life. This is a complex notion that I will call "identificatory valuation."

Against the backdrop of the philosophical literature I introduced in the second section, we will go to great lengths to clarify this very important concept. But we will also see that not only does identification involve people making these ultimate value choices; it also requires that they take responsibility for them. So if, say, a person really identifies with his mother's caretaking ways—if he really chooses them to be of paramount importance in how he conducts and evaluates his life—then we would expect him to take responsibility for consistently being those same ways himself. Anything short of this consistency would force us to conclude that he doesn't really identify with his mother as much as he thinks he does. And in general, we will see that any identificatory choice that a person makes is only as good as the degree of responsibility he takes for implementing it. A person carves character out of his valuational choices only to the degree that he stands behind those choices.

We will go on to discuss two fundamental ways in which people self-responsibly stand behind their valuational choices. That discussion will be in the context of understanding an existential tension that all people play out. On the one hand, everyone wants to be a character who is unique, individuated from all others; on the other hand, everyone wants to belong with one another in a community with shared character values. Life is about living out both poles of this tension—both character themes—by making the appropriate sorts of self-responsible valuational choices about character. At one pole, people carve out their personal self; at the other, their social self. In the first instance, we will develop the thesis that when people personally identify with something, they choose to assert its essential value for them as individuated distinctive selves, and they stand behind this choice regardless of what others think. That is, in part of their being, people choose to value certain traits in such a way as to make those traits parts of a distinctive character that is different from everyone else's. They value those traits because they see those traits as separating them (their character) from the crowd. And because they so very much want to be unique individuals, they stand up for those valued trait choices regardless of what others think. But we are also social beings. Socially identifying with something is all about a person's choosing to assert that something's ultimate value for him as a social self. That is to say, whereas qua personal identifier the individual stands behind certain values *regardless* of what others think, qua social identifier he makes value choices *because* of what others think. He chooses in concert with others because doing so expresses his solidarity with them. He is motivated to choose here because of his desire to belong to the group. But once chosen, these values become ultimate social values for him. Put simply, he really does believe in them. They are constitutive parts of his social self, anchoring his sense of social identity.

Finally, then: Autonomously choosing traits, choosing ultimately to value them, taking responsibility for those choices, doing all this in ways that carve out both a personal and social identity—those are the basic features of my analysis of identification. Those are the ideas behind the existential self-creation of character to which I will be bringing some new light. All this will happen in Part II. As I've said, however, before we begin examining these ideas, we will look at the psychoanalytic theory of identification and its developmental precursors. After all, people don't come into this life as full-fledged identificatory characters. They slowly develop into them; they evolve. Accordingly, not wanting to put the cart before the horse, we will move our attention now to the psychoanalytic theory of this evolution.

Part I

The Psychoanalytic Theory of Identification

CHAPTER 2

Object Relations Theory and Developing the Pre-Self

There is a debate among knowledgeable thinkers about when we start to develop our selves as characters. For different reasons, many philosophers of antiquity seem to think these matters begin on Day One. Some psychologists think so too. However, most current psychological theorists think self status is something that develops slowly and at different points in life. What I propose to do in Part I is to stake out the prevailing positions in each of these areas. My treatment of the philosophical views will be brief—a nod of recognition to the history of thought. That will be all I'll do, because most of these philosophical discussions have been *a priori* claims about the self as a metaphysical entity. Certainly the *a priori* claims are quite penetrating and immensely interesting. However, they are not what I am about in this book. Since my interest, after all, is in the psychological notion of the *empirical* self as character, I will be much more concerned with looking at what psychological theorists have had to say. Even here, though, I won't be covering the entire psychological waterfront. For example, I won't have much to say about the work of Piaget, Kohlberg, Gilligan, and company.[1] Instead, I intend to look almost exclusively at the psychoanalytic "self" literature. This is where the greatest commitment is found for understanding the role that *identification* plays in the formation of the self, and so this is the area that most closely speaks to our major concern.

As I pointed out in the Introduction, there are two psychoanalytic theories about the self that complement one another and constitute a very interesting backdrop for some of the insights about identification I will be developing later on. Psychoanalytic Object Relations Theory details the development of the earliest infant self—what I'll dub "the pre-self"—while psychoanalytic Narcissism Theory focuses more of its attention on the later infant/early childhood stages of self development—that self I'll dub "the rudimentary self."[2] Theorists argue that the rudimentary self evolves from the pre-self and that the adult character self that we are interested in evolves from both. Actually, I believe the theorists fail to pay attention to another intervening

27

phase of development, what I'll be calling "the latency self." Be that as it may, the theorists argue that the causal processes of the pre-self and rudimentary versions of the self finally give way to the process of identification. They suggest that identification fits into the psychoanalytic theoretical net of concepts. And indeed, I think they are right. All these concepts are a family of related notions; they are of a piece. But as I have said, I believe that psychoanalytic theory does far too little to show the detail of how identification functions in this family. I hope to rectify that in Part II, where I'll try to make an even better case than the psychoanalytic theorists currently do that identification is indeed a developmental extension of the pre- and rudimentary (and latency) self.

In Part I, however, I want to clarify what the psychoanalytic theorists are saying in their own terms. I will trace what they say about the self's development from pre-self to rudimentary self to latency self to character self. We will come to understand the psychodynamic processes that are central to each stage of development. In that regard, we will see how what is referred to as the process of infantile pre-self "introjecting" gives way to infant and childhood rudimentary self "grandiose mirroring," which in turn, after an adolescent latency self interlude, gives way to adult character self "identifying." In the present chapter, we will look at what Object Relations Theory tells us about the pre-self and its processes. Then, in chapter 3, we will see how Narcissism Theory extends the discussion to the rudimentary self and its characteristic processes. In chapter 4, we will see how the faint beginnings of a character self get underway in the form of the latency self, where the psychological processes best characterizing this phase of development involve a mixture of introjective and identificatory activity. And we will see how although this mixture persists even through pockets of adolescence and adulthood, character processes then come increasingly more into their own.

Although our central focus in this chapter will be on Object Relations Theory, I will begin the discussion by making good on my promise to give at least some general attention to relevant historical philosophical views as well as to some nonpsychoanalytic philosophical/psychological positions about the timetable for self development.

I

I am interested in the question of when the psychological self really begins. Let's appreciate, though, that this "when" question was originally a philosophical "what" question. The philosophers of antiquity prosaically asked the much broader question, What is the essence of human consciousness?, at first assuming that self and consciousness were one and the same thing. In this form, the question has a history some 2,500 years old. But there have been many turns in its form over the years. Side issues have often upstaged the underlying metaphysical concern about consciousness. Most notably, sometimes the question has been asked not for its own sake but rather for the sake of answering an ethics question: In virtue of what do we confer moral worth on people? Other times it has stood in for the question, What is the essence of personhood? Today, we quite often see it standing in for Can we simulate human thinking and feeling on a computer?, or What makes persons unique among the animal species?, or even Is there other intelligent life in the universe? The stand-in version of the question that we happen to be interested in in this book, however, is, What is character identity and the psychological processes that usher it onto the scene? We want to know what special compartment of consciousness is occupied by self qua character. We want to know what the complex processes of identification are which bring this part of consciousness into being. And right now we want to know *when* they come on the scene for persons.

Many philosophers have argued that the essence of anything must start on Day One. This idea has to do with the subtleties of sameness and change. In the grand Parmenidean sense, a thing's ever changing seems a tricky proposition. A thing has to be precisely what it is from the beginning of its existence—it can't really change—or else the thing is not that thing but rather some other thing. Quite simply, if something is different from how it was before—if it has changed—then it is no longer really the thing it was before. It is a new thing, different in *kind* from the original item. In order for a thing to remain the same kind of thing it was before—in order for us to justifiably recognize it as the same thing from beginning until now—there has got to be something unchanging about the thing, an essence. If there are to be any changes about a self-identical thing, it can only be peripheral properties that vary, not essences. Applied to persons, the argument has it that persons must have an essence—something that goes unchanged—if we are ever to attribute an identity to them. That essence is the kind of metaphysical Self we mentioned briefly in chapter 1.[3] Through the centuries, philosophers have provided many different candidates for this unchanging essential Self, for what it is to be essentially a person. Aristotle, for example, sees persons essentially as rational beings.[4] There is an unchanging rationality about all people, though of course rationality has accidental properties that can change over time (e.g., things like forgetfulness, argumentative acuity, creative insight, etc.). Descartes sees the identity of people in the unchanging material and mental substance they are born with.[5] They, too, of course, have changing accidental properties—some people are short while others are tall, some are emotional while others are dispassionate, and so on. For Berkeley, people are mental substance only, consciousness.[6] For Locke and his empiricist descendants, people are complexes of body and memories which must start on Day One and maintain at least a causal relationship to the Day One Self.[7] For Hume, the literal question disappears because Self qua personal identity is supposedly a fiction.[8] There are no real identity essences to anything, just clusters of properties which, to varying degrees, maintain relationships of constant conjunction with one another. For Kant, the Self is a logical construct, a transcendental thing, a set of organizing principles always functioning to gather perceptions and thinking under causal, spatial, and temporal categories, and more.[9] Here, too, Day One is the time of arrival for this Self, even if accidental properties of it change over the course of an individual's life.

Moving now toward the empirical side of things, let me briefly summarize what some well-known psychologists of the self (not the Self) have had to say in both an empirical and *a priori* vein. William James is usually recognized as being the first notable philosopher/ psychologist to veer at least partly from the *a priori* Day One versions of Self. On the empirical side, he was the first to suggest the importance of the process of identification for understanding identity, the latter being his term for self.[10] He saw a person's identity as the sum of what a person can call *his*—his mind, his body, his clothes, his books, and so on. These are things that the individual *psychologically owns*. For James, the premier sign of ownership are the *feelings* that surround a person's dealings with things. Things that are "mine" call forth—are associated with—feelings of intimacy and warmth. From these feelings I can recognize who I am.

But there was also a philosophizing side to James. Like the procession of metaphysicians before him, James was concerned with what necessarily has to be true of Selves/selves that seem to change some over time, yet remain *basically* the same. Sometimes, á la Kant, this appears to be something like a logically necessary transcendental entity. But more often one finds James talking about identity as a kind of logically necessary "spiritually same self" over time. One is the same spiritual Self/self today as she was yesterday, even though one's momentary psychological states most probably differ from yesterday's. For example, I felt hungry last night but I'm not hungry this morning; so I'm not exactly as I was yesterday, yet I'm still the same Self/self. For James, identity of an individual occurs in virtue of the fact that she resembles in important respects the person of yesterday and today. There is a continuity to Self/self phenomena to the extent that they fit together into some kind of coherent whole. The thoughts that I had yesterday belong to the same Self/self I am today in virtue of their fitting together—in some "coherence" sense of the term—with some of today's thoughts.

The psychologist Allen Wheelis offers another rich characterization of the character self and its central processes. In fact, his discussion picks up where James' leaves off. He says,

> Identity is a coherent sense of self....It depends upon awareness that one's endeavors and one's life make sense, that they are meaningful in the context in which life is lived. It depends also upon stable values, and upon the conviction that one's actions and values are harmoniously related. It is a sense of wholeness, of integration, of knowing what is right and what is wrong and of being able to choose.[11]

Wheelis's account is one that I quite favor as a barebones outline of being a character. Each of us has an empirical psychological core which, in important features, basically stays the same over time. This core is a psychological entity with a sense of wholeness, coherence, solidity to us. In fact, that sense of wholeness is the sense of meaningfulness we feel in life, to the extent that we feel such a thing. To attain wholeness or meaningfulness, however, requires a certain kind of psychological processing in us. That would be the choosing of stable values to commit our lives to. We bring these values to our practical life situations again and again and create a perspective that is uniquely ours, a perspective out of which we make our moment-to-moment choices about what to do in life. It is which values we bring to the world that makes our particular choices and character identity distinctive. To the degree that we fail to have such stable values (or at least the capacity to develop them), we are diminished in a sense of meaning, wholeness, and coherence; and we have that much less identity.

That is *what* Wheelis thinks character is. There are also clear implications here about *when* identity forms. For example, Wheelis would have no problem with the idea that identity is not a Day One developmental phenomenon. A sense of wholeness, coherence, solidity, and meaning in life are not in the scene on Day One. They develop. And so, accordingly, do selves. Even though the exact timetable for that development will differ slightly for each of us, it seems to be a general truth that for most of us the primitive seeds first appear in infancy. Wheelis says that, beyond seeds, we begin to develop a much fuller sense of meaning somewhere in adolescence.

On the heels of this "when" idea, Wheelis also has views about some of the required background conditions for unfolding a full identity during adolescence. Essentially, he focuses on the idea that all of an identity gets sculpted in social contexts. His thoughts in this regard are very similar to the views of their more well-known proponent, Erik Erikson. Erikson, too, believes that identity doesn't unfold until adolescence.[12] He believes that during adolescence we perceive ourselves in our own self-sameness and continuity over time. Most importantly, we perceive ourselves through what *others* say about our self-sameness and continuity. We are how others see us.[13] We are the roles we play for others, and we live out of what other people's role expectations of us are. Actually, Jung's idea of persona is a precursor to this view.[14] We become the totality of our roles. The other—whether this be a friend, family, society, or whatever—is always defining the individual's identity. Personal growth is inextricably tied to communal change.[15]

In sharing the same general thesis about identity with Erikson, Wheelis believes that the individual's life attains and maintains meaning only to the extent that one participates in the social process. Who one is as a meaningful character is conditioned by what one's culture is and by what one's participation in it is like.[16] But Wheelis's notion of "social" seems much more limited to the family than does Erikson's. According to Wheelis, the individual initially has an identity anchored by external means—family and relatives are the superego, the providers of acceptable values and behavior. They contribute the values with which one initially chooses to anchor her life. That is, one's initial values come from a social context. Eventually, a person develops her own internal superego, her own values. She develops a conscience that tells her what is right and wrong. However, conscience is just the internal embodiment of an abstract external parent a person continues to have guide her. The individual is forever trying to feel at one with her parents as the boundary makers of her life, even in the use of her conscience.

I am not interested right here in pursuing any dispute over *where* the idea of "the social" should be anchored—that is, whether it is with the culture-at-large or within the confines of the family. I am only interested in pointing out that "the family" idea fits quite well with most intuitive notions we have about who the major early contributors are to a person's character identity (whatever the role that the culture-at-large plays, too). We certainly start to have a sense of a person's character identity once we observe that she has feelings about right and wrong—or at least that she has a conscience about matters of right and wrong—and that these ideas initially come out of a family context. Empirical evidence of a superego is the watershed for most people's unequivocal claims about the existence of character identity. This is the view of character identity, anyway, that most thinkers on the subject seem to latch onto, some with deep Freudian "Oedipal conflict resolution" in mind and others with merely commonsense "now that you have a sense of right and wrong, there's something to you" in mind.[17]

In any event, while some thinkers see the rise of the superego conscience self as coming from familial social forces, others think that it's something that gets causally triggered by thoroughly nonsocial, private psychological mechanisms. (We will discuss the nonsocial option in the third section.) Whatever it arises from, however, the fact is that, for many of us, developing a conscience is a clear sign of an emerging character identity. Finally having values we are committed to live by is the sure sign of a character's being on the scene.

Moving on in our discussion now, there are still other thinkers who disagree altogether with the idea that it takes having a superego (which commits the individual to values) to have a character identity. Indeed, according to psychoanalytic orthodoxy, the seeds for character identity are sewn much earlier than any superego view would allow. In this view, although infants are not born with a self of any sort, self-related matters get started much earlier than the blossoming of the superego. There is no sense of a character self in our first years. Nevertheless, young infants are clearly engaged in a wide variety of complex activities that are purposive and intelligently conducted and that suggest a primitive form of a self, if not exactly a character self. In the very beginning, then, each of these purposive activities "proceeds in psychic isolation from the other."[18] The primitive person here is a mere conjunction of these mental activities.

That is the *very* beginning, where there is no clear self at all. But, according to many theorists, we seem to change quickly and move along toward different versions of self formation while still young infants. For example:

> The normal process of human maturation is the movement toward integration of these many engagements...of one single personal identity. This seems to be a constitutional given that arises after a couple of years or so of life. This self or person defines itself to itself by the distinctive inner avowals of self-identification, in effect acknowledging, *This* I am, and this, and this, but *not* that, or that.[19]

We have finally arrived at the point in our discussion that we've been aiming for. We are finally at a place where the views of Object Relations theorists and Narcissism theorists enter the scene. They, too, believe that self status begins early, during infancy. Moreover, they believe that there are complex processes (the tail end of which is psychological identification) taking place specifically during infancy and childhood that account for the very rich kind of development that the self undergoes during those years. The theorists make it their job to explore these processes. What they say about all of this is both interesting and important, and certainly quite relevant to what we will be arguing later about identification. Accordingly, what we are going to do now in the rest of Part I is immerse ourselves in their ideas and see where it takes us in our understanding of the developing character self.

Before we get down to the serious business of examining their views, however, there are two small correctable language errors the theorists make that we should put on the table and then dispense with. First, while they mean their discussion of developmental self-making processes to be about causal processes, as I pointed out in chapter 1, when they talk about these object relating and narcissistic processes of infancy and early childhood, they often imbue them with a very intentional tone—that is, a tone of noncausal conscious intent (e.g., "The infant/child introjects the blanket as a mother object," as though this wasn't something *happening* to the infant but rather something that she was volitionally *doing*). Finally, we will simply be looking past the intentional feel of their theoretical claims and understand that what they *mean* is really all about causal processes. This is just a case of perfectly normal adultomorphic misspeaking. The second error has to do with the failure of these theorists to make some important distinctions about *kinds* of selves. As I've said already, they run together ideas about a kind of mental organization we would better refer to as a "pre-self." They fail to distinguish this from the character kind of self they are most interested in explaining. They also fail to distinguish the latter from what I call "rudimentary self" and "latency self" ways of organizing mental activity, these ways being psychological organizations they say a lot about, even if they still lump them together under the rubric of "the self." They simply call too many different things "the self." No matter; we'll be forcing these needed vocabulary changes on them in the course of our discussion of their views, without doing any damage to their essential insights.

These errors aside, what the Object Relations theorists and the Narcissism theorists talk about is, as I say, of considerable importance both to our understanding of the process of identification and to our understanding of the development of self (by whatever name we call it). So let's get started with our examination of their views. We will focus on Object Relations Theory in the present chapter and on Narcissism Theory in the next.

We begin by sketching the big picture of self development according to Object Relations Theory. A central idea here is that the infant as a mental and physical entity—we'll use the term "mind/body" in order to remain as neutral as possible vis-à-vis the human's personhood status—starts out in life *seeking* some kind of agency for attaining and controlling her sexual and other need gratification. Indeed, there seems to be a built-in prime directive to do this.[20] She and all persons *must* seek having agency. But as the infant has no internal agency of her own yet, she seeks it from external sources. She enlists the aid of external objects in getting what she wants and needs. Mother is typically the primary early external source object. But whether it's mother or some other object the infant is trained on, the infant sees the agency she is seeking as being in the object and so she psychologically attaches to it in special ways.

Dovetailing with the directive to seek agency, there is another prime directive the infant responds to: the prime directive to return to the womb, as it were—to maintain one's primordial feeling of being loved by a central entity to which one is attached. The directive here is *to avoid separation*. In this context, object relating becomes a defensive reaction to separation from the primordial love object, mother. Once the infant senses a separation from mother, she spends a good deal of her time scurrying around in defensive reaction, forming relations with objects in an attempt to recapture in different ways the familiar primordial love relationship.

But if the infant is psychologically healthy, she will eventually give up the ghost and stop so doggedly avoiding separation. She will give up the second directive in favor of a third prime directive. Specifically, toward the end of the most intense object relating of infancy, she will slowly begin answering the internal command to become her own *individuated self*. She will slowly begin the long trek toward becoming an independent character agency, a solid character self independent of all other solid character selves. She will do this by engaging a new kind of psychological process that will come on the scene—that is, she will embark on a lifetime of psychological acts of identification.

In fact, these three prime directives complement one another. Simply put, in the heat of her most powerful object relating activity, the infant defends against separating from "mother the love object" (directive 2) who is also "mother the agency for sexual and other need gratification" (directive 1). Moreover, as she moves slowly toward becoming an individuated independent person (directive 3), the infant is at the same time becoming her own agency self (directive 1). Of course, as the third directive, about individuation, begins to gain power in the psyche, the second directive needs to abate. When things are working optimally, that's precisely what happens.

However any of this gets negotiated, though, the fact is that developing as a self involves the infant responding to all of these built-in prime directives. These three principles are what much of the human infant's developmental activity is organized around. That's the big picture, anyway. And Object Relations Theory is essentially about describing how all the detail of that picture gets filled in. With that in mind, what we are going to do now is proceed to the next section, where we will draw a closer bead on what the theorists have to say about that detail.

II

First, understand that, as advertised, I am going to refer to the infant here as a "pre-self." I do this because at this juncture "she"[21] totally lacks any internal agency. And I take internal agency to be an absolute requirement for being a genuine self. Of course, the infant is a person developing toward being a genuine self. So I give her the designation of "pre-self." This being the case, we will understand many of the claims of Object Relations Theory to be about the pre-self (although we will see in chapter 3 that many of their claims also pertain to the narcissistic rudimentary self of late infancy and early childhood).

As it is *Object Relations* Theory we are talking about, the first thing we should probably try to do is clarify what the "objects" are that pre-self infants relate to. The term "objects" doesn't refer to objects purely in the physical spatio-temporal descriptive sense. They aren't simply things like tables, chairs, lions, or bears. No, they are *psychological* objects, and they receive that status in virtue of their psychic significance as drive (need) gratifiers.[22] For example, mother's breast is an object for the infant in virtue of its gratifying the infant's felt need for nourishment, security, and warmth. There is an object relation when the infant in some prelinguistic sense comes to *see* (experience) the object as having the psychic significance of a drive gratifier. Most important for the classical Freudian theorists is seeing objects through their psychosexual significance. This means that in perceiving something as an object in her psychic world, the infant transfers libidinal energy to her recognition of the object. We say that she sexually *cathects* the object. The object becomes important as a way of gaining sexual satisfaction from the world. How the infant relates to all such objects becomes the life historical account of her psychosexual development. So, a given object may fulfill infantile anal, oral, or phallic/clitoral satisfaction needs, these all being stages of psychosexual development. Of course, there are more satisfactions that infants pursue through object relating than just the sexual. We just saw that in responding to prime directive 2, one can cathect objects in the service of fulfilling a basic need for love. And there are yet other kinds of object relating gratifications that are cathected— viz., protection, nourishment, psychic organization, aggression, and more.

There are different kinds of relations with objects the pre-self infant has, depending on where she is in her development. Mahler, Pine, and Bergman have systematically studied the procession of the kinds. The first pre-self stage occurs between birth and six months. It is understood as the time of *symbiotic object relating*. Here the infant makes no distinction between self and mother. The infant perceives no distinct subjectivities. The self-mother is *the* subjectivity, *the* self. This symbiotic relatedness to mother constitutes not one subjectivity among many but rather the total concept of what subjectivity is. For that matter, the self-mother is *the* object too. She is not one object among many but rather the total concept of what the object world is. In this composite sense, then, mother is to be thought of as the pre-self-*object*, first to be related to symbiotically and then later to be related to in other, developing ways. In any case, during symbiosis, the only concern of consciousness is a focus on the unity with mother. The infant certainly has a mass of wants and needs— for nourishment, sexual stimulation, locomotion, warmth, bowel relief, emotional comfort. But as we've seen, she (the infant) has no sense of having her own "internal"[23] agency that can get these wants and needs met. Rather, she is a pre-self center of psychic activity aimed at symbiosis. On some level, she recognizes that smiling, giggling, frowning, crying, cooing, and more will get done the job that needs doing. But it is mother—the "external" agency—who does the work. The infant has no sense of a *distinct* mother subject or object who does the job for her. Rather, it is the *symbiotically related-to* entity—what is called the "self-object"—that is perceived as getting the job done. The infant has no concept of how this is happening; the job simply gets done after some crying, cooing, or whatever occurs.[24]

At around six months, the infant typically begins the slow process of *separation* from mother. This normally does its greatest developmental work, however, during the second year. During this period, the infant begins to give up the symbiotic relation. A faint glimmer of a subject/object distinction appears. The first bid at individuation is underway. This is the first real movement toward self making, the first real movement toward experiencing a reflexive subjectivity that has some agency to it and is distinct from other subjectivities and other objects in the world. Still, though, the infant is nowhere near being a full self of the character variety. She is still more of an evolving pre-self than anything else. This newer pre-self stage is a kind of transition period, a time marked by the infant's having a different foot in each of two worlds, viz., one in the world of the self-object and its agency, the other in the newly emerging world of an internal agency subjective self. The infant has a chance to try out the new world without completely leaving the security of the old. She can make primitive forays into internal agency while holding onto a knowledge that she still has mother's agency at her beck and call. She can, that is, try out doing things for herself but always be able to return to mother as more of a "sure thing" for gratifying needs. For example, it's typical during the transition period that the infant practices autonomous functions, such as upright free locomotion, while maintaining her primitive psychic connection to the maternal self-object. She's trying out her internal agency on moving her body. Clearly, she hasn't fully mastered this part of internal agency yet. It's just the beginning. And it's just the beginning of her giving up her maternal symbiosis cathexis. She's giving up this cathexis in favor of cathexes of what are called "transition objects." These are objects *associated* with the power of mother's agency. Where formerly the symbiotically relating infant sought out the cathexis of her needs totally through mother's agency, now the infant gets it from an object associated with mother. So she may want the symbiotic comfort she had been getting from sucking on mother's breast. However, instead of going to mother for satisfaction, now she settles for a pacifier. It becomes an associated object that has the same self-object agency power for her that mother previously had. In time, such objects are seen not only in their associative significance but also as external objects in their own right. And even further down the line, the proxy psychic significance of such objects will eventually be cast out alto-gether and the infant will be able to cope with the fact that she is a discrete identity self in a world of such discrete selves. But until then, transition objects keep the maternal agency ever present. They substitute for what is of greatest value in the child's universe.

Transition objects serve another very important function. The infant enlists their power in order to stave off a *separation anxiety* that comes from trying to individuate oneself from mother. Separation anxiety is psychic fear or terror that is the terrible cost of giving up the "sure thing" self-object agency and beginning on some-thing that is only formative. That is, mother is still quite loved, still quite important. So, of course, separation from her can seem earth-shaking; it is tantamount to losing *all* of what one has known to this point to be the agency for getting one's needs and desires met. So when, say, mother merely leaves the infant's psychic scene (e.g., per-haps she goes to the store to buy some milk), the integrity of the infant's consciousness is threatened. To the early infant, when mother is physically unavailable, mother qua self-object no longer exists; consequently, the infant's sense of control over the world through mother's agency seems not to exist anymore either. Not having much of an internal agency backup, she is left with practically no sense of control at all over her life. And for any human being, infant or otherwise, the conscious expression of being totally out of control is anxiety. Quite appropriately, then, the initial threatened feelings of the newly separating infant are those of anxiety. She has neither enough of a consolidated subjective agency self to control her life nor enough to fend off the resulting anxiety.

Psychic evolution has provided for this infant's situation, though. This is where the other important function of transition objects comes in. Transition objects help defeat separation anxiety. What would human life have been like had we not developed the transition object? We might have become creatures who gave up altogether on the project of individuating; as infants, we might have returned fully to symbiosis with self-objects. However, had that in fact happened, human psychological development would have turned into something much different than it is. Indeed, humanity would have gone out of business as soon as the last self-object agency died off. For, at that point, there would have been no agency left to meet the needs of the symbiotically cathecting infant population. End of story. Alas, though, evolution *has* taken care of matters. The developmental picture that takes hold for humans has the infant unfolding an important mechanism for defending against and eventually overcoming her separation anxiety. And that mechanism is the transition object. By relating to objects associated with mother, mother doesn't have to be around in order for the infant to stay emotionally intact. These transition objects begin to come on the scene anywhere from twenty-two to thirty-six months, this period being known as "the rapprochement phase of the transition period." Because transition objects are present at rapprochement time to soften the blow of separation anxiety, the infant is better able to begin building the faintest sense of being a separate internal agency. The rapprochement period thus becomes a time of consolidating a primitive sense of self, that is, consolidating a primitive sense of an internal agency pre-self. It is a time when, for example, the teddy bear is cuddled with extra spirit, the pacifier is suckled with more zest, the blanket is clung to and deeply inhaled with greater gusto, and so on, as a way to stave off too much anxiety. Cathecting through these objects, the infant is able to take mother along in the mind even though she isn't physically present. Indeed, eventually the infant is able to take along just an ideational *representation* of the transition object as a means of mentally holding onto the security of the absent self-object agency.[25] The infant comes to know that even in the self-object's physical absence, something of it still exists. The infant stays functionally intact so long as the loved self-object or some transition surrogate or some ideational representation of either stays in view or in mind.

Pointedly, internalizing and holding onto relevant ideational *representations* allows the infant to reduce anxiety. The special benefit of the ideational representation is that it provides a new cognitive capacity that makes practicing agency in the face of separation anxiety more of a plausible proposition. Namely, it allows the infant mind to maintain a ideational *object constancy* for any psychological objects (self-objects or transition objects) that are otherwise "missing." Evidence that this capacity is finally on the scene is suggested by the infant's degree of comfort with playing games about disappearance (e.g., appropriate magic tricks and games such as peek-a-boo), with her watching mother go off to work and not falling apart, with her tolerating being left alone after a story at bedtime, and so on. To the infant, mother's absence no longer means solipsistic separation. When object constancy takes hold, a new sense of infant power and security obtains. Now a psychological object representation is almost as good as the real thing. The psychological object representation becomes an internalized psychological object. It is internalized as a constant, positively comforting, cathected image of some self-object.

As I've said, with the security of transition objects and their representations, the infant is better defensively equipped (against the threat of anxiety) to start practicing agency. In due course, not only is the infant trying out internal agency, but she's also starting to develop psychological structure around it. That is, more and more of her daily activities and more and more of her expectations about how the world is to function for her start to get organized around the idea of internal agency. Psychoanalysts sometimes refer to this developing psychological organization as the embryonic beginnings of "ego formation." It is what I refer to as the onset of "rudimentary self formation" and the final throes of the object relating pre-self. The focus on relating to psychological objects is gradually being transferred now to a new focus on creating and relating to the infant's own mind/body agency self.[26] She just now begins to think that she might not necessarily need to "hire" an external agent, as it were, to get what she wants out of life. Individuating her own mind/body as agency just might do the job instead.

Mahler, Pine, and Bergman claim, however, that well before the full unfolding of such an agency self organization, there first emerge seedling ideational *self representations*. These are self analogs of the ideational representations of *objects* I just mentioned. The infant takes on a mental representation of his being a separate agency self that is constant through time. We might think of this as a kind of "self constancy." This is an analog to object constancy, but turned inward. It's as though to say that to the extent that I now have a general sense of being something of an internal agency self, I am here as an agency self even though I am not always consciously thinking about it. I am now on my way to building up a repository of such self representations. These representations are the infant precursors to what later will unfold as identifications, the latter being crucial to one's eventually developing a full-blown character kind of self. "[The] establishment of mental representations of the self as distinctly separate from representations of the object *paves the way* to self-identity formation."[27] Much of the cathexis that had previously been invested in objects is now more and more invested in an enduring, continuous sense of the self.

Unfortunately, the transfer of cathexis from object to subject—from object representations to self representations—doesn't always proceed smoothly. For example, during rapprochement there normally occurs what is called "a splitting of the object world."[28] Infants at this stage are unable to consolidate what we would understand as positive and negative traits of their objects. They aren't able yet to deal with the idea that an object could have both kinds of qualities at one time. They have bifurcated the cathected object world into two distinct realms of goodness and badness. And they have come to experience the self-object as though there were an on/off switch running the show, so that sometimes the self-object is experienced as totally favorable and other times as totally unfavorable. Which is experienced depends on whether the object is successfully satisfying the infants' wants and needs. But now, just as objects are split, so too may one's self be split. And it's one thing to see psychological objects as split, but it becomes quite another to see the budding sense of self this way. Indeed, sometimes a damaged sense of self results because an unhealthy splitting of self representations has occurred. Here infants "make their own persons the objects of either love, admiration, and libidinal gratification, or of hate, depreciation, and destructiveness."[29] The rapprochement infant comes to form self representations that mirror these object representations—that is, now she has representations of her self that are either about being totally favorable or about being totally unfavorable. And this may, later on, also befall the developing character self. The individual may see herself sometimes as having a wholly bad self and sometimes as having a wholly good self. But such an individual can't experience herself as a consolidated blend of both tendencies as the rest of us healthier characters can. Indeed, such a pathological condition is part of the profile of what is known as the "borderline personality."

However the situation finally works out for this particular type of person, though, the point is that this is an unfortunate occurrence that happens as an aberration of normal development. By contrast, the norm for people is that they do not so harmfully split their developing self. Most infants are able to have self representations that do not mirror the splitting of objects. They are able to go from being exclusively object relators to enjoying the fruits of an emerging agency self that cathects healthy self representations. And they are able to experience themselves as a consolidated structure containing elements of both favorable and unfavorable traits.

III

I would now like to recast our understanding of the pre-self in terms of the *psychological processes* that are most distinctive in this period of self development. During the drama of "separating from the self-object and yet not being defeated by anxiety," the infant defensively keeps present something of the maternal self-object or its associated objects by trying out different kinds of psychological internalizing processes. As pre-selves, we process our psychological objects through *imitation*, *incorporation*, and *introjection*. Let's see what these are about.[30]

The object relating process that is probably least effective in moving the infant toward individuation is *imitation*. This is a copying of features of an object without any real attachment to it beyond one's simply wanting to copy it. This is a trivial sense of object relating, because there are really no enduring changes being made in terms of a meaningful cathecting of objects or emotional attachment to them. With imitation, the pre-self doesn't really move any closer toward becoming an independent self than before. Instead, the imitative infant merely play-acts at taking in some quality of an object. This does, of course, allow the infant to at least rehearse what it would be like to have the agency of the object he's imitating. And it is in this function that imitation has any importance at all in self development. It makes that agency *behavior* more familiar to the imitator. But it doesn't bring him any closer to genuinely internalizing the power of that object's agency as an internal psychological object. So it has no appreciable force in moving him closer toward forming his own self. This is just as true for the adult imitator as for the infant. When, as infants, children, or adults, we imitate another person, we try out an image of life, but we don't really make any honest headway toward creating psychological structure, or organized self representations. Rather, imitation just shows that we have some idea of the direction we would like our self making to go in. Imitation merely expresses how we *would* have ourselves be.

The process of *incorporation* is perhaps the infant's most dramatic and clearly most primitive response to the possibility of separation from the self-object. It is modeled on the infant's experience of physically taking in food, swallowing it. To hold onto a loved self-object, the incorporative infant tries to "swallow" it psychologically. In her desperate attempt to keep hold of the object through its representation, the infant tries to become the object by having it inside her mind/body.[31] She still makes no distinction between herself as a self and mother as a self. That is, "object representations completely lose their object character and are merged or fused with self-representations without distinction."[32] Clearly, incorporation can be effective as a way of keeping one's object world present. However, because it can't really move a person closer to forming her own separate agency self, its tenure is short-lived.

The process that is the most active one during the entire pre-self period is *introjection*. Introjective internalizations are less primitive object relations than incorporative ones. While through incorporation there is an attempt to fuse the object with one's mind/body self, through introjection one is bonded to the object by the *partial taking in* of some of its *qualities* but at the same time not attempting to make those qualities or the object a part of herself. The introjector takes in object qualities and allows them to work on her as *unassimilated* properties of the self. Introjects have their own special feel, as it were, somewhere between that of imitated qualities that are clearly experienced as belonging to the object (and not to one's self) and incorporated qualities that are experienced by the infant as having once belonged to a separating object (and former symbiotic object) and now to oneself. Introjects feel, in a sense, like object qualities on the periphery of the developing self.

Let me illustrate what I mean. Consider a situation for which we can imagine how all three kinds of object relating processes might get played out. Suppose a young boy's mother has died. What does this do to him as an object relator? Imagine that she had been the one to set the rules of moral behavior for him. He had no internal sense of being a moral self; he was too young for that. Rather, he simply followed her lead; she was his agency for morality in life. But now that she's gone, how is he to figure out what is appropriate moral behavior? How is he to deal with his object loss? One possibility is imitation. By simply remembering what mother's rules for appropriate behavior were, he is in a position to copy them. In this way, the boy would come to feel a clear distinction between himself, the lost object, and the recognized external rules that he is play-acting in order to get on with the job of living the moral life. The second possibility is incorporation. A regressive incorporative move would result were the boy actually to begin feeling as though he had become the person his mother was—that is, were he to feel that he had become the object qualities of his mother which he had related to when she was alive. This doesn't require that he actually think he is his mother, body and all. Instead, he might take on the mother's rules for defining appropriate behavior and believe that they have been of his own creation all the time. He might take full responsibility for these rules because he sees them as his own, although he has no explanation of why they don't seem to fit in with the rest of how he acts. They remind him of mother. And this is the crucial point. In having these rules as part of himself, he now feels that mother isn't really gone. He literally believes that part of her has become him.[33]

By contrast, an introjective move would involve the boy's feeling his mother's presence as something *partially distinct* from himself yet in some sense *within him*. Or perhaps he might feel an obsession with following the rules she used to enforce. In the latter instance, he is quite attached to the rules. He knows that he is now enforcing them. No one has to tell him, for, in a sense, he feels wedded to them. He feels mother's presence in his weddedness to the rules. But "weddedness" doesn't mean he has incorporatively internalized them as her agency. The rules don't feel part of who he is; they don't feel like they are his own. Rather, the boy feels driven by the rules, and he wants to be. The rules are a foreign force that he doesn't mind having function inside himself.

Generalizing from this case, we can understand all introjects similarly to be the welcomed partial working of an alien agency within oneself: foreign, yet, in some sense, part of him. But what else can we say about introjects? For one thing, they are object representations that are experienced as "existing within the confines of [the infant's] mind or body or both, but not as an aspect or expression of his subject self."[34] That is, they shouldn't be confused with agency self structure. Put another way, introjects have a different feel to them than ego components. They are felt as happening to us. We are passive to them; they are not of our own agency. But self functions are felt as active with a "self-originative" quality to them; they are of our own agency. Then, too, there is no real sense of intentionality, will, or activity about introjects. There is this sense, however, about genuine agency self functioning (i.e., about an identificatory self).

But having said this, I must also point out that all too often, people confuse introjects with agency self structure. There is an illusion of genuine agency that often accompanies introjects. People think that they have actively committed themselves to certain decisions about how to behave (i.e., committed themselves to genuine self agency), when, in fact, it is an introjected agency of some psychological object they are "borrowing" that is powering their decision making. For example, in introjecting, a person can take in (can borrow) the associated power behind some charismatic figure's forceful personality in making decisions. (We say he's introjected the charismatic person.) So one can appear as though he is forceful in making one's decisions, when in fact he is using the introjected other person to get the job done. The individual simply runs together what feels like his own agency power (but which is only borrowed) with genuine agency power. In this fashion, introjects *almost* feel a part of who we are as selves. We are *almost* full-fledged identificatory agency selves, but not quite.

What else can we say about introjections? In fact, they are the dominant kind of psychological processing going on during the *transition period* of development. Most often, they take the form of representational transition objects.

> In the process of introjection, a transitional internal object is created that somehow replaces the external libidinal relationship to the parent. The internalized object retains its transitional character, even as it becomes a part of the subject's inner world.[35]

Quite consistent with what we've already learned about transition objects, the subject here holds onto the lost object in the form of the new internal *introjected* representation of some features of the object. This introjection is inside him, the pre-self, so long as he needs it, so long as he can't fully "accept" his loss of the loved self-object—so long, that is, as he is in transition toward a more mature state where the evolving self can accept separation without fear of dissolution. At the point of *maturity*, the introject will either be totally dissolved or else assimilated by the self through the process of identification. Regarding the second alternative, the *content* qualities of what had been a foreign introject will still be present, but now they will be the content of an identification instead of the content of an introjection. And that, as we will see, makes all the difference in the world in becoming a full-fledged character agency self.

While an introject is functioning as a transition object, however, a person's psychological dynamics do some interesting things. It turns out that introjects have psychological processing mates—*projections*. It's not unusual for qualities that have just been *intro*jected as transition objects to immediately get *pro*jected out onto some real physical object in the world. Until the developmental phase of becoming an agency self unfolds later on, the person who no longer can depend directly on his parent self-objects to satisfy his needs has to depend on psychological connections that are in between being full-fledged external objects and an internal agency self. That is the introjected transition object. Its object qualities float around, as it were, as representations inside the primitive, still object relating pre-self. But sometimes having a "too alien" ("too foreign") object quality as a representation inside the pre-self isn't tolerable. So it gets projected out onto an object in the external world.[36] Suppose, for example, a child introjects his father's hostile aggressiveness as his way of getting what he wants. But also suppose he has been afraid of his father when his father has expressed that hostile aggressiveness. Suppose the child has been so afraid, in fact, that he fears having this trait as an introjected quality within himself. Well, like a splinter under the skin, such a transition object quality needs to be expelled from the pre-self, although not totally cast away. So it gets projected out onto someone else as a bad quality. He doesn't have to worry about himself being aggressively hostile now. In general, he so very much wants the introjected quality to be a part of some object other than himself that even though it isn't, he nevertheless imagines it is. To him, this external object now becomes the ultimate manifestation of the transition object. His object gratification now comes through his relating to this external object with the projected—that is, imagined—quality.

I have just described the context of projecting introjected *alien* qualities onto external objects. However, not all introjected qualities that then get projected are alien and undesirable. Suppose, for example, that an infant is weaned from breast feeding and fears a loss of his caring and comforting mother. He introjects these qualities. It may be, however, that they can be enjoyed more as some physical manifestation than as mere internal ideational content. So they may be immediately projected onto some other physical object in the infant's environment—say, these maternal qualities are now seen as belonging to the nursemaid. The infant sees her as being the same kind of person mother has been. The nursemaid has become the transition object, at least until the child can finally learn to deal with the loss of the mother self-object through the development of some semblance of an agent ego self. The same sort of thing might have happened to the child's pacifier, thumb, blanket, or teddy bear. The oral satisfaction he had from sucking mother's breast is introjected and maintained by sucking his thumb or a pacifier. The warmth and comfort mother provided gets introjected as abstract qualities and then immediately projected onto the child's favorite blanket or teddy bear. The transition object starts out in the form of an introjected internal representation and ends up as a projected object in the world. Both get cathected in their special ways by the infant. And if he fails to develop past this point in his dynamic growth, he will have a parade of transition objects taking on these needed-to-be-perceived-in-the-world qualities. So, for example, when social pressures force him to give up his teddy bear, he still might very well project the same object relating qualities onto a best friend, his bicycle, a movie star, or any of a multitude of other possibilities.

Psychoanalytic theory has it, however, that the normal need for transition objects eventually abates and the introjective activity begins to play still another role—a non–object relating one. A kind of rudimentary self structure begins to develop alongside of the still continuing, though diminished, pre-self activity. But not all at once. As we saw in the first section, many theorists think that the very first stage of genuine self-structure development arises in the form of *superego formation*. That initially makes use of introjective activity. More specifically, in resolving Oedipal conflicts, after competing with the same-sex parent for the affection of the other-sex parent, the child comes to a resolution of his feelings of lust and guilt by introjecting the values and desires of the same-sex parent: "If you can't beat 'em, join 'em." In this way, the child won't incur the same-sex parent's seemingly all-powerful wrath in the same-sex parent's envy of the child as the apple of the other parent's eye. Ultimately, down the road, the child will form rudimentary self structure by *identifying* with agency traits of the same-sex parent, an outcome of which will be the dissipation of his own fear and guilt because he no longer feels in competition with that parent. But this process doesn't occur overnight. In the beginning stages, the pre-self child introjects the same-sex parent's values as abstractions which haven't yet been fully assimilated as his own; they haven't been identified with as agency self structure. Rather, they are abstract *object* representations that are inside him, affecting the way he makes decisions about what is right and desirable, wrong and undesirable. They aren't yet full self-related superego functioning, although they are the immediate object precursors to that superego self formation.

The same thing can be said for the precursor role of projection. Sometimes the child projects these abstract introjected representations out onto the world in the form of what he sees as the world's objective "Moral System." Sometimes even society's law—the "law of the land"—takes on this projected object quality for him. In short, the child—say, the male child—introjects/projects the rules he lives his life by, where having these "object rules" to live by (which mirror those belonging to his father or society) gratify his need not to be overwhelmed by his seemingly all-powerful father or by society as a projected object stand-in for his father. Doing the introjective part of this is not *quite* the formation of superego. But it is what ultimately conditions superego formation. Finally doing the latter, however, requires that the child give up his object relating and instead start making use of his identificatory abilities for full-fledged self making.

All this activity is how things progress toward superego self formation when introjective/projective object relating is functioning normally. Sometimes, however, matters don't move along so smoothly. Damaged object relation functioning holds things up, sometimes forever. If, for example, the child never fully works through his Oedipal conflicts, he might never come to fully assimilate the introjected parent object values as his own. He might never come to turn them into identificatory self representations, the stuff of which a healthy superego agency self is forged. He is connected to the value rules, but never fully as part of his agency self. When this happens, it wouldn't be unusual after a while for the individual to experience the introjected/projected values as being so foreign that they finally feel like brutal rules of an oppressive society that he is forced to live by. He might even rebel against them as manifestations of his still live fear and hatred of the same-sex parent. The extreme of such a person would be the sociopath. That is one direction in which things might go. Another possibility, however, is that the introjected/projected values might be internalized in such a way that the individual is instead actually *obsessed* with *following* these values, although the felt tone of the obsession is a sense of "the rules come from outside, and I simply must follow them or I will get anxious." The law is father and it must be obeyed. The extreme of such a person would be the moralist. In either case—rebel or obsessive rule follower—the individual has not really developed full superego functioning. He is helplessly immersed instead in the precursor object relating activity.

I don't want to overstate the complaint here about introjective/projective object relating. Indeed, sometimes it can go haywire, as in the above two examples, and that can cause damage to the adult self. However, this does not mean that *all* object relating that remains in the individual's life past the transition period will be so damaging. The mated pairing of introjection and projection seems to weave its way throughout a person's psychological career without necessarily undoing him. We internalize what we need in terms of libidinal cathexes from the world. Introjection becomes the standard fare for doing this. We just as quickly push what we have taken in out onto something in the world. As we have seen, people seem to do this as much with negatively cathecting qualities as they do with positive ones. So, for example, an infant with a sadistic mother who is as likely to become very cold and angry as she is to become warm and caring toward the infant, might introject both pairs of qualities as part of his psychosexual development. This is what we referred to above as a "splitting of the object world." The reason for introjecting the positive elements is clear enough—it is the infant's way of "holding onto" the mourned-for lost and loved self-object. Why infants introject the negative elements is less clear. Object Relations theorists, however, speculate that they do this as a way of getting mastery, some control, over the feared and disliked negative qualities. It is as though the child were saying, "If I can take in these qualities that I dislike about mother, I can control them, and so I can also control her ever hurtfully using these dreaded qualities against me. I can defend against the undesirable parts of her agency." Clearly this would constitute a kind of adaptive defensive functioning.

Not everybody agrees with this view. Some theorists, for example, see the introjecting of negative qualities as an aggressive act by the infant toward the lost loved self-object. Mahler, for example, has pointed out that

> the less predictably reliable or the more intrusive the love
> object's emotional attitude in the outside world has been, the

greater the extent to which the object *remains* or *becomes* an unassimilated foreign body—a "bad" introject, in the intrapsychic emotional economy....In the effort to eject this "bad introject," derivatives of the aggressive drive come into play; and there seems to develop an increased proclivity to identify the self-representation with the "bad" introject or at least to confuse the two. If this situation surfaces during the rapprochement subphase, then aggression may be unleashed in such a way as to inundate or sweep away the "good object," and with it, the good self-representation.[37]

Then, too, there is this view:

The objects that frustrate primitive instinctual demands tend to mobilize an infantile rage, which is at once projected onto the objects and internalized as bad or destructive introjects.[38]

If mother is experienced in part as bad, the child will feel that he is bad or that he has a badness inside of himself that he can't fight. At the same time, though, the child at least can feel angry at the new object upon which he has projected the introjected badness. Perhaps he has projected his felt badness onto father. Since mother is necessary for fulfilling other required needs, the infant doesn't dare get angry with her. Father isn't so crucial to him at this time, so the infant can vent his wrath on the projected bad father. This is an economical way of dealing with aggressive feelings. Moreover, this kind of thing is even recognized as a normal part of psychosexual development.[39,40]

Finally, then, we've seen that introjects do many things and behave in many ways for people. But let's not forget what generated this discussion. I wanted to spell out the kinds of processes that prevail during pre-self object relating. We've done this now. And we've spent most of the discussion detailing the preeminent role that introjection has in the pre-self infant's holding onto the external object's agency.[41]

This idea in place now, let's also appreciate that after introjection has had its dominant run during this period, another process begins to emerge as the central player in the development of the self. What I've called object relating pre-self activity starts giving way to psychological activity of a different sort. *Identification* finally begins to emerge and do its work as the builder of an internal agency self. But even this identificatory move happens in stages. Pre-self object relating starts giving way to the narcissistic identificatory march toward internal rudimentary agency selfhood, which in turn will eventually give way to the identificatory building the latency self, which in turn will give way to the highest identificatory developmental project of building a character self.

Before we start looking at these later developmental stages, I'd like to close the present discussion by briefly making two points—one a general observation about two features of the pre-self that seem to stay with people throughout their entire psychological careers, the other a final word about how Object Relations theorists see identification as an improvement on the processes of object relating we've reviewed here.

IV

There are two striking central themes that come through in all of the pre-self process activity we've been looking at. One is that there is a human impulse for people to be enmeshed with an agency power external to and acting over them for the gratification of their needs. For all the obvious survival-enabling reasons, infants want to have a sense of belonging to something beyond just the mind/body. First we see this in symbiotic behavior: The infant's total immersion in the power of others defines who he is. Then we see the same thing in terms of the objects the infant transitionally connects to. The theme of connectedness just is important. But there is also a second lifelong theme that begins its expression in the pre-self. That is the human impulse to separate from others—to individuate—and make an internal unique center of power all of one's own. The object relation of introjection especially begins a person's journey in this direction. Clearly, these two opposing themes create the kind of existential tension I pointed out in the last chapter. Now we see that this tension comes on the scene as early as the pre-self stage of development. As a pre-self, one is disposed both to staying with and leaving the object. What's an infant to do? Of course, an even more imposing question to ask here is, What is *anyone*—infant, child, adolescent, or adult—to do? For we know that these two impulses which move us in opposing psychological directions stay with us throughout life. They are set in motion during pre-self activity, but we get to deal with them for the rest of our lives. Indeed, our earliest symbiotic predispositions get played out in the kinds of *social* character identities we create for ourselves, and our impulse to individuate is what the molding of our unique *personal* identity is all about. In other words, the two basic impulses that drive all the psychodynamic action of pre-self development stay with us and have a definite role to play in our character formation later on.

There is a second point I would like to make. The strategy in discussing Object Relations Theory has been to lay out this important context where identification gets talked about in psychology. Object Relations theorists see identification as the developmental high point of all the object relating activity we've been looking at; they claim that it is the ultimate object relation, where a person finally puts agency into his own self. So far, though, we've only been talking about identification's object relating ancestors. Clearly, we will want to see exactly how identification makes any kind of sense as their descendant. We will begin to talk about this in the next two chapters. However, let's be clear right now about how we will understand the general conceptual connection between identification and object relations. In fact, as I've just said, identification is often passed off as the ultimate kind of object relating process.[42] But while I have no difficulty saying that identification is the logical next step in the progression of psychic processes a person develops as he moves toward becoming a character self, I would rather avoid calling it literally "another object relating process." Certainly, one of the central ideas we've been talking about in this chapter has been that object relating processes are psychological responses to the feared loss of those objects that have psychic significance for the infant. As an object relator, a person is, in part, trying to hold onto the object as the important external agency that will help him gratify his desires. All the processes we have looked at are defensive maneuvers aimed at keeping the object present and functional as the infant's borrowed agency from the object. These moves may lay the groundwork for *then* being able to go on to create an agency self. But they are clearly in themselves not of self-making quality. All this being so, identification can't possibly be considered another kind of object relation. Identification is not a defensive posture taken by a person toward the possible loss of pleasure from the object. And most important, it is not a way of holding onto someone else's agency. The whole idea of identification is to finally create an agency self out of the infant. And indeed, it isn't as though the same theorists who call identification a kind of object relation don't also realize that identification is aimed at carving out an agency self. The problem is, the two notions don't fit together. If one acknowledges that identification is aimed at finally separating from the object world by creating an agency self, then, *by definition*, identification can't be seen as a kind of object relating.

Some theorists already recognize this. For example.

> Identifications carry the process of separation from the object
> a further step. In identification the object quality of the
> model [i.e., any loved object] is fully preserved....The object is
> acknowledged, accepted, and preserved as autonomously
> existing in its own right and as separate and independent
> from the internalizing subject. The tolerance for the sepa-
> rateness of the object is a mark of the autonomy of the par-
> ticipating ego (Modell, 1968).
> ...Each new level of structuralization is accompanied by
> a further evolution in the process of forming structure and
> internalization. Each progressive step diminishes the degree
> to which the inner world contributes to the constitution.[43]

Identification is, in part, a way of a person's being psychologically
connected to qualities or traits of an external object, but not in the
way we have understood defensive object relating. The identifier isn't
trying to hold onto the object as a helpful external agency. He is trying to make traits just like the object's into his own. He is trying to
internalize them and make them into his own agency. He acknowledges that the object's version of those traits is fully the object's. In
this regard, he is on his way to the eventual attitude of what theorists
call "mature object love," an appreciation of the object for what it is in
its own right. Here the full identifying person values some of the
object's traits for their own sake rather than for how the object and
those traits can better enable him to gratify needs and desires. In
this new kind of psychological world, the object traits are not "inside"
him in the way that introjects can be; there is no fantasy that he and
the object traits are fused to any degree in the object's being. The
identifier perceives the object and its traits as fully separate from
himself, it having its own agency that has nothing to do with him, the
identifier. At the same time, the identifier perceives his own
mind/body as having its own agency. This is his emerging sense of
having an autonomous self, a self that no longer has to depend defensively on the external object for its drive gratification. The mind/body
now is emerging as a psychological organization that can get the job
done. The more one comes to process experience through genuinely
identifying with objects in the world, the less of a hold the inner world
of introjecting, projecting, and so forth has on what and who one is.

CHAPTER 3

Narcissism Theory and Developing
the Rudimentary Self

In moving away from object relating, the infant puts less focus on her object representations and more on her self representations. This becomes the life-world of what Narcissism theorists call the infant's "nuclear self," what I refer to as her "rudimentary self." The *narcissistic* infant/child[1] starts to see herself in an entirely new internal way: She starts to experience her internal world in a manner that transfers agency for satisfying her desires to "her own" mind/body. She starts having more and varied ideas about the different kinds of internal agency control she has over various aspects of her life—moving about, grasping objects, orally gratifying herself, and so on. So not only is she able to do these sorts of things for herself, but she is now also having an ideational awareness—self representations—that these abilities are powered by an internal agency rather than by an external one. The sum of these self representations constitute the emerging rudimentary self. She is finally starting to have some control over her life by herself, and she is homing in on this focus more and more. In fact, she is getting so focused that there seems to be a conspicuous lack of interest in the world external to her mind/body. She is entering her own personal "age of Narcissism." Of course, we can't emphasize enough that what is going on here is just a beginning of selfhood. The developmental period of Narcissism merely trumpets the first call for the individual to experience her mind/body as agency. The self qua emerging self representations, though, falls a far sight short of being a full-fledged self; it falls a far sight short of what psychoanalysts understand as a solid core of complexly organized ego structure—what I am calling a "character self." Nevertheless, the individual is clearly now moving in the right direction.

In this chapter, I will explore how this rudimentary self unfolds and how it sets the stage for the character self. But before I get started, I want to once more quickly take care of some preliminary linguistic matters.

The first is still another point about what strikes me as a poor use of language on the part of some theorists. It appears that many

Narcissism theorists talk about the work of the narcissism period being a "cathecting of the self." In fact, they should be talking about a "cathecting of the *rudimentary* self." Since all that gets cathected here are merely individually emerging ego self *representations* and not ego self *structure*—the latter amounting to an internally integrated network of agency dispositions—it really makes no sense to talk about cathecting a self per se. Because we are going to understand a "rudimentary self" to refer only to clusters of these self representations, that terminology will do just fine for designating the self that appears during this time.

My second linguistic point is really just to say a clarifying word about the meaning of the other operative term in such claims about cathecting a self: "cathexis." In fact, this term has a complex theoretical meaning in psychoanalytic theory, and to unpack that meaning here would take us too far afield. So, for our purposes, when we use the term (as we will be doing again in this chapter), I simply want us to understand that any things that are cathected are items that become invested (sometimes consciously, sometimes unconsciously) with psychic energy (sometimes sexual, sometimes otherwise) because they play a role in gratifying standing important needs. Sometimes these are new items that have just come on the scene and are appreciated immediately (again, sometimes consciously, sometimes unconsciously) for their capacity to gratify certain needs; other times, they are items that have already been on the scene but until now haven't been seen as playing a need-gratification role. In the latter instance, for example, someone at work you may just have casually noticed for years as part of the everyday background might take on a considerable new meaning and significance in your scheme of things if you were to discover that she was a long-lost relative of yours. The idea of her becomes charged with new importance because of some familial need you hope she will satisfy. The idea of her is cathected. Or, to take an example of the former instance, the rudimentary self becomes cathected in the sense that it becomes something quite important and meaningful to the infant/child (we mean "becomes important and meaningful" in a prelinguistic sense) as it comes into existence. Obviously, too, it becomes a point of great focus for the infant/child. After all, it is the first blush of internal agency for the infant/child and, as such, it fulfills a very special need for her (prime directive 1 again). So naturally, as soon as it begins developing as a viable part of her functioning psychological repertoire, the continuance of that development receives a great deal of attention.

Large amounts of psychic energy are marshalled and trained on furthering along that development.

All this understood, we are ready now to proceed with our discussion. We will take it that what theorists call "infancy/childhood narcissism" refers to a particular developmental period when certain processes and themes about the emerging rudimentary self are cathected for the infant/child. They become the center of a lot of meaningful psychic activity that's generally described as narcissistic. Our job in this chapter will be to understand what this cathected narcissistic activity is all about.

I

Let's begin by sketching in this section how the infant finally breaks loose from functioning fully as a pre-self and begins ever so subtly functioning as a rudimentary self.

In *The Beginning*, there is the pre-self infant and its primitive wanting, or desiring, at the core of all its pre-self activity. Desires for getting needs met are raging and "insisting" on being gratified. We might think of the pre-self infant as being bundles of such desires. In no uncertain terms, the infant wants comfort, sexual gratification, warmth, and so on. But there is no centralized organization to these wants. There is no organized subjective self doing the wanting. There is merely the mind/body passing through the scene, as it were, forming wants as it goes along, responding to life's contingencies as they arise. From this perspective, a person's wants are her most primordial conscious-state responses to the contingencies thrown at her. But they aren't organized or recollectable in a repository of memory. That sort of thing would require a reflective center to connect earlier and later ones to each other. Instead, early infant behavior indicates that pre-self wants are discrete—indeed, indiscriminate— events. To put the point in different terms, the pre-self person qua "biological unit" appears to have a series of discrete want events that the biological unit's program "tries" to get met by enlisting the aid of an external self-object agency. When wants are met, there is a sense of momentary meaningful (cathected) gratification for the mind/body biological unit. But no moment of gratification is connected in a meaningful way to any other moment of gratification. A pre-self person is a series of momentary discrete sensory events, desires for sensory input or output, struggles for doing so, and fleeting meaningful gratifications or frustrations over meeting the struggles. But none of these elements is experienced as related to any of the others and organized by some subjective center.

Now, not only is the pre-self a bundle of unbounded wanting, it is, as we have seen, also one very complex defense structure that guards against the possible frustration of these wants. So it incorporates, introjects, and so on, to hold onto an external agency that will make certain its wants are met. During these early days, the pre-self infant has no inner reflective sense about a self that could do the job. Quite literally, the early infant is not yet "self-*interested*" although it is very much "self-*defending*." What I mean is that the pre-self is an organization of defense mechanisms. And not only am I emphasizing the "defense" element here, I would also underscore "mechanism." The early infant is a living causal machine which, through largely unconscious processes, is merely working out a preestablished biological program for survival. But the infant certainly isn't yet a human "being" with organized subjective concerns. She is a causally determinable servomechanism "trying" to maintain a steady state for continuing survival with minimal pain. The program comes with some learning capabilities for defending against the onslaughts of life, whether those onslaughts be physical (e.g., deprivation of nutrients) or psychological (e.g., loss of maternal affection). But there is no sense of a reflective subjectivity going on. There is just the expression of a complex survival mechanism. We are talking about a programmed biological machine here, doing whatever needs to be done to meet its wants and defending against anything that would frustrate them.

Just prior to the initial formation of self representations—the first hint of the emergence of a subjective self—the complex infant defending mechanism is immersed, for the most part, in the kinds of introjective states we talked about in chapter 2. The infant's introjecting self-objects and associated objects defend against the infant's suffering the loss of the highly desired (i.e., wanted) self-object, that and the loss of its promise of agency for meeting the infant's desires for nourishment, security, and so forth. Through introjection, the infant continues meeting its overriding desire to have the maternal self-object (in the form of surrogate object representations) as its agency for satisfying all of its other wants.

I'll assume the reader can make the appropriate parallel inferences about projection and wants (desires). In any event, at some point, this complex strategy for holding onto an external agency stops being optimal. At some point, it seems that life as an object relating enterprise must start to become tenuous, so that stand-in objects just won't do anymore. Patterns of cathected self representations begin emerging. Flickerings of agency experienced as "one's own" come on the scene. Infants more and more try out their own internal wares for getting the things they want. The more success they have here, the more they experience being their own agency, the more they cathect an internal agency self. The idea of self agency starts taking on meaning for them.

Theorists believe that one reason for this movement toward an internal self is the evolutionary benefit it affords. Simply, having a self agency to go along with the help of external agencies increases the individual's chances of survival as well as want/need gratification. On a more immediate experiential level, the first blush of internal agency normally gets played out as a very sensible response to too much imperfect maternal caretaking. Mother might be tired of putting all of her focus on the wants and needs of the infant—she might want to reclaim some of herself, might want to start focusing again on her own special wants and needs—or she might just simply start to develop a growing diminution of empathy for the infant.[2] In either case, the infant takes the message here as motivation for developing his own agency. It's a defensive move with survival value. Of course, there are other possibilities the infant might, and sometimes does, try first. Sometimes, in lieu of mother or an associated introjection of her, the infant tries enlisting the agency services of father or an associated introjection of him. Eventually, though, even this move will ultimately fail. Any external agency inevitably tires of paying total attention to the needs of the infant. And so the infant begins to try out his own mind/body's abilities to get what he wants. His awareness of his success in this regard gets expressed in the formation of self representations.

We might think of these self representations as being just over the psychic line, as it were, from object introjects. What before were object traits one was focused on are now internal subject traits that are focused on, or are cathected. The contents of what had been an object relation are now the contents of a self representation. That is, the very same traits that one saw in another and used with that other's agency to get his wants met are now taken inside, seen as his own, and used to get his wants met. For example, as an object relator, an infant might center on his mother's trait of providing sustenance when he's hungry. Either directly in the mother or in an introject of her, he focuses on the trait of "providing sustenance" and uses mother's agency or the introject's associated agency (i.e., object representation) to get the trait realized in the world. Then, as a rudimentary self, he is still focused on the same trait content he saw in the object; the object is still a *model* of that trait. However, the dramatic change that occurs is that the infant now internalizes the trait, applying a cathected internal agency to getting it realized in the world. In this particular example, as a rudimentary self, the infant sees food and decides that he can reach for and grasp it himself to satisfy his hunger. Of course, he probably has been reaching for and grasping food long before now, but that was all a causal affair. Now he reaches and grasps as an expression of a newly emerging sense of internal organized agency that can initiate its own activities. There is a clear sign of the difference here. There's a pride this older infant takes in his internal agency success, while there's a total lack of such a thing in the younger infant reacher/grasper. The older infant has crossed over the line from being an object relator to becoming a rudimentary self.

None of this change is clean, however; one doesn't make a discrete jump over some developmental line at a specific dramatic moment. Not surprisingly, the profile of the infant/child immersed in this stage of development is that of a person who really flickers back and forth between cathecting self- or introjective object representations on the one hand and cathecting self representations on the other. The two are run together, although the clear developmental movement is in the direction of cathecting self representations. More and more, self representations take on functions that objects and their representations had previously been performing. The more complex the organization of these self representations gets, the stronger the sense of a rudimentary self an individual gets.

II

Fine. We know that at a certain stage of development, a person begins to form self representations where before there were none. A reasonable question to ask of the theorists at this point is why they characterize these self representations as "narcissistic." What is the force of this descriptor? The quick answer is that the infant/child now is wholly preoccupied with himself. The only discernable psychological theme is that of straightforward mind/body gratification. For example, in speaking of infant narcissism, Freud calls it the attitude of a person who treats his own body in the same way in which the body of a sexual object is ordinarily treated—who looks at it, that is to say, strokes it and fondles it till he obtains complete satisfaction through these activities....Narcissism in this sense [is] the libidinal complement to the egoism of the instinct of self-preservation.[3]

Elsewhere, Freud speaks of the narcissist as a "whole individual who retains his libido in his ego and pays none of it out in object-cathexes."[4] In other words, Freud appreciates that the narcissist is preoccupied with his body identity and his ego self.[5] The infant/child at this stage does not look beyond the boundaries of what we would roughly understand as those things that are "his own." This is quite a departure from the prenarcissism days where the focus was on the object's agency.

The current Kohut/Kernberg Narcissism theorists have gone well beyond these early Freudian ideas about narcissistic organization and have extended the discussion to talk about "the narcissistic personality."[6] Although not a full-fledged self, the narcissistic infant/child, as well as the neurotic adult version of the narcissistic personality, is understood as a "bipolar cluster of self tendencies" set around issues of narcissistic *wants* and narcissistic *values*. We have just seen how the pre-self is filled with wants that have no self organizing them. Well, by contrast, the wanting that goes on during this next phase of development is organized around self related narcissistic themes. One involves emerging self representations about an internal agency that is aimed at satisfying what are referred to as "grandiose wants." These self representations are organized around the theme of "infantile exhibitionism and ambition." Clearly, we find ourselves once again steeped in adultomorphic terminology for describing infant/child behavior. So be it. Theorists presumably use these particular terms to describe infant/child attitudes and behaviors that would appear to adults to be an unashamed display of concern for the infant/child's pleasure-aimed desires—i.e., that's exhibitionism—and a dogged determination to get these grandiose wants realized regardless of what most of the outside world thinks about the project—i.e., that's ambition.

But these descriptions are only about our narcissistic wanting pole. Let's not forget the second pole, viz. narcissistic valuing. The valuing element is about an internalized image of what theorists call "an idealized parent *imago*." This is an image of an idealized self, that self composed of a set of self representations organized around the theme of certain ideal values that are derived from a self-object.[7] There are pieces of both organizational themes in earliest infancy which begin to seriously show themselves as budding self structure in late infancy and early childhood.[8] Let's see what both of these ways of organizing self representations are about, using the rest of this section to talk about the "narcissistic grandiose self."

The basic kind of consciousness that the emerging narcissistic internal agency self is aimed at controlling is the infant's wants. There is a way in which the quality of the wanting that's going on in this stage helps organize the new rudimentary self. What is this quality like? For one thing, the wanting is fully unfettered, unrestricted. One wants the things that will make her world *totally* under control. Of course, this description doesn't sound too different from the wants of the pre-self infant. And, indeed, the pre-self infant has narcissistic wants, too, in the sense that she narcissistically wants "her" nourishment, sexual stimulation, successful locomotion, warmth, bowel relief, emotional comfort, and so forth. But she allows—she demands—that the self-object will do the job. By contrast, as a narcissistic grandiose "wanter" qua rudimentary self, the infant/child seems to think that her budding agency can realize anything she wants. She isn't just trying out agency, getting practice; She is filled with wanting things for herself, and she behaves like a person who believes that her agency can bring them about, and she *expects* that these wants ought to be realized by her world, without any reservations. In short, she is grandiose with her wants. She is immersed in her "infantile ambitions," all of which she grandiosely thinks she should have satisfied and will have satisfied by what she does as an agency self. For adults, such grandiosity would normally be a defect, an unrealistic stance towards life. However, in the narcissistic infant/child, this grandiosity is no deficiency. It is part of normal psychological development.[9]

To understand "normal" here, we need to be a little clearer about what the general concept of wants is about.[10] If you will allow me some metaphorical license, I would say that the feel of a want is the feel of something missing, so much so that the wanter is pointed at doing things to fill the void of "not-enough." All wanters are seekers of the experience of "enough." In an ideal world, where all things would be equal, the wanter would always get what she's seeking. She would always experience the "not-enough" being followed by the "enough." In other words, ideally, all wanting is "meant" to be satisfied. Alas, though, the world isn't ideal. We have many wants that don't successfully lead us to "enough"; they don't all get satisfied. Even so, this doesn't deter us. We still continue to want. And even in the cases where a wanter is fairly successful at attaining "enough," wanting still doesn't slow down. Indeed, it's said that people never really have enough; we always want something. And when that's satisfied, we want something else. The process never ends. However, in everyone's life, a point is reached where we discover that we just can't always get what we want. We continue to want, but we stop expecting that our every desire will be fulfilled. We stop insisting on the land of "enough." We learn that we must mediate our wanting if we are to get along in the world with other wanters.

But how does wanting function specifically in the narcissistic grandiose infant/child? First of all, she experiences her wanting as the ideal I just mentioned. As a new wanter on the scene who hasn't yet been tossed around by the hard knocks that all of life's wanters inevitably receive, this babe-in-the-woods narcissist sees getting "enough" for all of her wants as her due. She genuinely acts as though she's convinced that "all things are equal" for her and her wanting. In a sense, she isn't being unrealistic. She is being prerealistic. She is working with a new primitive concept and trying it on in its pristine form. And that involves her wanting things without there being any limiting conditions placed on her situation; she sees total satisfaction as her due. Moreover, she insists on having all of her wants fully realized in this way. In the initial stages of narcissism, the infant/child's insistence is about the self-object using its agency to give her what she wants. But this soon evolves into an insistence that nothing get in her way for *her* bringing about her wants. Theorists say that she exhibitionistically flaunts her wants because, in a sense, they are the whole of who she is at this point. She has an unlimited package of wants for comfort, security, nourishment, and so on. There is no hint of compromising what she wants. And again, there is nothing psychologically deficient about any of this. It's natural, normal, albeit quite grandiose. It's certainly not realistic, but, by the same token, it's what can be expected of an infant who hasn't yet experienced the limitations that life places on wanters. Indeed, she will have forged developmentally appropriate self representations about her seemingly grandiose powers here that she will use in assertively announcing her rudimentary self structure to the world.

Now, if we are fully to understand the nature of the grandiose wanting of narcissism, we'll need to appreciate what theorists describe as the narcissistic infant/child's sense of *omnipotence*—that is, the all-powerfulness she experiences in her narcissistic wanting. To understand this, let's first appreciate the kind of power one experiences as a pre-self with wants. Again, as a pre-self infant, it seems that one need only have a want to then see it fulfilled. That is, with an attentive self-object at her beck and call, an infant's want gratification can become something bordering on the miraculous for her. Somehow the pre-self infant has merely to cry, smile, coo, scream, giggle, fuss, and the self-object will give her the affection she wants, the warmth she wants, the nourishment she wants, the security she wants, and so on. The success of these wants is empowering. The infant's awareness of success gives rise to the feeling of power across the full expanse of the pre-self infant's world. Let us realize, though, that while the infant feels power here, it is power she feels "out there" in the self-object. Or else it is power she feels as an introjection. In either case, although she certainly experiences power in having successful wants, she doesn't own that power. And she certainly doesn't own a sense of omnipotence.

In fact, at this point, the infant/child has a sense that the attentive *self-object* is omnipotent. With the dazzling display of the self-object's ability to satisfy the infant's desires, the infant can hardly help but see things this way. If nothing else, seeing things this way is the infant's *fantasy* about mother. After all, the greater the infant thinks the self-object's power is, the more secure she will feel in this world that she can't control in any other way. Eventually, that fantasized trait of self-object omnipotence is introjected by the infant. So she has this "outside" quality even nearer yet, although still not within her own agency.

But the infant finally does make the relevant self-object or introjected traits into self representations; she takes on self representations of traits that mirror the omnipotence of the self-object and introjects. That is, the infant's wanting things now triggers *self representations* of an agency that is all-powerful in meeting those wants. The more power that had been invested in mother as agency, the more it is experienced now in one's emerging rudimentary self. This is what theorists call the infant/child's "narcissistic mirroring" of mother's power. In a sense, the infant/child is happily crazed with the imagined agency she has over her wants. The wanting world is her oyster. No limitations, certainly no moral brakes. And as if that weren't extreme enough, in addition to this, the maternal self-object also now confirms the acceptability of this infant/child behavior, at least for a while. The infant is told that it is acceptable for her to have wants that she can be in charge of, as it were; it is her entitlement. She doesn't have solid enough core ego self in place yet that will do the full job of agency alone. So she depends on the messages from the self-object about which grandiose wants can be experienced as legitimate and viable.[11]

Think of the situation in this way. Although the self qua "internal agency that realizes its wants" is finally being forged, it is only beginning the process. It still needs, among other things, some support, a backup system of sorts. That is where the confirming parent is important. Through his sympathetic behavior, he confirms the legitimacy of the infant's wants, as grandiose as they may be. He loves the infant's having the sense of power she has in her unrestrained wanting. So he confirms for the infant that her behavior is perfectly acceptable. He even helps get her wants realized. In this process, though, he also confirms for the infant that she has her own internal power over her realizing her wants.[12] It is as though the confirmation from the parent enables the infant to believe more and more that she, the infant, can do it when it comes to fulfilling wants, and that it is good for her to pursue this regarding her grandiose wants. The parent is excited that his infant has these wants. That is because the parent knows that having wants is the first sign of empowerment. And when one loves someone, one wants that person to have and enjoy the fruits of empowerment. In his excitement, the parent would like to give the infant virtually everything she wants. So the parent is really fostering the infant's sense of grandiosity. He is confirming that it is acceptable to be this way. But he is also confirming that it is acceptable for the infant to meet her wants by herself. This is a very complex sort of consciousness for the infant. Her wants are felt both as being hers through the self-object and as being hers through her own empowered self. In a sense, she simultaneously experiences herself externally as the self-object agency and internally as her own agency self.

III

Just as pre-self and rudimentary narcissistic wanting are grandiose, so are pre-self and rudimentary self valuing that way too. Infants value totally, without qualification. Objects of grandiose wants are valued grandiosely and, as such, are the primitive versions of what adults would understand as being the purely good, the ideal. Just as infants want with abandon, so do they value with abandon. These are first-time phenomena and therefore occur in their unadulterated form. Infants and young children see their wants and the possible satisfaction of those wants as totally valuable, totally good. Only later in life do they learn about the less-than-perfectly-good and the gradations thereof. That is, only later do they learn to evaluate the relative strengths and merits of their wants. In the beginning, though, to value is to be connected directly to the totally good. This is certainly very empowering for the infant. Just as she is further empowered as a self by having her wants legitimized, realized, and confirmed by mother, so does her primitive valuing get treated the same way. Moreover, just as the former ultimately leads to the formation of self structure, so does the latter. It becomes another central theme for organizing self representations. Let's see how this works.

A life of unbounded wanting clearly would be intolerable for an individual. She would be out of control. Her frustration level would be well beyond anything that was acceptable for normal functioning. So the narcissistic infant/child needs some kind of boundaries placed on all that grandiose wanting. To bring this about, another rudimentary part of the self begins developing. Specifically, ideal values that "tell" the infant what to "aspire" toward are developed as self-representational structure. Initially, these items are introduced into the infant's repertoire as object relational matters. Her ideals are really the self-object's. But they are used in an object relational way to place boundaries around what the infant will do with her narcissistic grandiose wants. "From the outside," the self-object presents life goals about which kinds of wants are valuable—that is, desired by and acceptable to the self-object—and which aren't. Since the infant/child sees herself mirrored in the self-object, then since the self-object is seen as perfect, so is she. Moreover, the self-object is seen to be the bearer of perfect values, ideals, for the infant/child to mirror. As we discussed above, since her survival dependence on the self-object mother is so total at this time, it is only to be expected that the infant wants to see mother as omnipotent in every way. Now, for the very same reasons, we can say the same thing about *all* maternal *perfections*. For survival dependence reasons, the infant/child wants to see her mother as perfect in every way, including the kinds of boundary-setting ideal values she would have the infant/child live by. If the infant/child follows the value recommendations of mother, she will not only have her wanting under control, but that wanting will be under control in accordance with perfect limiting values. At least that's how the infant/child experiences matters.

Before any of these object relating values are turned into self representations, however, they first are internalized as value introjects. The infant/child introjects what we have noted is called "an idealized parental *imago*." That is, she introjects an idealized image of what, according to her perfect-seeming mother, is of value in life. These introjects set the first standard for what the infant/child should seek as desirable goals in life. Since the parent and the parent's valuing have been experienced as perfect, so, too, are the infant/child's introjects experienced that way. Moreover, because the source of these introjected values is the seemingly all-powerful parent, then the introjects are experienced as being all-powerful in the self too. That is, one is further empowered as a self through the mirroring of the parent's values.

What we have been describing amounts to a lot of feelings of perfection and empowerment. The infant/child's grandiose wanting is empowering; her introjected ideals are both empowering and perfect seeming. This sounds fairly wonderful for the infant/child. In fact, though, not everything is so wonderful. The new valuing empowerment and perfection actually cut into the sense of empowerment one has had as an unbounded grandiose wanter. And that's as it should be. After all, as we have said, it's the need to place some boundaries on grandiose wanting that gives rise to the development of narcissistic valuing in the first place. Once the infant/child is a valuing being as well as a wanter, she's in for some frustration. For quite often it happens that while the infant/child's wants may pull her in one direction of action, her values may push her in the opposite direction. This is a bitter pill for a newly formed omnipotent being to swallow. She is just getting used to wanting things with abandon, demanding that she get what she desires as her due. But now she finds out that she is sometimes to pursue courses of action that might run contrary to her wants—that is, what is desir*ed by* her isn't always what is now desir*able to* her.[13] Her grandiose wants aren't always in sync with her introjected perfect ideals. The introjective precursors to omnipotence-smashing moral brakes that will later have their way with the individual have now come on the scene. The infant/child can't hide from their force over her. And her sense of total empowerment is toned down accordingly.

Of course, there needn't always be a conflict between the infant/child's introjected values and her grandiose wants. And so her sense of empowerment needn't always be tempered. Narcissistic values aren't required always to be dampeners on the infant/child's grandiose wants and thus on her sense of empowerment, too. There are plenty of times when she can positively evaluate her narcissistic wants (i.e., when her ideals and wants complement one another). The Narcissism theorists have their own way of expressing this idea. As we pointed out earlier, as a pre-self introjector first emerging into a narcissistic self with some agency over her wants and values, the early rudimentary self is a bipolar cluster of grandiose wants and ambitions expressed in exhibitionistic ways, aimed at fulfilling (through the infant's skills and talents) the introjected values of the self-object. The early rudimentary self is a bipolar affair "driven" by ambitions (wants) and "led" by ideals.[14] When a person is functioning optimally, the two poles actually complement one another. Her ideals fit in with her wants. So her sense of perfection and empowerment from her ideals needn't always encroach on the empowerment she gets from having narcissistic wants. Only negative evaluations of a given narcissistic want need lead to that result.

In any event, people introject parental values and mirror them in their behavior and attitude. Sometimes this conflicts with their project of grandiosity and empowerment, sometimes it doesn't. This is pre-self and early narcissism stage activity. Eventually, though, the infant/child begins to evolve from being an object relator with ideals into being a rudimentary self with ideals. This means that her grandiose wants and her parentally defined values are now experienced as belonging to her self, rudimentary though that self is. She now cathects her thematically grandiose wants and perfect ideals as self representations. The narcissistic rudimentary self experiences herself not only as a grandiose omnipotent wanter who has the world of wants under her own budding agency control but also as a being of perfect ideals who, in the living of these ideals, has herself under control by some version of her own agency.[15] As with her narcissistic wants, her narcissistic ideals will become increasingly firm self representations—rudimentary self structure—the more she gets them confirmed by self-objects. The more support she gets from perfect, powerful objects in her life, the more she will really begin to believe in the power of her own value agency over her life.

I would like to look at this last idea a little more. To get a better grasp on things, though, we need to make a slight alteration in our vocabulary. What I want to say about valuing and the emerging rudimentary self is really best understood in terms of *esteeming* as a kind of valuing. Esteeming objects of any sort, including the self, is synonymous with valuing them highly, holding them in high regard, as measured by certain standards. Accordingly, valuing in the narcissistic infant/child's life is in part about esteeming the internal agency self, as measured by certain standards of value. As the infant/child moves into narcissistic development and begins to introject from mother and then to mirror a rudimentary sense of self, he learns what mother sees is and is not valuable. Through this process, he learns mother's standards of value. She is his paradigm for how an omnipotent-seeming self—mother's self—esteems things in the world. That is, not only is she his model of power and other perfections—that is, he mirrors her in these ways—she is also his model for what to value. It's as though to say, "If mother values something, it must be estimable." Quite simply, he mirrors her standards of value.

Perhaps most significant for rudimentary self development here is mother's behavior that as much as tells the infant/child that it is quite acceptable for him to act like a valuing agency self independent of her agency. She confirms for him that it is quite acceptable for him to esteem the things that he chooses to esteem and that it is quite acceptable for him to pursue those things as an independent agency self. In other words, mother confirms the acceptability of his esteeming powers as a self. And equally important, she esteems the infant/child as a separate valuing self; she values him in terms of *his own standards*. It is mother's esteeming here that gives the infant/child his first sense of what his *self's value* is all about. The greater the esteem mother has for the infant/child, the more perfect the image of being a valuable rudimentary self the narcissistic infant/child gets. This idea is the basis for the psychological cliché that if mother tells the infant/child that he is of great value—if she esteems him highly, if she simply *loves* him—he will have a core sense that he is valuable, lovable. An infant/child who is a loved self by the self-object—and therefore, presumably, someone who is lovable, at least to mother—experiences himself as a self of very high regard. An infant/child receiving waves of love experiences his emerging self as being something of greatest conceivable worth. If mother gives him something short of this message, then he will have a correspondingly weakened opinion of his self. She is his total determiner of worth at this stage of development.

There is something of a paradox about these ideas that bears mentioning. On the one hand, theory has it that it takes a loving mother to tell the infant/child that his emerging self structures are things of value and that it is acceptable for him to value them for his own reasons. On the other hand, one really is a valuing *self* only if he doesn't need confirmation from others about what he considers important. More pointedly, he is a self that truly sees his self as being of value only if he decides *for his own reasons* that his self is of value. The kind of being the narcissistic infant/child is trying to become— that is, an independent agency self—is someone who will no longer *need* confirmations of his worth. And so the idea that the more maternal love an infant/child receives, the more he will value his emerging self might seem a bit puzzling. Finally, though, it really isn't. We must remember that the emerging narcissistic rudimentary self is just that: emerging. We call it a self, but the force of my qualifier, "rudimentary," was intended to emphasize that the self-representational activity unfolding here is only about thematic organizational *tendencies*. At this time, there is nothing like the solid organizational *structure* that a character self will have in place later in life. For self structure even to start to become a serious possibility, the self tendencies of the narcissistic stage of development must be secured as conditions that are more than just tendencies. What the psychologists call "ego (self) structure" is more than *just* tendencies. These tendencies must become relatively permanent parts of the individual's personality repertoire, a consolidation of interlocking personality dispositions. To turn tendency into such a repertoire, there is still nothing quite so impressive as the work that *reinforcement* does. And maternal love of the infant/child self does precisely this kind of work. Mother's confirmation of the infant/child's being a rudimentary self slowly helps turn infant/child tendencies into self structure. Once that is significantly attained, the infant/child will no longer need mother's approval. Of course, this all occurs in degrees. Most people hardly ever are fully rid of the need for external confirmation of their self value. Most people depend on mother or other self-object surrogates for confirmation to some degree. Clearly, we expect this need to diminish as we develop as selves. But it rarely disappears fully. Nevertheless, it's the case for most people that once they reach some critical mass of self structure, they no longer need maternal approval in any significant sense. And so there really is no conflict between the ideas that narcissistic *rudimentary* selves (self tendencies) need confirmation of their value from mother while more developed selves don't.

Clearly, the valuing of self we are talking about here is really about how the budding infant/child self first establishes a sense of self-esteem. Finally, I believe that self-esteem can be *fully* experienced only by a developed character self. And that requires psychological development well beyond this infant/child narcissism stage. But the seeds for self-esteem are sewn during this time. The rudimentary self can have a reflexive sense of esteem and we can call it a kind of self-esteem. But we must understand that it is really only a primitive precursor to the real thing. It mirrors the love shown it by mother according to her standards. Later, however, if the individual has not been neurotically damaged, he will carve out a sense of self-esteem that is full, because it will come out of valuative standards that he has autonomously decided upon for himself. What we have been talking about in this chapter is how the process gets started in one's psychological history. Through infantile "self-esteem," the small gains in rudimentary self tendencies made during infantile narcissism are consolidated. This rudimentary self is held in place so long as one continues to esteem it, until that time when new psychological mechanisms—identifications—present further opportunities for the creation of even more organized self structure.

IV

Before leaving this chapter, I have some things I want to say about the rudimentary self that will set up some important discussions in Part II about the character self. The first is about the essential role that the valuing acts we have just been looking at ultimately play in building an agency self. For one thing, the grandiosity and perfection that the narcissistic infant/child feels about himself—his unrealistic sense of being a perfectly valuable self—become a model for how he later sees himself as a character self. Although as an adult he is a more rational being who knows that he can't possibly be perfect, he does continue to see himself as totally valuable. We say he is fundamentally still a "self-interested" being. As in his earlier narcissism, the adult character perceives his life as his most important commodity. He thinks the value standards he has chosen to set sail under as a character self—that is, he thinks the ideals he has chosen to live by—are, quite simply, the best. In those situations where a character starts having doubts about the ultimate value of his value standards, he either experiences a crisis in character identity or begins changing some of his value standards to sculpt a somewhat different kind of character, one that he will once again be able to think of as totally valuable because it arises out of new value standards that are seen by him as the best. The point is, the adult character self is an entity that highly esteems himself or else changes until he does. The model for being such a high self-esteeming entity comes in the forma-tive narcissistic rudimentary self stage of development.

There is a related point I should also make here. Selves cohere only so long as they have high value, esteem. A person will get some of that esteem from others in the course of his life. But most will be internally generated; most will be "self-esteemed." As an infant/child self, one's self-esteem is self-ascribed in terms of the standards of value the self has latched onto. Again, during earliest infancy, those standards are deter-mined by mirroring those of the self-object. The act of taking on values to make a rudimentary self by mirroring mother's becomes a paradigm for similar acts as they are performed in later life. In forming the adult character self, we mirror traits we see in other people besides mother. This is part of what it means to identify with other people. We find things about them we value and we mirror those things in our own character. The difference is that in narcissistic mirroring, we mainly live out a *causal* program that has us copying the values of the mater-nal self-object; in the mirroring that goes on later—when, as character selves, we identify with someone—we *autonomously choose* to make traits we see in others into some of the value standards by which we live our lives. No more dependence on mother. As we will see in Part II, this difference is of no small importance.

I would also like to say something here about the connection between the wanting of the narcissistic self and the wanting of the identificatory self. Narcissistic wanting stays with us throughout life. Even adults have pockets of it—we revert to the grandiose activity of a rudimentary self on occasion. On these occasions, all we can think about is how entitled we are to the satisfaction of our wants. Even though as rational adults we think of narcissism as a far stretch from reality and so, on the face of things, something neurotic in adulthood and to be avoided, still there actually can sometimes be something very healthy about having some narcissism. Why? There is a quality about narcissistic wants we can call "insistence." Since narcissistic wants in their purer form are unbridled—without boundaries—there is an insistence that they be satisfied. The paradigm image of this would be the infant throwing a temper tantrum because he wants something so strongly and he insists that the world accommodate him. But as adults, too, in our narcissistic moments, we go after want satisfaction with much the same gusto, although we usually try to stay away from throwing undignified tantrums. Still, sometimes things simply feel like they are our due. We insist on getting what we want. Where such insistence doesn't lead to antisocial behavior, it can be healthy. Often, such behavior leads to bettering our chances for getting what we want. Since wants in general are "meant" to be satisfied (all things being equal), the greater our socially acceptable wanting insistence is, the greater our chances of satisfaction. Moreover, there is something healthy about a personality that thinks that much of itself—that esteems itself that much—that it insists that it is important enough to have certain of its wants satisfied, even in a world where there may be others with competing wants. We see ourselves here as being *that* important.

What I am pointing out is that the rudimentary wanting self surfaces again in a person's life well after infancy and childhood. It is woven in with the more adult self of post-infancy/childhood development. And this isn't always a neurotic affair. In pockets of a healthy person's life, there are those occasions where he isn't disposed to scouting around for possible objections or boundaries that could put a damper on his wants. This stands out because as character selves, we typically are ready to evaluate our wants before we act on them. That's the rational way to be, anyway. My point is that as characters we are *not always* looking to evaluate our wants. If we were purely rational beings, we would constantly be evaluating our competing wants before we acted on any of them. Yet in many of our nonrational but nonneurotic narcissistic adult moments, we aren't disposed to continually poring over all the possible wants we have. We grandiosely go with the ones that feel clear and strong to us. We simply let things fly because we are worth it. No special self evaluation is needed. We leave it to the external world rather than to an internal disposition to challenge us. If the world insists on challenging our narcissism, the healthy person will probably listen. But he won't be sitting around just waiting for such challenges. Were a person to be always on the lookout for possible objections to his wants, we wouldn't see him as a healthy personality, for we would suspect that his self-esteem suffered some while his esteem for others-before-himself was thriving. The fact is, having some narcissism in adulthood is a mark of self-loving that is the spice of healthful psychological living. Phenomenologically speaking, one feels totally alive when he narcissistically lets out all the stops for wanting. For one feels a grandiosity and valuation about the self that is perfect—ideal—if not exactly realistic. In a sense, one comes as close in narcissistic consciousness to perfecting the self as he will ever come.

Obviously, these adult narcissistic wants can exist successfully only in pockets of life. Most of the rudimentary self has to stay at home, back in infancy/childhood. Otherwise we would have social chaos. Most of our effective adult wants are not narcissistic. We learn early on that our grandiosity had better play center stage only for the two acts that are infancy and early childhood. Our parents give us this gift in the service of their excitement over our growing into human personalities and in the service of our starting the outlines of a self that is independent of them and other selves. But in short order, these same parents tell us that the fantasy of our grandiosity which they have been feeding us is no longer so totally acceptable in the world we must share with them. There is a price we will have to pay for most continued narcissistic insistence ("If you don't quiet down, I won't buy you the toy I promised you."). We learn fast about the narcissistic fantasy and about expected reality behavior. As we have seen, in the service of peace, the human personality has developed psychological mechanisms for tempering its wants by itself. The boundaries offered by parental *imagos* and by our own autonomously chosen adult self values are what do the job. They rein us in, back to reality, thus keeping chaos in abeyance. We are left with wants that aren't quite so narcissistically insistent.

Our more realistic, nonnarcissistic wants exist on a continuum. Some of them are casual preferences. For example, I might think, "Better I should have vanilla ice cream than strawberry." I know what I prefer, but losing out on this preference would be no great disaster. We can take casual preferences or leave them. But there are greater degrees of preferences beyond "the casual" which eventually work their way into more firmly held wants. Indeed, by the time we get to the other end of the continuum of our realistic wants, we find wants we are quite insistent on satisfying even though they aren't narcissistic. These are wants that are related to constitutive elements of our adult self. These are wants that we identify with. They are part of what we sense as being our character identity. Similar to having narcissistic wants, we insist on living out these identity wants—they are quite strongly felt wants. But they are strongly felt for different reasons. We don't insist on meeting wants we identify with for the reason that we crave satisfaction as an end in itself. *That* would be true and definitive of a narcissistic want. With character identity wants, we relinquish the narcissism idea that the aesthetics of satisfaction is the end-all of wanting. Aesthetic enjoyment is not the ultimate justification for getting nonnarcissistic wants satisfied. We demand reasons now. In the specific case of wants that we identify with, we expect satisfaction of them because being able to live by or act out things we identify with, whether they are wants, ideas, principles, people, institutions, or whatever, is what it is to fully be the self we are. It is in the nature of things that a person lives by her identity. Of course, nature doesn't always get its way. Circumstances sometimes prevent a person from being herself. When that happens, a person feels that much less alive. She feels that much less herself. She isn't living her life quite as fully as she was "meant" to.

Details of this aside, though, the point is that all developmental stages of the self have something to do with the having of strong wants. One shouldn't automatically think that whenever a person is involved in a strong want, she is being a narcissistic rudimentary self. That is, to hold onto a want doggedly doesn't mean automatic narcissism. There are different reasons for having strongly held wants. Some of these reasons lead to people healthfully expressing pockets of narcissistic wanting, others lead to them healthfully expressing character wanting.

I would like to conclude this chapter now with a few preparatory words for our discussion in the next chapter. One can think of the narcissistic stage of development as the great divide in human psychological functioning. We come into narcissism basically as object relators and we leave it with a view of ourselves as budding internal agencies aimed in the direction of building character quality onto that agency. One would like to think that at this point a person is ready to go full steam ahead in identifying an agency character self into existence. However, this isn't so. And that's because of the kind of psychological processing a person is capable of at this point in life. We have seen that the processing responsible for the first blush of internal agency is the formation of narcissistic self representations. But it turns out that these self representations are only the most primitive version of the process of identification that is required for turning our new internal agency selves into full-fledged character selves. Mature identifications are self representations, but of a kind that's more reality-oriented than what we see going on in the grandiose self representing of the narcissistic infant/child. So the recently narcissistic child certainly isn't prepared to jump fully into character building. At best, she has been awakened now at the crack of dawn of her character building day. She is only now ready to *start* identifying.

Still, one is tempted to say that, even if she is only now starting to build character, at least the psychological processing that will occur from now on will be thoroughgoing identification. There will be no competing kinds of self processing that could throw roadblocks in the way of her character building activity. One wants to say all this, but, once again, matters aren't quite as tidy as we would like them to be. Unchallenged character formation doesn't really come in with a rush on the heels of one's infancy/childhood narcissism. The fact of the matter is, one seems to go through a period between her childhood narcissism and her adolescence where her mental life is equally occupied by combinations of pre- and rudimentary self processing along with the unfolding processes of identification. One practices her new identificatory processing, as it were, while continuing to stay with some of the old self processing stand-bys. And such a picture is the normal scene at this time. Consequently, one makes no great leap forward here toward becoming a character. The individual is just warming up for the fuller identificatory activity to come in adolescence and adulthood. This warm-up period I will call a person's self developmental "latency period."[16] All of us have to pass through this time of latency as we move closer to significantly becoming character selves. But even after we pass through this period in our lives, we still don't automatically have clear sailing ahead. Indeed, as I have said, even when one grows from latency into adolescence and then into adulthood, identification isn't the only self processing going on. The fact is, the self development processing competition for identification never fully disappears. Pre-self and narcissistic self functioning never totally vanishes. Life after infancy/childhood narcissism is never a fully univocal homogeneous identificatory universe.

The natural thing to wonder about at this point is what this less-than-homogeneous identificatory universe after narcissism looks like. We turn to this concern next.

CHAPTER 4

The Latency Self and Beyond

The central question we want to ask now is, What do selves generally look like during the latency period and beyond? Given that people are never pure characters but rather hybrid mixtures of pre-, rudimentary, and character self processing, what we will do in this chapter is make ourselves more familiar with the look of some of these different mixtures. We will see just how what is sometimes taken for a person's character is often, in fact, a mixture of character along with persisting primitive self processing. People grow character, but never in unadulterated form.

But there's a broader context in which I want to couch this discussion. We can talk about various hybrid mixtures of self in the course of evaluating two traditional psychological dogmas about identification and character formation—one of the dogmas arising from our everyday folk psychology and the other, a closely related view coming out of psychoanalytic theory. The folk psychology dogma states that people develop as selves in quite discrete stages; supposedly, once they finish with the exclusive self process of being an infant, they proceed to the exclusive self process of being a child, and then finally to the exclusive self process of becoming a mature adult self of a character nature. In our terms again, once they are finished with their pre- and rudimentary self development, they then are fully about the task of becoming identificatory character selves. More simply, infancy is one stage of life, childhood another, and adulthood yet another. The dogma has it that we are wholly different kinds of people in each stage, none of the stages ever overlapping. And so the psychological processes, too, of each stage are assumed to be differentially appropriate to its developmental period and never overlapping with processes from any of the other periods. In this view, people move along in life according to a built-in developmental plan, cleanly leaving one stage of life and jumping with both feet into the next.

The second dogma advances this commonsense piece of folk psychology into the psychoanalytic theoretic realm. It is the view that any adult self essentially is the extension of his earliest infancy/childhood identifications; supposedly, people don't change character that

77

much once their identificatory patterns have made their imprint during infancy/childhood. As backdrop for this view, the psychoanalytic proponents assume their own version of the folk psychology dogma. Specifically, they agree that people pass through discrete stages of self development. But those stages are not exactly as our folk psychology paints them. Rather, they are the now familiar developmental stages we have been looking at, where first we are object relating selves as infants, then grandiose self representing selves as infants and young children, and then primitive and increasingly advanced kinds of identifying selves as infants, young children, older latency children, adolescents, and adults. This is how our metamorphosis supposedly unfolds. And, leaning on an image we first introduced in chapter 1, the dogma would have it that just as caterpillars who once travelled about by crawling along the ground evolve into butterflies consumed with the activity of flight, so, too, do we, once we get through to the third stage of our self development, spend the rest of our lives pursuing a growing identificatory organization of our agency selves, as though we are fully done with the object relating and narcissism processes that preceded. In this view, we start becoming identificatory characters to any extent in infancy/childhood only *after* we *finish* with our jobs of infancy/childhood object relating and narcissism. Those jobs were about protecting us as developing infants and children while we were preparing to become full identificatory beings. Once the process of identifying was underway, though, the need for protection finally fell away. Then our lives became all about how and what we did as growing identificatory character selves. This point is where the piece of psychoanalytic dogma comes into the picture. The dogma has it that once we start organizing our self representations around the theme of identification, the earliest of these identifications condition the detail of all the identifications we will find ourselves immersed in as emerging adult character selves. Once the discrete identificatory process has begun in late infancy and early childhood, who we become as adult identificatory characters is directly traceable to who we were as infancy/ childhood identifiers. In this view, who one becomes as an adult can be explained as a sophisticated extension of his earliest identifications. Our character tendencies are set in place during the earliest days, and the rest of life is all about how we fill in the detail of those tendencies as we respond with those early identifications to the unique contingencies of life that we face each day.

Finally, I believe that both of these dogmas are false. And I will use my analysis of why I think this is so as the frame for the discussion in this chapter. Showing the flaws in these dogmas would be important in itself, for they certainly have had a strong impact on our cultural perspectives about character formation, and not always for the best. That reason aside, though, examining these dogmas also provides me with a larger stage to discuss my main concern in this chapter—viz., that of developing the idea that during latency and beyond, people are rarely pure characters but rather are complex hybrid selves. With this in mind, let's look at the two dogmas.

I

The folk psychology dogma is obviously false. People don't develop in completely discrete stages. Indeed, in terms of the psychoanalytic version of the folk psychology dogma, we have already seen the dogma's bankruptcy in our review of the kinds of claims made about infant/child self development. Specifically, we have seen that late pre-self activity and early narcissistic self activity commingle. Narcissistic psychological processing often involves pre-self introjective activity. Generally speaking, the processes typical of any given developmental stage just don't always stay put. They like to mix into other stages. But now, I'm also saying that such mixtures occur during latency and often into adulthood. Of course, in this folk psychology view, one would like to think that in development beyond narcissism, a person finally dispenses with his pre-self and narcissistic self needs and moves on to identifying his way into the life of the character self. But as I've just been pointing out in chapter 3, one doesn't start to become a character self all at once. Nor does one ever fully abandon his pre- and narcissistic self functioning in favor of the exclusive functioning of identification. The self representations formed in our narcissistic infancy/childhood are only a bare-bones start toward being what we come to recognize as a human self. Nothing approaching a full identificatory character really begins to come on the scene until adolescence. And once it finally takes shape there, we spend the rest of our lives reaffirming and periodically reassessing and changing that character self. But we do this while still continuing to function partly as primitive pre- and narcissistic selves in pockets of our experience during latency and beyond.

Let's look at an illustration of self processes continuing beyond a time that the folk psychology dogma would think appropriate. Consider the staying power of narcissistic tendencies in our lives past the developmental infancy/childhood narcissism period. Once we get beyond this developmental stage, ideally we start forging our identificatory character self. Ideally, as nonnarcissistic identificatory beings, we come to choose ways of being that are less grounded in the nonrealistic grandiose magic wish to have omnipotent control over our world and more grounded in a realistic, mature belief that we can produce a certain kind of character agency that will compete with other character agencies to get our wants met. The realistic character self is an agency that expresses itself to the world, recognizing that others are doing the same thing and that, in a spirit of mature compromise about competing desires of different character selves, it will sometimes have to defer to the control of others.

This image is an idealized version of the dogma at work. All of this is our developmental *aim*. We want to become the kind of selves whose organizing character agency allows us to be in control of ourselves. But, in truth, things don't always work out this way. Having this kind of control is never guaranteed—that is, *being in control through our character* is not always our reward as we age. The fact is, pockets of narcissistic demands for grandiose control intrude often enough. Even beyond our infancy narcissism period, although we are the agency for many things that transpire in our life—we are controlling bits of our life—we aren't always doing this as a *character* agency but rather as a narcissistic one. The obsessive personality often behaves this way. He is a person who, in parts of his life, has to be in control of what's going on around him, not allowing others their power as independent agents. This is narcissistic grandiose behavior, not character behavior. When such a person appears on the scene during his latency or adulthood, we see him as a kind of incomplete identificatory self. He is a far sight short of being a full character self of internal agency. We say that psychological forces are driving his "control behavior" (through introjects?) rather than that he is driving or choosing that behavior for himself through his own autonomous agency. The examples of this sort of person are endless: bullies, "me first" egoistic teenagers, ideologues, the armies of excessively insecure adults who put on arrogant false masks to hide what they really feel about themselves, and so on—all of these fall under this description.

This kind of case is one where a more primitive developmental state (narcissistic obsessiveness) infects a more advanced state (agency character behavior). Understand, though, that not all primitive states that are found persisting in later developmental periods are always *infecting* the advanced states of that later period.

Sometimes the primitive states are just neutral extra baggage, and sometimes they are actually quite functional for budding identificatory powers. We will see examples of both before we are through. Right here, however, I am only concerned with the general point of the example, viz., that there is a *persistence* of narcissistic tendencies that can interact with states that are otherwise mainly identificatory.

I think we could appreciate the point even more if we had an illustration that had finer detail to it. So let's look at such a case. I have in mind a most dramatic example of pre-self introjecting persisting beyond the pre-self period and interacting with more developmentally advanced identificatory processing. Specifically, I am thinking of the Oedipal activity that typically occurs during late narcissism just this side of latency (normally covering the years between 3½ and 6). As we saw in chapter 2, in becoming Oedipally engaged, the child both introjects and begins to identify with object traits he sees in his parents. His identificatory half starts looking at features of the parent world that he now at least acknowledges as being to some degree external to and independent of his mind/body. He is no longer wholly magically taking them on as his introjective self. But not only does he begin to see features of parent objects and recognize them as belonging to independent objects; he also now begins to do what he can to reproduce the same kind of features as his own agency. He now has an emerging sense that he can build his mind/body into such an independent agency with traits. In fact, if he chooses to do so, he can make himself into something of an agency that's similar to some of those same independent parent objects. This description sounds very much like it falls under the concept of identification introduced at the end of chapter 2. In other words, this individual is able to identify with his parent's traits.

We want to look at the kind of identifications that occur here. But first let's say something a little more detailed about the introjective moves the Oedipal child makes. Let's appreciate that the Oedipal child *needs* to continue being an object relator because he hasn't nearly enough organized identificatory agency yet to fulfill his drive-gratification needs in a character way. He isn't a solid enough character yet. We say that he doesn't have "enough confidence" in his autonomous functioning yet. So he continues introjectively to hold onto objects that do his agency work for him. Accordingly, the Oedipal child is someone who is carving an individual character self with one hand and defending it from possible damage with the other—that is, he identifies and he introjects. He performs both kinds of activities according to the Oedipal themes. Who he is revolves around the theme of his insisting on sexual narcissistic satisfaction from the parent of the opposite sex, this accomplished by his immersion into a sexual fantasy life involving a complex of sexual introjects and projections about the opposite-sex parent. The child also introjects some of the personality traits of the same-sex parent along with the practical life constraints valued by the same-sex parent. He does this partly on the theory that if the opposite-sex parent is attracted to those traits in the same-sex parent, she will be attracted to those same traits in him, too. But there is another reason for his doing this. It is his way of defending against a feared destruction by the same-sex parent because of the competition he fantasizes having for the favor of the opposite-sex parent. The Oedipal child fears destruction at the hands of the same-sex parent as a kind of ultimate punishment for his having sexual fantasies about the opposite-sex parent. Freudian theory has it that if the child introjects the opposite-sex parent's personality traits and values, the child will learn the boundaries of what are to count as acceptable traits, values, and behavior to the opposite-sex parent. The child's then staying within these boundaries will ensure his staying in the good graces of the same-sex parent in spite of his having sexual fantasies about the opposite-sex parent. The introjection of the parental values here extends to a very wide scene. For example, the child might project the feared parent's value preferences onto social institutions around him which he, the child, would then fear, perhaps instead of fearing the parent. He would also then introject the values of these institutions in order to stay within acceptable bounds of "parental" propriety.

Introjection aside, let's not lose sight of the *central* gains of the Oedipal period. I am referring to the birth of the identificatory process. Oedipal issues call forth the identificatory process in people. In our culture, anyway, this is probably because that is when our parents first *insist* that we make a stand about who we are to be in life as character agency selves. Up to this point, parents by and large only care to know what the child wants. They, the parents, then will take care of the child's gratification. But the Oedipal stage can be partly understood as that time when parents no longer are simply concerned with gratifying the child's desires. And they are no longer too happy with his acting as a grandiose agency whenever he cares to. Instead, they become much more concerned with his developing enough of his own agency to start effecting his own gratifications, that agency now being of a character variety. Up until this time, the

parents had no concern for moving the infant/child along in developing a character self; they were quite comfortable with his being a pre-
and rudimentary self. Up until this time, it was quite normal for the
infant/child to function with nothing but either the parents' agency,
introjections, or a minimal narcissistic self-agency. Up until this
time, the infant/child could have been totally involved in a pre-self
cathexis of sexual and hostile power fantasies (e.g., in the case of the
boy child, lusting for mother and hating and fearing father). But now,
with the appearance of Oedipal concerns, when the child starts acting
out his narcissistic demands involving sexual desires for the opposite-
sex parent and desires for destruction of the same-sex parent, there
normally occurs a set of demands by the parents to which he must
respond. As far as his parents are concerned, it is time for him to
start acting like a *real* person. And that means that it is time for him
to start becoming a character agency self. The Oedipal child's parents
begin to insist that he take on features of an agency character identity which he can enlist to defuse some of his Oedipal fantasy life.
The child is no longer to consider explicitly acting out his sexual
desires for his opposite-sex parent and he is no longer to express so
overtly his hostility for his same-sex parent. The child is confronted
and forced to respond to these parental demands. Real parental
power is now matched against the fantasy power of the child. There
is no way to hide from the confrontation. A person has to respond.
But whatever the full extent of the response finally is, it always
requires, at least in part, that the child make some sort of character
commitment. He must move to identify with certain ways of being
and at least partly make them aspects of an emerging character that
can deal with his Oedipal conflicts.

Just because the call is sent out for him to start the identificatory
life of character commitment, however, that doesn't mean he can
make good on the call. As we know, identification emerges slowly; it
doesn't just suddenly appear in full regalia. The child has to work his
way into being an identifier. And the first stage of the identificatory
life unfolds in large part as a kind of *imitation*. Remember that we
said some things about this in chapter 2. We saw it as a kind of object
relating in the weakest sense of that notion. In the present context,
we can also view it as a kind of identification in the weakest sense of
that concept. That is, while it is by no means a full-fledged kind of
identification, it is the first important step in that direction. It is the
Oedipal child's first effort at self representing as a character. It is
generally claimed that the Oedipal child "resolves" his Oedipal crisis

by imitating the parent of the same sex. We speak of how charming it is for the infant male, for example, to mimic his father, how adorable it is that he so "identifies" with his father now. In truth, we're overstating the case when we call this "identification." The child isn't really identifying with father yet, although for various reasons he does want to be like him. In any case, he comports himself in the manly way of his father. He mimics that air of authority that his father displays. He constantly quotes his father's value standards as his reasons for why he, the child, behaves as he does. Even if all of this imitative behavior can't be called full-fledged identification, the fact is that it is worthy of our notice precisely because it is the first evidence that the child is even thinking about forging a character.

The child is trying out a new game, as it were. And he's doing it by playing the game as his father plays it. Why not? He has to get started somewhere, somehow. Later, when he finally gets the hang of things—when he finally begins to identify successfully with his father and becomes a solid enough self so that he no longer needs introjective mechanisms to keep his gains for an internal self safely consolidated— he will no longer need to imitate. But until then, during the Oedipal stage, he tries forging a self that looks just like his father's. He first creates introjective object representations and then imitative self representations of traits that are like his father's. The kind of consciousness I am talking about here both is and is not perceived by the child as being distinctly individuated. That is, as an introject, a given trait is still partly under father's power; but as an imitation, it is a distinct replica of father's that belongs solely to the child. The sense of power and having the world under control that one feels in "being like father" during these times is an introjected power. The other sense one also has of having a personality trait that belongs to oneself (as part of who one is) is a self representational imitative happening. In so passionately wanting to be like his father, the child here seems so precious precisely because he is imitating. He has started becoming a little artist sculpting his own self in the world, even though the model he first uses is so predictably close to home, and even though the imitative moves he is making are, from an adult's perspective, so seemingly elementary. At this point, one's central life issue is all about getting one's feet on the ground with a new psychological activity that is crucial to living life as a reality-based individuated being.

Let's get our bearings now on what we have just been doing. I introduced this discussion of the Oedipal period so that we could look at a more detailed case of primitive psychological functioning persisting into more advanced developmental periods. In fact, we have seen that the Oedipal case is one where primitive object relating persists and interacts quite functionally with the advanced identificatory activity appropriate to the Oedipal period. We might think of Oedipal consciousness as being comfortably double-edged, with the identificatory timetable of life beginning now while fully sharing the spotlight with introjection. Clearly, a consequence of all of this is that the Oedipal situation debunks the folk psychology dogma we are concerned with— the dogma that claims that people move cleanly through discrete stages of self development. That acknowledged, it is time now to move on and look for more evidence of the dogma's failure.

We don't have far to travel to find what we are looking for. Persistence of primitive self processes mixing with advanced identificatory processes abounds where latency is in full swing. Indeed, that is how I'm defining the latency period. It is a time when the individual forges, consolidates, and defends his character agency identity gains by a total immersion into different varieties of combined introjection/identification states as well as by immersion into different varieties of combined narcissism/identification states and combined narcissism/introjection/identification states. It is only when a person has finally built up a kind of critical mass of character agency that he begins to slough off much of the primitive forms of self processing. Even then, however, he never fully lets go of these aspects of his past. Even in his more serious assault on being a full character agency during adolescence and adulthood, some of the old forms of self processing persist. In any case, during latency, primitive processing persists with vigor, along with the emerging new capacity of identification.

Interestingly, it is precisely because the latency child is so thoroughly a mixture of such developmental processes that we adults are never quite certain *who* they are when we interact with them. Developmentally speaking, we aren't quite sure from moment to moment what kind of person we are talking to. At one point, they seem solid in what they say and do; they seem to be independent character selves whom one can respect and admire. At other moments, they seem less solid and downright grandiose. At still other times, they seem less solid but at least imitative and, therefore, at least desirous of becoming solid. And at yet other times, they seem to have nothing of their own at the core of their selves, no strong identifications. Instead, they seem to be introjecting anyone with agency power around them, more concerned with the character agency of others than their own. In other words, every encounter with a latency child can be an entirely new proposition. No sooner are we proud of who we think our children are becoming as solid characters than they surprise us one more time by attacking some life conflict they are facing with some defensive introjective posture or some grandiose pose or some hollow, seemingly meaningless imitation of, say, what a media star would do in their situation. And then we are disappointed in them. But that's because we have expected too much of them. Consistent with our being under the powerful spell of the folk psychology dogma, we have expected character to rule their roost when, in fact, all that latency children are capable of is some mixture of object relating, narcissistic grandiosity, and shades of identifying.

There are certain stock contexts that characteristically exhibit these mixtures of self developmental processes during the latency years. I have in mind the passionate commitment children and teenagers make to complex states such as pretending, hero worshipping, idolizing, infatuation, romantic love, celebrity hounding, and more. Just as ontogeny recapitulates phylogeny, so do these complex states typically recapitulate the full spectrum of self development. Once again, then, the folk psychology thesis—that we move through discrete places on a timetable of self development processes—proves wrong. I would like to take some time now to drive this point home by devoting the next section to a discussion of some examples of these latency mixtures. However, let me say right here that I intend to be a bit greedy— or, if you will, efficient—in that discussion. For it turns out that some of these examples will allow me to kill two birds with one stone. I will be able to use some of these examples not only to crystallize the failure of the folk psychology dogma in describing what goes on during latency but also to crystallize its failure in describing what goes on during adolescence and adulthood. Many of the same mixtures of developmental states that are common fare for latency children are also visitors on the adolescent and adult scene, although with far less intensity than during latency and with far less influence on the general tone of one's stature as a character agency self.[1] So, in the spirit of finally putting the folk psychology dogma to rest in the context of what actually occurs during both latency development and the more advanced periods of development, we turn now to the following examples.

II

Case 1: Latency children love to get lost in pretense. They have a very large repository of clear images they've collected about what it would be like to be various kinds of independent agency selves. And they pick and choose from this repository, trying out one image or another in a spirit of pretense. This initially involves their introjecting traits of real or imagined people. In this way, they borrow the agency power of those people. But childhood pretense soon goes beyond just this pre-self way of functioning. The primitive incomplete kind of identifying we've seen imitation to be is also added to the stew of pretense. That is, children imitate the more obvious behavior of some favorite image without ever seriously having to think about making that image into who they really are. They are not willing yet to start fully identifying themselves with the character they are pretending to be. Instead, they are satisfied with trying it out in the form of play and imagination.

In fact, latency children have a vast network of games of pretense, the central premise of which is that it is acceptable to pretend identificatory characters. More than anything else, the context of pretense appears to allow people a chance to *practice* the general identificatory activity. They don't have to consider seriously the content as candidate for who they in fact might become. This is a latency period "timeout" from intense identificatory character building. Here children are playfully satisfied with exhibiting their developing *general capacity* for identifying with traits. They are merely trying out their identificatory skills without having to take responsibility for each and every considered trait they would make their own. The stakes are just too high to expect a person to jump into every considered identification. Certainly, the younger a person is, the more vital this idea is. For the younger a person is, the less able he is to cope successfully with all the responsibility he has in being a character. The young child would be overwhelmed by the social world that rewards and punishes all fully committed acts of identificatory character. He just doesn't have a full enough complement of a personality repertoire (not enough "critical mass") to defend against the possibility of a negative judgment. There's simply no survival value in jumping right away into being the character traits one first considers for himself. Social structures that allow pretense are a much better alternative when a person is getting started as an identificatory self.

It seems that all of us, not just the young, need a character practice area, a place where we aren't held accountable for who we *seem* to be as identificatory characters. The imagination is probably the best such location. That's where pretense is most protected from the possible slings and arrows of social judgment. That's where we can try out any way of being and keep it wholly private if we wish. But there are also more public arenas of pretense. We are given this sort of opportunity, for example, in the reading of fiction and in the participation in or viewing of theater and film. And there are countless other social structures of pretense that civilization has created to give people the opportunity to take a timeout from being characters and the opportunity to practice what it is to be an agency of various possible characters. These structures afford all of us the chance to practice what it would be like to have certain traits without having to take responsibility for really being that way. Of course, any pretender who comes to like what he has pretended can always proceed, if he wishes to turn imitative pretense into more serious identifications for which he is willing to take responsibility.

Case 2: Another important latency state of mixed self processes which prepare a person for a time in the future when he can more reasonably become a full identificatory character self is *hero worship*. Let's consider my Duke Snider scenario from chapter 1 again. When I was a 7-year-old, he was my hero. Recall that I was so very impressed with his athleticism. I worshipped him, just as my friends worshipped their favorite baseball heroes. Clearly, he was an important psychological object for me. I introjected qualities that I highly valued from the self- and Oedipal objects (i.e., mother and father), and then projected them out onto "the Duke Snider object." Highly valued parental power and control over threats to existence were partly embodied by Duke Snider's power and control. His overall hitting average and home run production indicated to me that he had both the control over which pitches to swing at and the power to hit many of those pitches a long way. I think the associations here with parental power and control are obvious enough. Moreover, my particular aesthetic twist on life that the narcissistic version of me had always craved was now being fed by Duke Snider's aesthetic pleasure-producing grace and power. In general, it is socially acceptable for any child to get these sorts of psychological staples of life in this same manner.

What I was doing, however, was not merely introjective object relating. Clearly, I was also exhibiting grandiose narcissistic self representations. In feeling connected to my hero, I was puffing myself up in the process. To the extent that I was seeing him as the ideal image of perfection, I was also mirroring him and seeing myself more and more as an agency self who was perfect, like him. I was seeing myself as an agency who could pretty much do what I wanted so long as I associated myself with Duke Snider. In short, I was grandiose.

But not only were there these introjective and narcissistic elements to my behavior, identification was also unfolding. A mixed triple consciousness was going on. Of course, let's remember that when I first introduced the Duke Snider example in chapter 1, I had no intention of billing it as a mixed consciousness. I explicitly introduced it as an illustration of childhood identification. And I was correct, but only to a point. What I failed to say was that *childhood* identification is not the *pure* identificatory item. I hadn't talked about object relating yet, and so we couldn't see that the identifying going on in this example wasn't pure. We couldn't know that, in truth, my hero worshipping was a mixed developmental state. Nevertheless, I wasn't wrong in calling what I was doing "identification." For there was also a fair amount of identificatory processing going on. I was recognizing Duke Snider as a separate individual with qualities valuable not only for their object relating powers but also for what I saw as their intrinsic worth. Power, control, and a comfortable aesthetic were now seen as being really out there in the world beyond me. Moreover, I was beginning to acknowledge that they were traits I didn't possess to the degree that Duke Snider did. But his excellence with those traits had become a model for what I wanted to become through my efforts. I was accepting myself as a separate, imperfect self who had something of an ability for developing my own version of those traits.

In different terms, I was beginning to see the world through nonnarcissistic eyes. I admired Duke Snider for himself in the sense that there was a separate being there who had qualities that I valued highly and that were not necessarily feeding some of my narcissistic needs, although clearly, on another track, they were doing that, too. In fact, part of this new edge to consciousness involved my acknowledging that there were many other beings with qualities of value I didn't possess and that didn't necessarily service any of my narcissistic needs. I subsequently began carving out more of a self through this process—that is, by seeing what I was *not* but might be. Through reality testing, I saw that I was no Duke Snider. But that didn't keep me from dreaming. As I say, he wasn't only a handy introjection and narcissism device, he was also a model of excellence around identity issues that were important to me. At first, I tried to imitate his behavior. I pretended to be him; I played at being him. Whether or not the imitation was accurate was unimportant. All that mattered was that *I* perceived that I did a good job of it. My emerging self representations were molded in terms of what I saw in him and how I believed I was accurately imitating him. But as time passed, my imitation played only a secondary role in my self representations. More and more, I began acknowledging my separateness. My pretense was toning down. Although I wanted to see how well I could approximate his general traits in my separate self, both my narcissistic grandiosity and my imitating were beginning to fall away. I acknowledged that he was the best and that we were separate.

All of this kind of mixed introjecting, grandiose self representing, and identifying amounts to hero worship. Children seem very preoccupied with this sort of activity as well as with playing games of pretense. And it's no wonder. Like playing games of pretense, hero worship affords latency children the opportunity to practice their emerging identificatory talents while still allowing them to hold onto their narcissistic fantasies about who they are and still allowing them to have the introjective agency defenses they need in order to meet the demands of the hostile world that would otherwise overwhelm them as not-yet-solid agency selves. It's no wonder that much of the latency period is spent with children arguing with one another about whose hero is the best hero to worship. The cry of "My *x* is better than yours" is one of the more important battle cries of the latency period. The latency child swathes herself with the cloth of the mixture of self processes that hero worship affords her. She continues in this way so long as she needs to consolidate her slowly emerging identity and defend against its possible dissolution. Heroes are stand-in character selves in this regard. If a child, through her own agency, can't protect herself yet from the onslaughts of others, she can borrow the traits and power of the hero agency to do the job for her. And she can also use her hero's perfections as anchors for a narcissistic rudimentary self that doesn't fully want to go away yet.

It's noteworthy that there is a variety of hero worship that we can give a slightly different spin to—*idolization*. In the generic hero worshipping we've been talking about, we not only see the traits in the hero object, but we also imagine that we can reproduce them in ourselves as a way of protecting our newly forming self through our own agency. By contrast, in idolizing, we think the traits we identify with are beyond us; we know we can't really reproduce them. Why? Because they are traits of idols, gods—a child's father, a teenager's heartthrob, etc.—not of mere mortals such as ourselves. Gods have many powers we mortals don't have. Gods can do with different kinds of perfection what we only wish we could do but know we can't. We are still partly attached to an early-stage narcissistic longing for introjecting the idol's perfection. But we know we can't really ever make the traits our own character. We have become too individuated and too attached to reality to allow early-stage narcissistic object relating to intrude. As adolescents, for example, people regularly idolize movie stars or rock stars whose perfections are in this way partly narcissistically aimed. We might idolize them for their sexual perfection or perhaps for their acting or singing talents. We could wish we had them ourselves. But finally, we know that we can't.

Clearly, latency children are heavily involved in both generic hero worshipping and idolizing. But it's not just *their* pastime. I just mentioned an example of adolescent idolization. Adults have heroes and idols as well. Consider an adult case. It is not unusual for academics—say, professional philosophers—to have their professional heroes, even idols, whom they worship. Indeed, it's common practice for professionals in the philosophical literature to jump on the backs of their heroes by responding to philosophical issues and positions that were originally framed by these heroes, whether these heroes are living philosophers or historical figures. Clearly, there is some identifying going on here. One may be identifying with the commitment to seeking truth, with the method of philosophizing practiced by the hero, with some philosophical position first put forward by the hero, or even with some very interesting mistake the hero has committed. In any case, one sees a kinship with the hero. But one acknowledges that the hero has already shown himself to possess the traits of the self that one values here. Indeed, the hero seems to embody these traits with a kind of paradigmatic perfection. The worshipper only hopes to possess someday the same self traits with something approaching the same degree of excellence.

But whether we are looking at adult hero worship or adolescent idolization, we don't want to forget the role played by introjection in either. Appreciate, for example, how an adolescent's idolization of a movie star also involves the adolescent in object relations with transition objects. The strength of the idolizing is partly determined by the varying degrees of cathexis from the objects—for example, from the movie star. The complex idea of the movie star sometimes cathects maternal security, grandiose power, and more. Movie stars just are teenage transition objects. But then, too, historical philosophers are sometimes transition objects for their adult philosopher hero worshippers. That is not to minimize the significance of the identification going on here. It is just to point out once again that that is not the total scene. In hero worshipping of any sort, the individual seems to need certain transition objects to introject in order to keep the unfolding identificatory self glued together, as it were. To keep oneself glued together as a philosopher, for example—to have "being a philosopher" as an ingredient of one's sense of identity—one may need to consolidate his recent identity gains by taking on a philosopher-hero as a transition object. Playing with ideas—a philosophical activity—is clearly a libidinal enterprise as well as an intellectual good in itself. That is, it is also aesthetically pleasurable; it is "sexual." The power some people feel from cathecting around issues of philosophical concern can be immense. It may, in fact, be an unconscious extension of their infantile cathexis of mother as a sex object. The pleasure and safety one got from nestling with mother might now be the pleasure and safety one gets from wrestling with philosophical abstractions. And just as one introjected and projected these relations with mother onto infantile transition objects to get what one wanted through the magic of fantasy instead of from one's own not-yet-developed agency, so may one later in life use one's profession as a cluster of transition objects to bring about the same results. He may get what he wants from the bantering, from the playfulness, even from the conquering of aggressive adversaries. In his fantasy, the philosophical idea qua transition object may get him all of these things instead of his own agency doing that for him. It may not be until much later that the adult professional philosopher comes to see himself as *being* a philosopher. He may not allow until much later that he has a self whose agent identity includes "the philosopher." And it is at that point where he has become a *full* identifier—someone who no longer needs to introject—where he finally no longer has any philosophical heroes, because he finally has no need for them. He gets his philosophical needs met by himself—that is, he satisfies his need for pursuing truth, his need to reason, his need to analyze and make distinctions, his need for aesthetic joy, his need for security, his need for power over adversaries, and more through his own agency. He has become someone (a character) who can do all these things. They are part of who he is. And so there is no magically protective introjective power needed here anymore.[2]

But until the time when one can so fully create such identificatory character, the philosophical hero worshipper and idolizer (and the adolescent idolizer too) continues partly to introject traits of the hero. In hero worshipping and idolization—and, for that matter, in any of the other forms of mixed introjecting and identifying (and, to some degree, in grandiose self representing)—the introjections are not yet totally dissipated. A person still needs that much external object agency to accomplish what he sets out to do. His own self agency isn't strong enough to do the job alone. So he stays in touch with the external powerful object any way he can, even through the magic of introjection. The introjector holds onto the lost object—in this case, the powerful hero or idol—in the form of a the new introjected representation of some traits of the lost hero or idol object. This introjection is inside of him so long as he needs it, so long as he can't fully "accept" his loss of the loved object—so long, that is, as he is in transition toward a more mature state where he can accept separation from the loved object without fear of dissolution. At the point of maturity we are all aimed at, though, the introject will be assimilated by him through the process of self representation, the ultimate expression of which is identification. Again, in this sense, most of us are never *fully* finished identificatory products. We always hold onto some introjecting well into latency and beyond. And, in the present context, this means that we always hold onto some heroes and idols. However, it's clear that the childhood disposition to involve ourselves in hero worship and idolization must abate considerably in the adult. We expect as much of a person of essential character identity, of a mature person.[3]

Case 3: Another arena of mixed developmental states during latency and beyond is found in *infatuation*. Clearly, latency children are easy marks for infatuation. And although the frequency of it dissipates as they get older, in adulthood it is still a force to be reckoned with. Whenever it occurs, though, infatuation is a lot like idolizing and hero worshipping, the difference being that infatuation always occurs where one's identifying and introjective object relating[4] are about traits of someone one actually knows, while this may or may not be so in cases of idol worship. Furthermore, the infatuated person has a degree of affection for the other. And although it isn't exclusively this way, quite often the infatuation is of a sexual nature. So the introjective component is typically more infantile libidinal cathecting than in the other complex latency contexts we've looked at. Thus, we don't think it unusual for an infatuated person to talk incessantly about the person with whom he's infatuated or even for him to swoon (an expression of his sexuality) over her. Object related sexual impulses work that way on people.

Infatuations are also typically short-lived. (By contrast, hero worship is typically longer lasting.) There is an interesting inference we can draw from this: I take it that the short-lived feature is explainable in terms of the introjective sexual component playing such a significant role here, a much larger role than it plays, say, in hero worship. And where an identificatory context has such a very strong introjective component and a comparatively weak identification component, solidifying more of a person's identity isn't really the main issue. Sexual pleasure and security through introjective fantasy are. As adults, we don't allow ourselves to indulge so thoroughly in such infantile fantasy mechanisms for too long, not unless they are ultimately also aimed at protecting a developing identity. Once infatuative relating to people is seen for what it is, we dismiss its appropriateness on the grounds that it is thoroughly infantile. Since infatuation doesn't seem in the main to be aimed at building identity—although *some* of that does go on—we demand that one let go of the infatuation once it becomes clear that it is mainly infatuative sexual fantasizing and not character self construction that is going on. "Oh, that's just an infatuation; he'll get over it."

Case 4: I won't pursue the matter, but I will at least mention here that *romantic love* is the clear adult extension of infatuation, but with a clear narcissistic component added. One's introjective fantasies and grandiose mirroring of traits from the love object run rampant during romantic love. For example, the lover "can't live without the beloved" in the sense that he so thoroughly depends on the introjected qualities of the beloved to get him through the day. Sexual pleasure and security through introjective fantasy is raging here. Of course, this isn't the way the love context is normally described in the popular culture. The popular way of describing it is in terms of *identification,* as in "lovers really identify completely with one another." However, this is another case where we fail to see the detail of what's going on. The fact is, there is a large dose of introjecting as well as some narcissistic mirroring at work. Of course, there is some identification going on, too. Lovers do identify with some of one another's traits. That is, lovers do sometimes effect real character change in one another. But this isn't the main psychological processing going on. When one thinks of romantic love, one thinks of the raging sexuality and the seeming imbalance that characterize it. Those aspects of romantic love are clearly introjective phenomena, not identificatory ones. Then, too, one also thinks of the grandiosity that typically pervades these contexts. The lover often feels as though he can "take the on world." The perfections he sees in his lover are mirrored back onto him as grandiose self representations that he then applies to his feeling of internal agency. Clearly, these, too, are a far cry from the reality orientation of identifications.

Case 5: Everyone is fond of *celebration*. Not only do we celebrate events, we also celebrate people; and in doing this, we make them celebrities. Let's see what the mixed self processing states are of people celebrating celebrities.

In treating someone as a celebrity, we are saying that she has a trait of identity we consider of great worth. She either has done something or possesses certain physical attributes that are considered part of her identity which we and possibly many others consider of extreme value. Heroes, beauty queens, Nobel Prize winners, sports stars, and others are prime examples of celebrities. Of course, so could one's mother be. She could be a celebrity in her family's eyes for the years of maternal perfection she has showered on them. But whether a person's celebrity status ranges far and wide or is just local, the fact is that a person possesses it when someone glorifies some trait of her identity. The celebrity possesses qualities that we observer/celebrators find highly admirable, so admirable that we empower her by giving her celebrity status. We see her as special to the extent that we offer her special agency power in getting what she wants. We may not allow her a full carte blanche range here, but we do offer her the power of agency far beyond what we allow the ordinary person. We give such empowerment to people because of their beauty, their dramatic talent, their athletic prowess, their bravery, and so on. When a whole culture generally values certain talents, physical qualities, and so forth, that culture celebrates those talents and qualities by conferring agency power onto those who possess them. Such people have a much easier time getting their wants met than the rest of us have. They have doors open to them that the rest of us only dream of having. Giving them this kind of agency power is our way of rewarding them for being the traited identities they are.

What are we doing when we treat people this way? I think the introjective aspects of this situation are familiar enough. Although it is certainly no law of psychology, people often introject the power they project out onto the celebrity. In being a "fan" and standing by and cheering one's favorite celebrities, one is often introjectively borrowing the agency power he has projectively instilled in the celebrity. In many contexts of celebrating a celebrity, one is in large part really using the projected agency power of the celebrity to do something in one's own life that he couldn't otherwise do as a character agency. The fan believes that his own character self isn't strong enough as an agency to get the desired job done, at least not as easily as it would be if he could share the celebrity's agency. So he stands by his celebrity.[5]

Of course, matters of celebration are rarely ever totally this way. Celebrating isn't all about object relating. In fact, the older we get, the more likely we are to use celebration as an arena to express our identifications. Celebrating a celebrity is often a communally joyful affair set around *our reaffirmation* and deep approval of some trait of *character identity* that we, in fact, have. We have it, but not to the point of perfection that the celebrity has it.[6] In fact, the celebrity often caricatures the perfection of the trait. We use him to stand for that trait and not much else, although in fact there is probably a lot more to the celebrity than we viewers will ever care to know. When we celebrate George Washington's birthday, for example, we are celebrating the caricature of Washington as the quintessential honest and patriotic American; he is our cultural paradigm for such virtues. In the same process, we are making our own identificatory claim on the virtue of this caricatured honesty and we are reaffirming our strong identification with American citizenship and the myriad of values which that embodies.

Creating celebrities is also an important way in which a culture can float culturally desirable character traits in the social winds. The goal is to send aloft certain caricatured traits that the public would consider for identification, whether or not it already did so before seeing the celebrity. Simply put, celebrities often act as role models for the masses to consider, role models the masses might come to identify with around the traits in question. We confer power onto celebrity role models *in exchange for* their maintaining their caricatured identity or at least maintaining themselves as symbols of that identity. Having identities as models of certain talents or qualities is that important to cultures. This practice provides the public an arena of values to *aspire* toward, values we would hope that all persons would identify with. As such, this practice of celebrity making provides a very significant source of public identification. And as such, the context of recognizing celebrities is a legitimate context of identification, no matter what one's age is.

Case 6: The cases we've looked at so far have been relatively playful examples where developmentally more primitive processes persist and mix with identificatory processes as part of the normal course of events. Let's turn now to a case that's a more sober mixed developmental state. Let's talk about the complex process of *mourning*. Everyone gets to mourn. Everyone gets the opportunity to grieve the loss of something of great consequence to them, whether it's an absent self-object, a broken toy, a deceased relative or pet, lost youth, an amputated arm, a favorite automobile, or whatever. And everyone does their mourning in different ways, depending on what their self developmental mix looks like at the time of their loss.

We can better understand the mixed state of mourning in latency and beyond if we first have the perspective of seeing how it behaves as a process during infancy. When infants and children mourn, it is most often in the context of their having to endure an interference with, or permanent loss of, some important object relation they have been enjoying. Given the roles we've seen that such objects play in the integrity of their pre- and rudimentary selves, infants and children who mourn are in an important sense mourning the loss of their "selves." Let me explain.

The younger the infant or child, the more inconsolable he is about his losses. He wails, he screams, he moans, he wrings his hands, or he undergoes any of a variety of other episodic states of sadness. Suppose, for example, that something associated with a psychological transition object has been lost, something that the narcissistic child has been and still is at least partly introjecting. In a very literal sense here, there is part of him that is experiencing a lost element of his narcissistic self. Since having the agency of those sorts of objects at his beck and call is at the center of his life at this time, certainly he experiences the loss of any of them as being extremely sad. So when, say, a parent insists that it is finally time for her child to give up the teddy bear he has always snuggled (we will suppose the bear is the projection of a narcissistically introjected feature of maternal comfort and security), then certainly the child will mourn the loss if the parent continues her demand. And it's not only the physical teddy bear that he's mourning—if he's really mourning that at all—it's more importantly the loss of part of his narcissistic self. Not only will he grieve over this, but he will also pout, be very angry, and possibly even fall into great despair. After all, he has lost something that he has taken as his due. If it is a narcissistic loss he is suffering, then, of course, in his grandiosity, he won't want to accept the loss. When the narcissistic child sees himself as all-powerful, he just assumes that he is an agency self who can avoid any losses. So when the narcissistic child has to face the reality that he can't always have what he wants—when he can no longer hide from some loss he, in fact, has suffered—his reaction is extreme rage, terrible unhappiness, thoroughgoing despair. It feels like a partial loss of the self—the rudimentary self—as it has developed to that point.

The same kind of circumstance occurs for the pre-self infant. The loss of any object relation renders him hopelessly mournful because of what's at stake for him—viz., the agency for getting his raging wants met. Without that agency, his life amounts to nothing. Since the heart and soul of agency for the pre-self infant comes from object relations with external agencies, when he loses contact with one of those external agencies or their psychological object representations, he loses part of what his self is at that stage of development. Naturally, the more primitive one's self development is, the more one will experience losing his self when he loses psychological objects. Naturally, too, then, the more inconsolable he will be. For a while there will be no talking to him, because there will be nothing one can say to bring back the external agency he needs in order to function. Most often, what brings an infant out of mourning here is the replacement of the mourned loss with a new object relation. Indeed, if the new replacement becomes an even more effective external agency for him than the old one was, his fickle heart will erase the love-memory of the very object relation he had been mourning (that is, if he has any memory to speak of in the first place). In fact, pre-self infants quite regularly run through these extremes.

But what of the latency child? What's going on inside of him? Clearly, to the degree that he has a mixture of some developmentally primitive self states still functioning in him, it is that much more likely that some of his losses will be grieved, at least in part, as much as his losses to his pre- and narcissistic self were grieved in infancy and childhood. His losses feel the same as they would have had he been an infant/child suffering those losses. So someone suffering those losses will be just as inconsolable as the infant/child. When one is spurned by a lover, for example, it wouldn't be unusual for him to react with this primitive kind of mourning. It wouldn't be unusual, that is, were a portion of the former love relationship narcissistically grandiose and appropriately introjective, as is often the case with romantic love. If one received total narcissistic grandiose agency empowerment from the lover, then her loss undoubtedly will leave an agency gap. That is why the spurned lover in the midst of mourning his loss is often found to be wholly listless, indolent, languid, depressed. Without the introjected perfect agency of his lover to affirm him as a narcissistic internal agency, he no longer can function as a "borrowing external agency" or as an internal agency. He has been that dependent on her. Such are the liabilities of romantic love.

Of course, that's just one scenario that better approximates a latency child who mourns than it does an adult (although we all know adults like this, too). Adults have a better chance at another kind of mourning, depending on how faded in persistence is their primitive self processing. It is certainly possible for the adult to experience "identificatory mourning." On one level of description, this kind of mourning is a less episodic kind of affair than the others I've described. In mourning a loss, the adult character certainly does go through his episodic emotional grief. However, that's just the first step. He eventually works past the emotional display, and he finally comes to a point where his mourning process is more of a cognitive affair. Specifically, he comes to a point where he believes that his loss cannot be undone. And with more focus on this acknowledgment, he eventually *lets go* of his episodic sadness feelings. In other words, the identificatory mourner finally comes to *accept* his loss. When he has succeeded both in consciously having and expressing his feelings of sadness and then finally no longer having and expressing them because he has come to really believe that nothing can be done to undo things, we say that he has "successfully mourned" the situation. This is often referred to in the "grief literature" as "the mourning process." It's one way of describing what I mean by "identificatory mourning."

How do we understanding this in terms of self processes? When a person exhibits identificatory mourning, that's a sure sign that he no longer is living in any significant way as a mixed developmental kind of self. Of course, once again, this is an ideal type; we are not going to come across a person who is *totally* this way. All of us grieve our *partial* object relating and narcissistic losses because those persist at least partially as the ways in which we connect to people and things. However, it is the aim of self development that we don't wallow in these pockets of how we relate to people and things. It is our hope that we can *primarily* function as identifying character selves.

So when as mature adults we suffer a significant loss, we first go through our bouts of episodic grief and then take over the mourning situation with our character selves. We recognize that we have the fortitude of a strong internal agency that can meet life head on, even in the absence of the valued objects we have lost. That is, as identificatory selves in mourning, we can accept losing objects, because those objects are no longer needed for our agency; we have our own. We have learned to see that the kind of loss we have suffered isn't really a loss of part of our character self but rather a loss of some objectively valued particular in the world, that valued particular being understood as something quite independent of the self, something no longer functioning as part of a psychological object relation. And so we are better able to give up both our strong desire to get back the lost item and the fantasy that getting it back is possible. We have a strong enough self in place so that we are able to let go of the psychological objects we have lost. We have accepted the distinction between the lost identified-with object and our self qua personal character agency. As mourners, we don't feel sad about our self being lost. We don't feel sorry for ourselves, as we do in the more primitive forms of mourning, for we haven't lost our selves. Rather, as mourners, we feel sad that the independent object of value—the loss—is gone. We feel sad for the object's sake only. We have learned to distinguish the lost thing from our self, and so we can finally accept the loss, even though we identify with the lost object. Put still one more way, in mature identificatory mourning, we feel bad about the loss *to the object*, while in the more primitive kind of mourning, we feel bad *for our self*, the latter being perceived as our own loss of self.

Finally, most of us are really combinations of the kinds of mourning[7] I have been talking about. So we probably never get to mourn purely in the more developmentally mature sense. The point is, though, we do have the ability to develop into this pure kind of character self here if we work at it. It certainly is not easy. Among other things, in our culture, there seem to social forces acting against this possibility. I am most certain that if any of us ever did fully become a character mourner, we would end up having to defend ourselves against the claim that we were being too stoical, too emotionally insensitive. People just do expect a full complement of sadness emotions when a loss has been suffered. They expect that we all lose psychological objects and that we suffer setbacks to grandiose images in our rudimentary selves. Ironically, a person who is too identificatorally strong is seen as someone who is morally bankrupt. Sometimes a person just can't win. Nevertheless, my point is that to the extent that a person can approach this ideal mourning type, we understand him as a mature identificatory self.

I won't say any more about mourning and we won't look at any more cases of hybrid self process states. I believe that what we have seen should drive home the point that latency children, adolescents, and adults, too, function as mixtures of self processing from all stages of development. Appreciating this, we have further established the failure of the folk psychology dogma. People simply do not pass cleanly from one self development phase to the next. They are a blend of identification and processing from all the developmental stages that came before.

Of course, we are normally ignorant of how we are faring as mixed introjective/narcissistic self representational/identificatory selves. We normally live the illusion that we are fully identificatory, never acknowledging the shared play of introjection and narcissism. There's even such ignorance where the primitive self processing far outweighs the identificatory processing. I have in mind what the psychoanalyst Winnicott calls the "false self."[8] He speaks of the person who appears to be acting as an autonomous character self but who really is unknowingly acting out of introjections. In the extreme, such a person will crumble at the first hint that the object he's actually introjecting has been devalued. He puts up the front of being fully an internal character agency. In fact, though, all of his eggs are in the introjective basket that is his primary psychological object. By all appearances, the individual is behaving like a character self, but this is a false self, a failed set of identifications. He has seen certain agency traits out in the world of people, and he thinks he has taken them in as self representations. However, he is wrong; they are wholly introjective object representations. And as such, the experiencing of them will still be satisfying for him. So, of course, the individual won't question their efficacy for him. But he nevertheless is wrong in his understanding of what kind of agency this efficacy is rooted in. When, for example, one feels bold in the presence of his hero or idol or lover or favorite celebrity, this could very well be because he is functioning as a false self. He might feel that his strength is coming from within, from character, when, in fact, it is coming from the introjected power[9] of the hero, favorite celebrity, and so forth. So much the worse for what we don't know about ourselves.

III

It is time that I say something about the second psychological dogma. This is the traditional psychoanalytic view that a person's basic identifications are formed during late infancy and early childhood and supposedly stay with her for the rest of her life, conditioning all she finally becomes as a character identity—that is, that the foundations of character are laid in the identifications formed during late infancy and early childhood with one's parents, siblings, and so on and that they hold causal sway over who she is as a character adult. Theorists claim, for example, that once the infant/child identifies with her parents' morality, that morality becomes hers for life. In general, this psychoanalytic thesis has it that any theme we see in the adult character can be causally traced back to what went on with her late infancy or early childhood identifications having the same themes. In this view, we leopards rarely change our spots.

Of course, this is claimed only as a general tendency about people. A person can stray on occasion. However, even with this qualification, the thesis allows that most straying pertains to the peripheral detail of identificatory themes. And on those rarest of occasions when even the main themes themselves are thwarted—on those occasions when a person really does veer from his early childhood identificatory tendencies in favor of more recent ones—we are to understand them as temporary *rebellions* against the identificatory norm, a norm to which the individual will return in due course.

This dogma, too, strikes me as false. We leopards do change our spots. Sometimes we even create new ones. That is, sometimes we form entirely new identifications that have nothing to do with who we may have been in our earlier years. Indeed, like Erikson and others, I believe that adolescence and adulthood are prime times for just such activity. Contrary to what the dogma supposes, this is when the weightiest character formation first begins. Only rarely is what goes on in our adult character an extension of our infancy/childhood identifications. My primary reason for saying this has to do with the nature of character identification. I will argue in Part II that character identifications are the products of autonomous volition and that it is an empirical truth that, for the most part, the latter isn't functional for people until adolescence and adulthood. So, of course, adult identifications are *not* the causal extensions of anything, from late infancy or any other time.

The proponent of the psychoanalytic dogma might respond, "But what about our late infancy/early childhood rudimentary identifications? They aren't chosen. They are the products of a causal developmental process unfolding during our infantile narcissism period. Mightn't those identifications account for our adult character identifications?" Clearly not. For although there are strands of rudimentary narcissistic identifying that unfold as a causal process during late infancy, these are not full-blown, freely chosen character identifications. So, of course, our character identity and our character identifications of adulthood aren't the causal descendants of our infancy/childhood character identity and identifications. For we have no infancy/childhood *character* identifications in the first place. As infants, we are not yet in the business of building character; we are too busy getting needs met. It simply makes no sense to say that adult identifications are causal extensions of infancy/childhood identifications. There's no character identifying going on in infancy for them to extend from.

Having said this, however, I must, at the same time, acknowledge that infancy/childhood rudimentary narcissistic identifications might be the causal ancestors for similar *narcissistic* identifications that make infrequent brief appearances in adulthood. These rudimentary sorts of identificatory strands are purely causal phenomena, and so they very well might have a lifelong causal reign beginning in late infancy. But infrequent narcissism in adulthood isn't what the psychoanalytic dogma is talking about when it talks about our adult character. The dogma's claim is about the full range of our adult character; and that goes well beyond any occasional narcissism that might appear. It is this full range of character that the dogma maintains is an extension of infancy/childhood identifications. Finally, given my view that adult character is crafted from autonomous processes, it comes down to a conceptual point that primitive narcissistic identifications couldn't possibly causally account for them.

I don't want to sell the dogma completely short, though. Beyond a person's continuing narcissism, might there not be at least some genuine character identifications that begin unfolding during childhood that have an impact on who we are as adults? I think the answer has to be Yes. Although the bulk of character identifications occur during adolescence and adulthood, casual observation should be enough to convince anyone that children have the beginnings of a concern for making their character. Children have *some* ability to make autonomous choices about their character. However, having acknowledged this point, let's also be quite clear that it doesn't support the dogma. For the dogma is a causal claim about the connection between who we are as characters and who we were as children (and infants). Admitting that children may tinker with character identification, though, isn't admitting that they are laying any causal roots for who they become as adults. Rather, admitting that children may now and then genuinely identify in a way we would generally describe as "character identification" is admitting only that they have the budding ability now and then to make an autonomous choice about who they want to be as a character agency. That, however, gives no causal status to these early life identifications.

What we *can* say about childhood identification is that it indeed might play a role in who a person is as an adult. But since there is no *causal* claim being made here, what we have to say is that some of a child's early character identifications may *endure* into adulthood. There simply are some free choices people make as children about how they want to be which endure as choices in adulthood for how they want to be. Parts of their character endure. The old didn't create the new. Instead, the old sometimes just stays around. Certainly all of us can see some of this in ourselves and others whose lives we have known well.

This is as far as I think we can go in making any concession to the spirit of the psychoanalytic dogma (even though we make no concession to the literal claim of the dogma). That our character has such a long memory is an appealing notion. However, we shouldn't go overboard with it. Let me summarize the reasons I have presented so far for saying this. Having acknowledged that *some* of our current character identifications come out of an endurance from the past, I must say that, consistent with my general denial of the psychoanalytic dogma, *many* of our current identifications don't, in any fashion. There simply are some early life identifications (whether they are narcissistic or budding character identifications) that have no bearing on who we become later as characters, and there are identifications we have later on that we first form well *after* our earliest identifications. Moreover, we have seen that young *infants*, in the first place, simply don't ever *identify* in the character related sense of that term. Rather, they are consumed with object relating. And while older infants and young children do begin to form self representations of an internal agency, those self representations are mostly narcissistic in nature. The fact is, there are only hints of the identificatory kind of self organization of self representations in later infancy and early childhood, and no hints at all during early infancy. Children do *some* rudimentary identifying with traits that they see out in the world, but not enough to account for all the psychological ancestors a person's adult identifying has. There is some endurance to some of their primitive identifications, but not that much. The fact is, *most* of a person's important identifications are formulated at different points throughout life but really only begin to work in earnest on the individual's personality well into adolescence and adulthood.

I have to say, however, that although I think the dogma is wrong, I also believe that the psychoanalytic theorists really *mean* to be saying something else—that is, there's a truth in what they mean to say, but they are saying it incorrectly. When all is said and done, I believe that when psychoanalytic theorists misspeak and talk about the causal connections between early infancy/childhood states and adult identificatory character, they are really talking about the causal power that infancy/childhood introjections have over introjective states in adulthood and the causal power that childhood mirrored grandiose self representations have over adult grandiosity. Our earliest self developmental processes just don't always go away. They are what causally condition a lot of the *non*character ways in which we function as adults. Indeed, as long as we don't have a *fully* reliable internal character agency that we can depend on to attain our gratifications as adults, we *should want* to be able to depend in part on the agency that a time-proven parental introjective transition object offers. And we do.

So imagine a psychoanalyst saying something like this: "She's always identified with her mother's way of caretaking. Like her mother, she just can't help but try to make things right for anyone who seems needy in the same way a helpless child might seem needy." What I'm arguing is that this is a muddling of identification with a state that is clearly introjective. If this woman really *couldn't help* but try to make things right, the dynamic is clearly that of introjecting the mother's trait as a way of holding onto mother's love, approval, and borrowed agency in these contexts. She fears separating from the strong agency of mother, so she carries the introjected trait of mother around with her. Maintaining the trait into adulthood simply proves that, to the extent that she has done that, she still borrows some of mother's agency self to get through life. I have no doubt but that we all do the same sort of introjective thing, to varying degrees, in our own unique life contexts. Regardless, the point is, it's quite easy to say that this woman is identifying with her mother. However, that is wrong. Her behavior doesn't have the autonomous volitional quality of an identification but rather the quality of a causal introjection upon which she can't help but act. In general, then, I believe that many of the *claims* that analysts make regarding what they see as their patients' identification behavior are really observations that are better described in terms of other more primitive self states.[10]

I suspect that the major reason that object relating and narcissistic causal states of infancy are often confused with identifications in explaining the life-historical roots of an adult's behavior is that when they appear in the adult personality, they frequently are part of the regular psychological repertoire out of which a person acts. Thus, they would appear to be very close to the heart of "who one is." "Who one is" is a reference to a person's identity; it's part of one's adult self. If one adds to this information the psychoanalytic *assumption*—an assumption that is entailed by the psychoanalytic dogma we are discussing here—that if some trait x is part of one's identity then x *must have been identified with* by the individual at some point, then one can't help but conclude that any feature of "who one is" must have been identified with at some point. And so, of course, one could fall into thinking that even traits that, in fact, were really introjective or narcissistic were identificatory. But the truth is, the assumption here is incorrect. There are x's that are part of a person's identity which are *not* identifications. Although we will be saying much more about it in Part II, I want to make the point here that in talking about "who one is," we need to distinguish between a person's "causal identity" and his "character identity." We will see that elements of causal identity are all too often spoken of as though they were part of a person's character identity. But the fact is, not everything that is part of one's causal identity is always something with which he has identified. He hasn't necessarily chosen it as a character trait.

There's another circumstance that's relevant at this point in our discussion. I have acknowledged that undoubtedly some of a person's adult character is traceable to identifications forged during his later narcissistic period of self development, and some is traceable to childhood identifications that have endured, and some is really not character related at all but rather continuing introjective activity that first formed during infancy. But now I would like to add to this list the idea that some adolescent and adult identifications are actually volitional *responses* to what started out in infancy/childhood as introjective and narcissistic activity. In this regard, it can make sense to say that sometimes people do genuinely identify in adulthood with traits that first arose during infancy/childhood. But understand that this means that what started out during infancy/childhood as a primitive causal self process was, as a result of choices the adolescent or adult made about who he wanted to be, later transformed into an identificatory process. Let me offer a brief example to clarify this idea.

I have a friend who is quite a liberal humanist. His father and his father's father before him were very much the same kinds of humanists. One would like to say that my friend first identified with his father's and grandfather's humanistic ways as a child and that that has conditioned the kind of character he has maintained into adulthood. In truth, though, it is more likely that during the pre-self of early infancy, my friend formed an introjective object relationship with the nest of humanistic traits he saw in his omnipotent-seeming father. They certainly would have continued into his later infancy/early childhood narcissism period. Here he probably would have added some grandiose self representations that mirrored his father's omnipotent seeming traits—that is, he would have mirrored his father's seeming omnipotence in his newly emerging internal agency. By introjectively and narcissistically living through these traits, my friend could borrow and mirror the omnipotent agency he saw in his father to get his wants satisfied. And given what we have seen about the lasting power of infancy/childhood causal traits for the adult personality, my friend might very well have held onto these introjections and grandiose representations as part of his adult causal identity.

But compare that interpretation of what went on with this one. Perhaps the truth is that my friend started out as an introjector and grandiose self representor about humanism and somewhere along the way really did develop into someone who genuinely identified with humanism. It happens. It is certainly understandable how such a transformation could take place. The fact is, a person identifies with traits he sees out in the world. And what traits could be more in front of a person (out in the world) than his own introjected grandiose mirrored ones? That is, when a person identifies with traits, he chooses from a menu of traits. The ones that are most likely to appear on any such menu are the ones he already has causally instilled in his psychological repertoire. He may simply decide to begin choosing to be the person he in part has already been for causal reasons. So, of course, there are definite connections between what an infant/child's identity is about and what he will tend to identify with as he grows up. But quite often that connection is between the traits he introjects or grandiosely mirrors as rudimentary self representations during infancy/childhood and his later identifications with those same traits. And that's because the introjected or mirrored traits are part of the menu of traits that are in front of him when he is developmentally ready to start forming his own character self through identificatory choosing.

There is yet a third way of interpreting what is going on in this example. It could be that somewhere along the developmental way, my friend formed a hybrid three-pronged introjection/narcissistic identification/character identification state around the context of liberal humanism. He may *still* causally respond as an object relator or grandiose rudimentary self to those traits, so that the fantasy of his father's omnipotent agency is still inside him. However, sometime after childhood, he may have *also* chosen to make this a part of his character. So now he responds *both* as an object relator/narcissistic self and as a character. He can't seem to let go of the need for at least some fantasized external agency in making his decisions in life, and he can't seem to let go of his need to see himself as grandiose. He can't make himself quite a full character self about humanism. But he has at least made himself partly that.

The point is, people sometimes make identificatory choices about what had started out in the personality as primitive causal self processes. Sometimes the latter are totally transformed into character and sometimes only partly so. In any case, this is certainly a perfectly acceptable sense of the idea that how we start out in life can have a bearing on how we turn out as a characters later on, although this isn't what the proponents of the psychoanalytic dogma ever had in mind.

Finally, in concluding this chapter, I'd like to mention a very important practical implication of our discussion for the human condition. With all the less-than-purely-identificatory activity from infancy/childhood that conditions our adult self, it should be no great surprise that I think people become identificatory characters only to different degrees. Some people hold onto a great deal of pre-self introjecting; some don't. Some hold onto large amounts of narcissistic grandiose self representing; some don't. Some approach being wholly identificatory, hardly introjecting or being narcissistic in exercising their agency at all. The latter sort are rare. Of course, where we find them, we are looking at human beings who are as "character solid" as people can get. These are persons of supreme self-confidence. They live to try to fulfill their own image of how they think life should be lived, not how others would insist they live. When they connect psychologically with other people, they do so for their own reasons, those reasons being *unrelated* both to borrowing the agency power of those other people and to effecting an agency mirroring of fantasized perfect traits. These people can't be bribed with offers of shared agency power or grandiose self agency. They are what is sometimes described as being "fully within themselves." We don't have to like the character they are, but we do have to acknowledge that they are fully the self they have chosen to be. We have to cope entirely with the character we see in front of us and not with some other versions of the self that have their genesis in infancy/childhood.

Again, though, people such as this are rare. People live as character selves only in degrees. It is difficult to hold onto this truth in the fast action of everyday living, however. The social world we all fit into insists that we communicate with each other as selves on an equal footing and that we not realize that, in fact, each of us is coming from a different place as a developed self. Something about the fray of social life causes us to blur these important developmental distinctions between ourselves and others. So adults normally treat one another as being of equal adult status, that status presumably making us equals in our interactions. That is, we normally just assume that all people are being characters pretty much as we are. However, in fact, *we are not really so equal as selves.* We may be equal in status as adults (so, for example, we talk the same general language, we put on the same general kinds of social masks, we have the same general kinds of social graces, and so on), but it is a mistake to conclude also from this that all persons who are fully adults also act fully as characters. For all the reasons I have reviewed in this chapter, the assumption of full character development parity among all adults is just not warranted. Indeed, we morally judge people *as though* they were wholly identificatory beings, when, in fact, they might be largely introjective or narcissistic and thus undeserving of much of that judgment.

Part II

Identification and the Character Self

CHAPTER 5

Causal Identity, Models, and Ownership

We have just seen that even after we finish functioning primarily as infancy/childhood object relators and narcissists, we are never really totally finished with these primitive modes of self processing. Their presence is with us as we move into latency. That presence is even a possibility as we move on through adolescence and adulthood. However, as littered as the landscape may seem to be with the remnants of earlier kinds of self processing, the radical shift in the general tendencies for how we are developing as selves after childhood is clear enough. We are becoming internal agencies, and we are pointing our agency powers in the direction of molding a character of our own choosing. The developmental process responsible for this profound turn of events is psychological identification.

Accordingly, what I want to do now is focus our attention in Part II on understanding this most significant of all the self developmental processes. I want to present an analysis of psychological identification that makes it quite clear how we identifiers pursue our life's work of carving out our character selves. I will begin by mapping out in this chapter the general lay of the land. I will talk about what it means, in the broadest terms, for a person to identify with traits of the world, that process somehow turning those traits into who she is as a character self. Just where does a person go to find the traits she would identify with? And once she finds them, what does she do to them to make them into parts of her character?

I

I am going to argue that there are two general sources we go to to find the things with which we ultimately identify. One is our already existing causal identity self. The other is the world of modeling objects beyond us. In this section, I will talk about the first of these sources. The fact is that quite a lot of who a person becomes through identification started out as parts of who she already was as a causal identity. To be as clear about this idea as I can be, I think it would

113

be helpful if I first said some things about what a person's causal identity self looks like prior to any identifying that might eventually get aimed its way.

Take me, for example. What has my causal identity profile been like? Who is the person I've been, as determined by causal factors? As an infant and child, not only was I powered by the causal forces of introjection and narcissism, I was also responding to the world through a battery of instincts that were to help me survive. So I had an instinctive fear of loud noises, an instinctive attraction to sources that would soothe my hunger, and so on. These causal instincts and my responses to them were part of who I was then. I was also causally conditioned by my genes. They gave me the body I have had all along, the body to whose demands I seem forever to have been responding. Laws of nutrition and physiology have controlled what my genetically determined version of a human body has needed in order to survive and flourish. I have grown according to the laws of physiology and the original causal genetic instructions for what my particular body would do with the nourishment I found for it. So if I were endowed with a fast metabolism, I would stay thin by quickly burning up my calorie intake. If I were genetically predisposed to being very heavy, I would be open to the possible causal consequences of heart problems. If I were genetically preordained to be tall, then tall I'd be. I would *be* a tall person, an overweight person, a person with green eyes, a person with a cleft chin, and so on. Who I am as a body identity is very much a causal affair.

Obviously, there's a lot more to anyone's causal identity. For example, behavioral biologists and ethologists tell us about the genetic determination of what they call the "release mechanisms" and "fixed action patterns" that are part of who we are. These are seemingly automatic, hardwired, non–culture-specific ways that all people have of responding to general environmental and social conditions. So when a person walks past another person and is greeted by him, the second person perceives the pattern of the greeting and automatically returns one of his own. The greeting response to perceiving social contact (that being a release mechanism) is a reaction pattern of behavior that is biologically built into human beings. Similarly, smiling is a fixed action pattern. This is one of a host of inherited complex motor action sequences. Other things being equal, people just do respond to smiles with smiles of their own. The important point, though, is that in our greeting others and returning their smiles, we are exhibiting part of who we are as identities. The special twists we put on our particular way of greeting and our particular way of smiling nails down even firmer those parts of who we are. But short of reflection about these things, we really have no say in the matter. We are biologically endowed with the release mechanisms and consequent fixed action pattern behaviors that are part of our identity.

As a causal identity, I am also me in virtue of the instructions my genes carry about my temperament. Because of one's biology, a person might have general lifelong psychological tendencies to be pensive, sober, shy, capricious, cheerful, confident, optimistic, hopeful, warm, calm, relaxed, laidback, sensitive, excitable, passionate, moody, brooding, gloomy, depressed, and so on. People just are some of these ways at the core of their identity. These are part of who they are, but from no determination of their own.

Obviously, there are numerous cultural and psychosocial forces at work on causal identity too. The roles our culture assigns to us and the social groups to which we belong causally determine a lot of who we become. So when I take on the role of being a father, for example, there are certain socially defined expectations immediately conditioning my behavior. To the extent that all of us are immersed in living out of a seemingly unending list of culturally defined roles, all of us respond in different degrees to general expectations of the culture. We aren't choosing our behavior; rather, we are responding to what social forces deem appropriate. The causal facts of identity are equally true about us as group members. Simply belonging to an ethnic group, a gender group, a religious group, a professional group, a political group, and so on commits us to certain beliefs and behavioral patterns conditioned by social-group forces.

We can stop our cataloguing here. I think the point is clear: Complex causal forces make us into complex causal identity selves. That kind of self is with us as infants and children, and it is with us as adults. Before we are done with our discussion in Part II, we will have a clearer idea of how many of these causal forces bear on a person's causal identity. However, we have seen enough to make the general point.

The claim I want to emphasize now is that it is causal identity that a person often looks to for her raw materials for identification. Who a person becomes as a character identity often starts out from who she has been all along as a causal identity. Then, by identifying with some of her causal traits, she transforms those traits into aspects of her character. What started out as traits that were wholly described in causal terms were transformed into traits that are now described in the noncausal language of character development. For example, we say that so-and-so was a chubby infant, a stubborn child, a frustrated adolescent. On the face of it, those sound like causal traits that arise respectively out of biological, temperamental, and psychosocial sources. As such, those would be traits that might be interesting to note about the person as straightforward causal facts true of her. However, their connection to character would be of even greater significance to us. And indeed, when we say of this person that she has grown into a chubby, stubborn, or frustrated adult, we don't have in mind that she has simply remained causally structured as she has always been since infancy, childhood, and adolescence. What we believe is that there are two different kinds of identities in play now—the causal one and the character one. We understand the chubby, stubborn, frustrated adult as someone who has *chosen* to respond to some causal aspects of herself in her own decided ways. She has come to actually identify with these heretofore causal traits. She has chosen how she would hang onto and develop her somatic chubbiness, temperamental stubbornness, and psychosocial-role- and group-determined frustration. By making choices about how she would respond to the causal self that external forces have determined originally, she has begun to add a volitional character identity to a purely causal one. Once this starts to happen, the whole game of understanding what a person's identity is about begins to change too. The universe of discourse has changed. Character identity exists in a different kind of reality than causal identity. It's a world where values and judgments rule. We want to know about, and we end up making moral judgments about, how people choose to fashion themselves into the characters they do.

Of course, even though a new reality opens here, we should remember that no one ever becomes a total character identity. As we saw in a different context in chapter 4, no one ever lives totally as an identifier. People vary in their identity not only in terms of the particular contents that get packed into it but also in terms of how much of their identity is, in the main, causally based and how much of it is volitionally based. People slide along this identity scale at different places. Most of us continue under the thumb of psychological and social forces, at least to some extent, throughout life. Temperament, too, never seems fully to quit. But much of this can be offset by reflective volitional capacities, these being the essential stuff of identification. Of course, in the case of those people who aren't very reflectively volitional, identity isn't so much a matter of character. The more reflective choices a person makes about the causal forces that play in her life, the more character is at work in her life. For example, against a backdrop of a psychosocial personal history that had her growing up in an economically deprived family with educationally deficient parents and emotionally disturbed siblings, such a person wants to confront these causal weights on her life and do something about them. She wants to focus and gain control over them. She wants to make choices about what she will do with those identity features. She asks: "How will I vary them? Will I hold onto them at all? Will I continue with them just as they are?" To the extent that a person seriously makes any of these sorts of choices about the causes that bear on her, she is finding a place on that sliding scale where she is turning causal elements of identity into parts of her character.

I will have more to say about these last points in the next chapter. Right here, though, let me just reemphasize the idea that identification often means a person identifying with traits that are part of her already functioning causal identity self. Identification converts what would otherwise be a causal psychological automaton into what we know as a character self with vital personality and moral quality. No small act, that.

II

There is a second well we go to for identification. Sometimes we go beyond our causal selves for things to identify with. We identify with things in the external world. Let me briefly replay a context we are familiar with now as a way of introducing this second arena.

Young children first have self representations around themes of internal character agency when they finally find powers in themselves to do things which they heretofore had only seen in others, powers they heretofore had only borrowed from others directly or introjectively. For example, consider the young child who has all along been using father's agency demonstrations of anger and aggression to fight off threats to his well-being from other children. In connecting with this trait of his father's, the child may point to it as his own source of power, as though that power really did belong to him, when, in fact, it actually flowed fully through his father. It wouldn't be unusual to hear the child say to a threatening source, "If you don't stop, I'll tell my father on you, and he'll stop you," as though these words—as an embodiment of his father's agency—would be enough to stop the other children. The child is using a specific trait of father's to defend himself against the aggressors; he's using the threat of father's agency over that trait to frighten the other children. In time, the child will probably move away from using father's agency directly. He will probably move toward introjecting different forms of this trait. For example, he might begin to use the same kinds of idiosyncratic anger expressions that father uses when he's angry. He might raise his voice in the same way and use the same vocabulary, speech inflection and cadence, and so on. He might do this as though the use of father's words in these ways was enough to enlist father's agency also over the power of anger. Such a thing would amount to the child's borrowing father's agency to defend against the threat the child perceives in the other children.

In time, though, identificatory self representations start emerging. A fundamental change occurs in how the child relates to his father. He uses him no longer as a psychological object to borrow agency from but, rather, as a real object in the world with traits (for angrily fighting off threatening people) that he (the child) now is trying to emulate under the power of his own internal agency. Alternatively put, in identifying with father and his traits now, the child is beginning to develop his own agency over those traits. In general, the more skilled he becomes in controlling such traits toward his own ends, the more we say those traits are becoming part of who he is, part of his character. In childhood, complete dominion over all, or even over any, of our traits is rare. Children are hardly solid characters. But they do improve as they age. One's original identifications grow more complex and one takes on new and evermore sophisticated variations as one moves from childhood through adolescence through adulthood. By this process of identifying with real objects and their traits, one becomes increasingly more solid a character agency with his own traits.

The point is that old introjective objects may eventually take on a different status for us. They may become a source of identificatory raw materials from the external world. But clearly they aren't the only kind of items a person plucks out of the external world for identification. There are plenty of objects from our experience we come to identify with which we never had anything to do with as introjectors and narcissists. Indeed, there's a special excitement we have when we come upon items in the world that are entirely new for us which we end up identifying with. Aspects of life that we never had an involvement with in any form now become part of who we are. We aren't converting something old into something new here. We are authoring something totally unique for us. And that just is exciting.

But whether we are addressing old material in this new identificatory way or new material in this same general way, the more important point is that, as identifiers, we are taking a special stance toward real objects in the external world, a stance that transforms some of their properties into parts of who we are as an emerging internal agency character. Obviously, we would like to know what this special stance toward the external objects is. But we will take first things first. Let's be a little more exact about what the external objects are like.

Clearly, most often when we identify with things in the world, we identify with other people—parents, friends, role models, sometimes even celebrities. But we also identify with other things besides people. We sometimes identify with other kinds of beings—animals, fictional heroes, deities. We sometimes identify with inanimate objects—cars, books, musical instruments. We sometimes identify with activities—playing basketball, writing a book, mountain climbing in the Rockies. We sometimes identify with ideas—philosophical positions, political ideologies, spiritual inspirations. And more. Undoubtedly, on occasion some of these categories reduce to some of the others. Often enough, for example, when I identify with a person, it is really some of her ideas or some special activity she does well or some concrete physical feature she has or some cluster of these sorts of things that I identify with. But however that works out in individual cases, the point is, there are a lot of different sorts of things people identify with.

We understand these various things to exist out in the world, *independent* of the identifier. In contrast with the developmentally earlier sorts of object relations,

> identifications...carry the process of separation from the object a further step. In identification the object quality of the model is fully preserved and is, in fact, one of the conditions of the internalization. The object is acknowledged, accepted, and preserved as autonomously existing in its own right and as separate and independent from the internalizing subject. The tolerance for the separateness of the object is a mark of the autonomy of the participating ego.[1]

In incorporation, introjection, and projection, the object and subject are run together. Acts of identification, by contrast, are signals that a person has finally managed to experience subject and object as distinct. The identifier may want to become like the other person in certain ways, but she recognizes that this will be a "likeness" of a trait that's a genuine objective trait of the other person, whether the identifier is successful in copying it or not. The other person will remain there with his traits, whatever a prospective identifier decides to do in terms of relating to him and his traits.

That's what happens when one identifies with a person. Recognize, too, that the point is just as true (if not as obvious) with all the other kinds of objects that get identified with. For example, were I to start identifying with some old building or with being in good physical condition or with believing a particular philosophical position about the nature of mind, I would antecedently recognize these "objects" as real and independent of me. I would have objectively observed them in the world and tossed them around in my mind for evaluation. I identify with a philosophical position only after I have heard it from others or developed it myself as a position that is subject to scrutiny in the objective world, whether I choose to scrutinize it or not. In fact, I know that I am not one and the same with the philosophical position. Rather, it is an idea in the world that can belong to anybody. Similarly, I can identify with a building and perfectly well know that I am not literally that building, even though in my identification there is something about it (e.g., perhaps its grace or sophistication) that I want finally to be part of me.[2] And, too, when I identify with being someone who is in good physical shape, I acknowledge that "being in good shape" is a condition that will exist as an abstract condition whether or not I become an instantiation of it.

But now, as identifiers, we don't *just* acknowledge the separateness of the object and its traits. We also strongly desire having those traits for our own. Because we have evaluated them as supremely *desirable*, we also want to take some of them inside us, making them part of our character. There is something so special about those traits that we would like to make them part of who we are. But we aren't aiming at *exclusively possessing* them; rather, we are only trying to *share* some semblance of them with the object. We give an equal billing to ourselves and the object as far as "being equal and distinct possessors of the trait one is identifying with" is concerned. If I identify with the idea of freedom, for example, I neither take it that this idea exists only as my idea nor that it exists only insofar as I am its sole instantiation. A trait may become part of who I am, but it also may be part of another person's character, too.

Exactly which objects and traits do people choose to identify with? Clearly we make distinctions among traited objects here; not everything is a candidate for identification. In the course of our lives, we spend a great deal of time being aware of an indeterminately large number of objects and their traits, hardly any of which time is invested in identifying with those traited objects. For instance, I see that there is dust on my computer screen and there is a lamp in the corner, but I don't identify with either object. And the same is true for most things in my experience. So what are the traited objects people do identify with? In a word, they are the objects the identifier perceives to be *models*. They are models of traits he would have as part of his character. All models are *paradigms* of traits that have great value for the identifier. Indeed, the model is seen to be a close approximation of a perfection of those traits. Developmentally, it should really be no surprise that models work this way for the identifier. For he is now simply carrying the modeling activity that started much earlier at a more primitive stage of self development into the next arena. Let's not forget the role that modeling played in his days as a narcissistic self. Any identifier has already gone through narcissistic introjecting and narcissistic self representational mirroring of traits that he once saw in the perfect parent. That is, any identifier once was a narcissistic self who took on the modeled traits of a parental *imago*. What I am claiming now is that one's identificatory modeling is an extension of this narcissistic modeling. How?

The narcissistic infant wants to take in the agency and traits of the all-powerful-seeming parent in order to get her wants met. One sees the parent agency and his value traits as a kind of perfection. So one narcissistically introjects this perfection. In a sense, the parent *imago* is the infant's paradigm for the perfection traits she so desperately wants to put inside herself. As an introjector, though, she can't really fully have the traits as her own. So she does the next best thing. She borrows them and her perfect parent's agency to feed her grandiose desires. In identification with an external object model, one sees the model in a way parallel to how the narcissistic introjector sees the perfect parent. The identifier sees the model as a perfect being vis-à-vis some traits of the model. Instead of having to introject the object's traits, however, one now has the psychological wherewithal to create self structure for her own agency out of the external object's traits. In ways we need to discuss, one *somehow* copies the traits and makes them her own. In both narcissistic introjection and identification, one sees some object as paradigmatically modeling certain traits that one perceives as being near perfections. The difference between the two cases is that while the narcissist tries to take the parental model's perfect traits and agency inside herself as introjects, the identifier tries to take the model's perfect traits inside herself under the control of her own agency. Also, while in narcissistic introjecting there is a running together of the model's traits with one's own (one *sees* the other's perfect traits *as* one's own), in identification there is an acknowledgement that the model's traits and one's copy of them are distinct.[3]

These differences aside, though, the upshot of what I am saying is that the "relating to models and their traits" found in identification doesn't just appear on the scene out of nowhere. It has its precursor in infantile narcissistic development. Now, moving on in our general discussion, what else can we say about object models and identification?

I would make the point that any given identifier's models are not universally admired as such by everybody. One person's model is often another person's yawn. I saw Duke Snider as a model of many perfections, but certainly not all other children agreed. They didn't see him as modeling anything for them. They didn't see him as a paradigm of traits they wanted to share. Instead, they had their own favorites who modeled traits they identified with. So why is it that some people are motivated to identify with a given object as a model and others aren't? The answer is that some people have certain character related wants and needs that are served specifically by identifying with the given object model while other people don't. These others either have different wants and needs or they get the same wants and needs serviced better by some different object model. Suppose, for example, person A's professional success depends on her finding ways to maximize efficiency. This has been a continuing condition of her doing her job well. But person B doesn't have this same need in order to do her job well. Surely, when both encounter a third person C who has efficiency skills, A will be much more disposed than B to engage C as a model of efficiency.

In a more general vein, we can say that it is a person's existing life plans, longstanding goals, existential projects that condition what objects she will treat as models for possible identification. Certainly in the context of early identity building, it is a person's preexisting causally built-in existential projects around issues like nourishment, security, comfort, and power that condition whom she considers models or not. Mother and father get the nod every time. As a person grows older, she immerses herself in new kinds of projects and takes on new goals—some of them chosen, many others the result of social forces. In either case, these, too, condition whom she will see as models. Group pressures and cultural role expectations could push her to set life goals around creating personal wealth, entering a profession, sending her children to status schools, and so on. Other people displaying some talent with these sorts of goals will naturally become models of identification for her.

It is important to note that these antecedently existing conditioning circumstances are in fact other parts of a person's identity as it exists prior to her new identificatory choices. By that I mean that they are either part of who she is as an already existing causal identity or part of who she is as an already existing character identity. Because of who one *already* is and what this entails about her wants and needs, she chooses to see one traited object or another as a new model to emulate. Only if some of an object's traits fit in with, and perhaps even bolster, some of the identifier's already existing identity features, or fit in with and bolster some of what she at least believes her existing identity features are, will she see those traits as desirable. And so only then will she see the object as a model.

Because antecedently we are precisely the identities we are up to that time, it is normally quite predictable what things we will treat as models to identify with and what we will not. Sometimes, however, the models we come up with are not so obvious. An object that may have always seemed rather inconsequential might one day exhibit some trait that quite by accident teaches a person how to figure out a problem area of her life. Antecedently, she might have been lacking a character trait that is needed to resolve that problem area. But she didn't realize this. Suppose, for example, you have never made any commitment to being a loyal friend. You don't realize it, but it is your deficit in this arena that is gnawing at one of your friends and causing her to be upset with you. You don't realize that the smallest sign of loyalty on your part would cure all the ills between the two of you. Now, in seeing how some other person (who seems otherwise quite unremarkable) deals with a similar gnawing problem, you quite conceivably might recognize the similarity and recognize the loyalty that this other person has firmly rooted in his character and is using to defuse similar problem situations occurring in his life. In seeing for yourself how loyalty could work for you, you might immediately raise this person to the status of a model.

Already existing identity states of the identifier are what condition the raising of objects to the status of models for the identifier.

Recognize, too, that these preconditions exert their influence by making object traits that may not have been noticed before quite desirable now. They are sacrosanct. Indeed, sometimes we *so* tend to positively value identificatory objects that we look past any of their deficiencies. We blow up the virtuosity of their traits, quite out of proportion. This is a tendency sometimes taken to an extreme, but one we are all familiar with. We see this happen most clearly when we identify with charismatic figures—for example, with political persons or parent figures whose traits of social power might be the core of what we are really after for ourselves. But it also can happen to a person identifying with a religious institution or ideological system. It just does happen more than we would like to admit when we identify with modeling objects. Because of our attachment to the modeling object, we sometimes get extravagant with the traits we want to make our own.

When we get extravagant like this, we sometimes end up being fortunate. A person sometimes takes on traits she hadn't bargained for which benefit her life. However, sometimes people aren't so fortunate. Sometimes an identifier's extravagance distorts her view and even eventually gets her into trouble because of the influence the object has over her. She gets stuck with traits for which she hadn't bargained. One might imagine, for example, an overweight child coming to so identify with the idea of being thin that she becomes bulimic, a condition not only physically debilitating but also psychologically disturbing vis-à-vis her sense of identity. Or we might imagine an adult who is so desperate to have a sense of belonging in the world that she latches onto the first crowd of people who accept her, even though they are a bunch of thugs and unsavory characters. In both examples, the individual's identifying clearly has a bad influence on her life. But just as clearly, the individual didn't pursue identification with the traits that led to these bad consequences *in order to* experience the bad consequences. That is, she didn't identify with those bad consequences. Rather, they were *causal results* of the traits she did genuinely identify with. Presumably, she would rather extricate herself from these results if she could.

I'd like to relate our talk about models and traits now to our discussion in the first section. This involves making an important distinction about the models with which one identifies. The kinds of models I have been focusing on in this section are all things independent of the individual identifier. They fit the classical psychoanalytic picture of identification, where an individual looks *outside of herself* at external objects for traits that she then copies and takes in through identification as qualities of her unfolding character. This is the prototype notion of identification. I am going to call this "identification with externally modeled traits," and I am going to distinguish it from "identification with internally modeled traits." The latter is, in fact, the kind of identification described in the first section. Not only do we identify with traits out in the world; we also identify with traits that are already part of our internal causal identity. If by causal temperament I am a friendly person, I may at a certain point become aware of this fact and decide that I very much like being this way. I may, that is, begin to identify with this heretofore causal aspect of who I am. Now I start to take responsibility for this trait as part of who I *want* to be. I have picked it to identify with from a model who just happens to be me-as-a-causal-identity. That modeling causal self is external to my character. The modeled traits are certainly part of who I am, but they aren't part of my character. So when I am about the business of building my character by looking to models for prospective traits, I look to all of the world beyond character. What I am saying now is that that world includes a person's causal identity self as well as the world of external objects. Because they are both "beyond" our character, they are grist for the kind of identificatory mill we've been talking about in this section.

So, people are internal and external identifiers. The raw materials for identification come both from modeled objects independent of them and from their own causal identity self. Now that we have these ideas in place, it would behoove us to turn to the main event, that being an examination of the identificatory act itself. What does it mean *to identify* with a model? Since we have focused most of our attention in this section on identification with *externally modeled objects*, I propose to continue in that arena in answering this question. Understand, though, that what is said about the identificatory act here will apply just as aptly to identification with internal models. In a manner of speaking, talking about identification specifically with externally modeled objects will be my model for discussing all forms of identification.

III

"Identifying with a model" is a relationship between the individual and her model. I want to work up a general sketch of the required conditions of that relationship now and then do the fuller analysis in the chapters to follow. It happens that there are actually a number of different candidates for what the identificatory relationship is—a number of possibilities, each of which, on the face of things, has some initial credibility. But only some of them are truly necessary conditions. So with that in mind, what we are going to do in this section is inspect all of them and separate the wheat from the chaff.

1. The first candidate for the identificatory relationship has it that when someone (S) identifies with some object trait (x),[4] he normally likes that object trait, in the sense that he *values* it. I want to be clear about the significance of the "value" idea. Sometimes a person says he identifies with another person in contexts where he has a liking affection for the other person. And he talks as if to identify with that person is to like him. In trying to convince us of his fondness for the other person, he tells us "he's a great person and I really identify with him," as though affectionately liking him *is* identifying with him. Clearly, this is a mistake. The individual identifies with his friend *because* he has affection for him. Because of his affection for his friend, he has come to see what his friend is made of, what his friend's character is about. If, as a result of this process, he also comes to *value* the makeup of that character, he might then *also* come to identify with his friend. That is often what happens between friends. But the point I must emphasize here is that identification depends on "liking" being done in the context of "valuing." We often, though not always, end up identifying with people we like in this sense. Perhaps this is because we like them in virtue of their having certain qualities of character we *already* identify with. Or perhaps they have qualities of character we don't *yet* have ourselves but we nevertheless value. In either case, it is valuing on top of affection that we have in mind when we say that we identify with people whom we like. When S identifies with x, S likes/values x.

Also, the *extent* of identification often parallels the degree of liking/valuing x. That is, if a person likes some x, he often identifies with x in some comparable measure. So if I say I identify with being a philosopher to the point of actually becoming one professionally, part of what we believe about me is that I very much like/value being one. I value that kind of life to the extreme degree that I have made it part of who I am. Some people have been known to like their dog or even their car to the point where they would claim to identify with it. It is perfectly understandable for me to say that to the extent that I love my family, I identify with it. To the extent that I like my current writing project, I identify with it. None of this is to suggest, of course, that one can't have momentary lapses from liking while still maintaining identification. And it isn't to say, either, that momentary lapses sometimes don't evolve into fully changed minds. A person can totally stop liking something. But when that happens, he also begins weakening the bonds of his identifications. People tend not to identify with things they don't like.

Is this always so, though? Don't we sometimes end up identifying with things we apparently don't like/value? Suppose, for example, I am identifying with the pain a friend is telling me he has gone through. He might be telling me about the death of a relative, and I might very reasonably respond by identifying with this pain. Clearly, I don't like/value pain. But given my view of these matters, how can this be? How can I deny liking/valuing pain if I am identifying with it? The fact is, although the pain may be undesirable, I am identifying with it only to the extent that this is an expression of the *value* I have *for my friend*. I am not really identifying with pain per se. I am identifying with it only as a stand-in for how I feel about my friend.

That is one sort of answer to the objection. There is another. Granted, people sometimes just *are* ways they simply don't like being—that is, these unliked ways are part of their identity. And they wish they, as people, were different. For example, what if a someone sees himself (his identity—who he is) as lazy? Moreover, what if he not only sees himself this way but also doesn't like it? Isn't this clearly a case of a person identifying with laziness yet *not* feeling good about it?

No. In this sort of situation, the problem quite often is that a person's character identity—what he identifies with—is in conflict with elements of his causal identity. A lazy person is usually someone who, because of temperament or circumstance, has developed general dispositions towards laziness. He has developed causally triggered habits of mind and behavior which we describe as laziness. And although another person in his situation might feel different than he does, he doesn't like this causal component of his identity. But this isn't really a counterexample to the claimed connection between identifying with x and liking x. For as we now know, just because something is part of a person's *identity* doesn't mean that it is automatically something a person *identifies with*. Having causal identity traits needn't involve having identifications with them. And in the proposed counterexample, there is no reason to believe that the individual in fact identifies with being lazy. That trait is part of his causal identity, but there is no reason to suppose that he also identi-

fies with it. Indeed, the very fact that he doesn't like being this way—
that he disvalues it—is ample reason to suppose that he doesn't think
that it is part of his character. There is no conflict between what a
person likes here and what he identifies with. There is only a conflict
between on the one hand, what character he likes and identifies with
and, on the other, what causal identity he possesses.

There is one other example that I think is relevant to this particular discussion. The psychoanalytic claim that people sometimes
identify with their enemies flies in the face of what I am saying here.
Surely one doesn't like/value his enemy at all, yet the analyst tells us
that he can identify with him. Obviously, I disagree with this idea.
It seems to me to be clearly another case where a person is using the
term "identification" but is really talking about the phenomenon of
introjection. The so-called identifier-with-the-enemy certainly takes
in features of the enemy, but not in an identificatory manner. Rather,
he introjects some of the enemy's traits in the spirit of protecting himself from the enemy. What's called "identifying with the enemy" is a
defense mechanism through which one actually introjects hated and
feared traits of the enemy so as to have the fantasy of controlling
those traits. It is as though to say, "If I can be these hated and feared
ways, then I have control over all such activities and I don't need to
worry about them being turned against me by others. I control all
expressions of such traits." In fact, this sort of general behavior is
paradigmatic of what we saw, in chapter 2, psychoanalysts refer to as
an introjective "splitting of the object world." That they would also
decide to call such behavior in this special "enemy" context "*identification* with the enemy" is just careless talk.

2. "S identifies with x" often conveys the idea that S *wants to become*
the kind of person who embodies certain traits of x. Indeed, I opened
the discussion in this book with this idea. In talking about a person's
becoming someone he likes, I distinguished between the ideal images
a person has about what his version of a good life would be and his
actually bringing those images to fruition through his character
development. And I said that the process of identification was the
very thing that moves a person toward this end. Linking what we
said there with what we have been saying here about identification,
it appears that the identifier sometimes scans the environment for
modeling objects that possess traits that incorporate the ideal images
he has of a good life. Other times, he has no prior set of images he
brings to his scanning. Instead, he discovers an object that has traits

he *then first decides* will be part of what he now will see as traits of a good life for himself. In either case, though, someone who identifies with an object x necessarily wants certain traits of x to be part of who he is.

Now, I can imagine someone objecting to this idea. One might point out that when a person doesn't like who he is, he also normally doesn't want to be that kind of person. So *if* a person could identify with traits he didn't like, he could identify with traits he didn't want either. Well, I hope it is clear that this argument in fact fails for the reasons I just cited in case 1. Simply, a person can have traits he doesn't want, but he has them as part of his causal identity, not as part of his identificatory character. And so I am still confident that wanting x is part of the concept of identifying with x. Of course, merely wanting certain traits is not the same as actually having them. But that is only to say that there are more logical conditions of the concept of identification that must be met besides "wanting."

3. Sometimes "S identifies with x" means that seeing x and certain of x's traits confirms for S who he, S, already is. When TV network programmers decide to put on a certain show because they think "a large portion of the viewing audience will identify with its subject matter" (say, for example, they air a show about parental dilemmas with teenage drug use and target it at the parent population), they mean that a large portion of the viewing audience will figuratively see themselves in the show. They will as much as say, "Yes, this is me; this is who I am. I've got the same parental problems." Identification in this sense of the term is about a person's getting zeroed in on some traits he sees in some object and surmising that those traits *already exist* in himself. Here, S doesn't take on certain traits as a means of *becoming* a person with those traits. He already *is* that person.

I think that because this sense of identification misses the central idea from the second section that has identifiers learning something about traits from the external object world and then taking them inside as part of their expanding agency self, we can't accept it as viable. It is a mistake, albeit a perfectly understandable one. For it seems that someone might slide into this mistaken view because he rightly sees identification as involving "person S's possession of traits that are seen out in the world of modeling objects." The mistake comes in not being clear that in genuine identification the identifier S learns something from the modeling objects about what traits he, S, will then take on. The mistake here is in getting things backwards.

It is true that understanding something about the modeling object's traits is crucial to acts of identification; but the advocate of case 3 brings those traits as a *fait accompli* to his encounter with the object, looking to get his view of who he already is here confirmed by his viewing of the object, instead of first making the traits he sees in the object into part of who he will become.

I don't mean to suggest that there is something untoward about people looking for confirmations for who they are by finding examples of themselves out in the world of modeling objects. Such a thing quite legitimately gives a person a sense that he is not alone in possessing certain traits that he would rather not be alone in having. It also more sharply clarifies for the individual what the traits in question are exactly. That is, it further clarifies for him who he really is. And that's all valuable material for living life. The mistake here simply is that the wrong term is being used to designate this phenomenon. It is a lot like identification, but different enough not to warrant the designation.

4. Another sense of "identifying with x" is "being able to imagine being x-like." Sometimes we claim to identify with a situation where what we have in mind is that we can imagine being in that situation ourselves. For example, a perfect stranger recounts a tragedy he has experienced. I react and say: "I can really identify with what you're saying; I can relate to it. I can just imagine what you were going through and how you must have felt." I don't know the stranger, so I don't fully empathize with him. But I hear enough so that I do take an imaginative stance toward a hypothetical situation I might have gone through. I believe his tragedy called forth character traits in him that would be similarly called forth in me were I in his shoes. I imagine that the stranger goes through precisely what I would go through.

Like case 3, this sense of "identification" seems to me not to be the kind in which we are most interested. The imagining going on here is actually a kind of discovering or testing of what my identity is like. But it is a discovery or test about what my identity was like *antecedent* to the imagined situation. The imagining really is an occasion for the kind of reconfirming of who I already am that we spoke of in case 3.

Another problem with the proposed analysis is that there are cases where I say that I can imagine certain ways of being but where there is clearly no identification going on. So I might be able to imagine what it would feel like to live under a totalitarian rule, but that wouldn't mean that I would identify with that state of affairs. Indeed, I wouldn't. And the reason I wouldn't is related to the first sense of identification. Because I wouldn't like/value totalitarian rule, I wouldn't really identify with it, even though I could imagine it. The point is, imagination of any x is linked to identification only to the extent that that x is already something I believe to be true and valued about my character.

What is the final disposition, then, of the connection between "being able to imagine being x-like" and "identifying with x"? If these expressions don't really mean the same thing, why do we sometimes use them in the same breath? The answer is that imagination provides a person with a knowledge of the *limits* of what he is able to identify with. For example, if I couldn't in any way imagine what it would be like to be a homeless person, then surely it would be wrong to suppose that I could identify with being one. Or if one weren't able to imagine what it would be like to have a criminal mind, then surely one wouldn't be able to identify with criminals.[5] Where a trait x is something about another person and one has no image of what that kind of x-like character is like for the other person, then, of course, one also has no image of it about himself. And so he couldn't identify with it. He might be able to *be* that x in the sense of having x as part of his *causal* identity, but we wouldn't expect that he would be able to *identify* with being x as part of his character identity.[6] In the final analysis, imagination just does set the limits of identification.

5. There is a special sort of imagination that applies only where x's are other persons (or, in rare cases, animals, too). What I have in mind is *empathic imagination*. Sometimes we loosely substitute saying "I identify with him (some person x)" for saying "I empathize with him." Friends, for example, typically both empathize and identify with one another. However, it would be wrong to conclude from this that the two concepts mean the same thing. For surely we sometimes identify with people we don't empathize with and we sometimes empathize with people we don't identify with. The fact of the matter is, the two concepts are closely related in the sense that people who already identify with one another highly like/value one another; and the latter is typically motivation enough for getting people also to empathize with one another. But that's as far as the relationship goes. Actually, as in case 4, empathy tells us something about the *limits* of one's identifications. If we can and do empathize with something about a person, then we have made being that way a possibility about our own

character too. When we want others to know this about us and our character, we let them know this by mixing the two expressions.

6. Sometimes a person means by "I identify with x" "I have *compassion* for x," where x is an individual or a kind of individual. When we say of a political candidate, "He really identifies with the minorities who have systematically always received the short end of things in our society," we mean that he is compassionate with their concerns. We assume that he knows the particulars of what they are about—their central traits—and he responds to this knowledge with sincere compassion for them. This identifier has no intention of taking on the traits of the people he claims to be identifying with. Unlike in cases 2 and 5, he doesn't want the modeling objects' relevant traits to become part of who he is. In fact, not only will he keep his distance from ever taking on those traits, but he will also probably do what he can to help the modeling objects get some distance of their own from those traits.

Finally, this use of "identification" is simply too off the mark. Not all identifiers have compassion for their modeling objects. The most we can say for why people sometimes confuse the two concepts is that "identifying with x" sometimes is a causal condition of "becoming compassionate with x." There is no logical connection between the two concepts, though. Secondly, and more damning, the identifier in no way wants to acquire the relevant traits he sees in the modeling objects. He doesn't want to become that same kind of person himself. And since, as I claimed in case 2, I take "wanting to become like the model" to be one of the central aspects of the concept of identification, the "compassion" notion of "identifying with x" can't be right.

7. Sometimes a person means by "S identifies with x" "S can copy, mimic, simulate, or imitate being x-like." So we say things such as "He acts just like his father. He really identifies with him"; "She walks and talks just like her favorite athlete. She must really identify with her." These kinds of claims are certainly not unusual. In general, we take it to be a sure sign that someone identifies with someone else if he can accurately copy him. The fact is, though, a person's being able to copy someone's traits might be a sign that he has successfully identified with him, but that doesn't justify concluding that "identification" *means* "being able to copy." Indeed, we made the point in chapter 4 that, at best, imitation is identification in the weakest sense. What we meant by that in chapter 4, and what we mean by it now, is that although imitation is a necessary condition for

identification, it isn't enough by itself. For example, if a person were *merely* imitating a certain way of being humble, then we most definitely would *not* allow that he identified with being humble. He's just playacting. At the very least, actual identification requires a kind of sincerity about one's actions that mere playacting misses. Mere reproduction of behaviors won't do as a sufficient analysis of identification.

8. "S identifies with x" is sometimes used to mean "S knows a lot about being x-like." The teenager who learns all there is to know statistically about the basketball career of Michael Jordan, who collects all the relevant sports fan magazines and tabloids, who finds out about the family life of Jordan, and so on, is someone we say strongly identifies with Michael Jordan. And in general, we expect that if a person really identifies with a model, he will know a lot about it. The less he is able to exhibit the relevant knowledge, the more we doubt that he genuinely identifies with what he says he identifies with.

Of course, this is all true. However, once again, here is a condition of identification that isn't sufficient for a full analysis. Obviously, we can know a lot about plenty of things without identifying with them. A physicist may know all there is to know about quarks and pulsars, yet we wouldn't be surprised to discover that he didn't identify with them. A sportswriter might know all the above sorts of things about Michael Jordan, yet we wouldn't be surprised to find out that he didn't identify with him.

I think we are starting to run out of viable candidates for an analysis of identification. So let's pause. Where are we in our discussion now? The views we have looked at so far are typically presented as though they were serious candidates for definitional—that is, necessary and sufficient—conditions of identification. In fact, however, they all fall short of the mark. The analyses that we have looked at really present a variety of *kinds of conditions of identification*, with no analysis individually (nor any combination of them jointly) constituting logically sufficient conditions for full identification. The variety is such that some of these analyses are logically necessary conditions, some are causally motivating conditions, some are causal consequences of identification, some are what we might call background context-setting conditions, and some are just a bit off as any kind of conditions and are in need of some reformulation. For example, we can understand analyses 1 ("like/valuing x"), 2 ("wanting to be like x"), 7 ("imitation"), and 8 ("knowledge of x") as necessary but not sufficient logical conditions of identification. We can understand analysis 5 ("empathy") as a causal motivating condition, analysis 6 ("compassion") as a causal consequence of identification, and analysis 4 ("imagination") as a background context-setting condition. We can understand analysis 3 ("confirming identification") as careless, just plain wrong, and in need of some reformulation. The point is, none of these kinds of conditions is fully definitional. What more do we need to be talking about?

What is conspicuously absent from our discussion is the role that *ownership* of traits plays in identification. All of us carry around a myriad of images of who we are as characters, of what our traits are like. But we all know that who we say we are and who in fact we really are are sometimes two very different propositions. Among other things, we sometimes delude ourselves. And we don't discover this until some difficult life situation calls for commitment on our part toward a trait that we have all along been claiming was part of us, only to discover now that we have no intention at all of standing up for who we have been saying we are vis-à-vis the trait. We have been more talk than anything else. What we are seeing here is that a person doesn't always own the character he says is him. This comes down to saying that he doesn't always identify with who he says he is. Genuine identification is most essentially about ownership. Put another way, when a person identifies with certain traits, they become part of *his own* character. As the philosopher Bernard Williams has stated the point,

> To be an expression of character is perhaps the most substantial way in which an action can be one's own.[7]

From my point of view, one could want, value, be able to reproduce behaviorally, and know a lot about a trait and still not necessarily have it as part of his character. The trait could still be outside of his self, as it were. Indeed, even a modeled trait of one's own causal identity is outside of one's self qua character. It looks good to the individual, but it still doesn't belong to him. The special trick of identification is to be able to take what has been only outside of oneself and somehow get it so inside the personality repertoire that it actually becomes part of one's self. Somehow, one internalizes the object traits and takes them inside himself to where he becomes a *psychological owner* of them.[8]

Alas, though, there are a number of components to psychological ownership. And each one is quite complex, far too complex for us to analyze within the confines of this chapter. So instead, I am going to spread the analysis over the remaining chapters and argue as follows: I will press the now familiar idea that identifiers take ownership not only of externally modeled traits but also of the internally modeled traits of their causal identity. I will try to make sense of the existential notion that as identifiers we *choose* ourselves into character existence. We make special kinds of choices about traits that we heretofore have just seen in models. And it's in this special kind of choosing that we actually constitute our character, that is, that we actually take on the traits as our own. We will also see that there is a *valuational* component to the identifier's choices—I'll argue that one furthers one's ownership of traits when one chooses to treat those traits as having "ultimate value." We will also see that, as owners of our character traits, we necessarily *take responsibility* for the character choices we have made. We are willing to stand up for who we have become. I will then finish the discussion by detailing the two general arenas of ownership that people partake of in character development—*personal identification and social identification*.

That's the capsule summary of where we are going. Now let's go there.

CHAPTER 6

Character Choosing

When a person identifies with a trait, he makes it his own. I am going to argue in this chapter that a character is someone who takes psychological ownership of various traits in the world in the sense that he makes *reflective choices* about them. Some of the reflective choosing has to do with traits that are already part of a person's causal identity, some has to do with traits out there in the modeling world beyond his causal identity. The first kind of reflective choosing becomes the individual's creative response to causality, the second becomes his consideration of what the outside world has to offer of quality for filling his character. We will discuss the kind of reflective choice that goes on in both of these arenas. Then we will proceed to discuss some other crucial aspects of identificatory reflective choosing. These will include the role that reflective choosing plays in creating character structure, the role it plays in the self constitution of character, and the role it plays in defining the autonomous nature of identification.

I

In this section, I would like to look at the kind of reflective choosing that is a person's creative response to causality. To begin, though, we need first to say some things about the life of choosing, with a special concern for showing how reflective choosing matches up against other kinds of nonreflective choosing.

Once in full swing, we humans are choosers, spending much of our time making choice after choice after choice. Most of these choices flow from our own agency or are caused. Even where there is some break from either kind of choice-making action, we seem constantly to be either playing out the implications of choices, fine-tuning their detail, reaping their rewards, suffering their downsides, or covering over some undesirable unanticipated tracks of their outcomes. Indeed, the narrative of a person's life could be viewed as a complex network of responses he makes to his procession of choice-making acts. This description, however, is a reality we only begin to develop as children and then more completely as adults. We need to understand that, by contrast, from the earliest of times during infancy and childhood, we do many things automatically, without thinking and without choosing. As we saw in our brief chapter 5 description of the causal self, we are ordinary animals that often act from instincts to satisfy our cravings for things like hunger, beauty, sex, and so on. We have instincts and other "hardwired" mechanisms for pursuing these cravings. We have releasing mechanisms, built-in traits of temperament, and so on to trigger our responses to our environment. And we do all of this without much need for thought.

Very little choosing is going on. And of what there is, very little is reflective. Indeed, there are contexts of early life where such a thing would be wholly inappropriate. If we had to reflectively think out choices before *every* action, we would not survive as a species. Instead, we depend on an instinctive egoism (a part of our causal identity) to save us. No choosing here. Then, too, even when we do make choices during infancy and early childhood, most of them are causal rather than reflective. Usually, they are causally conditioned by causal identity features that are already in place. For example, perhaps the temperamentally shy child can't help but choose to steer clear of joining social groups. He simply chooses without any reflective consideration of his response. Or how about the pleasure-seeking infant? If he has to choose between the pleasure of mother's breast and continuing a reverie, he surely doesn't reflectively weigh matters. He chooses as the causal forces dictate. Theory has it that he just decides as a matter of narcissistic causality. The point is, when infants and children do choose, much of that choosing is of the causal variety.

As we get older, our choosing gets more and more reflective, less and less causal. But that doesn't mean that these two kinds of choosing exhaust all of our volitional possibilities as we grow. There is also a kind of "fiat choosing" that is neither reflective nor causal that we carry from childhood into adulthood and give a fair amount of play to in both places. As children, we all too often seem to choose a course of action by fiat, either lacking the time to think things through or else simply refusing to do so. No reflection and no causality. This spontaneous choosing is, in fact, one of the defining features of being childlike. And adults, too, certainly sometimes behave the same way—childlike. We can choose or act impulsively, without any thought. But at least we try to hold such behavior down to a minimum. Spontaneity is nice and sometimes even exciting, but only within limits.

The fiat variety aside, though, our choosing does get more reflective as we grow. But that is not to say that reflective choosing thoroughly overwhelms our causal choosing. The social sciences have made us all too painfully aware that it doesn't. The truth about us right through adulthood is that a lot of our choosing activity remains heavily laced with causal influences. Not only do we find hardwired causal factors such as temperament continuing to exert a heavy hand on our choices, but there are also the psychological, cultural, and societal conditioning forces that now work on us, creating behavioral and cognitive habit choices that become quite grooved parts of our identity. For example, as children, it is difficult even to imagine, let alone actively fight, the power of parental approval over what we choose to be like when we make choices about how to be a person in various situations. This psychological causal power holds sway even into adulthood for many of us. Then, too, we know how social pressures condition who we are as children and adults. Pressures to conform to certain socially approved role expectations make many of us what we are. Our choices follow the script of our roles to the letter. Social forces have defined our identity for us in terms of the expectations of the roles in which we are cast. The choices we make in life had better be consistent with those expectations if we want to conform to our socially defined identity. Theater, film, and television tell us how we are to see ourselves as social beings. This means, for example, that we had better choose a life of the consummate consuming materialist if we want to fulfill the conditioning dictates of commercial America, dictates that rule the airwaves. We had better choose politically correct positions if we want to be acceptable citizens as defined by TV news shows. And so on. Unless we make the "right" choices as determined by psychological and social contextual forces, we will not be socially acceptable. This is the plight of socially defined causal persons as choosers.

Of course, although a lot of this nonreflective choosing we do stays with us throughout adulthood, it eventually is joined on center stage by reflective choosing. We reflect and choose about many things. Shall I have chocolate chip ice cream now or not? Shall I do research next year in Thailand or not? Shall I mention more examples of nonreflective choosing now or not? Think, evaluate, and choose; think, evaluate, and choose. This is a favorite adult pastime, a favorite rational cycle—reflective choosing. But these particular examples are not really at the heart of the kind of reflective choosing we need to understand in this chapter. We are interested in the reflective choosing that people do about *character* identity *traits* and the daily reflective choosing that flows from the parts of their character that is already in place. Social forces and the other causal factors provide us with a menu of the internal traits we may come to identify with. And what this means is that we may make reflective choices about these traits in such a way that some of them ultimately become new components of our identity. But they become parts *not* of our causal identity but of our character. These choices are *not* seen as causal consequences of antecedent events. They are often related in interesting ways to antecedent causal events that are read off the social menu, but they are not caused into existence by them. Rather, these reflective character trait choices are the essence of one's *own* choices.

Another way to make the point is to recognize that the identity of psychological beings at some juncture starts to develop beyond just the merely mechanical. While causal identity continues to play an important role in how we experience the world and how we present ourselves in it, as we develop, its centrality to who we are shifts more and more toward the character identity that we create. This character identity is something forged in part through the thematic reflective choices we make about what life sends our way, when viewing what is sent our way through the lens of the causal identity elements that are already in place. We make reflective choices, that is, about how we will allow ourselves to *respond* to our causally configured life. The more of a role that reflective choosing assumes in how we finally respond to life situations, the more we are acting from what we come to understand as character. Our volitional two cents is really worth a lot more than just two cents here.

Think of matters this way. Part of the causal identity that has been forged since a person's earliest days can be understood in terms of clusters of deeply entrenched personality dispositions that are related to one another in lawlike ways—biologically (i.e., temperamentally), behaviorally, and psychodynamically. Certainly our primitive narcissistic identity values, wants, hopes, beliefs, emotions, and the like can be understood in this way. But as we grow, reflective choice starts making itself felt. We start confronting ourselves, confronting some of the causal states that have become so much a part of who we are. Sometimes we reflectively choose to accept parts of who we have causally become. We have given our stamp of approval, as it were, on who we have been all along. We act in the same ways; only now it's the strength of our character agency that is generating this behavior. We are quite happy with what we have seen in ourselves and simply choose to affirm it as it is. The only difference is that now we have taken volitional ownership of what has all along been causally true of us. Of course, sometimes we look at who we have been and decide to shake things up a bit. That could mean that we decide to embellish how we have been all along. We could add new wrinkles to how we have been, variations on a theme we basically still accept about ourselves. A more extreme response would have us choose to contravene our causal behavior and strike out in a new agency direction, perhaps even toward building new disposition states that we would be able to respond to the world with as "new character" in the future. After all, we don't always like what we see when we start to see who we are causally. Sometimes we value other traits we see modeled outside of us instead. So we try to modify our identity. We choose to intervene in the flow of our causal identity and behave in traited ways other than what to that point have been causally automatic for us. If we disvalue the old traits enough and their causal bonds are not too overpowering, we will stay on top of matters over the long haul. So whenever the causal identity trait in question is triggered in the future, we will choose and rechoose and rechoose again the more valued way of behaving on which we have decided. The more we reflectively choose for the valued modification and its enhancements, the more we take the modification to be part of our growing character.[1]

Why do we do all this? Quite simply, these reflective choices that we make about our causal identity are, in a sense, occasions for our being born as characters—our own birth experience. Before any of this, we literally didn't exist as character agents. Our life experience then was totally different than it is now for us as characters. The point is, most of us come by our sense of being alive as character agents through our active, reflective choices about *going beyond* the causality that would otherwise drive who we are. Unchecked, causality is overwhelmingly acquisitive and it jealously guards what we do. It wants to control all of who we are and deny us our agency. It is in the nature of causality to spread itself far and wide, until it is checked. Reflective choosing is the attempt in the human sphere to check it, to stop its progression in our lives. So to carve out a feeling that we own ourselves as character agencies—to come by a sense of finally having been born as creatures who author our own destiny— we fight the good fight to get beyond causality. In reflectively choosing to maintain a caused identity state or in choosing to modify or override one, we are effectively getting that job done. We are being an active authoring character agency rather than a passive series of causal events.

So, the point has been driven home: Making reflective character choices is a requirement for getting us beyond the passivity of our causal life. Having said this, however, I must also acknowledge a paradox that seems to revolve around this contrast between character and causal identity. Allow me a moment to set the backdrop for the paradox before stating what it is. I have said that character is formed in the reflective choosing we do. But surely not just any volitional response to our recognition of a causal identity trait will count as evidence of character commitment. I may reflectively choose once in a certain way, for example, and never do it again because I don't like its consequences. *Simply* choosing reflectively about a causal trait, then, is not enough to say that one is doing something to form character. A given choice must be made again and again, on recurring occasions when the causal trait would normally be triggered. In order to legitimately make character claims about a person and his choices, there must be evidence of something like a cumulative effect of his making thematic choices again and again. When a person begins to regularly choose for the same reflection—whether, by the way, such choices have been made consciously, unconsciously, or preconsciously—we can legitimately say that that choice is becoming part of his character.

Here is where the paradox takes shape. The fact of the matter is, after any of a person's thematic choices have become repeating regular choices—after they have become repeating regular volitional responses to given sorts of situations—they are correctly recognized to be automatic, causally based responses in their own right. Indeed, we don't just recognize things this way, they actually happen this way. Our character responses to situations eventually become causally grooved in much the same way that causal identity traits are. Character trait responses eventually form their own causal networks. They become what we might call "volitional habits." After a while, we don't have to go through all the deliberations we went through earlier as prelude to the decisions we made about how to be in the general kind of situation. What started out as autonomous reflective choices really do end up becoming causally determined choices. The individual will now automatically respond to what has become part of his character identity. And this is a paradox. If this regularity of the same choice turns into a new causal structure of the personality, we are fully prepared to call this causal structure (this new "automatic" response) a part of his character. The more that a person's decision about how to be takes the form of volitional habit, the more it is a part of his character. We simply do not normally expect a person deliberatively to make himself over as a character on each occasion of an old causal identity trait—we don't expect him reflectively to redecide each time. Volitional habit will get the character job done far more efficiently.

What are we to say about this paradox? Mainly, that there are two things which, in fact, make the situation seem not so paradoxical after all. One grows out of our expectation that the person acting from character would *take responsibility* for his automatic character choices; the other grows out of our expectation that he would have *reflective reasons* for acting as he is, reasons that were initially reflectively instrumental in his making the decisions he made about his causal identity traits. Looking at the latter factor first, we would expect that, if asked, he could, to some degree of success (depending on variables of memory, linguistic facility, emotional clarity in the given situation, and so on), call forth some of these reasons. So, for example, we would expect that he could point out that he chose in favor of a particular initially causal identity trait because it fit well with other very important life projects that either were part of his character self already that for other reasons he was unwilling to change or were part of his causal identity self already that for other reasons he was unwilling to give up. The point is, we would expect that the individual could marshall *something or other* about his initial deliberations in defense of his being the way he is. Even something as weak seeming as "I just like being (i.e., I just like making decisions like) this kind of person" would count as a reason that indicates character is in play and not just automatic causality. Generally speaking, in this kind of case, we assume that the individual's reflective reasons were the essential ingredients in his making the choices he initially made. And now it is in having these reasons at his disposal (to some degree) that really makes us say the individual here is acting as a character. Even though he has taken on new causal mechanisms as part of his identity, the fact that these mechanisms are connected to reflectively derived reasons for their very being is enough for us to call the individual a character. The fact that people are able to turn what starts out as difficult reflective choosing into new causal behavior is not what is crucial to character formation. That is just a convenience. Instead, it is the having of reasons that went into the original choosing that's important. Of course, if people weren't psychologically equipped to turn recurring choices into automatic causal behavior but instead were stuck with having to go through the same reflective reason-giving processes each time they faced a questionable preexisting causal trait, then that is how we would understand the person of character to be. Such a person would have to remake himself every time he confronted the preexisting caused identity trait. And as I noted above, from our perspective now, that would seem like a lot of work, a real nuisance, and a process of questionable survival value. It is our good fortune that this isn't how people really are.

Having made the possession of reasons so important to the notion of reflectiveness, I do feel a need to qualify what I am saying. First of all, when a person involves himself in *full* reflective choice, he is normally calling forth reasons, pro and con, for his acting as the character he is. "On the one hand, I could do this or this or this; thus and such and such might be the consequences. On the other hand, I could do this other thing or that other thing or that other other thing; and these other thuses and suches might be the consequences. Whatever shall I decide?" When a person chooses for or against a trait he sees as part of his causal identity, he sometimes makes such full reflective choices. These are the clearest cases of character building. However, in fact, these are quite the rare events. When most of us think back over our lives, we just don't recall all that many moments when we so fully chose our character traits. Reflective character choosing is seldom the pure dramatic and fully conscious event. Very few reflective character choices are experienced by us as reasoned, drawn-out affairs of great importance. And so it's not all that often that a person actually remembers a defining moment when he weighed the pros and cons that then led to a considerable decision about the kind of person he would become around a given trait. Nevertheless, we all have made reflective character choices, great numbers of them. Even though many of these choices might not stand out in consciousness— that is, even though they were not *fully* reflective—we know them as occasions of a person's acting *on purpose*. That's enough to constitute "reflectiveness." Bells needn't ring and fireworks needn't explode. "To act on purpose" sometimes means that a person does caused behavior that he *knows* he is doing while he is doing it. Moreover, he wants the caused behavior to happen and he knows that he wants this. In the case of an individual reflectively choosing for the way he has been all along, he is allowing the causal pattern he knows about to go unchanged. A person acts on purpose vis-à-vis some of his identity traits precisely when he knows that he is doing what he is doing and that these states that he is acting out of are wanted, second-nature, caused parts of his psychological personality network.[2] Knowing what he wants and what he is doing, he chooses not to force the issue; he chooses not to break the flow of his particular network of psychological causation, although he could, all things being equal (e.g., no brain lesions, no severe neuroses blocking his volitional capacity, etc.), break the flow if he chose to. All of this constitutes reflective, albeit not noticeably monumental (not *full*), choosing.

There's a second qualification I need to make about reasons. Sometimes it happens that what starts out as clearly recognizable reflective character choosing goes beyond merely becoming a causally grooved, volitional character habit. The volitional character habit is actually transformed into rote habit and takes its place among the elements of one's *causal* identify self. In this particular kind of situation, we have to acknowledge that character identity has died and has turned into causal identity. This sort of thing occurs when a person no longer has any reasons for why he decides for the trait for which he habitually decides. He has actually lost any knowledge of why he had been choosing for the trait all along. And that's because the reasons he had way back when are no longer his reasons for acting as he does; they are no longer reasons for him to know about. He's acting from rote habit.

A person may fall into this condition without necessarily even realizing it. I have in mind situations where a person claims to act as a character, and when asked what his reflective reasons are for his character behavior, he responds by presenting what, according to public standards, would count as good reasons for acting as he does. However, merely being able to call forth good reasons isn't the same thing as really having those reasons as *his functioning reasons*. People often enough deceive themselves about such matters. Sometimes a person is facile at citing, after the fact, what the public deems good reasons. That is, he can figure out what the public would consider to be good reasons. However, that doesn't mean that those reasons really were his reasons before the fact—that is, it doesn't mean that those reasons were really what were *motivating* his choices. He is just clever at uncovering what the public would want a person to have as good reasons for given choices before the fact. A person can be a superb *rationalizer* about his actions without those actions really having been a matter of genuine volitional quality. A person's being skillfully able to show that something looks like a good reason for making a certain choice isn't the same as establishing that that reason really was what was working for him at the time. The choice still might have been fully habitualized, even though the rationalizer can, as it were, make it look good, even to himself.

I want to offer yet a third qualification about reasons and reflective choosing. We shouldn't lose sight of the fact that even as a character eventually loses the need to make himself over as the same kind of person on each new appropriate occasion, we expect that he *could* do so if he were asked. He could trot out some semblance of the reasons for why he decided to be the way he is, even though he isn't normally thinking about them on each occasion of his automatic rechosen activity and even though they didn't necessarily have any dramatic moment for him when they first started becoming functional. Moreover, we expect that in being the character he has become, the individual is open to formulating some *new reasons* for slightly altering his basic character themes. So, along with his now automatic character tendencies, the individual is also making new choices about how to tailor the automatic recurring character trait to the unique features of each new situation that triggers the trait. There will always be something slightly different about each new situation. So he's got new reasons to alter slightly his general character pattern to fit the situation. For example, when a person responds to situations that his temperament has preexistingly grooved in one way and he subsequently has volitionally grooved in another, he will, as a volitional character, always have to vary his volitional response to meet the precise changing conditions of each new circumstance giving rise to the general chosen trait. Were a person to be a character trait rubber stamp who simply applied the same general trait stamp to every situation that called forth the trait, his life would suffer. Each of us has to take into account the subtleties and textures of life's everchanging circumstances. This requires that we fine-tune our rubber stamps to fit the precise specifications of each unique situation. So even a person who has causally grooved his general character trait choices will need to be open to the requirement of fine-tuning in each new life situation. He has to be open to accepting and enforcing new reasons for choosing.

The general point, though, is that, in one form or another, a person has reasons for his reflective character choices. And we have seen that it is in having reasons that the paradox of a person's developing into a causally grooved character disappears. But let's remember now that this isn't the only reason for the paradox disappearing. I've also said that something about "taking responsibility" is a factor here, too. I'll be brief about my thinking here, for I'll be returning to the issue in detail in chapter 8. The point is that we know that a person's automatic identity choices are acceptably part of his character self when we see that he is willing to take responsibility for both making those choices and accepting their outcomes. In contrast, when choices a person makes and the outcomes that those choices lead to are solely the product of external causes or external agencies, we neither hold that person responsible for those choices and their outcomes nor do we expect him to take responsibility for them. So when we see a person taking responsibility for a choice that seems automatic and causally grooved, then, assuming that he isn't making some kind of conceptual mistake—that is, that he is not confused about what in general he should and shouldn't take responsibility for—we can conclude that he owns this choice. We can conclude that the choice is part of his character. Even though his choosing here has become automatic, it is something that he has created. He's taking responsibility *for himself.*

One implication of what I am saying is that when a person refuses to take responsibility for himself around the issue of some causally grooved traits he has been exhibiting, he's as much as telling us that those traits aren't the result of any reflective choices he has made. When a person does take responsibility, though, this is a sure sign that there is character at work even though the automatic grooved behavior of causality is all that appears on the surface.

II

What we have done thus far has been to look at reflective character choosing as it applies to a person's creative response to causality. I'd like to shift our attention now to the other main character arena. Not only does the identifier come to own traits that have been part of his causal identity, he also comes to own traits that have been modeled by objects distinct from him. It is time to say something about the role that reflective choosing plays in this "external world" context.

First of all, who and what do we choose as externally modeled traits with which we would identify? One relevant factor in deciding is proximity.[3] It's no accident that people tend to identify with the ideas, institutions, physical objects, and other things to which they have been most exposed. Take, for example, the case of identification with family members. Those people happen to be the most available when we identifiers are looking for models on which to base parts of a character. Because of the various object relating roles that parents especially have played in our early want and need gratification, they normally become the people we value quite highly. Certainly this is clear in our infancy narcissism. And our favoring of them continues beyond this because they continue to keep their agency on loan to help meet our needs. It's no wonder, then, that when we finally reach that point in psychological development where we start forming our own agency, we tend to favor the idea of taking on their traits. They are our first models. We choose many of these traits to be our own—to help define our internal agency—simply because they belong to these antecedently valued people (models). Our focus, of course, is on those modeled traits of theirs that we think might be of particular benefit in helping us attain our desires, goals, and other causally installed motivational states. But it is just our parents' proximity to us that accounts for what modeled traits we happen to choose. We decide parts of who we would be by seriously considering the modeled traits we just happen to have in front of us. On a certain level, who we become here is quite a haphazard affair. I mean this in the sense that had we had parents with a very different character than our actual parents in fact have, we would have turned out to be very different characters ourselves, because we would have been picking traits for our agency selves from a very different kind of source.

Proximity is important for determining which objects will become models for an identifier to reflectively make choices about, but it is not an absolute requirement. People can go beyond "the proximal" in choosing modeled traits. People have been known to discover and eventually identify with new ideas with which they have had no proximity. "Alien" ideas, institutions, objects, and so forth can present new identificatory opportunities. Certainly, for example, people do eventually go beyond family members for their models. They discover that other people share some of the same kinds of desires, goals, and so on that they (the identifiers) have. And some of these other people have character traits that are more effective in attaining these desires, goals, and so on than any of the family members' character traits. So the identifier chooses them as models for the traits in question. When a youngster is concerned with athletic excellence for who he is, for example, he is more likely to choose a sports star as his model than one of his parents. Of course, here, too, which sports stars one happens to have a knowledge of will certainly be a major determining factor in the kind of character traits the identifier will have a chance to develop. Had he known of different sports stars that met his same needs, he might have turned out quite differently.

Another important factor in determining what will become models for the identifier revolves around the question of what things have traits for meeting the same kinds of momentary desires, life projects and goals, and so forth that the identifier typically experiences. That is, as identifiers, we reflectively choose traits to own that we see doing an effective job of meeting the same kinds of desires that we have. So the models we choose are effective possessors of those traits. That is, we choose something as a model of a trait in the first place because of the way we see that the model has effectively used the trait in attaining the appropriate desires. We reflectively choose to identify with a particular model because we have become convinced by the model's success with the trait as part of its agency. We pay special attention to the detailed way the model uses the trait in question in its agency. And we choose to be the same detailed traited way. Obviously, merely reflectively choosing to be this way doesn't automatically make us so. But it's a start.

What else can we say about reflective choosing in the "external world" context? We should understand that the encountered model is not just a casual manifestation of the trait we are interested in; it is the model of it in the chapter 5 sense of it being the *paradigm* of how the trait is best to fit into a life. So, an impressionable teenager may see "sophistication" in many movie stars. But it is only his favorite star who seems perfectly—paradigmatically—to model the trait. So he zeroes in on his favorite star's version of "sophistication." The other sophisticated celebrities pale in comparison. In general, the same thing happens regarding all identifications with things beyond us. We choose to see the object as a paradigm for some trait that we highly value.

With the modeling object in focus, we try copying bits and pieces of its traits that interest us. We do this in ways that parallel some of our identifications with causal identity traits. Sometimes we choose to follow the model as it is—we choose to act out the trait just as we see it in the model. Here we are fully affirming the modeled trait, and we want to make it our own just as it appears in the paradigm. More often, though, we try to modify what we see in the model—we choose our own unique variation on the paradigm's theme. We want the same *kind* of trait, but with our own unique version of it. Clearly the model is still all-important to us, for it is the holder and teacher of the thematic trait we so value. But we don't merely want to learn our lessons about the trait for the sake of being accurate copiers. We want to put our own unique imprint on it as a means of making it part of our character. Accordingly, the identifier here becomes invested in a dual role. He is both trying to be like the model and yet working matters out in his own unique ways. He may try out many different variations on the modeled theme before he is satisfied and finally settles on how he will choose to express the trait in his life as the appropriate situations recur. Suppose, for example, a child identifies with his father's social aggressiveness. Father is his model, but he has to figure out how he will choose to express the same trait, given his own unique experiences in the social world. Suppose he writes short story after short story expressing his aggressive feelings toward people. Each time, he works out his feelings in a slightly different way. It is never quite what father is like, for the boy doesn't feel quite what he believes father feels like. The boy will write stories until he gets it right according to his image of the valued trait.

I should point out, too, that a lot of what we saw in the first section about reflectively chosen traits moving in degrees toward becoming automatic deeply grooved choices applies just as much to reflectively chosen external traits. We don't have to call up all the reasons we may have for choosing a particular kind of trait every time we want to act through it. We expect that the choosing of the particular kind of trait will more and more become a volitional habit. If a person chooses to act out of a certain trait on recurring occasions of a particular kind of circumstance, and the results of his actions get him things that he wants, then his choosing will become progressively more habitualized. After seeing the benefits that acting from an externally valued trait brings him, he eventually will no longer have to think much before choosing for the trait. Again, the survival value of such an efficient volitional shortcut is obvious.

In concluding our discussion in this section, I want to acknowledge a very different notion of "reflectively choosing traits from the external world" than we have been talking about. Not all traits that an identifier has an interest in owning as part of his character are found by seeing if some model meets preexisting gratification needs. Sometimes a person simply wants to author a new part of his growing character self, not because he values the trait for what needs it helps him meet, but, rather, because he has decided to make it valuable in and of itself. He may want to try on the trait, as it were, and see what it makes of who he is—all in the name of pure authorship. Typically, in this sort of situation, the identifier doesn't even look for a model to emulate. Pure authorship requires more than surmising what some model would usually allow. It involves creatively positing a trait as something one considers inherently valuable enough to make part of his character. This is risky business, for one has no model to use as a gauge of success with the trait. In any case, from time to time, people do engage in this kind of character trait choosing.

III

We have now completed our discussion of the reflective choosing that people do as identifiers with both causal traits and traits from the external world. It is time that we move on to other aspects of reflective character choosing. To introduce what I have in mind, I'd like to recall briefly an idea we first broached back in chapter 3. There we made the point that the most obvious difference between the budding internal agency that unfolds during infancy/childhood narcissism and the mature adult character agency is that the latter involves complex psychological structure while the former doesn't. We contrasted the self representational activity that goes on during infancy/childhood with that which goes on in the adult experience. During infancy/childhood, that representational activity is only about organizational tendencies set around narcissistic themes. The tendencies are fleeting, however. They occur as intermittent strands of self representations. Most of what goes on here is accounted for by causality. There's very little reflective self choosing in the air, although there is some. By contrast, in adulthood, one's self representational activity has solid organizational *structure* set around a complex network of character trait themes that are enforced by one's internal agency. One is a full-fledged chooser now. And through the reflective choosing that goes on here, the adult character agency actually creates this structure. He creates a consolidation of interlocking character dispositions that constitute relatively permanent character trait fixtures of his personality repertoire. One wants to say that the reflective choosing that goes on here is the key difference that is responsible for the development of character structure. I want to pursue this idea more in this section.

Before we say anything about the choosing aspect of these matters, let's say just a few words about the notion of "character *structure*." People often treat their character as though it is something about themselves which, once in place, can't be tampered with. They see it as something which, once chosen and committed to, is locked in place as a set of solid unchangeable personality structures. Indeed, they are equating the idea of structure with unchangeability. So they say things such as "I can't help doing that; it's who I am." This isn't a claim most people would object to. How are we really to take it, though? There clearly is one sense to this idea of "one can't change structures" that is totally acceptable. There is a commonly accepted presumption that, other things being equal, a person has something of a *right* not to be *required* to try to change parts of his character once he has set them in place in his personality. "I can't help doing that..." here means that the individual has made his particular choices and since this project is about *his* image of how he wants *his* life to be, anyone else insisting otherwise is not allowing the project of character building to proceed. (Indeed, if the individual followed someone else's instructions about the kind of character he should be, he wouldn't be building his character but, rather, the other person's image of character.) In short, then, in this sense, "I can't help doing that; it's who I am" means "I have a right to be left alone here (other things being equal)." More to the point, "I can't help..." means "Leave me alone. I have rights, so I *shouldn't have to change.*"

But while there is this value sense to "I can't help doing that...," when we consider this expression in the more literal vein of "what's *possible* for a character to do," we have to recognize the claim's limitations. Having character structures doesn't mean that one's character is *unalterably unchangeable*. It *tends* not to change. But that's not a claim about what is possible in the character arena. There's always some give to who we are. No matter what a person's character is, he *can* help acting through it. He can help what he does. Reflectively choosing for character traits entails the possibility of reflectively choosing against them. That's the nature of reflective choice. If a person couldn't choose against having a given trait, then it wouldn't be reflective volitional character we were talking about but rather insurmountable causal forces acting on him. In fact, it *is difficult* for a person to help what he does as a character to the degree that his choices become less consciously reflective and more (preconsciously) habitualized. But "difficult" is a far cry from "I can't help myself," that is, from "it is impossible for me to help myself." A person *can* help it, but he simply sometimes does not because he doesn't want to. Why change things when one likes the way he has chosen to be?

So although character choosing does result in the formation of relatively stable character structures, those structures are not wholly unalterable. The point is, character choosing doesn't lead to unchangeable ontological features of one's being. But obviously it does lead to something basic, something relatively solid, something with strong tendencies. That understood, although I will talk about the content nature of such structural tendencies in chapter 7, what I want to do now is talk about the general nature of the reflective character choosing that leads to character structure. Just why is it that these sorts of choices effectively lead to character structure while other sorts of choices people make aren't nearly as effective in attaining their ends?

I'll begin by noting that there is no clearly definable point where a particular choice a person keeps making moves from being an ordinary contingent fact about him to becoming a psychological structure of his character. Reflective character choices are relatively effective in creating character, but there is no set quantity of choosing that all people have to do to bring this about. We don't have to choose for a trait seven times, for example, before what we choose takes on structural character status. I am certain that in some cases, one episode of choice is enough; in others, structural character gets formed only after many bouts of reflectively fine-tuning choices. By the same token, it is true that the more we choose for a trait, the more structurally entrenched it becomes as part of our character. And we can recognize where contingent choosing has finally turned into *a clear case* of structural character choosing. We just have a difficult time saying what happened in between. At one point, there was a person making ordinary contingent choices about traits he wanted as his own but didn't yet have. At another, that same person was making the same choices that were now character choices with structural tendency status.

So what accounts for the effectiveness of reflective character choosing? Here is where I will take my Nietzschean stand about the self-constitution of the self. Consider the following. If I were a college student who wanted to belong to a fraternity, I could choose to become a candidate for membership. If I then was to fulfill the requirements of membership, I could become part of the fraternity. The structure of the fraternity would be enlarged by one. But my choosing would have been independent of my actually becoming part of the fraternity's structure. The two are causally connected but logically independent phenomena—"choosing x" and "being x" are not the same here. In the case of character formation, however, things are different. My Nietzschean-styled thesis is that *reflectively choosing* to take on *character* traits in an identificatory manner is actually part of *being* a *character* with those traits. It is my view that character structure is created precisely in the consistent reflective choosing for one trait rather than some other in the recurring instances of a circumstance. Character structure in part *is* this consistent reflective choosing, not something lying behind, causing it. In the identificatory choosing of one trait rather than some other, a person is *constituting* a self out of that chosen trait.

I don't intend to pursue this Nietzschean perspective with elaborate argumentation. On the other hand, I'm not submitting it as an unargued assumption either. Rather, I see it as an empirical hypothesis. In fact, not only can we observe that in the consistent choosing of a trait of character, a person gets closer to being that character, but we can also observe that it is precisely that consistent choosing that *counts* as one's character behavior. Moreover, one can observe that in making character trait choices, the self is *reflexively* creating the self. Let me say some things about this idea as a way of putting more meat on the bones of my Nietzschean thesis.

For clarification purposes, let's distinguish "reflexive creation of the self" from a *non*reflexive kind of creating that is also related to the self. Specifically, as infants, our mental activities—our minds—create the pre-self and the rudimentary narcissistic object relating self. There is no reflexive choosing of a self going on here. The self is not making choices that constitutively create the self. Rather, during infancy, self related matters unfold as causal processes of introjects and projects. The mind causally creates psychological objects to relate the mind/body to. The mind introjects and projects in different combinations and permutations. What come out of these causal processes are pre- and rudimentary selves whose introjected and projected psychological objects are external to—that is, different from—the mind/body. Here the mind's self is a mosaic of psychological objects ultimately powered by causality. By contrast, when the mind creates the character self, it chooses traits that do not end up as psychological objects powered by causal processes. What gets chosen ends up as self (qua internal character agency) structures. Better, the mental activity of choosing character traits ends up as the very essence of the character one is choosing the traits for. That is, this kind of choosing is what it is to be a character. Moreover, it is one's character that is doing this choosing in the first place. That is, character is constituted by character's reflexively choosing itself. It reflexively chooses itself into existence.

How are we to understand this? Talking about the idea of ownership can be of some help. What I am claiming, in effect, is that in reflectively choosing character traits, the self is reflexively taking ownership of itself. We can contrast this kind of choosing with the ordinary choosing of physical objects we do every day. When I choose an object out in the world, that doesn't automatically make it mine. I can choose to wear the diamond ring I see in the store window. But merely choosing it doesn't make it mine. Many cases of choosing are like this one in that we are simply intending to try out something. We are trying to better imagine how it might feel to own the object. More than that, we are really just reflecting on what we *want* for ourselves, on what traits we want to own. In the case of character, however, things are different. At first, the choosing may amount to this same kind of "trying out" of a trait. A person might have some idea about the kind of person he would like to become down the line. But this is really just a statement about a person's character trait ownership *desires*. To actually *choose to be* a certain trait goes beyond mere desiring. When a person *chooses being*, that is precisely what it *is* for something *to be owned* as part of his being. It's what it is to *be* that trait of his character. So identificatory being qua the choosing of a trait becomes the person's *being* that trait. And this is a reflexive activity of the mind. It chooses traits from a model it values to become the self; and in the choosing of those traits, it has chosen itself that much more into existence.

Now, that's my general view about the constituting of character through reflexive choosing. While I feel quite satisfied with what I have said, however, I suspect that some people may not share my feelings. For on the face of things, there does seem to be a terrible logical problem that leaps out at us, an unavoidably uncomfortable intellectual hot point. To say that we choose ourselves into existence is one thing, to make clear sense of it is another. One wants to scream about the seeming absurdity of a thing's choosing itself into existence. "If it is first coming into existence now," we fret, "how can we sensibly say that there's a selfsame 'it' there *before* that point, ready to create itself?" That's certainly a reasonable question.

Clearly, something needs to be said. While I will be offering the discussion in chapters 7 and 8 as the fuller picture of what the self constitution of character through reflexive choosing looks like—a fuller picture of what the 'it' looks like—I would like to say something here about this challenge to the very logical possibility of there being a self that could choose itself into existence. One hypothesis for answering the challenge might be the suggestion that a preexisting homunculus self somehow chooses the character self. However, that kind of logic does us no good. For the existence of a choosing homunculus would certainly need accounting for, too—who chose *it* into existence? Right away, we recede into an infinite procession of underlying homunculi. And that reduces the hypothesis to nonsense. So we need some other account that will get at the above question more sensibly. What I have in mind is admittedly a speculative hypothesis, but one I believe is plausible. We will end our discussion in this section by taking a look at it.

In its earliest stages, genuine character formation processes simply start to unfold consistent with principles of evolution. For adaptive survival reasons, the human psyche starts to make character-creating choices. There is something of an evolutionary built-in existential directive to create some kind of character self or other. *That* a person starts making these existential choices—that there is this built-in directive—is an evolutionary causal affair. But once the mechanisms of this fact are in place, many of the individual choices a person then makes are of his own reflective doing. What has been a wholly causal object relating mind aimed at special external agencies up to this point now starts to make some choices about how to be as an internal agency. It starts to identify with character-making traits of the world. Specifically, it makes some choices about traits and it gives structural agency self status to them.

Once this early character with structural self status has been created, what there is of character at that point takes over the rest of the job of character making. It does not literally create itself. What it does is grow *newer* character. It creates new parts to add onto what started off as a mere evolutionary happening. I am imagining something that parallels what happens in cellular mitosis, where one-celled organisms divide and, in so doing, multiply themselves into complex creatures. I am imagining that identification works in a similar way. I am imagining that identification just *is* the special psychological process out of which the one-celled psyche, as it were, creates character agency for the mind and body. It is as though a single "self cell" has been created by causal forces. This cell has a particular property unlike anything belonging to earlier versions of the self. Namely, it can make reflexive reflective choices about many matters. One crucial matter is about what character traits to consider and give structural status to. Now, that is surely a very special kind of choosing. The character self can choose itself into existence, but only in the sense that it can choose, and thus create, structural status to *new* character elements. The original volitional cell has the ability to create new character cells, to choose new modeled traits. It is in this sense that we are to think of character creating itself—the given mass of cells can choose further traits. At any point in time, we have a cluster of self cells that constitute a character. We say that the person owns certain traits at this point. However, we understand that that means that earlier clusters of cells have chosen the newer members of the cluster into existence. There is no person, separate from his character, actually owning a separate character. There is only the cluster of character traits that have been chosen into place by earlier forms of that reflective and reflexively acting cluster. The character self continually chooses new parts or rechooses old ones.

IV

Since this chapter has been all about reflective character *choice making*, I think I would be remiss if I didn't say something before we finished about where autonomous choice—free will—fits into the picture. Clearly, I believe that character choices are autonomous choices. So I'd like to say something here and then later in chapters 7 and 8 about how I understand this. Naturally, I don't intend to fight the whole free will/determinism battle. I do, however, want to make a broad suggestion about how an understanding of autonomy can fit in with our concerns. Basically, I want to argue that if determinism is right in holding that there are always causes for our psychological states, it turns out that some causes are far less offensive than others. And where these less offensive ones are in force, that is where we can say we are choosing and acting autonomously. That is also where we can say moral responsibility can be comfortably enforced.

My view falls in line with the view of the philosophers Harry Frankfurt, Charles Taylor, and Gerald Dworkin.[4] As I pointed out in chapter 1, their basic thesis is that a person is able to make autonomous choices and that this amounts to his reflectively choosing to act or refrain from acting on his first-order conscious states. That is, a person experiences his will as free to the extent that he acts on reflective decisions he has made about his wants, beliefs, principles, feelings, emotions, and so on. His reflective decision about these states is referred to as a "second-order" phenomenon. The states that get reflected upon (the wants, feelings, beliefs, etc.) are called "first-order" phenomena. And in general, first-order phenomena are part of what I have referred to as a person's "causal identity." That is, these philosophers agree that all of one's first-order states are causally driven. Accordingly, making second-order reflective choices about our first-order causal self is where freedom lies.[5] This idea should sound familiar. For what all three philosophers call the arena for autonomy is precisely what I have been calling one of the arenas for identification. We identify with aspects of our causal identity (i.e., our first-order conscious states) precisely in the making of reflective choices about them. Clearly, then, what Frankfurt and the others are talking about is of some interest to us here. Identification and autonomy are intricately tied to one another. I will show exactly how in the next two chapters. However, right now, I want to focus exclusively on showing where my view of autonomy fits into the discussion of these other philosophers.

Again, their view is that it is in deciding which of our first-order states to prefer realization for that a person expresses his free choice. Contrary to what is necessary for making the point of determinism, they believe that people don't just function on the level of first-order consciousness, although surely we do that a good part of the time. The degree of commitment of a person to act as a reflective consciousness on the level of second-order consciousness is an expression of that person's autonomous nature.

Now, although I agree with these philosophers that it is in reflective consciousness where we find autonomy, I also have to say that all three fail to take seriously the obvious objection that a determined determinist would doubtlessly raise here about the origins of our second-order reflective preferences; to wit, that a person's second-order reflective states are just as causally explainable as his first-order wants and beliefs are. And so, can we really say that second-order reflectiveness makes a person free? Is there really a palatable sense of autonomy in any of what they say?

This seems too obvious a pitfall for any of these three thinkers to have missed. And in fact, I strongly suspect that they haven't. They simply don't take it as a serious objection. Why? It seems to me most likely that all three really must be what philosophers call "soft determinists"—that is, they believe that *all* conscious states (*including reflections*) are caused, but that we are free too. So they see their job as that of describing what we *mean* when we call a particular caused state "free." They simply believe that if there is (and, in fact, there is) anything we *mean* and *experience* when we talk about making free choices, we have in mind these second-order states, caused though they may be. I too have no great difficulty accepting such a *general* soft determinist move, as long as it allows the difference in experience between what a person calls his free choices and what he understands as his caused states—that is, as long as it still allows for a *distinctive sense* for what is experienced as free will. However, just as an empirical matter, I would disagree about the details of which level of consciousness a soft determinist should say free will is to be found on. Indeed, many people acknowledge a level of third-order consciousness. This level amounts to a reflective awareness about second-order preferences that can be causally traced back to either the individual's genetic temperamental endowment or to causal unconscious psychodynamic factors working on him. That is, on a level of third-order consciousness, many people are aware of their second-order reflectiveness being causally rooted. For example, a person might be aware that he regularly tends to choose reflectively (on the second level) in favor of his first-order egoistic wants whenever he faces choosing between one of his first-order egoistic states and one of his first-order altruistic states. He might be aware (on a level of third-order consciousness) that when reflectively choosing (on the level of second-order consciousness) between these first-order states, he has causally explainable tendencies to opt for his egoist wants. If this individual is introspective enough to reflect on this level of third-order consciousness about the causal nature of his second-order reflections, one would suspect that it is on this level of third-order consciousness that the individual feels his freedom.[6]

Many more people than one might at first suspect clearly live on the level of third-order consciousness at least some of the time; enough, anyway, to cement their being autonomous characters. All one has to do is think about some of the embarrassing rationalizations he has made in the past about matters he hasn't wanted to face, and the point is made. In the terms we are concerned with here, what is a rationalization and what is it to become aware of one? It's the level of third-order consciousness where a person recognizes that he sometimes rationalizes when he reflects (a second-order conscious state) on his wants (a first-order conscious state). That is, he sees that his second-order reflective state was an inaccurate interpretation about some first-order conscious want. Such rationalization is a frequently employed defensive mechanism people use to "hide" from becoming aware of the real first-order states that drive their behavior. That's what rationalization is. However, what I am saying is that a person reflects often enough to become aware of the fact that he has been rationalizing. He reflects on a level of third-order consciousness about the second-order rationalization. Because of what he recognizes on this level of reflection, a person may then refuse to go along with his rationalization. This certainly has been known to happen among more honest and strong-willed people. They reflect that some of their second-order reflective preferences for some first-order wants are really (unconscious) rationalizations for conforming to some features of their temperament—that is, they reflectively acknowledge that unconscious causes sometimes play a role in their second-order thinking. And as a result, they might choose not to go along with their rationalizing tendencies. Accordingly, my point is that to reflect on possible second-order reflective choices and to make decisions about them on this level of third-order consciousness is where a person feels he is being as straight and honest with himself as he can be about the causes working on him. This is where he is reflectively freely choosing and not reflectively rationalizing. And we can find most fully formed character selves living part of their mental existence right here.

While this level of third-order consciousness is, as a matter of contingent fact, currently in vogue as a place to reside in introspective consciousness, living beyond this point currently is not. Undoubtedly, it is possible to live on such higher levels of consciousness, but doing so would hardly be comfortable for anyone at this point in the evolution of human consciousness. So, for example, it is a contingent fact that most people today have no level of fourth-order consciousness about third-order reflections. Certainly, the science of psychology and the practice of psychotherapy do not (on a level of fourth-order consciousness) investigate any causal processes about third-order reflections; not yet, anyway. And none of us lay people are aware of such fourth-order introspectiveness in ourselves.

Ultimately, what I am arguing is that, as a matter of contingent fact, it is the level of third-order consciousness where more and more people stake their sense of being autonomous individuals. At least, this is how many of us are equipped to conceptualize volitional matters right now. Of course, if psychology begins to delve into causal factors that weigh on third-order consciousness, and if psychologists develop concepts to clarify these causes, and if these concepts find their way into the lay vocabulary—and, finally, also into the lay person's experience—then matters will change. For people will have taken on a newer version of the boundaries of the causes working on them and the boundaries of free will.

But I would argue a more general point as well. It is that our concept of free will is always about making choices at a level of consciousness just beyond where our current conceptual scheme places the causes in our mental life. Indeed, consistent with this idea is my belief that because of the popular infusion of psychoanalytic information about the unconscious into our everyday working conceptual scheme, we *experience* our second-order reflective psychological states more and more as being caused. We experience a lack of felt freedom on that level. Accordingly, I believe that claims about free will really are an empirical matter about how far a particular concept happens to have developed at a given point in time. At the current cultural moment, the reigning concept of free will has us making our free decisions in third-order consciousness—that is, the level at which we deliberate about our reflections. When, in the future, the concept becomes stretched even more regarding causes (i.e., regarding what it entails about the causes working on us), then so will the boundaries of free will move to another level of consciousness.

What does this view about where free choice lies mean for the rest of what I have been saying in this chapter about character choosing? Simply, reflective character choices are autonomous and often occur as third-order conscious states. I say "often" because all of us frequently are autonomous also on the second level. We simply needn't always reflectively doubt the straightforwardness of our second-order choices. That is, there just aren't always unconscious causes at work on the second level for us to reflect on. And so we don't have to reflect about second-order causes in those cases. Rather, we can just reflect on the second level about first-order causes. In these instances, autonomous character choices occur as second-order phenomena. And indeed, for people whose conceptual knowledge of psychological causes just has not yet developed *at all* according to what I believe has become the cultural norm (i.e., the norm of taking the unconscious into account), character choices are *entirely* second-order phenomena. So that's where they find their autonomy. But whichever of these positions we find ourselves in, it is clear that making autonomous character choices is more than viable. They happen on some reflective level of consciousness or other.

Finally, where have we come in this chapter? Remember that the strategy by the end of chapter 5 was for us to talk about what goes into an identifier's *owning* the character traits he identifies with. The first part of that discussion was to be about the importance of reflective choice. That's what we have been doing. We know now that a crucial element of taking in a trait and finally owning it involves a person reflectively choosing it as part of his character, choosing it off of a menu of traits offered up by his causal self or else by models in the external world. We also know that character structure, self-constitution, and autonomy play roles in all of this. But there is still more we need to discuss about our reflective choosing if we are to come to a full understanding of the psychological ownership in identification. We want to know more about the *content* of our character choosing. We want to know what are the kinds of choices about traits one needs to make in order for traits to end up as part of who one is. We go to this discussion next.

CHAPTER 7

Identificatory Valuation

What we have done thus far really has been to paint a picture of the concept of identification with wide brush strokes. We know in general that in order to make ourselves character selves—indeed, to own who we are—we need to reflectively choose traits that are either already a part of who we are as causal identities or else modeled by objects out in the world beyond us. That's the big picture. It is time now to start providing the appropriate detail. And so in this chapter and the next, I am going to do precisely that by laying out the core elements of my theory of identification. What I would like to do specifically in this chapter is talk about the valuative component to all of this volitional activity. In choosing traits to be parts of our character, we don't merely choose them in a disinterested way. In owning who we are, we choose traits to be things of supreme value to us. I am going to argue that we choose them to be the value standards we try to live our lives by, endlessly reaffirming and readjusting these standards in the flow of everyday social intercourse. The act of choosing such standards is what I call "identificatory valuation." This concept will be our central focus.

I

To provide a context for understanding the concept of "identificatory valuation," I want to revisit my chapter 1 discussion of the ongoing philosophical debate about the role that character values play in character development. Among other things, I discussed the claim that Frankfurt, Taylor, and Dworkin make that it is a person's ability to reflectively *evaluate* at the second order her first-order conscious states that makes her a person in the fullest sense of the term.[1] Persons are essentially evaluators. Taylor makes much out of what exactly the appropriate kind of evaluation needs to be—he prefers the "strong evaluations" we make about the moral worth of our first-order states to the "weak evaluations" we make about the convenience, satisfaction, attractiveness, and other quite subjective features of our first-order states. For Taylor, what stands out about persons as strong

162

evaluators is that they make objective moral value judgments about their first-order states, as opposed to the subjective weak evaluations about first-order states that all other animals are limited to making.

When all is said and done, I think that Taylor's distinction here is interesting but not all that important for delineating the unique features of what it is to be a person. Strong evaluations are not all that much more important than weak evaluations as central features of personhood, or features of the character self. In fact, strong evaluations are not really that critical to being persons at all. Certainly a person might not *identify with* the life of strong (moral) evaluation at all, yet he still would be considered a character self, a person. Specifically, he would be the person characterized by whatever *else* he identified with. For example, the sociopath always throws moral caution to the wind, yet we wouldn't say that he wasn't a person with some kind of character. Rather, we would say he was an immoral, perhaps despicable, character. But he is a character, nevertheless. It is our identifications with first-order states (internal causal traits) and externally modeled traits that make us characters. Since *moral* or any other sense of strong evaluative identifications are only a small part of this total identificatory package, we must reject Taylor's thesis.

But neither are we merely weak evaluators. Who we are is more than just the most intense or most convenient or most satisfying or most attractive first-order states (i.e., causal self traits) or externally modeled traits we happen reflectively to evaluate in favor of. We are more than just our first-order conscious state itches. No, the fact is, we are weak and strong evaluators and *more*. We evaluate first-order states not only in terms of moral content and subjective itches but also often in terms of aesthetic content, political content, religious content, and much more. We are multi-dimensional identifiers[2]— often enough, we pick which first-order state or externally modeled trait to act on because of how well it meets our aesthetic concerns, our political concerns, and so on. Perhaps, though, the category of contents that gets the lion's share of evaluational work is what might be called "practical content evaluation." That is, we mostly decide on which first-order states or externally modeled traits to opt for by seeing how well the competing candidates among them measure up to our practical concerns about matters such as friendship, money, leisure time, work life, intellectual curiosity, and so on. These are the everyday concerns of people living out their lives with one another. These are our life projects. Subjective itches and moral concerns are certainly part of this package. But they are not, by a long shot, everything. They are certainly not categories that always dominate the rest in our evaluational life.[3]

But whether one's philosophical preference is weak evaluation, strong evaluation, both, or any of the others, the point is that people are evaluators of many varieties and that there is something or other about their being evaluators of lower-order conscious states or externally modeled traits that is quite important to their being persons. However, if we were to rest at this point in our analysis of character, I think we would have settled for an incomplete story of the valuative feature of being persons. In fact, the ability to make any kind of evaluation is only a secondary feature of the story. In this chapter, I am going to press the idea that it is not in evaluating per se that one becomes a person, a character. Evaluating is significant only because it is an *expression* of an even more fundamental kind of valuative act that is unique to us. That is the act of *identificatory valuating* that I have mentioned.

The fact of the matter is, when people make any evaluation, they are making a value judgment about something, and they are making that judgment against a backdrop of value standards that are already in place for them. Opting for a particular first-order desire because it is the most convenient among the viable candidates, for example, means having some value standard in place about what is to count as convenient. Opting for a particular first-order desire because, as Taylor would be inclined to have it, it is morally or "spiritually" superior (the latter being an amended view of "strong evaluation" offered by Taylor[4]) among the viable candidates, or because, as I would be more inclined to have it, it is "practically" superior, means having some value standard in place about what is to count as moral or "spiritual" or "practical." In other words, the very capacity for any of us to make any evaluations presupposes our having value standards already in place. Having value standards are our reasons for making the evaluations we make. And I believe that it is each of us who puts those standards in place for ourselves. Each of us chooses what to value as standards. That choosing is what I am calling "identificatory valuating." In this kind of valuating, each of us chooses traits that are to be our image of the valuatively good life. And, consistent with what I just argued in chapter 6, in our choosing of this image, we are constituting our character selves.

In sum, then, it isn't so much the evaluating of first-order states that makes us into persons (characters) as it is the identificatory valuating—that is, the choosing of the value standards—on which we base that evaluating. The fact that we have these underlying value standards and that we have chosen them into existence is more fundamental to our being persons than the capacity to evaluate first-order states is.

What does Taylor think about these matters? Actually, he seems to be at least vaguely aware of part of the distinction I am making. He seems to be vaguely aware of the basic distinction between evaluation and a presupposed set of value standards (however it is that those standards come to appear on the scene). Unfortunately, he sometimes collapses his vocabulary so that he uses "evaluation" to refer to both concepts. As a result of this equivocation, he often fails to appreciate the significance of the second value notion—choosing value standards—he is talking about. For example, he says that the

> notion of identity refers us to certain *evaluations* which are essential because they are the indispensable horizon or foundation out of which we reflect and *evaluate* as persons....A self decides and acts out of certain fundamental evaluations.[5] [italics mine]

Clearly, "evaluate" here refers to reflective evaluative judgments and "evaluation" refers to the backdrop value standards for these judgments. But because the former notion has far and away received the most ink in his writing over the years, Taylor often runs the latter together with the former and assumes that we are talking about the former. We won't assume this, though. And, in fact, Taylor doesn't *always* do this either.

For example, sometimes Taylor talks about evaluations in the context of "foundational values," "horizons," "frameworks," and "inchoate values." So, he speaks of

> evaluations which touch my identity...[where identity] is defined in terms of certain essential evaluations which provide the horizon or foundation for the other evaluations one makes.[6]

> My identity is defined by the commitments and identifications which provide the frame or horizon within which I can try to determine from case to case what is good, or valuable, or what ought to be done, or what I endorse or oppose.[7]

> Frameworks provide the background, explicit or implicit, for our moral judgments, intuitions, or reactions....To articulate

a framework is to explicate what makes sense of our moral responses. That is, when we try to spell out what it is that we presuppose when we judge that a certain form of life is truly worthwhile...we find ourselves articulating "frameworks."[8]

These background standard evaluations are the yardsticks against which we make reflective evaluations in the first sense. But Taylor believes that there isn't really much of a yardstick for looking at the background standard evaluations. Or rather,

> it is not exactly that I have no yardstick, in the sense that anything goes, but rather that what takes the place of the yardstick is my deepest unstructured sense of what is important, which is as yet inchoate and which I am trying to bring to definition....I am trying to open myself, use all of my deepest, unstructured sense of things in order to come to a new clarity....[W]hat is at stake is the definition of those inchoate evaluations which are sensed to be essential to our identity.[9]

Instead of asking the obvious question about origins for these values, he simply is satisfied with stating that this horizon is "inchoate," bubbling in an unstructured manner beneath the surface, waiting to be used to make the strong reflective evaluative judgments about what is better or worse, right or wrong, and so on. That is, he lets "horizons" and "inchoate" remain in something of a conceptual haze, choosing instead to focus his attention on the evaluating we do with these values.

Clearly, what he is talking about here comes close to what I am calling "identificatory valuation." So what I would like to do now is ask some more questions about Taylor's notions as a way of moving us into consideration of my notion of "identificatory valuation." I would like to ask, What are our "value horizon frameworks" and such all about? What's going on when we choose framework standards of value by which to live our evaluative lives? What are the essential valuative acts of framework choosing about—that is, what are the essential valuative acts of identification about? What are the contents of value frameworks, or of identificatory valuative acts?

II

Let's begin by considering the last of these questions, adding some detail to what we have already said about the content of character valuations. Taylor believes that our value frameworks are about deep moral commitments. He says that to

> know who you are is to be oriented in moral space, a space in which questions arise about what is good or bad, what is worth doing and what is not, what has meaning and importance for you and what is trivial and secondary.[10]

Moral space, moral value. I don't think so. Just as we saw in the previous section that much of our evaluational life is of nonmoral concern, so, too, can we say here that many of our foundational value concerns are about practical life issues of sex, politics, friendship, love, marriage, leisure, work, education, sports, money, freedom, truth, justice, beauty, God, and much, much more.[11] How we create value standards in these arenas are our responses to the general contexts of living that our social life presents to us. That is, we can hardly avoid interacting with other people sexually, politically, and so forth, because sex, politics, and the like are the general contexts that make our life what it is. So we take valuational stands about the kind of persons we choose to be in these human arenas. We create standards for how we choose to see value—the good life—in these arenas. We create images of what it is to lead a life of good sex, a life of good leisure, a life of good work, a life of good aesthetic pursuit, a life of good intellectual pursuit, a life of good religious pursuit, and so on. These images define a life of meaning for us. And, like Plato and Aristotle, we spin our yarn about the good life in these different contexts without necessarily talking about any moral content.

To take another example, when I identified with Duke Snider, I chose to make him a standard for what counted as baseball playing excellence, and perhaps a standard for much more—for example, a standard for psychological power and aesthetic perfection in life. My focus here was not with being moral. It was with being a certain kind of good baseball player. The point is, we can identify with virtually any content. Virtually anything is a candidate for what can fill in our value framework. And people do sometimes identify with the most amazing things. I could choose to make counting blades of grass part of my standard for what image of life I think I should pursue. I could choose to make being an efficient worker part of my standard for who I am. I could choose to make wearing flashy hats part of my standard for being myself. I could choose to make pursuing musical activities part of my standard for what my life should be like. I could choose making a lot of money or being trustworthy or being a scrupulously loyal friend or being a Republican. As I say, virtually anything goes here.

So, *what* the contents of a person's value frameworks are like is unlimited. However, *where* the framework values *come from* is not. Of course, we know that one must find the candidates for such standards either in the stock of causal first-order psychological states that are already part of his psychological repertoire or in the externally modeled ideas, objects, social institutions, and so forth he sees in the world. Either he reflectively chooses to make certain causally definable first-order states into traits of a selflike being that he values, or else he chooses certain externally modeled traits of ideas, objects, social institutions, and the like in a similar vein. In choosing value standards for traits from either repository, he is making those traits his own—he is constituting his character. We saw how all of this worked in the last chapter.

For instance, we know that in the first arena, a person is equipped with causal states such as introjects and other object representations, temperamental tendencies, emotional habits, unlimited wants and beliefs, and more that are the caused first-order motivators of action. At any time, one can reflectively choose any of these causally induced first-order states as new standards for what he will henceforth consider of worth in life. For example, while I might be a shy person by temperament and, thus, unthinkingly causally disposed to acting in shy ways when people are around me, I could go beyond merely having this as a causal feature of me and reflectively choose to treat this shyness as a way of being that henceforth defines for me what is a good way of being in life. I would now reflectively and enthusiastically stand behind being this way. I would care about it as an issue of the self I value being. I would do things to highlight and vary its subtleties. In choosing to do these sorts of things, I would be constituting it as part of my character identity, where before it was merely a facet of my causal identity.

Obviously, too, one can create character by valuationally choosing *against* a causal identity trait. Sometimes a person becomes aware of an aspect of his causal identity that he thinks is harmful to him or is inconsistent with other aspects of his identity that he likes. So he chooses to change. He chooses to value the contrary of his causal identity trait. If, for example, a young woman becomes aware of the extremely overdependent relationship she has had with her mother since childhood, it would be perfectly natural for her now to choose to make herself into a person who values independence in herself. In working to deny an aspect of what her causal identity has been, she is making independence into part of the value framework that constitutes her character self.

Creating value frameworks out of the external world is straightforward. Sometimes we reflect on modeled traits and, if we like them, choose to make them our value standards for how life should be lived. When, say, someone identifies with being a philosopher, he reflects on what he observes in his experience about philosophers and chooses to make certain of these modeled philosopherlike ways of being into his standards for living a valuable life. He might, for example, decide that the only kind of legitimate good life is partly defined by a person's being concerned with foundational questions about existence, with making abstract distinctions, with having good reasons before acting, with being speculative about the meaning of life, and so on. In choosing these as his standards of the valuable life, he would, in the same stroke, be constituting them as traits of his evergrowing character.

Of course, too, a person wouldn't necessarily need to have a model off of which to choose valued traits. He could create his own ideas about what his value standards for the good life should be. He would only be limited by the limits of his imagination. Once his imagination spoke, though, it would be his job to turn the imagined value choice into character.

What we have been reviewing in this section answers the question we posed at the end of the first section: What are the *contents* of identificatory valuative acts and where do those contents come from? Now let's move to the question, What are the essential valuative *acts* of identification (identificatory valuation) about? We will see that there are two basic acts, one having to do with what we will call "brute valuation" and the other having to do with "ultimate valuation." Mastering these two concepts will round out our understanding of identificatory valuation as the value ingredient to identification.

III

Let me begin by setting the proper context for our discussion of "brute valuation." We saw in the previous chapter that identificatory choices normally don't appear on the scene as singularly dramatic events, decked out as fully finished products of a clear and strong character. Rather, we normally choose to be a certain way and then try it out. We slowly build a character trait by trying out the chosen value and expressing it again whenever a relevantly similar situation calling for it arises. That is, a person can choose to mark his life by valuing a particular trait in a certain way and subsequently repeat the same valuation in future situations. Or he can re-mark it over a life-time in a parade of subtle variations on the trait's general value theme. Over a lifetime, most of us face large numbers of subtly different kinds of situations that sound the call for the trait we have identified with. We re-mark that identification in each of these situations by tailoring the particular value standard to fit the particular context. Indeed, it is normally *because* a person learns to make *variations on* a given valuational *theme* that he becomes recognized as that traited person. He becomes known for the trait, for being that particular character. The important point here, though, is that all of this happens during the process of the individual's building up a procession of occasions where he chooses to convey his presence in the world through the central value. The fact that he sculpts variations on the general valuational theme only serves to solidify further the valuational commitment he has been making to the general value trait.

That's one aspect of the valuational life. Another involves the idea of hierarchy. A person's valuational framework is a hierarchy of value standards he chooses to embody in his character. There are the most fundamental valuational standards and then there are lower levels of standards that get generated from these most fundamental ones or from the less fundamental ones in between. When a person chooses what's important in life, sometimes he does this based on what other things are *already* deemed important. The former are what I mean by the lower levels, the latter the higher. Except for the choices found on the most fundamental (higher) level, all the valuational lower-level choices a person makes are, by definition, based on the reason that they are entailed by or psychologically associated with higher order valuations and one's decision to commit himself to those entailments and associations. So, certainly, I could choose to embody a life of being charitable to needy people and logically base that choice on prior character commitments I have made to being a moral person. Being moral is higher up on my character hierarchy and being charitable is lower down. One entails the other. But *both* are parts of my character, my valuational framework. Both count for me as value standards by which I live my life. One is simply more fundamental than the other. But both are standards, and so they become the stuff from which my everyday evaluations of how I should behave spring.

Although both higher and lower levels of valuational choice are part of the character value framework, the higher order ones are far and away the most conceptually interesting. Those are the ones where the *central processes* of character value choosing are found. And those are the ones I will spend the rest of this chapter discussing. They are what I am calling "brute valuations." When we choose to see some x as a highest-order fundamental standard for our living the good life, we are brutely choosing x. What does this mean?[12] It means that we can't, as we can in evaluating, go back any further to find still more underlying value standards on which to base our choices. Our brutely chosen value standards are our self-created value premises or axioms for living as valuing creatures. When, for example, I brutely choose to make the honoring of friendship a part of my character, the fact that I honor friendship does *not* follow from other prior standards determining "best ways of being." There are no objective character "bests" to appeal to. Rather, what's going on is that I am throwing myself into choosing friendship as a primitive standard for living my life and then seeing what becomes of me and how I fine-tune that choice over the years. In trying to understand how any person's valuing life works, we can't keep going back, always expecting to find more primitive underlying value standards to justify her every value attribution. There must be a starting point, a place where a person posits value premises or axioms to which she appeals in making later value judgments. This is the originative source of all of any individual's character valuing activity.[13]

Where a person does appeal to prior value standards, those standards become *reasons* either for her lower-order character choices or else for her evaluative decisions and actions. "Brute choosing," by contrast, is *not based on reasons* about prior value standards. But I don't mean by this that valuation choices are irrational in a Dostoevskian sense of "capricious choice"—where there are no reasons of any sort for a person's choices[14] and so she no longer acts, in any sense, as a rational being. Rather, all I mean is that they are not based on any *prior value* commitments. We identifiers just *do* sometimes brutely choose to value things in certain ways. Of course, although there are no antecedent value standard *reasons for* our brute valuations, there nevertheless is usually *reason to* them. So we might brutely value a particular way of thinking and then try it out. At that point, although we wouldn't have prior value reasons for the original valuational choice, we would proceed to act as rational beings by looking to see if we like the results of the original choice. Something akin to a rational reconstruction of principles of operant conditioning would seem to be in play here. That is, after we assert a choice, we test the consequences to see if there is a "comfort" to them that would justify the choice after the fact. We look to see, for example, if the consequences of our choice fit with other valuations we have previously made into a regular part of our value standard repertoire. We check to see if a valuational choice fits consistently with the rest of who we already are as character valuators. We check to see if there is an internal coherence or cognitive and emotional consistency with the rest of our life. We want to avoid the discomfort with which value standard incoherence or inconsistency of any variety would strap us. If we find such discomfort, we might back away from our valuational commitment and, in a trial-and-error spirit, strike out in a new direction to try a new valuational commitment. But if the comfort is there in the first place, we will probably choose to valuate in the original valuative way again when appropriate contexts present themselves. In this fashion, we slowly build our character by choosing and rechoosing the same general valuations over time and new circumstance. There is that much *reason to* our lives as valuators.

There's a second, quite different sense to the idea that there is *reason to* our brute valuational activity. It is that valuating is its own existential reward. All other rationality aside—that other rationality consisting of the formulation of "comfort" strategies aimed at insuring that our valuational choices lead us to a life of happiness—it is rational to brutely valuate, because that is what it takes to become a character. One might say that being brute valuators is our existential requirement for personhood. We have to put ourselves out on a limb by brutely throwing in with a kind of value life that we aren't certain about before the fact. We have to take the chance, because doing this is a significant part of what persons qua characters are. It is what makes us unique individuals. It is what ultimately makes us the authors of our own lives. Were we to depend on prior value reasons for the character value commitments we made, there would be nothing unique about us. Moreover, we would have become life plagiarists, not life authors.

So on a couple of counts, there is *reason to* our valuational life. At this point, however, I would like to explore a difficulty that I can easily imagine someone feeling about the "no reasons" thesis, the thesis that we identifiers have *no reasons for* our valuational choices. Since we have no reasons for our valuational choices in the arena of our fundamental framework values, it might appear as though I am saying that a person could just as easily have made other brute choices in life as the ones he has, in fact, made. And that might make it seem as though I am putting too much contingency into who a person is. The critic wants to take me to task here and say that our character identity is so centrally important to us that any view allowing that it could have been wildly different than it is must be wrong. Like a similar argument that we discussed in the last chapter, this argument in effect claims that there just must be something necessary about the way each of us is. Otherwise, how could we so value our *particular* lives?

Well, I understand the sentiment. However, when all is said and done, it is an extravagant one. A life can be important without its needing some preordained blueprint for it to be a *necessary* response to. A life can be of value—more importantly, *our* life can be of value *to us*—just so long as we *decide* to value it. We don't need any reasons other than that it is our life that we are constructing. Our life is our most important product, so we might as well treat what we put into it as being of great value. In fact, we do just that. And the way we do it is by positing great value to the traits we make ourselves into. We *could* do otherwise, though. We *could*—and sometimes, in fact, we do—choose not to value ourselves. But that would take us out of our full personhood and into a state of improper functioning. The norm for selves is to choose for a self trait that will count as a standard of value for us. (See the sixth section.) So our lives are important just so long as we choose to value them through acts of character valuation. There need be no specific script of *particular* valuational choices that we necessarily follow. We can choose virtually any value we could imagine. Thus, what a person's character is like could, indeed, have been wildly different than it is. These matters are that contingent.

Of course, as we saw in chapter 6, once we commit ourselves to a certain way of being, we can't say that just anything goes anymore. We have created psychological structure to our character now, and that puts requirements on how we are to be with people. But the initial *making* of that self is brute in the sense that, on the face of things, we have no good initial reasons to pick being one way rather than some other wildly different way. While I know that this manner of putting things has a *prima facie* sound of absurdity to it, I believe it really needn't be so disturbing. Initial character valuation choosing is brute in the sense that it is our spur-of-the-moment response to contingent life circumstances. We can imagine a vast number of alternative character choices we could have made, choices that have a different set of consequences to them (although that couldn't have been known before the fact). And any of a multitude of still other character choices could have done just as well as what we actually chose to be like. Indeed, I think that most of us know this already. In fact, we actually sometimes use this idea to tease ourselves about "what might have been." Every one of us can look at our lives and imagine that at any of our momentary "character choice points," we could have chosen otherwise. Sometimes, because we don't like the consequences we have endured as a result of the particular brute character choices we have made, we think about how nice it might have been had we actually made different ones. Here we have no problem thinking that there was nothing necessary about the choices we, in fact, made. We enthusiastically believe that we could have chosen otherwise without doing violence to who we are. We still would have been the essential us, but things just would have been a little better. Certainly, if we can accept here that different brute choices would have been acceptable in this situation—that they would not have gone against some law of nature requiring that a person necessarily be exactly the way she has turned out—then we can accept the general thesis that *any* of a person's brute valuations are contingencies that could quite acceptably have been otherwise.

Consider an example where we tease ourselves in fantasy about this truth. How many married people fantasize about how life might have been different, perhaps even better, had they married someone other than their spouse? Someone twenty years into what has become an unhappy marriage might be such a fantasizer. She wishes she had married her high school sweetheart instead of the man she met when she first started working two lifetimes later—after she finished high school, finished college, and moved to a new city and job. Each of these new context changes saw additions to her character, for she had to meet new kinds of social circumstances that the ever-growing social contexts were providing her. That is how the life of adult character development normally proceeds. When it came time for her to consider marriage, she was a different character than she had been in high school. We can suppose that whom she chose to marry fit in well with who she had become. But years later, things soured (they began "growing away from one another") and she began wishing she had chosen differently.

Clearly, such scenarios as this are proof that we accept the idea that people could sensibly choose differently without doing violence to the integrity of who they are. However, in all fairness, we should point out that sometimes such fantasies get out of hand. There are *some* limits to the brute valuations we can sensibly make. Indeed, I think that happens in this example. While it illustrates how a person's brute choices could be any of many possibilities, it also illustrates the point that a person isn't always in the best position to imagine accurately about all the possibilities she thinks up. What I mean is this. The star of our example imagines in great detail how her life would have been desirably different had she married her high school sweetheart. She imagines how her life would have been different had she made one of her character commitments the "brute valuation of her high school sweetheart." In fact, though, I believe she is involved in a bit of a confusion of a general sort that a lot of us get into when we indulge in such reverie. She judges how happy she would have been through the eyes of the person she was back when she was in high school. But she was a different character self then. In the passing of twenty years since her choosing the man she married, she has forged valuational choices about a whole network of character traits connected to her life with her husband. And these choices have molded her valuational self. In her reverie, however, she is thinking about her high school sweetheart through the eyes of the girl way back when. Perhaps that historical self would have been happier, given who she was *then*, with the high school sweetheart as the center of her growing character self. But that historical self wasn't who she was when she, in fact, made her choice to marry. And that historical self certainly isn't who she, in fact, is now. Were her high school sweetheart miraculously to appear suddenly on the scene, and were he exactly as he was in high school (as she is hoping), she would see that she couldn't possibly really want him instead of her actual husband (although she still might have perfectly good reasons to prefer *someone or other* instead of the husband she is unhappy with)—not, at least, because he had the traits of the old high school sweetheart of twenty-plus years ago. For now she is a totally different person than the high school character. The truth is that it is her *memory* of who she was back then that she uses in constructing her fantasy about the high school sweetheart. She mistakenly thinks that her fantasy is a judgment that comes out of her current character self. Her current character self, though, is in a position to evaluate only what is going on in her life now and what she would want it to be like in the future. And it is done against a backdrop of who she has become with her husband. So, were she actually to make a life decision about staying married or not, and were she to base that decision on the high school fantasy, she would be making a grave error. Were she to leave her husband and try to find the old high school sweetheart in hopes of marrying him, for example, she would be working under a conceptual confusion. Of course, she might get lucky. It could turn out that the high school sweetheart has coincidentally grown into a character who is quite what she needs and fits well with, given her current character. But that outcome wouldn't have been *based* on her fantasy of what he used to be like.

There are some limits, then, to the kinds of brute valuations it is reasonable for a person to make, even though there is a general sense in which a person could choose to be virtually any kind of character he could imagine. Let me add another qualification to this idea. When I talk of brute character choosing as "being so contingent that had one chosen otherwise, it might have been perfectly fine," I don't mean to imply that on each repeated occasion of a general kind of circumstance a person could sensibly choose totally differently. I only mean that that *initial* choice was so thoroughly contingent and not based on any reasons. But once a person has made an initial choice about a particular trait, and he has committed himself to having that trait constitute part of who he is, he must choose the same general kind of trait on subsequent comparable occasions if he is really to be the character to which he has committed himself. Of course, he certainly can tailor the subsequent expression of the trait to suit the unique features of any new circumstances. But the general trait must be expressed. It must be there, not as a matter of full causality, but as a matter of his having made the decision to make the given trait into who he is. General consistency and repetition are required for this to happen.

What I would like to do now in closing the discussion about "brute valuations" in this section is consider a possible challenge to the basic thrust of what I have been saying. Specifically, I want to look at what Taylor has to say critically about what he calls "radical choice." For, on the face of things, this concept looks like a close cousin to "brute valuational choice." He argues that radical choice is a confused concept, and so, by implication, my notion of brute valuational choice would seem to be a defective linchpin for understanding identification.

Taylor begins with a review of the concept of radical choice that he sees explicitly in Sartre and implicitly in Nietzsche. In much the same spirit as I see brute valuational choice, Sartre believes that radical choice is a person's choosing to value one course in life rather than another and not basing that choice on any value standard reasons. To make this point about Sartre, Taylor offers an illustration of Sartre's in which a man considering going off to war has to choose between staying home to take care of his ailing mother or going off to join the Resistance. Sartre believes that there is no basis for the choice here. There is no way of adjudicating between both impressive claims on the individual. He must simply choose; and the choosing becomes its own value justification. Generalizing from the example, Taylor says that Sartre believes that all moral decisions are, in this same regard, radical choices people make—that they are based on no prior value standards.

Taylor thinks this example is a paradigm of Sartre's general notion of radical choice. But since Taylor also believes that when we look closely at the example, we must see that there really is *no* radical choosing going on in it, Taylor also concludes that the general condition for which the example is supposed to be a paradigm is also devoid of any real radical choosing. That is, there is no such thing as radical choosing in our moral lives. Taylor's strategy: Destroy the validity of the paradigm and you destroy the general conceptual point. Well, I want to argue that Taylor's selection of this example as a paradigm of radical choosing is, in fact, unfortunate for our understanding of Sartre's concept of radical choosing. Part of what Taylor criticizes about this example and radical choice is quite right. However, he goes on to conclude from this some other things about radical choosing that are unwarranted. Let me explain.

I think Taylor argues convincingly that both of the example's dilemma options have strong claims on the young man *precisely because* there *is* some standard of value or theory of right action he has considered when he thinks about his life. The strength of any such claim on a person presupposes the existence of a good value standard reason giving rise to the claim. As far as Taylor is concerned, in the example, the young man clearly has *already morally evaluated* his situation and has seen that he is faced with a dilemma. And so the young man really did no radical choosing.

By the same token, Taylor acknowledges that if the dilemma is *thoroughgoing*, then, of course, the young man ultimately has to make a choice about what he is going to do. And if the reasons on both sides are effectively of equal weight in his considerations—and they would be just that if the dilemma is thoroughgoing—then the choice he finally goes with will be something of a radical choice in the sense that he will just have to throw himself into one course of action rather than the other, equally good one. He won't actually use a set of reasons as the basis for his choice. But at this point, Taylor goes on to say *rightly* that it doesn't follow from this idea of radical choice that *all* other moral choosing contexts are about radical choosing. Specifically, evaluating what went on leading up to the dilemma—for example, morally evaluating the import that his leaving would have on his ailing mother's life—certainly wasn't a radical choice. Clearly, when people in general make most moral choices, they evaluate their options based on independent standards they antecedently have at their disposal. Moral evaluation is always based on independent standards people rationally put into play. That the young man in Sartre's example made a radical choice wasn't so much proof positive for how one makes moral decisions as it was for how one moves past genuinely full-blown dilemmas by throwing oneself into action. In the final analysis, then, Sartre's example actually equivocates on the notion of radical choosing; that is, there are two different ideas of radical choosing going on in it. On the one hand, if Sartre was trying to show us the kind of choosing that normally goes on in being a moral agent—if he was trying to show us that it was radical in the sense that it involved no prior consideration of any values—he failed. On the other hand, if he was trying to show us the kind of choosing that normally goes on in resolving genuine dilemmas—if he was trying to show us that it was radical in the sense that it finally was not based on taking any prior set of value reasons to be better than some other set—he succeeded. But for Sartre to run the two together and conclude that we are radical choosers in the first instance because we are radical choosers in the second is a mistake. In this regard, Taylor is right that Sartre's example is flawed. The concept of radical choice has problems.

However, at this point, Taylor seems to take his turn in making mistakes. He seems to conclude from this victory over Sartre's example that radical choosing of the first variety *never* makes sense in value decisions.[15] And the fact of the matter is, I believe I have shown that it sometimes does. Perhaps radical choice makes no sense for strong moral evaluating, but it is quite relevant for the choosing of many of the value standards we go on to *base* our evaluations on. Each person's idea of the good (i.e., his standard of value) is radically chosen in the sense that it is a brutely chosen valuation—that is, that it is not based on any prior value standard reasons. That, anyway, has been the thesis I have been advancing. Indeed, I believe this view is also both Nietzsche's and Sartre's thesis, although the particular

Sartrean examples that Taylor chooses to focus on are clearly about strong moral evaluations and not about the valuating standards for the good life that Sartre talks about in other places.

Finally, then, what I'm saying is that Taylor's view about the poverty of radical choice really has no bearing on my concept of brute valuational choice. Taylor has certainly shown that where a person is *evaluating* his moral situation, his choices do presuppose value reasons—he has shown that there is no radical choosing going on here (in the first sense of "radical choosing"). But nothing he says shows that in those different value contexts where a person is being a *valuational character self*, his choices presuppose anything about value standards. Indeed, I believe I have convincingly argued that they don't. And so I think Taylor's criticisms of radical choosing have no real impact on my claims about brute valuational choosing.

IV

I will leave our examination of brute valuational choice now and begin looking at the second essential kind of valuative act of identificatory valuation (identification) that I promised to consider. Not only are many of our character values brutely chosen into existence, but all of them are also seen by the chooser as having what I will call "ultimate value." Accordingly, the act of identification involves the act of "ultimate valuation." In choosing to embody certain valued traits as one's character—in choosing them as the standards by which one wants to live and grade his life—a person chooses those traits as having a kind of perfection about them. In ordinary terms, we speak of one's having *ideals* by which he lives his life; or at least he grades himself on how well he lives by his ideals. That's simply the way the context of character choosing behaves. In choosing about character, one just is positing a trait as having *total value* for himself. One just is an idealist when it comes to the character self. And so nothing is more important to him than being the character of his choice. Choosing one's character self into existence through the choosing of value standards by which to define the good life—that is, through character ideals—is the act of choosing for perfection in one's traits.

We should understand that there is a psychological history preceding this aspect of the identificatory act that makes it only natural that we develop as beings seeking perfection in ourselves. There is precedent for our trying to embody ourselves in our value trait ideals. One has only to recall the Narcissism Theory discussion of chapter 3 to see that the idea of "ultimate valuation of one's character choices" is a developmental extension of the infant/child's narcissistic grandiose attitude toward his emerging rudimentary self. For one thing, we know that the narcissistic infant/child comes to think of his every want as being of supreme importance in the world, unmediated by any other considerations. It turns out that with the emerging of identificatory character activity—that is, with the emerging of the process of valuating an internal agency self into existence—the young child extends this attitude toward his wants to his newly unfolding valuations. Something about his mental life is still of supreme importance in his world. Specifically, certain of the goods he comes to posit have supreme importance for him, although now he is better able to mediate some of them when practical circumstances make such a thing prudent. But there's also a second aspect of narcissistic infant development that gets extended into our lives as ultimate valuational adults. The primitive narcissistic parental *imago* is the value precursor to the adult ultimate valuator. Where, during narcissistic development, an infant's parents set a value standard of grandiose perfect proportions that the infant mirrors and creates self representations around, as an identificatory being, the adult sets his standards by himself and he endows them with ultimate value proportions. In other words, grandiose valuing gives way to ultimate valuing; and the causally initiated mirroring of the grandiose values gives way more fully to the self-creation of ultimate values.

We don't have to lose ourselves in discussing the detail of this rudimentary self development. The above reminder is enough. The point is, it really should be no surprise that identification involves a person's choosing to embody perfect values, value ideals. He has been involved in this process in one form or another well before he's become a serious identifier. Of course, the version of seeking something perfect, ideal, about the self that comes in character construction is different from the rudimentary versions of infancy and childhood. In seeking to create character ideals, the adult *commits* himself to his valuating activity, as though doing so had ultimate importance for him. By contrast, infants make no commitments to the things that are important to them. Things are important to them (e.g., need gratification), but they have no developed capacity to commit a self to those things. Adults, though, have character self agency at stake. Having our own character agency with which to try to effect some degree of control over our world is of crucial importance to each of us. It's what is of ultimate importance to us. It's what we have seen the whole march of self development is aimed at. Consequently, building and maintaining an agency character self through the positing of brute valuation is our ultimate life project. The degree of commitment is a sign of the value ultimacy of any project. So, of course, we commit ourselves wholly to the valuational process of identification.

There are yet other distinguishing features of adult valuation ultimacy. For one thing, as a character self, the adult is concerned with *intrinsically* valuing the traits of his character. To intrinsically value anything in life—not just traits of character—implies that a person sees it *unconditionally* as good. He sees goodness as a part of the unconditional nature of the thing. The thing is an ultimate good. By contrast, when a person valuates a thing in a less-than-intrinsic manner, the value he sees in the thing is wholly conditional. For example, were he only instrumentally valuing something, he would see good in it only to the extent that it was instrumental in his attaining some other good. The possibility would always be open that under circumstances where instrumentality was seen not to be present, he would not see the thing as being good. But this doesn't happen with intrinsic valuation. When something is intrinsically valuated, what is valued is valued unconditionally. That is precisely the state that the character trait valuator is in. When as a valuational chooser of a new character trait a person ultimately values the trait, he is unconditionally focused on and valuing it.

Our character valuations are also of ultimate value in the sense that they define the conditions in which good can ever occur in our lives. Since they define the standards for what we see as good, then only through their creation can goodness in life ever be part of a person's experience. Only through their creation do we have conditions that make it possible for us to ever evaluate what we are experiencing as good. With this in mind, laying out such conditions would seem to be something of ultimate value for any of us, for it provides the context in which we can come to have enjoyment in our lives, this presumably being one of life's built-in *desiderata*. Consider this exercise. Try right now to genuinely posit a new brute valuation in your own life. Try simply deciding to see some way of living that you haven't until now valued for itself. For example, try positing a new brute valuation for cooking or for being totally devoted to God. Recognize that you are not reevaluating the worth of cooking or devotion to God. So you are not deciding for some preexisting value reasons that cooking or devotion to God will be valuable to you. Rather, you are simply positing your brute valuing of them. You are deciding to see them henceforth as valuable where before you didn't. Once you have really made these valuations, you begin to enjoy cooking and the life of religious devotion. When you are in the realm of what you really see as being good, taking a positive attitude toward them in your thought and behavior is genuine. Faking or playacting a preference for cooking or devotion would have no place here. When being "the cook" or "the religious devotee" becomes something you posit as a part of who you are, then when you express this way of being in the world, you are exercising the good, your ideals. What could be more enjoyable?

Our valuations are ultimate in one more sense. It is that they define what we see as a good life *for anyone*. We can get some assistance with this idea from something Sartre says. He claims that when a person chooses the kind of life he will live, part of the "radical" quality of his choice is the fact that not only is he choosing what is to be a standard of value for himself but he is also choosing what is to be a value standard for all humankind. In my terms, ultimate valuation involves choosing for humankind. Sartre says that when we make a value choice about how to live our lives, "what we choose is always the better; and nothing can be better for us unless it is better for all."[16] When a person chooses a way of life, he isn't only choosing to make that way of life *his* standard for what is to be considered valuable in life, he is choosing for *everybody*. Actually, he is *prescribing* for everybody. Were he *not* to do this, his valuations would not be quite so ultimate. If a person's identificatory choosing is to confer *ultimate* value on a trait, then of course that person isn't going to think that there could be any better way to be. Had he thought *that*, he would have chosen for the better values, for the values he saw as better than the choices he was considering. It simply is the case that the prescriptive feature of "being the very best values to live by for humankind" is built into the very concept of character value choices.[17]

Of course, the obvious problem here is that everybody feels the same about things. I prescribe my character valuations as best for humankind, but so do you and so does she and so does he. And so on and so on and so on. We are all prescribing for one another what is of ultimate value. Obviously, there is no real sense in which we can say that any one of us is "right" about matters here. It isn't that one of us has *discovered* the best values on which to mold his character. Rather, each of us by ourselves has *created* values of ultimate worth. If part of that ultimacy involves our prescribing them as "best" to others, then so be it. As we saw in a different context in the last section, it doesn't mean that they *are* best in any evaluative sense (where "best" is the result of applying some commonly agreed upon standard of value). Our prescribing them for others as though we thought they were best is just the way of characters. It is simply part of the behavioral repertoire of ultimate valuators.

In concluding here, I want to say that finally it is in a person's *brutely choosing* certain traits to *ultimately value* that makes for what I have called "identificatory valuation." It is these two features of valuation that are the heart and soul of how a person valuatively creates himself as a character. When someone genuinely identifies with certain traits from the world, he chooses to treat those traits as special (ultimate), so special that they are actually posited—brutely chosen—as the value standards defining his character. These are the traits on which one focuses his agency activity. These are the instructions one gives his agency for how he wants his life to be lived. In consistently abiding by these instructions, one eventually transforms the valued traits into psychological structures that constitute his character.

V

I am going to shift gears now and make some comments about autonomy and identification. I have already said some things about them in chapter 6. We know that autonomy involves a person's making higher-order reflective decisions about lower-order conscious states. Given this view, I would like to further analyze autonomy by taking into account what I have been saying about identificatory valuation in this chapter. I would like to develop briefly the idea that it is through valuational acts that a character self becomes an autonomous being.

I can best make my view clear by elaborating a bit on Professor Frankfurt's analysis of autonomy. He thinks that a person has a will at all (we are not yet talking about a *free* will) to the extent that he has first-order desires that are effective, that is, that actually can and do motivate the bringing about of their aims. So if I go to Moscow but I don't do so as a result of any desire I have (imagine that I am skyjacked there), then my going there isn't a matter of my will. If I have a desire to break into show business, but because of my overwhelming fears of rejection I never act on that desire, my will would be considered weak, if not altogether nonexistent around the issue of my desire's aim. In neither case is a certain first-order desire about some aim (going to Moscow or breaking into show business) a motivator for realizing that aim. That is, in neither case is a relevant desire effective in bringing about its aim. So we say that my will plays no role in what happens to me. On the other hand, if I desire to finish writing this book, and that desire really motivates me to do what I can to finish it, that desire is an effective first-order desire. And we say that I willed finishing the book.

But what about *free* will? Frankfurt believes that a person has a free will through his second-order reflective desires. A person can reflect on various first-order desires and form evaluative preferences for certain of them. If a person then desires (on the second order) his preferred first-order desires to be his will, he is moving in the right direction toward being autonomous. However, merely having this second-order desire isn't quite enough. Finally, it must also be true that his second-order desires be "effective"—that is, it must be true that having second-order desires be enough to bring about the success of his first-order desires. Then the individual will have acted freely.

This view is all well and good, but there is something missing. A person could have this kind of second-order desire in cases we would *not* call expressions of free will. Suppose, for example, that a person successfully chose to do things that were instrumental in his becoming a physician. It is always fair to ask if those choices were an expression of autonomy. Suppose he had earlier evaluatively chosen between his strong first-order desire not to become a physician, his very much stronger first-order desire to please his grandmother who wanted him to become a physician, and some specific physician-becoming desires that resulted from his desire to please his grandmother. In reflectively evaluating these three sets of desires, he opted for the second and third. He had a second-order desire to have that desire be his will. And it was. He did the things necessary for becoming a physician and, in the process, for satisfying his desire to please his grandmother. In other words, his second-order desire here was effective. It was effective, but I don't think we would say that he freely chose to become a physician. Perhaps his grandmother freely chose for him to become a physician, but he didn't. What's missing here is that he did *not identify with* becoming a physician. He wanted to please his grandmother and so he formed wants to do what it took to become a physician. But he didn't identify with the latter wants. That is, he didn't identify with the things he ended up doing to fulfill his first-order desire to satisfy his grandmother. He fulfilled his grandmother's desire for his becoming a physician, not his own.

It is my view that a person's choice is free only when Frankfurt's kind of conditions are met *and* the chooser *identifies with* the choices that have been effective. The individual in my example *did* choose to please his grandmother. And, no doubt, he identified with making *that* choice. So *that* choice was free. But what about the particular desires he formed and chose to act on as the means for fulfilling his grandmother's wishes? Were those choices free? For example, he wanted to apply to medical school; he wanted to get good grades; and so forth (even though he no doubt also had wants conflicting with these things). These "means" sorts of wants were certainly effective in the sense that he chose to act on them and he did. So Frankfurt would say that this individual freely chose to do the things he did to become a physician. But this can't be right. This person wasn't being an autonomous agent. At worst, I would say that in a very straight-forward sense of the term, all the things he chose to do here he was "coerced" into doing. And at best, I would say that all the things he chose to do here he willed, but not freely. The autonomous person doesn't simply want his wants, as it were. He also identifies with them. If the wants he acts on are not *his own*, then they don't flow from his autonomy.

Let me reframe Frankfurt's analysis of autonomy to cover not only desires but all varieties of conscious states about which we say a person makes choices. This refers to things such as convictions, feelings, beliefs about the traits of some external model, and so forth— that is, first-order conscious states that are either part of one's already existing causal self or about some externally modeled traits. And let me reframe how identification makes its entrance into the discussion of autonomy. There is something about second-order (or, as we saw in the last chapter, third-order, too) reflecting on first-order states (whatever variety they are) that is crucial to autonomy. But I don't believe that Frankfurt's second-order reflective evaluating of first-order states by itself is what makes for autonomy. These second-order reflective choices are just instances of a more general condition that is what's really at the center of autonomy. It is a condition that takes into account what we have been saying in this chapter about identification. The autonomous person *valuates* certain of his first-order states as well as externally modeled traits. That is to say, a person (or any other being) is autonomous to the extent that he iden-tifies with the first-order states (and externally modeled traits) by which he effectively evaluatively chooses to live.[18] It happens that evaluations are normally choices about states with which a person identifies. For example, when I evaluate whether or not I should steal an apple from the fruit stand, I might decide not to endorse my first-order desire to steal and instead endorse my first-order desire to be honest. I certainly would be identifying with my first-order desire to be honest here. (I could also be identifying with the other desire to steal, only less so.) And certainly I would be practicing my autonomy.

Both identification and autonomy are the norm for evaluation contexts. But there is nothing necessary about this. One could, as we did in the physician example, imagine a person's making a "forced" evaluation; that is, we could imagine a person's deciding for a first-order state yet not identifying with it. And so that evaluation would not have been an autonomous choice. Let's consider still another example. An individual would rather not choose between two friends, say, who are competing for an award. He doesn't identify with either possible first-order choice. But pressure is brought to bear. Suppose there is even a gun put to his head. He would rather not choose, but he does. And his choice amounts to an evaluation of the relative merits of the case that each of his friends could muster on their own behalf. It doesn't seem to stretch matters here to say that his evaluation wasn't autonomously formed. He evaluated—he chose—but he wasn't autonomous. He wasn't fully behind the first-order state he chose. He wasn't fully behind, say, this first-order belief that friend A should win the award over B. Yet he chose in favor of that belief. Clearly, he didn't identify with it. And he certainly didn't identify with evaluating in terms of it. That is, he didn't identify with the act of choosing the first-order state that was the product of his evaluation. Normally, evaluators identify with both the first-order state they choose for and the act of evaluative choosing. So, normally, people evaluate autonomously.[19] But it isn't their evaluating that makes them autonomous. Rather it is the identification—their valuations—that their evaluating presupposes which makes them autonomous.

Finally, I believe that *where* we find autonomy is in our reflective second- and third-order decisions. So what we discussed about autonomy in the last chapter really was important. But the point I'm adding to the analysis now is that what happens in second- and third-order evaluative decisions is that a person brutely valuates some trait as having ultimate value and he uses that valuation to decide reflectively (evaluate) what to do about some lower-order state he is considering. We say that he identifies with the lower-order state, but what this *means* is that he has brutely valuated it on a higher order and so naturally chooses to favor it when it appears as an option about a lower-order choice.

VI

In closing the discussion in this chapter, I would like to do two things. First, I would like to consider briefly a critical sentiment that I suspect many readers have found themselves raising. Second, I would like to place what I have been arguing in this chapter into the broader perspective of the more general argument of the book.

1. The critical sentiment I have in mind might sound something like this: Are all identificatory characters really, as I have suggested they are, in pursuit of creating standards for leading the good life? Is the process of identification always so perfectly aimed at the good? Isn't it likely that we at least sometimes make valuational choices that are about things other than standards for the good life? That is to say, aren't there some evil characters around, so chosen if only to make themselves uniquely different from other characters, to make themselves really stand out from the crowd? And if not opting for evil, don't people at least sometimes identify with the various shades of gray in between evil and one's idea of the good? All of these are reasonable questions. And they are aimed at denying the central thesis of this chapter—that identification is about brutely choosing and living out ultimate standards of the good life. When all is said and done, however, I think the aim of these questions falls flat. Let's see how.

In the spirit of these critical questions, *of course* there are some evil and otherwise less-than-good persons in the world. But that doesn't defeat my thesis. Saying that there are some evil people in the world is always done from a perspective about what the good life is all about and how those particular people have failed dismally at it. One person's evil might always be another's virtue ideal. Judgment about evil is all in the eyes of the beholder—or, in this case, in the eyes of the character valuation creator. With Aristotle, I believe that no one ever really accepts as evil the valuations they themselves make. As identifiers, we only brutely choose and pursue what we see as the good, whether this be the moral good, the aesthetic good, the economic good, the practical good, the epistemic good, and so on. When we claim that there is evil and other less-than-good in the world, we are saying that by our standards, other characters aren't fully up to speed. That is our egocentrism. The truth is that people do choose and pursue traits in a fashion so as to confer ultimate goodness on those traits.

The idea that we might think that some characters are evil or shades of gray in between good and evil is really more of a commentary on *our* view of *our* standard of good than anything else. "Evil character or the less-than-good character" is a description of the negation of our own personal valuations, of our own way of "doing" life. It is a third-person perspective of the character world beyond ourselves. Indeed, this chapter's thesis that character valuations are each person's privately posited view of the good, as though our standard, á la Sartre, is the ultimate best that we are prescribing for everyone else, actually *entails* that we see all other people as exemplifying valuation less than the correct (i.e., our) standard of value. So of course each of us sees evil characters and any number of shades of gray characters in the world.

"Alright," someone might say, "what about Hitler? Is he an example of pursuing the good life?" Am I claiming some kind of relativism where there is no evil in the world? Are all valuations morally equal? Let me briefly say why I deny this relativism. For many different moral reasons, Hitler *was* an evil force in the world. But that is for *moral* reasons. In contrast, for reasons pertaining to what it is to be a *character* self, Hitler was just being himself. And that was a self *he* no doubt saw as being in league with the good. However despicable he might be from the perspective of our own personal standards for a person's leading the good character life and from the perspective of some communally agreed-upon moral vision, he certainly appears to have thought that he was doing good things and aiming to lead the ultimate good life. And he had cohorts who also identified themselves with the same sorts of traits and who also saw themselves as pursuing the perfect image of the good life. It turned out that they were wrong, at least on moral grounds and from our personal perspectives. They and Hitler were being responsible as characters per se but evil as *moral* characters specifically. But even the morally evil person experiences his life as pursuing the good. As a rule, people don't see themselves as having a *bad character*.

That's the way it is as a rule. But of course, we can all point to parts of our own experience where we haven't always felt so good about who we seemed to be as characters. Each of us can think of plenty of occasions where we have knowingly fallen down on our ideals and have felt bad about it. One wants to ask, Weren't we still full characters there? So doesn't my notion of ultimate valuation seem faulty for our analysis of the choosing that's essential to being a character self? Again, I don't think so. The fact is that when a person does feel bad about the way he is behaving, he may be feeling bad because his behavior so contradicts what he knows to be his genuine character. In other words, he may see this behavior as aberrant in the context of who he really is. Of course, this doesn't always accurately describe the person who feels bad about how he has been. Sometimes the individual's behavior is an accurate expression of his full character, not an aberration. In this kind of situation, I would submit that were a person to feel bad about who he is as a character self, that fact alone would be enough to trigger the beginning of character change. When we don't like who we are, we are no longer holding valuations that are our standards for what the good life is to look like. This simply is an intolerable condition for people. It is part of being a normal-functioning person that we have such standards working in us. When they aren't, change to obtain this condition becomes the order of the day. I don't consider what I am saying here question begging. The fact is, one need only look at what really happens in the world. When a person claims that he doesn't like who he is, he is already in the process of changing to a new valuational ideal self. He is already looking to take on a new modeled trait that he sees as a new standard of the good life. Psychotherapists' offices are filled with such people.

These are all cases where a person has been less than an ideal self and has felt bad about it. How about the cases where a person doesn't feel bad? Can't someone have aspects of his character he simply doesn't see as good? Perhaps he is indifferent to them. Once again, I can only repeat that although this certainly is a logical possibility, in fact, it isn't a real-world possibility. People simply don't function that way as character selves. When a person chooses about his character being, he always chooses the (perceived) good. And he always throws commitment behind that choice. For a person to admit otherwise about himself is for him to be mistaken about who he is as a character. If he judges negatively about his actions or if he is genuinely indifferent to how he is acting in the world (and he doesn't feel bad about it), then how he is in either situation isn't part of his character. It is simply part of how he is behaving. We might even consider it a dispositional part of his personality. However, he is not identifying with his way of being.

Finally, can't a person have a character with quite imperfect traits and not have any feelings about his situation one way or the other because he is just not aware of what his character is? Well, in fact, this case brings us full circle. For although this person's traits needn't be so imperfect as to be deemed immoral, the case really boils down to a nonmoral version of the point we made about the above

Hitler case. The fact is, this person's traits appear imperfect in the eyes of *the observer*. And that is tantamount to saying that the observer wouldn't choose those traits as *his* standards for a good life. However, this doesn't warrant concluding that the possessor would see them as imperfect were he made aware of having them. Indeed, without any evidence to the contrary, one should assume that the possessor would think the traits to be quite valuable were he to become aware of them. One should assume that he did valuationally choose them for himself. The choice just wasn't a fully conscious one. One has to assume that the individual *uses* these traits as his standard of the good but isn't aware that he is doing so. He isn't aware of who he is, yet he still, in fact, is valuationally positing his particular traits. And without any other strong evidence to the contrary (evidence other than what some observer claims *he* thinks of the possessor's character), the critic has no real case for his point.

2. The broader perspective of this book has found me basically contrasting the character self with the causal picture of infancy and early childhood. So, we saw how the object relating infant is really no self at all but only a pre-self. He is simply a very complex nest of mostly unconscious incorporations, imitations, introjections, projections, and any number of other psychic defense mechanisms that keep him from missing out on libidinal and other satisfactions through the conduit of the maternal self-object. The narcissistic infant is a rudimentary self. He is focused on having his raging wants met. He does this by enlisting the aid of mother or anyone else who would care to join in. He is clearly a personality with wants, strong emotions, perhaps beliefs (about how to get what he wants). However, all other conscious states seem to be structured around supporting, defending, and realizing these wants. Of course, mirroring and the creation of parent *imagos* come into play in the cause of helping the infant better carry out his mission of satisfying his wants. But the main theme is his having and satisfying wants. In this regard, the narcissistic infant/child is the paradigm case of the Frankfurtean notion of the wanton. He only knows that he has wants and that these need to be satisfied. Sometimes he even has second-order wants. But these are based on nothing other than a second-order narcissistic desire to have his first-order wants receive the attention they are "due" from the whole world. Nothing internally mediates these or his first-order wants. There is no pause for consideration, no thought of denying a single want from either level. The infant rudimentary self simply has

itches and tries to get all of them—if not only the most pressing of them—scratched without taking any alternative possibility into account.

The process of identification takes the infant/child out of the world of the narcissistic self and into the world of the developing character self. Here one reflexively and autonomously authors into existence his character self as an agency through which he can satisfy his desires by himself. How does this work? The self is basically a reflective being, a being that, among other things, can reflect on what would otherwise be raging narcissistic first-order wants. He can reflect on and mediate his first-order wants with any of a number of other conscious considerations. With Frankfurt and Taylor, I have argued that a character self evaluates his competing first-order wants (as well as other first-order conscious states). But the key to reflection is the introduction of second-order value states. And key among our reflective activities is the taking on of a certain kind of stance toward value. Before this point, the human isn't a valuer. Character selves go beyond object relating and develop the capacity to choose to brutely value. Creation of values is uniquely something that human selves do. It is our new psychological act. We create value where there would otherwise be none. These created values then go on to become the standards we use in evaluating the world of events and in strongly (morally) evaluating our experience. Without value standards we would remain mired in our first-order wants. Because of the introduction on the scene of values, a person no longer simply wants things. Nor does he simply want to want things. Instead, he wants to want things because he values wanting them.

What finally turns us into character selves that we own is our taking a very complex valuational stance in consciousness and placing it under the control of our internal agency. We create our own ways of valuing as moral beings (e.g., we valuate things like human dignity and respect for our fellow beings), our own ways of valuing as aesthetic beings (e.g., art and music are now seen as "important"), our own ways of valuing as practical beings (e.g., things such as work efficiency, having manners, spending leisure time, being normal, and so on become points of focus for what we think we ought to do in life), and so forth. When we place these valuational ways of being under the auspices of our internal agency, we are very much acting as character selves. But for the complex identificatory capacity of character selves, there would be no valuing in the psychological universe. There would be only the wanting of beasts and of pre- and rudimentary self humans.

Put another way, a character self is most centrally what it is in virtue of its reflectively choosing the very value standards according to which its evaluations are made and then realized in action under its own internal agency. These self-created standards become the stuff of which mediation of first-order wants is made possible. In becoming a self, the child comes by mechanisms that intervene in the heretofore uncompromising activity of his wants. Now, with a character self in the form of standards for living the good life, the child can evaluate which, if any, of his first-order desires he should cater to. He has the ingredients for a self agency that can realize his chosen first-order desires. He needn't depend on parent objects or object relating defense mechanisms anymore to get him what he wants. With his character traits qua "valuated standards of the good life" in place under the control of his agency, he has a basis for making choices about what to do in life and how to do it. And he's got the agency to do it. There is a *center* of self now instead of a jumble of free-floating wants. When a child begins to valuate standards of what he imagines the good life looks like and puts them under the control of his internal agency, he is in the process of converting from a rudimentary self to a character self. He is reflexively creating a very different kind of human psychological organization. Wants are no longer the crux of matters for the emerging internal agency. Values are. Wants and other conscious states are important to a self only insofar as they are *identified with*, that is, only insofar as they are brutely and ultimately valuated.

Through our discussion of valuation in this chapter, we have come a long way down the road of understanding psychological ownership and the concept of psychological identification. However, we are still not finished with our journey. There are other important aspects of identificatory choosing that we need to clarify. Of particular importance is the notion that a person doesn't fully valuate standards for the good life unless he takes responsibility for making those standards part of who he is. A person doesn't fully own his character until he takes responsibility for his valuated traits. Understanding this idea will be our next order of business.

CHAPTER 8

Taking Responsibility for Ourselves

A person who says that she is a certain way but doesn't show that she is committed to being that way, or doesn't show that she is committed to dealing with the consequences of being that way, isn't really the character she says she is. By contrast, a person acting as a full character self *takes responsibility* for who she says she is. This isn't always easy. For when someone acts through her character, there are normally consequences to her actions which were unforeseen and not always pleasant. Nevertheless, as a full-fledged character, she is expected to take responsibility for both her actions and their consequences. As a character, she is expected to own and own up to whatever she has done. Her willingness to do this is perhaps her strongest kind of affirmation that the valuational choices she has made in the name of being her kind of character really are constitutive of who she is. Indeed, the more fully a person takes responsibility for her valuational choices, the more fully those choices actually become who she is as a character.

Let me put the point slightly differently. To fully psychologically own the traits that one would have as her character—to identify fully with them—it isn't enough that one only reflectively choose and valuate them in the ways that we have discussed in the last two chapters. Were one only to go that far, she would have a reflective image of what she saw as the good life, but that image wouldn't yet be who she was as a character. What's missing in this picture is self-responsibility. It is in one's taking responsibility for being the ways (traits) she ultimately valuates that one genuinely starts becoming those ways as a character. Self-responsibility is the energizing force that turns a mere valuational image of character into a living, breathing character being.

In this chapter, we are going to round out our analysis of the identificatory psychological ownership of character by taking a look at various components of this energizing force. We are going to examine the phenomenological feel of a full-fledged character taking responsibility for who she is, that is, taking responsibility for the value image of life she has carved out for herself. We will proceed by

193

looking at a series of descriptions that are most commonly associated with the general concept of self-responsibility and see how they fit into the particular context of character self-responsibility.

1. The first description is about the stands a person is willing to take in the name of her character. What strikes me as most obvious about a self-responsible character is that she is someone who "stands *for* who she is," "stands *up for* who she is," and "stands *behind* who she is." Although there are certainly subtle distinctions that could be made between what these three expressions entail, I am going to focus on the meaning they share. A person who stands for or behind certain ways of living life and stands up for herself in that regard is someone who plainly cares about what she has shown of her character to the world. Those are the aspects of her self that most matter to her. She doesn't want her character taken lightly. And she certainly doesn't want it abused. She wants it respected, just as, other things being equal, she respects it herself. The degree to which she stands behind the values she claims to be her chosen standards for the good life is the degree to which she is taking responsibility for them. It's the degree to which "who she is being" is important to her. Indeed, it's the degree to which she really is who she says she is.

How do we recognize the self-responsible person in these terms? A person who is disposed to standing up for herself (etc.) is a person who is disposed to doing what it takes to protect and maintain the integrity of who she is, and she does this intentionally. In the most obvious of such circumstances, for example, when a person is threatened with bodily harm, she defends herself because she cares about maintaining the integrity of her bodily self—that is, because she ultimately valuates the bodily aspect of who she is. She is intentionally willing to fight to maintain her bodily integrity. But let's be careful to understand properly the scope of "intentional" here. Certainly having a *nonintentional* willingness to defend one's own life is true of all sentient creatures, whether they have psychological character selves to protect or not. Turtles, trout, and house flies defend their lives, as do nonidentificatory infants and children. Nonintentional *instinct* guarantees that much. There are no "intent-defining" reasons behind their life-defending behavior. There is only causal mechanism. All beings stand up for themselves at least in this regard. But someone's standing up for herself as a character is done in an *intentional* vein. It's done on purpose—viz., for her reasons. A person who takes responsibility for herself stands up for herself here in the sense that her bodily self *matters* to her. She values it. And she does what she does in order to maintain what matters to her. By contrast, preidentificatory infants and children fight for survival because of a biologically nonintentional, programmed instinct to do so.

Protecting and maintaining oneself in the intentional sense is true not only about one's bodily identity but also about the rest of who one is; that is, it ranges the entire gamut of one's valuational life. The self-responsible identifier defends her valuations if they are really to be her valuations. She has created an image of the good life all by herself and she has made her whole being answerable to that image. With so much on the line, it's no wonder that the self-responsible identifier typically does whatever it takes to stand up for that image. Human beings qua character selves protect their wholeness, their integrity as character selves against challenges to their worth. This doesn't always have to entail a physical defense. Characters more often defend who they are through argument. When her bodily or psychological survival is threatened, one fights or argues for who she is for all she is worth. There's no issue in life that matters more.

But now, let's be careful again not to confuse this activity with some similar-seeming activity of nonidentificatory children. All too often, children have the appearance of being identity selves in this regard when, in fact, they are not. That is, they often make a lot of noise in their own defense, when, in fact, they are not really acting as self-responsible characters standing up for who they are at all. Sometimes, for example, children get into fights with one another over beliefs they appear to stand for, that is, over apparent character value commitments. At the very least, bickering with one another over what "the best" this or that is—the strongest father, the best baseball team, the hippest drug pusher, the best way to succeed at cheating in school, and so on—is a favorite childhood pastime. This sort of thing certainly gives the appearance of people defending very definite identity characteristics. However, as I hope I have convincingly argued in this book, a lot of this is just appearance of character activity, personality fluff.

The fact is, there is no solid core self yet in children. There is no self there with which we adults can deal. That doesn't stop them from making bold claims about how life should be. Their bravado about such matters is legendary. However, we aren't shocked to see them all too often fall flat on their faces when it comes to practicing what they preach. We even expect them to fall. That's because we know that they haven't reached the psychological maturity yet of persons who have finally started to take responsibility for the images they have about the ideal life. But when we see them finally begin to carry out some of their bold claims about how we all should be, our dealings with them begin to change. As parents, for example, either we rejoice over the changed child's having entered into personhood in the fullest identificatory sense or we struggle over it because we don't particularly like some of the identificatory choices the child has made and is now taking responsibility for living. In either case, though, as parents, we know we are finally talking to a different kind of psychological animal than we heretofore have been. The quality of love we feel for such children probably will not have changed, but something significant about our parental stance—indeed, usually something in any adult's stance, even nonparental stances—toward them as serious selves probably has changed. These children are simply now seen as relatively solid selves to be taken more seriously. When they defend who they are now, we listen in a different way. These are characters addressing us now who are finally taking responsibility for how they are seeing the world. They are as intent on defending the character they are as we are on defending the character we are.[1]

The point is, however, that up until this time, they have not been the solid character selves they have now become, even though the heat they often have generated in the defense of their would-be selves might have been extreme and sometimes convincing. The reality is that children are, for the most part, "causal personality machines" powered by biological, psychological, and social causal forces that sweep across the human landscape. From their narcissistic development right up to the point of full character identity formation, any semblance of a character self is partly accurate but largely illusory. What we have instead is a person who stands behind beliefs dogmatically due to social causes, psychological causes, or biologically determined temperament causes. Of course, such a being is an individual with strong wants, emotions, and beliefs about the world. And in standing behind her wants, emotions, and so forth, she certainly presents the *form* of being a self-responsible, committed person. However, she is simply not yet a full character self, a person of her own intentional choosing. What's missing?

Were we to probe a bit, we would find out in short order that the child didn't really know why her commitments were important to her. She might be able to provide some causal explanation for why she is committed as she is. For example, she might point out that she is committed because her parents are committed that way. But obviously, being able to formulate such a *causal explanation* for her commitment is not the same thing as being able to give a *justification* for being a particular *character*. Causal explanations aren't the sorts of things that count as *good reasons* for one's having chosen to be the way one is. And we don't find such reasons in these contexts, because, in fact, there aren't any relevant kinds of character choices she has made yet in the first place. Indeed, if you ask most children for good reasons for their value standard commitments, they normally haven't the faintest idea of what to say. And that's because they are committed to value standards that they haven't reflectively chosen. Those standards aren't part of character. They are part of their causal identity. Although there are other causal possibilities often enough in play, children are usually just causally narcissistically mirroring or mimicking their parents' standards and passing them off as their own character. So if the causal winds in their life start to blow in a different direction—if their parents start to send out different value messages—their value dogmas will often enough change, too. But this isn't a character change. It's just a change in what children mimic. The truth is, they have some distance to go developmentally before causality bows to the power of autonomous character choosing.

The point is that the child who, say, through her argumentation, *appears* to be standing up for herself isn't really standing up for *who she is*. She is just following one causal program or another. She is not yet a person who is taking responsibility for herself. When the preidentificatory child stands up for a point of view at all, she doesn't know why she holds it (in the sense of having good reasons for it). She is often perceived by the adult character community simply as a "little grown-up person," an adult self in approximate form only.[2] What is conspicuously missing from the picture—and why we still think of her as "*merely* a child"—is the fact that she hasn't freely chosen her values and so she hasn't come to have the consequent beliefs at issue. Any choices she has made at all are either the mere playful trying out of the volitional activity—that is, it's fun to try out agency within oneself—with no real understanding yet of being committed to those choices, or else the tail-end of causal activity. In both cases, the individual hasn't yet taken on the full profile of "the brute yet rational chooser *committed* to who she is" that the rest of us have taken on to varying degrees. Because she hasn't yet become the full profile of the autonomous chooser of value standards, she hasn't yet climbed to the next step either. She hasn't become a being who takes responsibility for such choices. She isn't really standing up for her character self.

Often when we adult identificatory characters defend who we are, we present arguments justifying why we behave as the characters do. Obviously, in the case of lower-level character trait valuations, we argue by appealing to our commitment to higher-level ones. In the case of standing up for our higher level character valuations, matters are a bit stickier. By definition (of "brute valuation"), we can't give "prior value" reasons. What does count as "standing up for ourselves" then? Sometimes we appeal to claims such as "This is what makes life meaningful to me" and "This is what fits well with the rest of who I am" (the latter being a kind of "character coherence" argument). But more often, we point out that we simply are doing what persons who are character selves do. We point out that we are willing to put the full weight of our entire being behind our valuational choices *because* they are *our* valuational *choices*. We are asserting that we are willing to be held responsible for our autonomous choices and their consequences. Infants and children don't have this sensibility. Moreover, unlike children, we show the sincerity of our commitment to our autonomous choices by asserting and reasserting our valuations over and over again in our actions. As was noted in chapter 7, we decide to make ourselves this sort of person or that by consistently sticking to being these autonomous chosen ways. That just *is* the way of genuinely being a character self. Of course, doing these sorts of things doesn't really amount to any kind of logical defense—justification—of who we are. Logically speaking, these moves only beg the question. ("This is who I am because this is who I am"; "This is who I am because it bolsters up that other part of who I am, which in turn bolsters up this part of who I am"; "This is who I am because I am willing to reassert being this way"; etc.) But psychologically speaking, this just is the way that properly functioning character behaves.

Interestingly, while we might not have a logical justification for why we choose the particular brute valuations we do, often enough we *use* those *valuations* themselves *as justifications* for why we do what we do. This move is another feature of "the proper functioning of character." Let me explain. When we claim a character valuation as being part of who we are, we also put ourselves in a position to use that valuation as a *definitive* kind of *justification to ourselves* for certain of our actions. Appealing to something I said in chapter 6 (but changing my focus now), sometimes we answer challenges to something we have done by saying things such as "That is just part of who I am," "It's my nature," "I was just being myself," and so forth. In other words, we stand for certain valuations from which such an action follows, and our standing for those valuations is justification enough for us for why we did what we did. Sometimes our character just will out. And we take it that when it does, mentioning that we are acting on a character valuation is supposed to be some kind of final justification for our action, at least to ourselves. We would only hope that others see things that way, too. We would only hope that others would see that we were just honestly being ourselves in what we did, and that that should be good enough to justify the action. Aristotle has something like this in mind in the *Nichomachean Ethics*, where he argues that the moral person is someone who acts from his character qualities.[3] I am not interested in this as a claim about morality. However, I am concerned with the idea that there is something nonmorally "natural" about expressing our character values in our actions. I think what's in play here is a commonly unspoken, but nevertheless universally accepted, truth to the effect that a prime directive for being a self is that any character self should (nonmorally speaking) *be itself* and, usually, not anything else. Just as livers, hearts, and kidneys have their proper functioning as biological organs, so do character selves have their proper functioning as "personality organs." Acting from character is a central functioning of developed personalities; so, as best they can, people ought to act from character. Moreover, when they do do just that, they can point to the fact that they are doing that as a kind of supreme justification for the action that stemmed from it. For example, we say things such as "It was my right to do that" or "It was what I saw as my duty to my comrades" as though to say, "Of course what I did was justified. I was only acting naturally; I was only being myself."

Put another way, for a person to stand for a given value is to use her self as the final justification for acting as she does (viz., consistent with that value). Whether or not some publicly determined set of standards sanctions one's actions, one still feels justified in what she does when she acts consistently with the valuations she stands for. Of course, in the name of abiding by general social mores, social forces, and so on, it is certainly possible for a person to act against her character valuations and to point to those external standards as her justification for her action, even though she doesn't really believe in those standards. Here a person opts for getting along in the world instead of affirming herself. Clearly, if the world is to go around with a minimum of turmoil, it needs this sort of compromise from everyone once in a while. People must sometimes put aside their concern for being themselves in favor of the well-being of the world-at-large.

They must sometimes put aside using their character as final justification for action. This is just a principle of prudence for many of us, even if it is a brutely chosen principle of morality for others.[4] Even so, it still isn't optimal psychological functioning. The more a person develops as a character, the more she uses her valuational self as the definitive justification for her actions. This doesn't mean that she won't listen to the value claims of others or society-as-a-whole when they vary from hers. She will listen. Perhaps she will even acquiesce from time to time, at least if she wants to get along in the world. However, when she is in the mode of taking responsibility for herself, she will act from character valuations and use them as final justifications for why she acts as she does. In common parlance, we say such a person is someone who has "taken charge of her life." Others may be impressed by this or not.

2. The next feature of identificatory self-responsibility is its *"ought-ness."* Plenty of people only *partially* identify with ways of being. And that is to say that they too often fail to carry out their valuative choices. Plenty of people talk a good game. They have their ideal character pictures but they don't always get serious enough about them. They haven't really committed themselves to acting on them when the chips are down. They don't act on them as though they *ought* to. By contrast, other people are more serious about their character ideals. They follow through more often. And that's because they have actually *obligated* themselves to live out the ideal standards of the good life that they have brutely posited.[5] They have dedicated themselves to this. When people are significantly willing to stand up for themselves, they have created a sense in themselves that they *must* proceed along the track of behavior laid out by their character traits. Let's understand, though, that this sense is *self-generated*. It isn't an externally initiated command about how people should be. It isn't a feared sword that is wielded over them from the outside, perhaps from the "objective" rule-setting realm of social norms. Rather, identificatory "oughtness" is a command that people create for themselves and to which they willingly surrender. They welcome it as an internal sense of law about how they are to be as character selves. They welcome the opportunity to give themselves their own self-ruled direction in life. In short, they welcome the *autonomy* that goes along with choosing to be ruled by character. The power of their character in fact depends on how willing they are to use their autonomy in this way. The significance of their lives as character selves is measured

according to their willingness to put themselves under the rule of character law. Autonomously *demanding* that they live by certain traits is what dedication and commitment to being those traits are all about.

All too fallible, of course, even a genuinely self-responsible character self won't *always* follow through on her autonomously created "oughts." She won't always follow her own laws. She won't always act in character. There's a little anarchy in all of us. However, her commitment to trying her best has nevertheless been made. Through her self-generated demands, commands, or imperatives about how she ought to be, she quite willingly now is disposed to making her character actions speak louder than her words.

3. Clearly, self-responsibility is part of a person's ownership of her character. If she really owns who she claims she is, she will take responsibility for it. That is an assumption that is presupposed by the discussion in this chapter. However, there is another way of seeing the connection between self-responsibility and ownership that I would like to discuss. Actually, it is part of an interesting relationship between self-responsibility, ownership, and the delineation of psychological boundaries. Let me explain.

When a person thinks she owns something (when she claims ownership of it), in her mind, she has placed that something within her psychological boundaries. As far as she is concerned, that something *belongs to her*. But it isn't just part of her physical space, as is what we normally think to be the case about "legal ownership" of physical objects. It is also something that is now within her psychological boundaries.[6] In other words, as far as she is concerned, it is now literally a part of her, part of who she thinks she is. Moreover, in general, the things within one's psychological boundaries (the things that are part of who one is) are the things for which one takes responsibility. That's certainly the basic thesis we have been arguing for so far in this chapter. It follows, then, that the things a person claims ownership of are things for which she takes responsibility (i.e., she stands up for them). Now, as I said above, we already know this to be the case. ("That is an assumption that is presupposed...") But now we know it to be the case in terms of the connection of these concepts (ownership and responsibility taking) to the concept of psychological boundaries.

This connection has some interesting implications. For example, it helps to explain why property disputes are often so horrendous. In determining ownership of a physical object, there is more than the location of the object at stake. One's psychological boundaries are at stake, too. So, say one owns a house. It belongs to her and consequently she does things to take care of it. She takes care of it not just for the sake of the house itself, but also because the house is something within her psychological boundaries. She sees it as something that's a piece of herself. In part, she maintains and protects *her self* by maintaining and protecting the house. Now, imagine that a perfect stranger suddenly opens the front door and walks into her house. Clearly, she is going to feel outraged (not to mentioned frightened and any of a number of other emotions)—not only because of the legal error on the stranger's part but, more importantly, because of the invasion of her psychological space, the tampering with her psychological boundaries. The basic structure of her self would have been challenged and shaken. If the stranger then went on to actually claim ownership of the house (even though he had no legal basis for his claim) and insist that she move out immediately, her sense of calamity would be heightened even more. For she would experience this (probably not in these terms, though) as an attempt to destroy her psychological boundaries, her self.

The same general point applies to all kinds of boundaries. If one country thinks that its borders should be extended to a position not acceptable to its neighbor, there is trouble on the horizon. To maintain itself as an intact entity, any agent simply must have its boundaries of what it is the sole responsible agent for maintained and respected by itself and others. Certainly, national borders fall into that category for the citizens of any country. The borders are part of who the citizens *are*. In a manner of speaking, the country's geographical borders are within their psychological boundaries. The borders are part of their causal bodily identity, their causal psychological identity, and their valuational identification with both—that is, they identify with living within these particular geographical borders. Accordingly, when the borders are challenged, so are the citizens' psychological boundaries. War may occur not just to settle legal disputes but also to protect part of the citizens' psychological boundaries.

On the other hand, we would expect that citizens who felt no responsibility for the ownership of their nation's borders (they wouldn't take care of those borders, they wouldn't be willing to defend them) wouldn't identify with them. And so those borders wouldn't be within their psychological boundaries. Where there is no responsibility taking for ownership, there is no full-fledged identification going on. In general, someone who fails to take care of her things (i.e., fails to take responsibility for them) is someone who doesn't really see those things as belonging to her in the deep sense we are talking about. Or if she does see them as her own, we think that she doesn't really value herself as she should in the first place. She doesn't esteem herself enough to stand up for what is hers. In either case, the norm is that a person who has some item she *sees* as belonging to her is a character who is *defined*, in part, in terms of that item. But she is that person only if she also responsibly does things to ensure the value and safety of that item. She stands up for herself in the sense that she stands up for any of the items within her psychological boundaries.

I know that this view of equating who a person is with what's psychologically owned within her psychological boundaries is controversial. Plenty of people would say that I am particularly straining the point with my examples. They would distinguish the boundaries of one's "core psychological self" from *physical* boundaries, treating *physical* boundaries as mere peripherals. The psychiatrist Irvin Yalom makes a clear statement of this view. In discussing one of his clinical cases, Yalom laments:

> I had helped him understand that he had lost sight of his personal boundaries. It is natural, I had told him, that one should respond adversely to an attack on one's central core— after all, in that situation one's very survival is at stake. But I had pointed out that Carlos had stretched his personal boundaries to encompass his work and, consequently, he responded to a mild criticism of any aspect of his work as though it were a mortal attack on his central being, a threat to his very survival.
>
> I had urged Carlos to differentiate between his core self and other, peripheral attributes or activities. Then he had to "disidentify" with the non-core parts; they might represent what he liked, or did, or valued—but they were not *him*, not his central being.
>
> Carlos had been intrigued by this construct. Not only did it explain his defensiveness at work, but he could extend this "disidentification" model to pertain to his body. In other words, even though his body was imperiled, he himself, his vital essence, was intact.[7]

Clearly, I believe that Yalom has done his patient a disservice here. Yalom has *assumed* an unthought-out view of the self and has imposed it on how he does therapy. In this particular case, his doing this may have had pragmatic benefits for his patient. (His patient died of cancer shortly after this interpretation. The timing of the death was no surprise. Yalom's words probably made the patient's last days more comfortable than they would have been otherwise.) However, if it's truth we are concerned with, I believe that Yalom's unthought-out view of the self is off the mark. We *are* our identifications; and those identifications have no limits as to what can instantiate them, including physical boundaries and material objects and their traits. Those sorts of things are not peripherals if one psychologically owns them. Those are the sorts of things for which we legitimately take responsibility.

Finally, in owning one's character life, a person actively takes responsibility for the things that she valuates as elements of (standards for) the good life. That means that she maintains and protects them. She does what it takes to stand up for the integrity of boundaries of the valuated elements because they are the psychological boundaries of her character self. Each person's claims about where the lines of integrity are to be drawn for her character valuational relationship with the world are always claims about the location of her psychological boundaries.

4. To self-responsibly stand up for a trait, one must be able to exercise a modicum of *control* over how that trait gets acted out. It is to be able to be the person one thinks one is at a moment's notice. Normally, this means that one has turned her traits into the volitional habits we talked about in chapter 6. She has made their acting-out second nature. But if not this, it means that one is at least able to try hard at behaving in ways consistent with her stated character and that she often succeeds in her efforts. In other words, in genuinely taking responsibility for who she is, a person makes herself accountable for getting to a point where she finally has the execution of her character behavior under control.

Obviously, I am talking about reflexive control. One might think of the situation as the self reflexively honoring and surrendering to the power of the self over certain kinds of behavior. If I really identify with being a loyal friend, for example, then in being committed to this image of myself, I have chosen to live the image and its subtle contextual variants in the unfolding drama that is my life. I take responsibility for it. I hold myself accountable to myself and others for how consistent I am here. I further ensure a consistency in gaining a firmer control over living out the loyalty image. I thereby make loyalty behavior more me. The existing self reflexively does what it takes here in order to be itself more fully as the new self with the expanded capacities for loyalty. The self actually extends itself incrementally into a larger self, as it were, when it gains more control over new valuational domains of character. The more control a person gains, the more she perceives the trait to be part of who she is. Where a person has *total* control over a trait, one part of who she is *is* that trait. She is that kind of character. At that point, she no longer has to think about things. The trait unfolds in context automatically, without thought. Of course, in situations where there is a conflict of deeply entrenched identity values, a person is sometimes forced to think in order to decide anew about her commitment to being one kind of self or another. Or a person sometimes simply acts, being as interested as any spectator might be to see which character element will win the day.

I hope it is obvious that this control over who a person is happens with different traits to different degrees. But, then, one's identifications in part happen to different degrees for precisely that very reason. Just look at cases where a person can't control things at all even though she might want to control them. For example, suppose she would like to control her body but she is paraplegic. Certainly, such a person doesn't take as much responsibility for being the master of her body as she formerly did. She doesn't feel nearly as much the owner of what she formerly could do. Her body identification here fades away.[8] On the other end of the continuum, a person who feels total control over certain traits she exhibits normally experiences full identification. And places of control in between are obviously places of relatively partial identification.

5. Another aspect of responsibility taking (self-responsibility) has to do with *self-respect*. C. R. Snyder believes that it is how a person responds to his loss of self-respect when things have gone wrong in his life that tells us about how that person takes responsibility for his life and, consequently, about who he is as a valuational character.[9] When a person owns up to seemingly negative consequences of something he has done through his character, he feels bad about what he has done and bad about himself. To the extent that he then tries to turn things around for himself so that he can recover his self-respect, we say that he is taking responsibility for himself.

Taking responsibility here is about the individual's admission of guilt as an imperfect valuational character. It is about his embracing his loss of self-respect over this imperfection and his subsequently doing something about the situation. This amounts to his willingness to make restitution for what he has done. When a responsible person suffers a diminished sense of self-respect, he no longer feels quite as confident about being the person he has been. To shore up his flagging self-respect, he goes through the restitutive process, whatever form it may take. That is the payment a person expects from himself for the transgression he feels he has committed.

On this account, being a self-responsible person all depends on how one responds to a loss of self-respect. Let's understand that in my terms the transgression one responds to boils down to acting in ways that are inconsistent with some of one's character values. So it is valuational inconsistency that one pays for in part with feelings of diminished self-respect. One isn't quite the whole person he would like to be. Other things being equal (e.g., he's not intensely neurotic), he is willing to do just about anything to make those feelings go away and reclaim his full sense of self-respect. His feelings here are actually what propel a person toward restitution. Of course, each of us has our own internal sense of *value equality* that gets us moving. Each of us has our own rules for *character justice*, rules about what it would take to "make us even" after our transgression. One person's views about the degree of his transgression regarding his spoken valuational ideals might be very different from another person's. People always seem to be willing to tell others that they (the others) should hold themselves more responsible than they appear to do. That aside, the point is that wherever one draws the line regarding his own sense of character justice, it is in insisting on this justice in order to reconstitute a fuller sense of self-respect—whether others see the individual's restitution as *enough* (or perhaps overdone) justice or not—that we say a person is taking responsibility for himself.[10]

Now, what I want to say is that while such a view certainly strikes a familiar chord, finally I think it is overstated. Snyder seems to insist that a person is a responsibility taker *only* in the context of making a comeback from diminished self-respect. While this is, in fact, sometimes the context where a person takes responsibility for himself, it is *not* the only such context, and it doesn't seem to be a necessary one. Accepting certain kinds of gains is another quite legitimate context here. Certainly a person could feel quite good about who he is—there might be nothing diminished about his sense of self-respect—and he could still be someone who takes responsibility for himself. In fact, my view is that *whenever* a person is trying to be—and is standing up for—the ideal value images he has brutely chosen as his standards of the good life, he is taking responsibility for himself. Sometimes this might get spelled out as his willingness to endure the negative consequences (part of which include a diminished sense of self-respect) of character misbehavior, that is, a willingness to demand and endure character justice. But other times it simply means being committed to doing whatever it takes—painful or pleasant—to live by one's ideal valuational images.

6. Now, I want to follow up what we just said with some comments on a related aspect of self-responsibility. That would be the notion of *self-accountability*. We know that when a person takes responsibility for being who he is, he is willing to live by the consequences of his character behavior. Quite importantly, he is willing *to be held accountable by himself* for both character transgressions or successes. Clearly, consistent with what we have just been talking about, this can sometimes mean a willingness to suffer some punishment without much complaint when on the road to restitution and recovery of self-respect. Here the account is settled and he can, with a clean slate, resume making life decisions through his character. But a person can also be accountable to himself for ongoing character successes. Instead of experiencing a reclaimed self-respect, he experiences a heightened sense of self-respect and *pride* about who he is and continues to be. Pride is the accountability payoff when things (issues of character) are going right for a person. But whether it is working toward wiping the slate clean or basking in one's pride, the point is that this "accountability to oneself" is the more fundamental notion. The former are causal consequences of the latter, and, as such, they derive any significance they have for the concept of self-responsibility from that fact. That is, the payoffs of slate-cleaning self-respect or a heightened sense of pride are only secondary self-responsibility phenomena. Self-accountability is a primary one. The obvious question now becomes, So what about this idea of self-accountability? How are we to understand it?

In one view, a character takes responsibility for himself when he holds himself accountable to what *others* would have him be like. Of course, this view can't be right. Public values just can't be what determine a person's *self*-accountability. They can't be what determine what it is for him to *take* responsibility *for himself*. Certainly, it is true that a person can be *held* accountable for doing things that offend the value standards of others. But being *held* accountable comes from the outside, from the public, not from himself. While it is true that on some standard of public morality, a "responsible person" might be expected to make amends for any public offense, that doesn't amount to his being responsible in the sense of being accountable to himself. Moreover, while I suppose that in some sense when a person accepts public condemnation and atones for his public wrongdoing, or accepts public adulation for his living by the public's standards and continues doing so, he could be said to be "*taking* responsibility for what he has done," this, too, isn't the same thing as a person's "taking responsibility for himself" in the sense of self-accountability.

In contrast, where a person *really* takes responsibility for himself in the self-accountability sense, all the relevant activities stem from his paying attention to *his own standard of value*, not from his paying attention to the public's. So, for example, when a person feels bad about having transgressed against another, it is because he has decided for himself that "transgressing against others" is undesirable that he feels a loss of self-respect. He feels bad *to himself* about not honoring the person he identifies with being. He doesn't feel bad that he has failed to measure up to some public set of standards. When I take responsibility for myself, I am willing to suffer and make restitution when it is called for by my sense of justice. But we want to be clear here that the justice envisioned isn't determined by the judgment and value standards of others. Indeed, it often comes about in spite of what others do. It has a completely internal source—namely, what the self does and the judgments it makes about what it does. That's self-accountability.

Clearly, this view is in line with what I have already been arguing about character creation. Specifically, the character self *is* the reflexive assertion of a set of valuations (ultimately valued character traits). In living the life of a self, one asserts some such set of values—and in so doing creates them as "one's own"—and lives the ongoing project of trying to consistently match up what he actually does in his actions with what he values as a character self. In other words, he has a set of value standards for what his self should be like. As he makes himself accountable to living by these standards (or not), he feels good about himself (or not), he has self-respect and pride (or not). The central idea is that he is the source of his "self-ing" activities and of the rewards and punishments for consequences of character acts for which he is holding himself accountable. The responsibility for character creation and judgment is entirely his.

Put another way, when a person taking responsibility for himself says, "I did it" (this being an expression of self-accountability), the focus really is on the "I." To be self-responsible is for a person to see his particular mosaic of being—his cluster of identificatory valuations—as constitutive of his self. And so when one refuses to take responsibility for behavior that *others* would have him take responsibility for, he is insisting that the behavior in question is *not* part of his self. It is not one of his identifications. For example, when one is held accountable negatively by others, they are telling him that his behavior has been inconsistent with a trait of character they insist he ought to have. When one is held accountable negatively *by himself*, one is telling himself that he has failed to live according to a trait of character upon which he insists he ought to be acting.

However, that a self-responsible person is someone who is willing to be held accountable for consequences of his actions as judged against his own value standards can't be *all* there is to a character self's responsibility taking qua self accountability. There certainly are people, for example, who are willing to hold themselves negatively accountable by their own standards but who we would not call responsibility takers. A masochist is usually more than willing to accept the negative consequences of his action as defined by himself, and then some. But he certainly isn't the type of personality we would say is taking responsibility for himself. While he is more than agreeable to being accountable to his standards, what's still missing from his situation is that he isn't willing to do things to right his perceived wrongs. He isn't willing to do things to solidify the character traits he accuses himself of having transgressed. For a complex of psychological reasons, he is bound and determined to keep punishing himself with negative personal judgment. However, inasmuch as he goes out of his way not to do anything to improve his flagging character self, we say he is failing to take responsibility for himself. Not only, then, does the true responsibility taker hold himself accountable for who he is in the sense of passing value judgments on his worth as a consistent self; he also must do things to solidify that self according to the dictates of those judgments. He has to show that he *cares* about being the character he claims to be. That's a fuller kind of self-accountability the masochist just isn't interested in. He has other fish to fry.

7. Another telltale sign that a person is taking responsibility for his character can be found in the *confidence* he displays about his valua-

tions. That is, solid selves walk around with a general feeling of confidence about themselves. Even in those unavoidable contexts where a person finds himself conflicted over which course of action to take, as a solid individual he is confident enough about the *rest* of who he is so that he can be honest and forthright about his conflict and uncertainty about what is "best" in the current situation. Of course, every one of us seems to have places in our lives where we lack some confidence in ourselves, no matter how strong we are otherwise. This tells us something about the solid character self. It tells us that the ideally self-responsible person is someone who has no fears about losing his identity; he doesn't see that as even a possibility. He has enough confidence in who he is. He is neither afraid of challenges that others might raise about who he is nor afraid of the self-initiated challenges that arise in one's being aware of his sense of conflict and ignorance over what course of action to take in a particular circumstance. By contrast, the less than fully solid character is someone who does have these fears. He defends against the possible loss of self, or at least against the possible loss of the sense of self that he has enjoyed. He is "a defensive person" about that part of his self.

Certainly challenges to confidence about who one is arise often enough. Now and then they arise as a matter of honor between two unlikeminded people. Each person might have special reasons why he thinks his character traits should be acted on and not the other's. And so the challenge is boldly entered. There is no hiding from the fact that one's self is on the line here. But as unpleasant as this sort of thing can sometimes be, it is just one kind of confidence-challenging situation. There is another kind that is much more fundamental to our nature as persons and much more invasive: The very fact that another person in the first place would pick a different character mosaic than we do to mold his life with is a challenge to our confidence. We will see in the next chapter how the human condition requires that all of us try to pick character identities that we believe are, at least in part, unique. To the extent that we are successful at this, the human condition necessitates that we are all challenging at least parts of one another's character all the time. We may not always feel the challenges as intense confrontations; nevertheless, the stance of challenge is there. That is, we may prefer tolerance to rancor here or we may just avoid a conscious awareness of our built-in character differences with others, but the differences are still there. And the fact that there are these differences means that there are challenges, too, regardless of how we decide to respond to them.

But this is just the point. It is how a person responds to character challenge that tells us about his solidity as a self. If he responds with genuine confidence, then even though we might not approve of the self he has sculpted, we still must acknowledge that it is a solid self. It is something to contend with; *he* is someone to contend with. He is someone who is very responsible when it comes to following his character image of life. The degrees of confidence he has in the decisions that stem from certain of his traits tell us something about the degrees of his successful identification with those traits. They tell us how responsible he is to living out those traits.

8. Consistent with this last point, the more responsible a person is to the task of being himself, the less defensive he feels about any criticism of his character, although, as we have seen, that's not to say that he isn't equipped to justify his character decisions if he wants to do so. I am only suggesting that he doesn't defensively apologize for being who he is. The more defensive a person is about a challenged identity trait in this sense and the less in place the trait, the less secured is the self. His defensive maneuvers are not expressions of a full character self. He is not expressing his confidence in his trait-related decisions. He has no such commitment. Now, some people hold that "not being defensive" is different from "being confident." I certainly agree that a person who isn't defensive about the challenges to himself doesn't automatically always experience the feeling of confidence. But then, too, he doesn't experience a lack of confidence either. I believe he simply isn't aware of what he is here. (And that happens all the time with regard to many other sorts of psychological states too.) In fact, though, he is a confident person here, whether he is aware of this or not.

The nondefensive person we are talking about is someone who is *self-accepting*. The degree of a person's solidity and the degree of his self-responsibility is the degree of his self-acceptance. Such a person accepts the value or worth of the character self that he has sculpted through his identificatory valuations. He has self-respect, self-esteem, and pride. He doesn't respond to challenges to the worth of his self by defending that worth. That issue is a closed matter. He *assumes* his worth and so doesn't even speak to the issue. Persons who totally accept themselves in this fashion are a rare breed. We recognize them by their unflinching calm and sense of conviction when challenged. They *know* their worth. But most of us are this way only in degrees. And we are this way in contrast to the defensive person. He finds it necessary to argue for his worth. But, as we discussed the matter in our treatment of self-responsibility feature 1, the only kind of defending that a solid person does involves doing what's necessary to get others to allow his character trait-related decisions to stand; that is, the solid person stands up for himself. Such a person is actually celebrating the self, not fearing the possibility of the self's immanent demise. Clearly such a person is different from the defensive individual. Moreover, this is confidence if ever there was any. A person who accepts both who he is and the value of who he is is a person who most fully is who he is. By contrast, the person who is open to self-doubts about both who he is and the worth of his character is a person continually defending against a final dissolution of the self. Therein lies the basis for a lot of the neurotic activity on which people embark. One defense mechanism gets piled on top of another. People use these mechanisms to hide from (to remain unaware of) their doubts about the real contents of the self and its worth. They use them to protect an odd self-image that doesn't accurately reflect the traits they have really identified with.

9. What else can we recognize about the self-responsible person? The individual who takes responsibility for herself increases her stock of what we can call psychological self-empowerment.[11] When one stands up for herself, she is a psychologically stronger figure than before. I am not saying that taking responsibility for oneself *is* self-empowerment. Rather, self-empowerment is a phenomenological expression of self-responsibility. It is the final touch in recognizing the psychological backdrop of the relatively solid self. So, what exactly is this self-empowerment?

Colloquially, we say that the self-responsible individual is relatively *decisive* in her actions. She has the *conviction* of her beliefs, of her character valuations. What such a self does, she does *wholeheartedly*.[12] There are *relatively few* self-*doubts* to be found. The individual just feels that she is perfectly right in her character-based decisions. The standards of the good life that she valuationally posits she posits with a relatively full sense of the kind of *confidence* we just talked about. However, as with everything else we have been looking at, the phenomenon of power I have in mind happens in degrees. Each person is empowered by any of her character values to different degrees. That is to say, the more a person stands for her self valuations, the more decisiveness, wholeheartedness, and the like she feels about herself as a character. The more responsible a person feels for her value standards, the clearer and less hesitant she is in expressing them in her actions.[13]

To the extent that a person genuinely wants to do, and feels that she ought to do, what she does in acting out her valuational commitments, the self-responsible person has no questions about who she is. And it is only natural that she acts with conviction. After all, the degree of "oughtness" she has in taking her stand for her valuations *entails* dismissing possible challenges to the legitimacy of her decisions, leaving room only for valuational convictions. In standing for what one stands for, a person in effect decides away the possibility of value competitors. One might think of what I am saying in the following way. Before a person takes responsibility, she is just a complex of valuational *possibilities*. But in then taking responsibility for herself, she makes a commitment to a particular set of those valuations by committing herself to being fully those valuations. Recognize that she isn't grandiose as we have seen the narcissistic infant/child is. Her feelings of empowerment aren't a narcissistic fantasy. Rather, they are the legitimate result of having taken responsibility for being the separate character individual who she is in the world of separate character individuals. This person is now as fully a real self as one can be. In living through convictions, a person feels whole, unfragmented as a self. One feels the integrity of one's identity. Before this point, she was, to varying degrees, just playing with possibilities of chosen self traits. With all the clarity, confidence, and conviction that taking responsibility entails, though, naturally such a self feels powerful. After all, to be confident, clear, convinced about one's values' ultimate worth is part of what it *means* to be self-empowered.

Of course, such a person isn't always guaranteed successful outcomes for her efforts. One doesn't always get done what she wants to get done. There may be others who are more powerful than she is. Or life's unpredictable contingencies simply may have their way over what she does. One can't always be assured of successful outcomes from her character behavior, but she can assure herself a full *effort* to deal with whatever the outcomes finally look like. Facing the essentially incalculable future with the courage of one's convictions is a person's way of being herself in the fullest sense. It is one's truest test of power. Indeed, the more one actually confronts life's indeterminacies with commitment to one's character, the more power about that character one typically comes away with and is entitled to. We say the individual has proven her mettle, she has proven her character. A person of power is someone willing to try to live through her values and possibly "lose." Trying fully to be the self that one has brutely chosen to be is worth any effort, even an effort to deal with the essential incalculable future consequences of one's decisions. It is worth *everything* to the psychologically developed person. And that's because "being worth everything" is always defined in terms of the image of the ideally developed human character that each person envisions for herself.

Indeed, as we noted in a different context in chapter 7, if there were no tough, incalculable life contexts, we could always act on rational formulae in our decision making. But there would be a sense in which it wouldn't be us as *individuals* who were taking responsibility for the decisions we made (unless, of course, we identified with being purely rational beings). Instead, it would be, after a fashion, our principles and the rules of logic that were really most instrumental in doing the deciding. The act of taking responsibility is what separates the full-fledged persons from the automata. Incalculable circumstance, then, actually helps make us persons. Overcoming such circumstance further empowers our self. In order to be self-empowered character selves, we *must* involve ourselves in incalculable circumstances from time to time and depend on our character effort and some luck for the outcomes.

Planning the consequences we would have our character behavior lead to, then, is not fully determinable. Many of us get to be character heroes in this regard. We sometimes *take risks* about goals whose attainments are not totally within our control. Moreover, we even see such risk taking as part of the spice of life. It makes character life seem more worthwhile and exciting than a life that is filled with "sure things." In taking responsibility for who one is here, one's sense of power certainly soars.[14]

This will conclude our discussion of the salient features of self-responsibility. It should be clear now that in order to become a full-fledged character agency who psychologically owns her claimed traits, merely having reflectively chosen valuational images of the good life isn't enough. A person simply can't avoid also taking responsibility for realizing those images in her thoughts, feelings, and actions. That's what finally makes her a real character self, that is, the kind of fully developed character agency at which human self developmental activity is finally aimed. Obviously, we all find ourselves at different points in our battle to become such responsibility-taking beings. One thing is for certain, though. How much we are willing to fight the forces that would act against our self-responsibly being the character selves we would be is really up to us. The challenge of *trying* to be our ideal character selves—*taking* responsibility for ourselves—is completely within our province. And, given our discussion in this chapter, we know a little bit more now about what that involves. Specifically, when we decide to take up the challenge, we find ourselves, to differing degrees, immersed in a life where we stand up for our valuational choices about our image of the good life; we approach the living of our valuated traits with a sense of self-generated "oughtness"; we delineate our psychological boundaries; we have degrees of control over the acting out of our traits; we hold ourselves accountable to ourselves; we have degrees of confidence in the expression of our traits; and we enjoy degrees of self-empowerment in living through our character selves. We are self-responsible individuals to the extent that we carry out our valuational choices of character traits in the spirit of this mosaic of qualities. To the extent that we can successfully bring this about, we are people who are living life as genuine characters.

Before moving on to the next chapter, I would like to address myself to two matters. The first has to do with the autonomy/identification connection that I have talked about in the previous two chapters. Now that we have seen the crucial role that self-responsibility plays in the identifier's creation of his character, we are in a position to appreciate something quite important about the relationship between autonomy and identification. What I have been arguing in the last two chapters is that autonomy entails identification. But now I think we can also say that identification actually entails autonomy. Not only must the autonomous person identify with his choices, but the person who identifies with traits (i.e., the person who valuationally chooses those traits as his own) necessarily is autonomous in his choosing them as his own. *Character selves are essentially autonomous selves.* Character selves are beings who autonomously choose themselves into existence. Why do I say all of this?

There are three traditional philosophical tests that an analysis of autonomy would have to pass in order to be considered a serious analysis. One test requires that when an autonomous person chooses, he decides by himself—he is self-ruled in the sense that his choice is *not coerced.* A second traditional test requires that the autonomous person *not* have his choices *influenced by causal factors*, be they either external forces or internal psychological forces. The third traditional test has it that the autonomous individual be someone who can *do what he wants to do*. My analysis of identification passes all three tests. We know from our discussion in chapter 7 that when a person identifies with something, he brutely chooses to value it as his standard for leading the ultimately good life. Now we also know what it means to say that he takes responsibility for his choices in the sense that he puts himself in a position actually to carry out the program of his chosen standards. I have to believe that brute choosing and taking responsibility for living those choices are as close as we are going to come to a description of autonomous choice. It passes the test of being a choice that is uncaused, at least on our soft determinist's account of causality (see below). And it passes the test of being self-determined, not coerced. A person's freedom amounts to the fact both that, by himself, he can choose the things (traits) that make his life valuable for him and that he can effectively choose to take responsibility for making that life his own by carrying out their program in the first-order choices he makes. A person who does these things is clearly self-ruled. He creates the rules for his own life; he creates the standards. Moreover, he is able to do the things he identifies with doing. And this, I believe, is the essence of one's choices being uncaused and uncoerced. Moreover, the analysis handles the third test insofar as the autonomous person is someone who has put himself in a position where, through having taken responsibility, he can effectively live the life with which he identifies (other things being equal) and so he is able to do what he wants. He can effectively be himself.

Passing all three tests, the character self is indeed essentially autonomous. When a person identifies with anything in life, he is at the very same time making an autonomous choice about how he will conduct his character. In other words, being a character self (by choosing character) is being an autonomous being. Autonomy in this way is built into the act of identification. And so, when philosophers of the self traditionally have made claims that the essential feature of being a person is "being a being with autonomy," they have been right. What I hope I have done here is to have provided a reason why this is so. Autonomy is part of identifying. So naturally a person qua character self is essentially free.

Of course, there is still the determinist's objections to contend with. And there is also the objection that, in embracing the "bruteness" of choosing, this view of autonomy comes close to sounding totally irrational (sounding something like Dostoevsky's "caprice"). But, finally, these objections have already lost their steam. We acknowledged a version of soft determinism in chapter 6—that is, if someone is going to insist that we can always find causes for whatever a person does, then we have to say that some causes are certainly less objectionable than others, and these less objectionable ones are what we *mean* when we talk about our experience of freedom. They are what we mean when we talk about human choices being uncaused. Furthermore, I think that what we said about "brute choosing" in chapter 7 helps us dispense with the "irrationality" criticism. In the various ways I specified there, brute choosing has quite a lot of *reason to* it, although it is not *based on value reasons*. Claims of irrationality make no sense.

The second matter I would like to address is this. We have seen the importance of self-responsibility for the development of character. But it turns out that there are two basic themes of self-responsibility we haven't talked about that pervade each person's experience, two themes that we really need to get an understanding of if we are to appreciate the full texture of the identificatory life. These themes are about the basic ways in which a person stands for who he is. Simply, sometimes a person stands for certain valuations regardless of what others think, and sometimes he stands for valuations precisely because of what others think. These are the two primary contexts defining how a person takes responsibility for creating and using his standards of value for living his life. The first encompasses one's living life as a "personal identity." The second is about his living life as a "social identity." Personal identity is that portion of one's valuating that is aimed at giving him a sense of character uniqueness; that is, it is aimed at giving him a sense of being valuatively unique in the world of human valuating characters. By contrast, social identity is that portion of one's valuating that is aimed at giving him a sense of character likeness with certain others in the world; that is, it is aimed at giving him a sense of social belonging and camaraderie with others because of shared valuations. Standing for values regardless of what others think and standing for values precisely because of what others think are crucial to attaining each of these respective aims. Everything that matters to a person is in the service of one or the other of these two character self tendencies. This being so, and since our project in this book is to understand fully the concept of identification, it behooves us to come to grips with understanding what these new concepts are about. We turn our attention to this now in the final two chapters.

CHAPTER 9

Personal Identity

Personal identity is certainly a concept that gets bandied about a lot. It's one of those ideas that has a place both in psychological theoretical discussions and in ordinary parlance. And there really is no singular agreed-upon sense of the expression found in either arena. That's unfortunate. Matters don't have to remain this way, however. In fact, I believe that if we look at personal identity from the context of what we have been saying about identification, there is definitely some welcomed order we can bring to the concept. I am convinced that part of what lies dormant in many of the different uses of the term has to do with my ideas about the self-responsible valuational life. I will argue the case for this in the present chapter.

I

The first thing I want to do is show what the evolution of personal identity development looks like. With that in mind, what I propose to do is briefly review in this section some of the Part I material about self development and then explore in the next two sections the particular kind of valuational development that is peculiar to personal identity.

To begin, let's remember one of the basic motivational forces in the infant's psychological development, a force that plays on a person throughout life. I have in mind the drive toward individuation. Along with developing a self agency for getting satisfaction of all varieties of needs and desires, the impetus to separate from the self-object and become an individuated being is taken to be another of the major lifelong, seemingly biologically programmed, internal prime directives by which a person lives. We are always trying to individuate into unique selves, and the action begins during earliest infancy. I am going to argue that the carving out of the individuated self vis-à-vis creating valuations is the main accomplishment of personal identity formation. But the developmental ball starts rolling during earliest infancy.

The infant pre-self becomes a locus of psychological defense mechanisms all aimed at getting a host of needs and wants met (e.g., sexual satisfaction, security, comfort, etc.). These mechanisms all emanate from the infant mind/body and they serve to preserve her survival. There's nothing like a reflective consciousness in force yet under which all of these defensive moves are organized and evaluated. There's nothing like a self-conscious being. Rather, the infant is more like a mechanical servomechanism, a sophisticated goal-directed device run by a set of programs that are "thermostatically" aimed at survival. She is a "unified theme" in this sense. Ascribing anything more than this thematic set of programmed behaviors to her—ascribing anything like, say, an adorably coy personality when she coos and giggles or in other ways "responds" to adult prodding—is pure fancy. Intentional personality qua character doesn't really exist here. It is only projectively put there by the infant's beholders—us. What is real is that psychological mechanisms such as incorporation, imitation, introjection, and projection are all functioning and aimed at mind/body survival. In the early stages of this pre-self activity, the program calls for symbiotic immersion with the caretaker. The aim of this immersion is to enlist the aid of an agency to get the mind/body's built-in needs met. Symbiotic immersion into that agency, primarily through incorporation, is the center of activity at this point. That symbiotic connection is the most primitive human precursor to what developmentally later becomes the character self. When the caretaker begins to lose interest in continuing the symbiosis, new built-in infant programs aimed at immersion in stand-in caretakerlike objects unfold. At this stage of pre-self activity, the still singular theme of bodily survival is played out through introjective and projective object relating to caretaker substitute objects. It gets done with both new material objects and ideational (fantasy) stand-ins. These are attempts to defer any *final* separation from the symbiotic reality with the caretaker.

At the same time, there's another, seemingly conflicting program unfolding. While, on the one hand, the infant is object relating as a way of being part of a symbiotic reality, she is, on the other hand, now beginning to behave in ways that suggest a concern for individuation from the caretaker. The pre-self infant in these complex ways is still "trying" to survive as an entity in the world. But where, to this point, she has enlisted the agency of something beyond the mind/body to get the job done, now things start to change. Symbiotic relations become too precarious. So the infant now begins to show signs of "concern" for becoming a separate self, as though she is meeting a new causally programmed prime directive. She insists on the paramount importance of her wants over those of any competing beings in the world, as though there is something unique about herself that needs catering to. At the same time, she uses mechanisms of object relating to hold onto the fantasy of not being separate from the loved caretaker. Separate and not separate (i.e., individuated yet safe)—the best of both worlds.

We recognize this new phase of development as the major theme of infant narcissism. Infant activity is now aimed at acknowledging, consolidating, and celebrating the infant as a unique entity of special value, value beyond that of the other discrete entities in the world. Narcissism structures come into play as new templates to be laid over experience along with the battery of object relating mechanisms. But the object relating still keeps the fantasy of symbiosis seemingly viable. At the same time, the new narcissism mechanisms pump life into the infant's new fantasy that there is something uniquely special about her as a separate entity. Of course, the new mechanisms along with the object relating ones are still powered by survival interests. But now there are hints of movement toward developing an agency within the mind/body; that is, there are hints of the development of a subjective self, a self-consciousness, a character self with its own internal agency. The budding "rudimentary self" is now on the scene.

The aim of this version of the self is crystal clear; everything is centered around the theme of having one's wants satisfied. These are what we described earlier as pure wants, wants totally unmediated by any reflective considerations such as the deferring of gratification for some greater good, the denying of gratification, and so on. The infant now is a causal mind/body identity that is the locus of a complex of wants. Being unmediated by any self-consciousness, these wants are unbridled; virtually every want "insists" on satisfaction. In this regard, the infant appears grandiose. She appears to be an entity acting in the interests of herself as a distinct and important being. And she gets some help with this suggestion from external sources, too—parental figures try to help the infant meet her every desire. For a while, anyway.

Eventually, parents stop trying to satisfy the infant's every want. They start placing demands on her. But in doing so, they start treating her as though she were a separate being, a separate self. And they convey this idea to her. The parents start esteeming the infant now, not so much when she behaves as a creature of unbridled wants, but more when she acts as an individuated being, a being who can do certain things on her own. The parents provide the ground rules for her becoming an individuated being who can still count on parental assistance for agency once in a while. By showing their notion of what is to be valued in life—through their insistence that the infant behave in certain ways and not in others—the parents become models for the child's first brush with the concept of values. These values become the "parent *imago*" that follows the infant for the rest of her life. The infant learns to behave according to the *imago*. This is her ticket to receiving esteem (love) from the parents. But this esteem isn't just the adoration that infants get in the earliest stages of development. It is esteem for being a special being, a unique "person" of value. The bargain has now clearly been struck. If the infant learns to behave in ways that the parent values, ways that often require deferring wants, then the infant will receive esteem from the parent, not to mention continued parental agency in getting infant wants and needs satisfied.

Two oppositional tendencies are raging now in the infant/child: one, to have her every unbridled want met through the agency of the parents, without any consideration yet for developing an internal mind/body agency; the other, to act as an individuated entity aimed at developing "her own" agency, that individuated entity being defined partly as a being with grandiose wants but also as a being who is beginning to defer some of those wants in the service of meeting the value demands of the esteeming parents. In time, the oppositional balance becomes functionally impossible to maintain—the infant can't continue to play out both tendencies. There wouldn't be optimal survival value in that, for honoring one of the tendencies weakens the other. With the help of the parents' eventual desire to separate from being the main agency for the child's survival and satisfaction, late infancy/early childhood development takes a dramatic turn in the direction of self agency, a self agency blossoming under the organizational theme of becoming a character. In the process, psychological development heralds in the complex mechanism of identification. The infant/child—actually, more the young child—slowly begins becoming a thematically reflective choosing, valuational, responsibility-taking being whose behavior more and more gets placed under the control of an emerging internal agency. All of this now becomes the infant/child's central life project. She very slowly starts becoming aware of her first-order narcissistic wants as well as other first-order conscious states. But being aware of these isn't enough. She also begins reflectively choosing values (valued modeled traits) to use as standards of value for deciding between her first-order wants. She very slowly begins valuationally choosing which of the heretofore narcissistic first-order states will be the ones of preference in her life. But she also starts making valuational choices about certain value states that heretofore had been causally installed by her parents—those parental *imago* values. Up until this point, these were working on her in a causal way. Now it is up to her either to choose to value these values for herself, to change them, or not to make any choices about them at all. From now on, there will always be something of a battle going on inside of her between merely acting in a causal fashion though the parental model of value—that model guaranteed to feed her fantasy of parental love and acceptance—and brutely choosing to value those values for herself or not, as well as brutely choosing to value other conscious states (e.g., some narcissistic wants) as standards for the good life or not.

In doing all of this, the human being is finally opting for creating agency in the mind/body through what we know of as reflective consciousness. It does this by reflexively creating the character self—that is, by creating itself as a reflective conscious chooser of a good life, a life of self-determined and self-responsible value. This doesn't happen overnight. It is a long, drawn-out affair. In very young children, this identificatory activity is only very sporadic. There are only very sparsely arranged dangling threads of self-aware brute valuation going on in the early years. There are only brief glimpses of this new kind of organizational pattern for experiencing the world. But the new pattern definitely is on the scene. Now, instead of functioning exclusively as a being who is merely aimed at *satisfaction* of raging grandiose narcissistic wants, the young child starts forming self representations. In different terms, she starts exhibiting a psychological organization that moves her away from mere want gratification toward more and more *brute valuation* of pieces of a vision of the good life. This new valuational capacity actually constitutes a character self that is the locus of valuational activity and the locus of the consequent evaluations and actions the self brings to living. As long as this activity is still sporadic, however, a person hasn't become a full-fledged character self. What else needs to occur?

Identifying one's self into a fully grown character self seems to happen in three stages. It appears that there is something of a critical mass of valuations (we will call this stage 2) that has to obtain before children begin even to experience life as a character agency.[1] Before that point, one's most primitive identifications are just the self-aware valuational strands I just mentioned (stage 1). And, in fact, we wouldn't even call these valuations a character. That comes with the arrival of the critical mass. And when *that* finally happens, that's *still not* a person's becoming a *full-fledged* character. That won't start to unfold until adolescence, stage 3.

What a stage 1 infant/child experiences is something of a bare-bones valuational existence, an awareness that there are certain things unfolding which he now uses to define some globally nebulous sense of who he is in the world as a discrete individual. But talking about his seeing himself here as a being with a character makes no sense. According to some child psychologists, a person normally begins having this bare-bones sense of self by the age of two.[2] In my view, perhaps the first of these strands appears with the narcissistic infant/child identifying with his body. Up until this time, the body and its behaviors have only been part of the person's *causal* identity. Before now, he hasn't identified with any of this causal activity, as he hasn't had any capacity for any identification until now. He simply has been protecting that part of his causal identity according to bio-logically determined programs. Since bodily survival seems the centerpiece of the human agenda, then it is only fitting that the earliest of valuational acts be aimed at brutely valuing the body. While, before, one's body was part of one's (causal) identity even though it wasn't reflectively *one's own*, now one brutely chooses to see it quite pointedly as one's own and as something of great value. Since there is only one body per customer, a person brutely chooses to make the maintenance of it one of the value standards defining his image of the good life.

Making this value choice and taking responsibility for it is tanta-mount to making that way of valuing a constitutive part of who one is. Part of being this emerging nebulous self involves standing up for the integrity of the body. That is, people from the earliest age defend themselves. And as we saw in chapter 8, they do this not just as a matter of programmed instinct (as in the case of very young infants) but also eventually as a matter of genuine valuational concern for themselves. Once this part of a person's causal identity is valuation-ally affirmed, from that point on, one always measures any of his prospective life choices against this standard of value. One measures any of his life choices against his valued physical survival, as well as against other valuational standards that develop along the way.

Identifying with one's body, then, is undoubtedly among the first identifications a person has. However, although surely it is a strong and centrally important peer among early identificatory peers, there still is not enough of a network of identifications in force to constitute any reasonable facsimile of a character self. There's certainly no network that's complex enough to constitute the critical mass required for being a character self. There is mostly a self-awareness of one's being a self-valued physical body. Such a person is only moving toward character identity existence. His main existence, though, is still as a causal identity. Indeed, as I have said, in the earliest stages of identification, there is a battle going on between, on the one hand, causal narcissistic object relating and, on the other, striking out in this new direction of becoming an individuated identificatory self agency. Causal object relating doesn't just roll over and die once valuations of the body appear. It takes some time before the infant/child begins to "trust" his identificatory powers. So it is likely that in the beginning, identifications occur along with the occasional narcissistic desire. And this pairing goes on for quite a while. What, then, finally marks the coming of the critical mass of the identifying child? When do we adults think we are in the presence of a "real" identificatory self when we are around children? When does the child self become someone to reckon with as a solid person? When do we begin to believe that we are dealing at all with what Erikson and Wheelis (chapter 2) call an "integrated self"?

The answer: when a child shows signs that he values himself as a coherent historical psychological being. That is, when we sense that he identifies with his personal history—when we sense that his personal history has been posited by him as an item of ultimate value—we are well on our way to believing that he is becoming a full-fledged character identity. Identifications with one's personal history are the critical mass events that mark the coming of the character self. But let me be very careful now to explain what the idea of "identifying with one's personal history" amounts to, for there is much room for misunderstanding here.

Everybody has a personal history at any age. Clearly such a thing is always part of one's causal identity self. It is during childhood that one begins to become aware of this part of his causal identity self. Even the infant starts to become aware of his personal history in the sense that he shows evidence of knowing what his daily routines have been and will probably continue to be, who the people of significance in his life are, what it is reasonable to expect of his need gratification in the immediate future, and so on. As he grows older, he becomes aware of his detailed life with his family, his play with his friends, his part in social institutions, and much more.

Knowing these things about himself is a very important part of his life. But what I would like us to be careful about understanding right here is that a person's knowing his personal history is *not* the same thing as his identifying with it. And so when I claim that the critical mass necessary for becoming a legitimate version of a character self involves "identifying with one's personal history," I want to be certain we are clear that I don't mean by this that the individual who knows a lot about who he is vis-à-vis his personal history is a person who therefore is finally a character self. A person could know a great deal about who he is as a causally created personal history and yet not be much of a character self.

Unfortunately, sometimes people mistakenly run these two ideas together. This mistake is often made because there are two uses of "identifying" that people confuse with one another. When a child knows a lot about his personal psychological history, it surely is the case that he is able to *identify* who he is in the sense that he recognizes the detail of his personal psychological history. But this epistemic notion of "identify" doesn't transform a person into a character. One can, of course, identify his personal history qua causal identity. However, again, knowing about one's causal self—being able *to identify it*—isn't the same thing as *identifying with* it. And it is the latter that gives a person enough identificatory critical mass to start becoming a genuine character self. Well before he begins identifying with his personal history, the child is able to identify it. Indeed, he might well be reflective—self-conscious—about this part of his causal self. But he can be reflective about this and yet not be identifying with it.

Let me give an example of how this confusion can occur in adulthood. Suppose I am driving home, thinking about the projects of the day that are in different states of completion, incompletion, maybe even disarray. I am thinking about the indefinite immediate future— a part of my unfolding personal history—I have in front of me. It constantly meets me head on. Perhaps I am considering the meal I am going to prepare and the work I am going to do after dinner. This is common enough, innocent enough. But, then, a lot of consciousness is filled with such mundane moments. A lot of our personal psychological histories are about our being immersed in these sorts of concerns. Such moments often enough seem to be so much the very heart of who we are. It's tempting to say that they are the very heart of our character. Tempting, but wrong. What's indisputable is that such moments are central to our continually unfolding personal histories. And we want to believe that our personal histories, with all their common and subtle bumps, contours, and pieces, are one and the same with our character selves. We are tempted to believe that who a person is from moment to moment is primarily about a self-conscious involvement with life's passing concerns. Certainly we recognize, clarify, sometimes rationalize, often have complex emotional responses to, evaluate, plot out strategies for, suffer and appreciate the consequences of, and nominate as permanent fixtures in our personal history such passing concerns. And we do precisely the same sorts of things for the more dramatic concerns of life. The fact is, though, all of this is about the epistemic stance we take toward our causally based personal history. Just because a person experiences things that happen to him in the personal and social flow of life, that doesn't mean that everything he experiences is part of his character self, that is, that doesn't mean that he's identifying with it. What we can say for certain is that it is always part of his *causal identity*. But simply knowing that one is a certain causal identity way isn't synonymous with identifying with that way. Knowing about identity isn't the same as identifying with that identity.

What are the telltale signs that a person finally has started identifying with his personal history? Quite simply, when we are convinced that he is *attached* both to his memories about his life and to what is unfolding about his life before his very eyes—that is, when we are convinced that he is attached to his past history and to his immediate history. He won't let go of any of these items very easily. He treats these historical events as ultimate valued occurrences. Understand that I am distinguishing here between (*a*) "not letting go" of facts about one's personal history in the *epistemic* sense that one won't deny what he knows to be true about himself as a causal identity and (*b*) "not letting go" of facts about one's personal history in the *identificatory* sense that one will stand behind parts of his personal identity and take responsibility for the value of being those ways. He incorporates the items of his personal history into his standards of the good life. He treats them as standards against which he will evaluate the worth of what he and others do in life. Say, for example, he identifies with being a member of the aristocracy, where before he simply knew that he was. In now identifying with this part of his personal history, he is positing it as a filter through which all his interactions with people will henceforth pass and be judged.[3] This part of his history has now become part of his character.

The point is, through his budding identification with his personal history, the individual—and normally this would be the latency child—has started organizing enough of a critical mass of identificatory valuations for us to call him a character, although not yet a fullfledged one. He is not quite there yet, but he is definitely moving in the right direction. Brutely and self-responsibly valuing parts of his history constitutes his owning that history. And an owner of a psychological history is someone we all can deal with as a relative equal in terms of what kind of selves we are. He is someone who falls under the general category of character. Of course, as a latency stage individual, there is a lot of filling in he needs to do yet—moral education, improved rationality, social graces, and so forth. But at least now he is in the right ballpark.

What will make him a full player? What we are still waiting for from him apparently doesn't really begin in earnest until adolescence (stage 3). And then that gets enlarged or transformed with varying degrees of change throughout the rest of his life. This third stage is marked by the appearance of what we will understand as the "personal identity self." The latency child valuator for some time has been brutely and self-responsibly valuating in order to create an individuated value self. The adolescent and adult do this, too. However, they add a new wrinkle. Not only are they interested in individuating character agency, they also *matter to themselves* as *unique, distinctive, character selves*. Let me explain.

Up until this point, there was no mattering of the self to itself. As an infant, there were, of course, many raging narcissistic desires that the individual went to great insistent lengths to have satisfied. But that wasn't "having wants that mattered to him." "Strong insistence for satisfaction" is conceptually different from a thing's "mattering to a person." For something to matter to a person, that person must value that something. The infant's having raging wants that are programmed for satisfaction is not the same as his valuing those wants. The stage 1 and stage 2 identificatory self can valuate and thus be said to value certain of his narcissistic wants. So, too, then, can those wants be said to matter to him—they matter to that person. They matter to him a lot. They become "issues" for him. As the individual takes on more valuational mass, more things matter to him in this way. During these two stages of identifying, the individual starts ultimately valuing one life project after another. However, in none of this mattering activity is the individual mattering as a self to himself.

Eventually, though, one begins to value ultimately the identificatory self itself. It isn't until the self begins to do this that the individual becomes a full-fledged self. This is stage 3, the time of personal identity. Here the self reflexively valuates the self as the definitive character object. This happens through its third-order consciousness of itself as a reflective second-order character consciousness. It is in ultimately valuing (on the third order) what one is becoming as a valuational self (on the second order) that one becomes a personal identity, or a full-fledged character self. In plain words, when one finally becomes a personal identity, one is self-consciously concerned with really being a person of quality. One is concerned with doing what he thinks needs to be done to realize himself as something distinctively good in a world of selves. Moreover, consistent with what we said in chapter 8, such a person is also finally a fully autonomous character self. Being a character qua personal identity self entails being autonomous, and vice versa.

Again, adolescence and adulthood seem to be the time for getting the job(s) done. These are the times for getting focused on who we are. They are the times for making certain that we stand out as someone special, at least in our own eyes. In this regard, adolescent high school and college students have a lot more than just hormones chaotically churning away inside of them, driving their behavior. Reflexively carving out character is playing at least an equally important developmental role for them. Of course, a person's identificatory processing doesn't end with the work they do here. As I say, it is really a lifelong affair. However, it happens with a definite intensity during adolescence. And character issues seem most dramatic during this time. There certainly is a more rapid turnover of new choices during this period. Moreover, the holier-than-thou earnestness of adolescents toward what they mistakenly see as the various "best" character choices they have made is legendary. Adolescents often become insufferable to their parents, who have to hear about all the supposed virtues of their newly born-again personal identity children and about the supposed parental character bankruptcy that these same children are so expert at pointing out. But besides this unpleasant edge to the adolescent emerging personal identity, there is also an admirable existential component that appears. Adolescents seem to get the idea that personal identity character building is something that each of us can only do for ourselves. They realize that they have to go it alone. And normally, by this point, they also have enough internal agency strength and enough nerve to start carrying this out. That is, they marshall the nerve to stand alone with commitments or at least to start seriously testing the personal identity waters. They try out being alone with certain values, finally discovering, and in some cases even celebrating, the meaning of solitude. They try out, that is, taking full personal responsibility for the living of their lives. An awesome undertaking, even if it is a rather tenuous proposition at this stage in life.

II

Where are we now in our discussion? As a character self, a person is about the business of meeting the primitive prime directive of becoming an individual. So she eventually begins to identify a self into existence. But as an adolescent and then as an adult, a person becomes specifically a personal character identity. She works toward making a self that matters to her, a self that matters to itself. All of a sudden, she starts caring very much about the detail of who she is as a character.   And in particular, she cares very much about becoming a *unique* individual, different from all others. In growing as a personal identity, she takes more and more pride in living a valuational life in precisely certain specific terms and not in others. She self-responsibly stands up for herself as a unique individual.

With all of this in mind, what I would like to do in this section is sketch the big picture of what a person is aiming for when she tries to sculpt herself into a unique, distinctive individual character. What is the life of personal character really about? Exactly how is it that one's buying into that life leads a person to a sense of uniqueness? To get the discussion of this underway, I want to offer the following two preliminary caveats.

The first is a caution about what I do and don't mean by the role of uniqueness in identity. It's important to keep separate the notions of a person's unique personal character identity and her unique causal identity (what we can call a "personal causal identity"). There are aspects of a person's causal identity which make her quite distinctive, without her having to valuationally lift a finger. For example, nobody ever is precisely the same locus of bodily causal relationships as anyone else. Each of us has a causal bodily identity that is one of a kind. Moreover, in our conceptual scheme, one and only one bodily identity is allowed per person. A similar situation holds for a person's causal psychological history: one per person, and much of it is unique. Yet we want to be careful not to confuse these kinds of unique causal identity with what I have in mind by the valuational notion of personal character identity.

We can make the point in a slightly different way. Although in becoming a personal character identity the individual is carving out a distinctive character self, there will always be plenty of her personality repertoire that is distinctive but not an expression of her character. In particular, part of any person's distinct causal self will remain just that—causal and distinct—and have full play in her life. She only senses some of her unique projects—viz., the ones she most centrally identifies with—as part of who she is. There will always be some other projects that are part of a distinctive "her" but that she doesn't identify with. And so she will often undertake these other distinctive projects, not for reasons of valuations she has posited, but rather because of various sorts of preference, the latter being part of her causal identity self. For example, getting a fence painted might be a unique project I have as a preference. However, since painting fences isn't a standard on which I grade my character—that is, I don't identify with being a fence painter—then doing this distinctive job well or at all will in no way directly affect how I feel about my *character self*. I won't directly take identity-related responsibility for this part of my distinctive self (although I might make some aesthetic judgment about the job I've done). Indeed, doing the job well or at all will affect how I judge my self only if this unique project is *attached* to other unique life projects that are part of my character identity. For example, I might identify with being a promise keeper. So if I have promised to paint the fence, then doing so or failing to do so will be something that affects my view of myself. But fence painting per se won't enter the realm of my identity. And in general, we can say that a person never becomes so much of a personal identity that she is always putting her self on the line in everything she does. A good chunk of the human experience is, and will always remain, living out of pockets of existence where one isn't acting as a character self but rather as a causal self or no self at all. Only some of what we show the world in our unique being is our personal character identity.[4]

The second caveat has to do with the struggle that becoming a personal identity often involves. Although people fight to carve out a personal identity aimed at making them distinctive in the world of valuative selves, they do this against a tide of events that would move them in the opposite direction, away from uniqueness. For example, we are endowed with causal temperamental traits that would seem to make us anything but unique identities. Most of the time, our temperamental traits are genetic copies of temperamental traits belonging to our parents or other ancestors. We might in general be trying to be different from other selves, but right away many of these temperamental traits defeat the uniqueness project. Temperamental sameness is difficult to fight.

Difficult, but not impossible. Sometimes we take our causal temperamental endowment and give it "our own special character." Either we decide exactly how to affirm valuationally that temperament or else we change our responses to it. We take responsibility for how we will act out our causal predispositions. We autonomously make them our own, as opposed to allowing them to remain something that happens to us. That is to say, we try to give our *chosen* valuational style to how we act on the *causally* endowed general temperamental similarities we share with others. Our own special twist on what we share with others becomes our uniqueness maker. Because of this, we believe that we are not exactly like our forebears. The same can be said of the other *non*causal traits with which we come to identify ourselves. The traits we first see modeled in the external world and then make our own are our copies of things in the external world, but copies with distinctiveness. That is, identification involves some amount of making ourselves similar to things in the world, but only to a point. We finally demand putting our own particular spin on any general traits we share with others. Any general trait category that we value we value in our own special way. My point is that even though we work hard at making ourselves distinctive, we are fighting a tendency that would move us in the opposite direction.

These two caveats understood now, what can we say about the general profile of a personal identity? As with everything else we have seen regarding self building, personal identity building starts with primitive activity that only eventually works its way into the real thing. So we have to start this profile by taking this primitive activity into account. It is a primitive uniqueness-making kind of valuation that begins during early childhood and doesn't quite have the unique *character* features we only start seriously developing later. Put another way, it is only aimed at not-*quite*-yet-character aspects of a unique personal identity.

We take this first crack at valuational uniqueness by focusing on the kinds of things I talked about above; namely, our bodily and psychological (personal) history valuations. We continue the process here we started during infancy/childhood. In continuing to treat our own body and psychological history as being of ultimate importance in the realm of all human bodies and psychological histories, we make our first kinds of bold statements about just how unique we see ourselves as being. Consequently, quite early on in our identificatory careers, we already have nailed down for ourselves a self that is distinct in the world of selves. And we continue embellishing it as we grow. We go around in life doing what it takes to keep the integrity of our unique embellishments intact. Most of us, for example, groom ourselves in our own favorite ways in an effort to present a bodily self to the world that has its own distinctive marks. We comb our hair, flash our smile, dress in a certain style, and so on, all with the aim of presenting a self we think is uniquely us. Then, too, many of us master the physical expression of our bodies in what we intend as varying distinctive ways of being a bodily self of ultimate value, as in athletic activities, body building, dance, sexual encounters, and much more. The valuational activity aimed at a person's body is a lifelong project; only death finally stops it. The same can be said of our psychological history. We maintain its integrity through our memories and how we make those memories the coherent backdrop of our response to experience at any given moment in time. At any given moment when I am acting on the world, I do what I do always in the context of my belief that I am simply continuing the line of events that are part of the unique integrated valuatively ultimate history I know of as mine. I respond to that particular distinctive psychological historical backdrop and not to any other. Each of us is this way. On the rare occasion when a person doesn't do this—as, say, when a person ultimately valuates a psychological history already spoken for (e.g., when a person believes he is Christ or Napoleon) or when a person ultimately valuates many psychological histories (as in the case of acute multiple personality disorder)—we say her identity is in crisis (at the very least).

But this bodily and historical personal identity that begins for us so early in life isn't nearly enough for any of us as full-fledged characters. We insist on much more distinctiveness than just what our unique body and history offer. So as adolescents and adults, we begin more earnestly to brutely value many things in the world beyond body and psychological history. We make life projects out of friends, work, social institutions, abstract ideas, and much more. That is to say, we so value some of these things that our involvement with them is actually constitutive of who we are. And we reflectively see the sum of these projects as a unique set of traits that constitutes our personal identity. How is all of this more "mature" personal identity activity to be understood?

Actually, the philosopher Richard Rorty says some things that fit nicely into the picture I have in mind. I am referring to what I pointed out in chapter 1 about his notions of "final vocabularies" and "ironism." Slightly tailoring Rorty's ideas, we can say that the unique valuations of our life projects are expressed through our final vocabularies. Rorty says,

> All human beings carry about a set of words which they employ to justify their actions, their beliefs, and their lives. These are the words in which we formulate praise of our friends and contempt for our enemies, our long-term projects, our deepest self-doubts and our highest hopes. They are the words in which we tell, sometimes prospectively and sometimes retrospectively, the story of our lives. I shall call these words a person's "final vocabulary."[5]

Rorty believes that the way each person fashions his own particular final vocabulary makes that person distinctive. Each of us has our own special set of words that tells the story of our life. In my terms, each of us has our special set of words that outlines our image of our very distinctive personal identity. These words correspond to our special sets of valuations which are uniquely ours. Of course, these words have the same general connotations that other language users put to them, but there are subtle nuances of meaning that are uniquely ours. And the final package of words is different from any other final package. (And where, miraculously, we discover that this isn't so, we go on to make it that way, just so that we can continue to feel unique.) Inescapably, each of us is the mosaic of our unique final vocabulary about what is of ultimate importance to us in life.

Knowing a person's final vocabulary, then, is another way of having a fix on a person's personal identity. While I obviously like Rorty's idea here, he unfortunately goes on to draw what I think are some faulty inferences. Since these inferences are instructive for our discussion, we will take a moment to look at them. Rorty believes that since each of us has a final vocabulary, we also end up being "ironists" about such matters. Again, what this means is that people with final vocabularies ought to realize that no one's final vocabulary—unique or not—is really any better than anyone else's. For each of us has simply posited the words we have decided on as our final vocabulary. (In my terms, we simply have posited the vocabulary's ultimate value.) But we could have chosen (posited) otherwise. And so we ought to realize that any final vocabulary is open to revision by its possessor. This is the mindset of the ironist. Rorty goes on to further conclude that ironists' renunciation of the attempt to formulate criteria of choice between final vocabularies...puts them in the position which Sartre called "meta-stable": never quite able to *take themselves seriously* because always aware that the terms in which they describe themselves are subject to change, always aware of the contingency and fragility of their final vocabularies, and thus of their selves.[6] (italics mine)

Too bad for the ironists. That, though, is what Rorty thinks is the acceptable price we must pay for the luxury of having our own unique final vocabularies.[7] Clearly that is *not* my position about our final vocabularies. While we certainly ought to renounce any attempt to formulate criteria of choice between final vocabularies, we also certainly ought to take our own final vocabulary very seriously. Indeed, we do, and rightly so. Sartre's meta-stable person is someone who hasn't yet come to terms with her final vocabulary as identifications. Her "bad faith" with herself here—her not being able to take "who she is" seriously—is her own particular psychological problem that's a predicament for anyone who has special difficulty in psychologically identifying. Such a person indeed cannot take herself seriously. However, that's not the general human condition. Rorty has failed to appreciate that most people have final vocabularies not as disinterested vocabulary window dressing but rather as fully invested valuational commitments to who they are as personal identity selves. People stand up for their vocabularies because these vocabularies are words designating who they are as special beings. And often enough, people stand up for their vocabularies even in the face of extreme disagreement from others. They stand up for their vocabularies regardless of what others think. So while, as we saw in chapter 7, who people are is a contingent matter (they could have been otherwise), who they are is not a fragile or disinterested ironist self. Rather, they are a self of serious moment. They are a self which, while identification with what their final vocabulary designates is in force, is relatively solid and relatively unopen to self-doubt.

The point we can glean from this is that not only is the personal identity expressed through our final vocabulary unique, but this is a uniqueness that each of us *stands up for regardless of what others think*. We defend the specialness our character has for us in the face of whatever anyone else has to say about it or in the face of any external challenge to change it. Contrary to what Rorty's ironist would do, we don't blithely let go of who we are as a personal identity. In genuinely identifying with certain traited ways of being, we self-responsibly stand up for those traits regardless of what others think. After all, it is *we* who have chosen for our character uniqueness. We *want* to be unique. So, of course, we stand up for our uniqueness in the face of any challenge. If we finally cared more about what others thought made for good character values than what we alone thought, it wouldn't be *our* unique character we were creating. It would be someone else's. We wouldn't have the seriousness of purpose about personal identity building that's required of full-fledged characters. So naturally we stand up for our valuations regardless of what others think.

Of course, matters can change when we have new valuations and corresponding vocabularies conflict with the reigning ones in our life. But that isn't the norm over the long view of one's tenure as a particular kind of personal identity self with a particular final vocabulary. Change is the exception, not the rule. The rule is that we spend a good deal of our time autonomously expressing, fine-tuning, and taking hefty amounts of responsibility for our valuational choices. And we do this not because we have to but rather because we want to. Moreover, we prune these valuational choices so that they become what we believe are unique variations of a general valuation that anyone else might share with us. So, not only is an identificatory solid person serious about her final vocabulary, she is also serious about the unique nuances that its words have for her.

But what are the particular words like in our final vocabularies? What are the general categories and what do they tell us about personal identity? The words are about the deep commitments we make to how we think we ought to live our lives, the projects we ought to pursue. These words can vary in style. Sometimes people take the broad view in describing their character selves; they dispense with any interesting detail. For example, an intellectual person might describe herself as basically someone who, because of the choices she has made, can't help but pursue a life of knowledge which she values so highly. A superpatriot might define herself in terms of her extreme valuing of her country. An egoist might identify with being someone who values her own survival most highly, and so she might grade herself on how well she does the job. These examples are quite general descriptions of a person's character. They just describe general tendencies. There is clearly much more to the individual than just such generalities, though. In fact, there is usually an overwhelmingly vast complexity about who a person is that she takes pride in. So one's final vocabulary goes well beyond blanket terms like "intellectualism," "patriotism," "egoism," and the like. What do some of the more specific, less broad terms look like?

Most of us would probably begin answering this by pointing to a list of moral virtues. "Who am I? I'm the unique person who believes in and stands up for the importance of honesty in life regardless of what others think. I'm the person who believes in loyalty to friends being sacrosanct. I'm the person who believes in selfless altruism," and so on. Whether and to what extent we actually live by such things is another question. The fact is, we typically define ourselves in part by some such set of moral virtues. And most of us draw from the same general list that Western civilization provides, although the lists of virtues from other cultures no doubt would do just as well. Wherever we draw our moral virtues from, though, each of us goes on to put what we believe is our own particular slant on them. And we go on to stand up for them regardless of what others think.

Moral virtues, though, aren't nearly the half of what goes into a final vocabulary and personal identity. In fact, there's no limit to what could count. As we know, people brutely value traits that allow them to function in the everyday practical contexts of life. In this regard, it is the general categories of social life that condition the kinds of traits that people even consider. So, for example, most of us formulate clusters of value standards around issues of work, friendship, politics, religion, sexuality, leisure time, love, marriage, food, play, money, and more. Most of us have a complex of valuational attitudes toward how we conduct our marriage, our money, and so forth. These attitudes are not adventitious. Rather, they are part of who we are. They are either valuations of first-order conscious states we have about marriage, food, play, and the like, or they are valuations of responses to these social contexts that we have seen modeled in the world beyond ourselves.

Whatever the source of our valuational content, though, the fact is that, in order to distinguish ourselves from others who would face those same general social circumstances, we make our particular attitudes uniquely part of who we are. Moreover, as personal identities, we stand up for these particular attitudes regardless of what others think. We are serious about our practical concerns. The relevant contexts here range anywhere from the profound to the mundane (mundane as far as the rest of the world is concerned). But whichever it is, in answering a challenge in practical life, we are often quite serious, at least when we are answering through our personal identity, through our deep valuations. For example, we all commit ourselves to our own special vision of sexuality that we bring to the various social contexts where sexuality is an issue. That vision gets spelled out in subtle, complex behavior repertoires that evolve through the changing sexual contexts of our life. We generally describe the subtle ebb and flow in simple blanket value phrases. But even though they are simple and general, these phrases are really doing quite complex descriptive duty that it would take a veritable psychoanalysis to fully unpack. So where a person might describe herself as "basically a person who is after sexual conquests" or "basically someone for whom sexual pleasures are accept-able only after an honest sense of intimacy has been fashioned," these descriptions actually are simple designators of very complex central valuational tendencies that are seen as unique and quite important to the individual. There are whole clusters of value attitudes toward sexuality that fall under each of these blanket phrases.

Perhaps the clearest indicator that a person is acting through character and not through some aspect of causal identity is the appearance of attendant emotions and final vocabulary emotion-packed terms.[8] Where emotions (and an emotion-packed final vocab-ulary) tend to accompany how a person is being, how he is being tends to be who he really is as a personal identity. Put another way, peo-ple regularly identify themselves with their emotions—typically the stronger ones—and the character valuation states that surround them. A person can be working out the details of a social encounter with another person and not have the faintest idea that there is any-thing of his character self or the other person's character self on the line. The social objects might seem to have a life of their own and have nothing to do with the two individuals' selves. But once emo-tions start flaring during the encounter, both people know quite clearly that selves (and final vocabularies) are at stake and to what extent. They both begin to pay more attention to what the two of them are so emotional about, suspecting that they both have a char-acter self stake in things. And they are usually right. If, for example, a parent gets extremely upset because his child has lied to him, it is a good bet that the parent both identifies himself with his anger and disappointment as well as with the ideal of honesty. Part of who he is as a personal identity ("the honest one") has been denied by his child, not to mention that his child has expressed an aspect of her own self that the parent would rather be different.

Whatever kind of personal identity indicators we have available to us, however (there are others besides strong emotions—just ask a stoic), the fact is that in the commonest of situations, people confront each other with their personal character selves. Clearly, in these situations, people make their accommodations with one another. They try to get along with one another as best they can. But this is always done against the backdrop of people trying to be distinct in their responses to the common social world they confront. In that regard, a lot of life can be viewed as requiring negotiation. The aim is to let everyone be themselves but also to find a common course of action in any given practical context so that there isn't anarchy or war between them. In other terms, the aim is to let everyone have his own final vocabulary but also to find a common vocabulary through which civility can flourish. Life is a tenuous balance in this regard. Each of us as a personal identity is trying to live out our unique valuational image of life and speak the final vocabulary that constitutes us. But, at the same time, we are trying to allow others their way in life, too.

Obviously, we don't always get the hoped-for social harmony here. In living out her value standards—in being the personal identity one is—a person sometimes ends up offending the life standards that others hold. Indeed, that is precisely the kind of story we hear about Gauguin. He valued the project of being an artist; he valued it as constitutive of his self. That project was "the given" against which all else was measured in his value scheme. Its words were part of his final vocabulary. It was part of his personal identity. But in order to be the unique personal identity self he wanted to be, he had to leave his family. Not everyone was happy about that. One person's personal identity statement sometimes becomes another's personal identity disaster. This is true of all of us and the life projects we make into our standards for living. I might get into a debate, for example, with a student over issues of racism. It could become clear in short order just what's at stake in our affirming our respective positions. One of us might define himself in terms of the ideal of justice, racial or otherwise. The other might define herself in terms of being superior to people of color. That is, one person's sense of personal identity gets expressed and affirmed by spreading justice whenever he gets a chance. The other's gets expressed and affirmed when she can compare herself favorably next to what she wants to see as a racially inferior person. For both of us, to be ourselves will probably end in one of us stepping on the other's toes. Such is life.

None of this existential disharmony is something I think is obvious to everyone. Nevertheless, just look at any life being played out on the social stage. You very quickly see the special personal identity that each individual sees himself as, conflict or not. All of us confront one another through our final vocabularies, often unbeknownst to us. That is, people often fail to see that what they are interacting about might be of ultimate self value to the other person and themselves. Of course, sometimes we catch on. We see that the other person is really standing up for the project she is talking about regardless of what we think about it. She is standing up for it as her unique commitment to that project. And what's at stake isn't just some inconsequential project. What's at stake is something that is constitutive of her personal identity. It is at moments such as this that we appreciate the uniqueness of one another, even if we don't always like it. This becomes obvious in just thinking about the most common of situations where we have found ourselves in heated debate. Something quite personal is at stake. In short order, we are willing to go to the wall over issues of, say, freedom or how we will spend our leisure time or how we should spend our money. We won't allow anyone else to dictate their terms to us. Our response is so essentially us. We start reflectively appreciating our valuational choice here about how we want to live life. We start appreciating our value commitments as being personal, as being distinctively who we are and something we won't let go of without a fight. We see that the same is true of the other person. It is in the most common of contexts that such a profound understanding of life arises. These realizations of ourselves make for perhaps the most personal and some of the most exciting moments in being alive.

Everyone is like this. But perhaps adolescent children are most vocal about it. They exert a lot of energy in showing all who would pay attention just how different they are from their parents and just how pained they are about any suggestion to the contrary. Obviously, finally, they aren't all *that* different. But it is their human due to try to become as different as they wish. Most of us spend the early part of life having to listen to adults tell us just how we are the spitting image of one parent or the other. And as I have said, when we reach adolescence, the internal directive to become a unique personal identity most decisively becomes fully functional. We are ready to begin seriously carving out an identificatory self beyond just body and psychological history. Since we have heard our whole life long about our similarities with our parents, we do whatever it takes to break loose from this image. Sometimes that involves valuational rebellion. Other times, it involves developing our own talents in our own special ways and integrating them into our lives in our own unique fashion.

But whatever we do, it is always about how we will respond to the practical contexts of everyday life.

Let's pause now to get our bearings on where we have come in the discussion. Our concern in this section is to give a general profile of personal character identity. So far, I have been arguing that a distinctively unique personal identity emerges in the individual's taking responsibility for valuating images of the good life vis-à-vis her body, her psychological history, and the traits she would use in navigating the common contexts of social intercourse. What these valuational images are about can be seen in the final vocabulary a person uses to express her life. She isn't an ironist about this vocabulary at all. That is, she is quite serious about living specifically the valuational images of life that she's chosen and no one else's. We make this point by saying that the individual stands up for her valuations regardless of what others think.

Now, these ideas certainly capture some important aspects of the life of personal identity. They show us some of what it is for an individual to be aimed at meeting the prime internal directive to individuate, to carve out a distinctive unique character for himself. But this isn't the whole of matters. Let's see what else we can say about the profile of personal identity.

We know that we can't help but share some general categories of responding to our social environment with many others. There just aren't enough responses on the menu of possible responses to go around. So to continue individuating into selves, we bring our special commitments to what a given valuated trait *means* to us. The self makes its traits mean something to itself in the sense that it chooses its own unique degree of self-responsibility (commitment) to living those traits. Each of our character traits has a distinctive special meaning to us that others can't share. We autonomously stand up for our character traits in our own inimitable way and to our own chosen degree, regardless of what others think; and, in so doing, we perform the finishing touches on constituting them as part of who we are as personal identities. In this way, people *make their own meaning* in life. How?

Essentially, we choose what we would put of ourselves on the line in the defense of a given trait. That is what the "meaning" of that given trait is to us. "Meaning" here is what a person is willing to do to hold onto a part of himself.[9] And what we put on the line for a given trait is another part of the character self. We show that living by a given valuational trait is so important that we would be willing to sacrifice the expression of some other part of who we are in its defense. We would be willing to interfere with one part of us in order to protect another. And that other part we would be willing to interfere with in turn gets its special importance defined by yet other character valuations with which we would be willing to interfere. A willingness to give up a part of the self is as much an individual commitment to a way of being as anyone can expect of a person. After all, the character self is as valuable an item as there is to a person. It is the ground from which all of his value life springs.[10]

What we have here is a personal identity that is a *hierarchy* of valued ways of being. The individual commits to all of his valuations, but always on a hierarchy he has chosen. After all, he needs to be able to cover himself in conflict situations. The particular style of commitment to each element of the hierarchy is defined in terms of the relative importance each element has to the others. Clearly, the most dramatic of such hierarchical commitment relations is seen in the person who is willing to die rather than compromise some ideal for which he lives. What this situation amounts to is that the individual, who presumably valuates physical bodily survival for at least the reasons we discussed above, has determined that his valuation of, say, freedom is of greater character importance to him than his valuation of his bodily survival. They are both important, but the ideal of freedom is *more* important than bodily survival. "More important," of course, sounds odd if we have acknowledged that any valuation is an *ultimate* value standard for the good life. However, there is a sense to the expression. One valuation on the hierarchy is more important than another in the sense that the *degree* to which a person is willing to take responsibility for his valuational commitment can vary from valuation to valuation. The relevant consideration here is about how much of his self (the other parts of his self) he is willing to give up as a way of standing up for who he is. How much does a given trait mean to him? In our example, if a person can manage to live out both valuing his bodily integrity and his concern for freedom, that will be the best of all worlds. But if he can't—if they are in conflict—he will opt for defending the ideal of freedom, because that's the ultimate value for which he takes more responsibility. It is that much more meaningful to him. Indeed, our nation has always depended on the expression of freedom being higher in a person's character hierarchy than bodily survival. Playing to the cause of freedom has always been the prime mover in getting young men (and now women too) to go off to fight our wars. It is part of the American character—that is, the typical American character self—to find meaning in valuing freedom over everything, even bodily life.

In any such case, what the individual is doing is whatever it takes to defend the highest parts of his character. For if he didn't, more of him would be "character dead" than if he compromised the value standards he holds on the lower level. More of "who he is" would be gone. We can imagine such a person saying something to the effect that his life was no longer worth living. In a straightforward sense, this means that a particular highly placed standard (on the hierarchy) of what defines a life of value (worth) has been extinguished for the individual. In failing to express this standard, he hasn't been himself. Life has, accordingly, lost the most important value for him.

The hierarchies for most of us are not structured like this example. Although we might be willing to die for freedom, it is a different story when it comes to most of a person's other values. No matter what we may *say*, most of us have bodily survival quite near the top of our character hierarchy, if not at the very top. So when another character value conflicts with bodily survival, we opt, sometimes hesitatingly, for survival. We might feel terrible about the choice we have had to make. But we live with it because we've held onto what is of *most* value to us. Pity the person whose hierarchy has a lot of deadlocks, whether they are deadlocks between bodily survival and certain ideals or just between the ideals themselves. When conflicts arise between the stalemated elements, the individual doesn't know what to do.

Whatever the hierarchical relationship between parts of our character are, though, the point is that we become distinctive individuals for ourselves insofar as we make our unique complexity out of these hierarchical relations. Of course, it is logically possible for two persons finally to have identical hierarchical composition. I suppose if this were to happen to two people, we would simply have to say that they weren't fully unique. Each would have to say that there was someone else just like him in character. Of course, at that juncture, most people would go on to appeal to the fact that at least their valuated bodies and histories were different. That fact would seem to protect their personal identity distinctiveness. And if someone were to press even this point by pushing the logical possibilities to cover similarities with body and psychological history, too (as some philosophers are disposed to doing), that would cloud the issue of personal identity distinctiveness still more. But even this possibility wouldn't finally defeat a person's claim on distinctive individuality. For each of us is so fully immersed in our experience of what our character parts mean to us in terms of the relationships they have with other character parts that this immersion itself is enough to affirm our distinctiveness. The act of making meaning is itself a uniqueness-making activity.

There is just one more aspect of a person's character uniqueness that I want to talk about in this section. It has to do with the idea that what a person stands for as a unique individual quite often comes out in the *claims* he makes about certain *rights*. As a personal identity, one's responsibility taking often presents itself in the form of his *claiming rights for himself*. Let's see what this idea amounts to.

First of all, exactly what is meant here by "claims"? While it is a person's actions that are so important in evaluating what he stands for, what he says still has a great deal of importance, too. Specifically, it is in what a person says about his character values that we can see what values he lays *claim* to. Not only are there these values that he is willing to be held accountable for, but, perhaps more important, he is also willing to *express himself* essentially through them. That is to say, he has decided to make these values the expressions of his central way of being in the world, and he is willing to tell the world this. He is willing to tell the world that this value image is his choice of what's best in life. It is his choice for how he will be; no waffling by him allowed anymore. There's nothing defensive in this stance. Rather, the individual now is immersed in the act of most fully expressing the self. He is as alive as a character person can ever be. To the degree that he is standing for certain values, he is finally really being that image of a personal self that he has imagined. Claiming that image as his self is tantamount to telling himself and the world just who he is and what his feelings of integrity, self-esteem, self-respect, pride, and individuality will revolve around.

If this is what "claiming" is, what is it a person does as a personal identity when he lays claim to certain valuations as his *right* to live by? One's personal identity valuations are always valuations he feels entitled to act on. This feeling of entitlement and his assertion of it to both himself and the world are what "claiming a valuation as a right" is all about. That is, in laying claim to value standards we have chosen to live our lives by regardless of what others think, we are *asserting an entitlement* we believe we have for acting on these values. That's not to say, of course, that all the rights a person has are things he lays claim to. There are some rights that are externally designated formal entitlements, entitlements that political entities anoint a person with but that the individual doesn't necessarily lay claim to. We might think of these as "social rights," valuations one's group of choice considers important enough to make into group entitlements but that the individual nevertheless disregards. He just doesn't focus enough on them to have them count as being values he stands for regardless of what others think. In other words, he doesn't assert this right as a personal identity valuation. Indeed, voting is often viewed in this way. A person may have the political right to vote, even though his apathy has pushed him to a point of not laying claim to this right. His fellow democrats share the social valuation of voting. However, he doesn't care about expressing himself through the vote. And if he does express it, it is only by force of habit. In any case, he doesn't lay claim to this formal entitlement as his own. He doesn't stand up for it.

Now, what about the person who *does* lay claim to his rights? He generates and asserts the entitlements he feels. He stands up for his valuations regardless of what others think. Were he to fail to stand up in this way for a value that he sees as an entitlement, then, to that extent, he would fail to take responsibility for life. Claiming the valuations we genuinely care about as our rights is an important part of what it is to take responsibility for our lives as personal identities. A person who doesn't claim as a right what is so centrally his is just not fully involved in his life. Moreover, he isn't respecting himself either. A person who respects the worth of his self insists that his valuations be honored in the arena of human interactions. Insisting in this way—laying a claim—is how selves function when things are running optimally. Just as computers compute, baseball players play baseball, and so on, selves assert, insist upon, lay claim to their cared-about rights. These are the people whom we generally acknowledge as taking responsibility for their lives.

Claiming rights, though, goes beyond just asserting entitlements. It involves a willingness, other things being equal, to make certain that what one sees as his entitlements are honored by others. In making authentic rights claims, an individual is insisting on being treated as a person who is entitled to the personal identity valuations he has made. In standing for certain personal identity valuations, the self-responsible individual doesn't let other people step on his right to live those valuations. He goes out of his way to make certain that his rights are honored. Suppose, for example, I am denied a promotion to becoming a senior partner in my firm even though I have met all the requirements for it. Because I care about who I have made myself in my professional persona—that is, because I know that this is fully a part of who I have become—and, presumably, because I know that I have done what it takes according to public standards to receive such a promotion, I will assertively demand that I be promoted. I will fight the good fight if necessary. Were I not to say anything and, instead, assume that I would get the promotion at the next opportunity, I wouldn't be a person of self-respect. I probably wouldn't really be a person who fully knew what he identified with around the issue of the promotion in the first place. With either of these factors working on me, I wouldn't be taking responsibility for my self. The point is, a person who takes responsibility for his personal identity self stands up for his rights, where this requires his knowing what his entitlements are and his claiming them because he respects the self (*his* self) that has them. He is willing to take on the world for his rights if that becomes necessary; he is willing to defend himself as a unique individual. Of course, this doesn't mean he is always inviting such a challenge. There's nothing objectionable about having one's entitlements acknowledged by others. In that case, one can go about the business of living as an individual through accepted claimed rights without having to make *special* claims.

III

That completes the profile of personal identity uniqueness. There is another feature of the identificatory life, however, that is part of the organizational theme of being a mature personal character identity that we need to talk about. It is no less important than the distinctiveness-making activities we looked at in the second section. It is the idea of *valuational consistency*.

When an individual starts getting serious about carving out a distinct personal identity, he begins to think much more carefully than before about consistently practicing what he preaches regarding his ideal vision of the good life. Now that he reflectively sees his identificatory valuations for what they are—his unique character self—he becomes even more invested than before in being that particular self. His self now matters to him as a global character phenomenon. The surest way of being that self is to live out consistently his valuational commitments. Anything short of that consistency is a piece taken out of his being. If, for example, a person claimed a strong commitment to a life of honesty and then told us lies every five minutes, we would conclude that he really didn't have the commitment. His behavior wouldn't count as his "standing up for who he is (for what he valuates) regardless of what others think." And so his character wouldn't really be as settled as he suggested it was. If he continued to claim the commitment, then we might conclude any of a number of things about him—that he was lying, that he was confused about the concept of the given value, that he was crazy, that he was evil, that he was insincere, that he had a lesion on his brain, that he was weak-willed, that although he wanted to become a person who held this value, he, in fact, found it difficult to do because of old conflicting value tendencies, or that he thought he would like to be a person who held this value but, in fact, was just deluding himself.

Valuational consistency, then, is certainly a very important component of being a personal character identity self. But realize that I am not talking about the knee-jerk consistency required by our concept of rationality, the kind of activity belonging to a causally driven kind of consistency. That is, I am not talking about the person who is driven by some causally built-in command of rationality to be valuationally consistent. Rather, what I am talking about is a person's autonomously choosing to be consistent—his deciding, for his own reasons of ultimate valuation, to be committed to acting consistently on what he believes he stands for regardless of what others think. Let me put it this way: Autonomously generated consistency is the *fundamental way* of *expressing* one's commitment to a valuation one has made. It shows that the given distinctive character trait matters to the individual as much as he says it does. It is the crucial evidence that the unique character trait really is his very own.

Of course, although a person's giving a full effort to being consistent shows who he really is, we have to realize, too, that to every rule there are exceptions. And this rule is no exception. Inconsistency for a personal identity might be allowable once in a while under certain conditions. Surely, for example, we would accept that a person is occasionally forgetful. Passions could momentarily cloud his memory. It is conceivable that a person committed to honesty could, on rare occasion, forget his commitment and "act out of character" in the emotional heat of a situation—for example, in some political fervor or intense religious debate. But this would have to be a rare occasion. What's more, we would expect the individual naturally to experience and show great psychological pain when it was pointed out to him that he temporarily forgot about his deep value commitment.

There is another context where we actually would *expect* less than total consistency between claimed valuations and behavior from a personal identity. I have in mind situations of internal valuational conflict. Here we would expect our hierarchy to determine which value we would act consistently on and which we would not. Life can sometimes be unfair in this way. We can all expect such conflicts once in a while. That's what makes a real-life dilemma a dilemma. We would rather not have to choose against one of our valuations, because there is so much accompanying psychic pain. However, there is no avoiding it. That we are able to make such painful choices is still another mark of what we recognize as a full-fledged personal identity. We care enough about being the self we have posited that we would struggle with such situations. Were the individual to find himself in similar conflicts between inconsequential desires, he wouldn't struggle, and he wouldn't suffer any particular pain in having to act inconsistently with one of them. He would just cheerfully move on to the next order of business. With our valuations, though, it's a different story. We really care about being consistent, because it is the core us that is at stake in the process. Of course, sometimes in order to avoid any pain and the need for choosing between valuations, people unconsciously engage in the psychological process of denial, self-deception. Sometimes that is all a personal identity can really be expected to do to protect itself from intolerable amounts of pain.

I must point out, however, that valuation inconsistency in conflict situations doesn't always end in either deep internal valuational struggles or self-deception. There are many circumstances where a person doesn't practice what he has preached in one context but does in another, yet he feels no qualms about the apparent inconsistency. As a matter of fact, some social psychologists have actually raised this idea to being a norm about persons. Benzion Chanowitz and Ellen Langer, for instance, point out that people routinely perform complex behaviors that might involve inconsistency but that lead neither to a sense of internal psychological struggle nor to self-deception. And that's because the person simply places those behaviors in different cognitive universes. He sees them as apples and oranges. And so what might appear to an outside observer as an inconsistency doesn't appear that way to the individual. A person might have one set of values he identifies with in business, for example, and yet be untroubled by any conflict this set might have with other values he identifies with in different contexts—say, in the moral life of his intimate relationships. Chanowitz and Langer ask how these distinctive values and the distinctive sets of social behaviors they give rise to in two different contexts can so routinely get accomplished without an awareness of the difference leading to internal strife. They answer this way:

> For each social environment, a socially situated identity of
> the person (i.e., a social "self") emerges that exhibits a knowl-
> edge of the skills and conventional standards that are appro-
> priate for action in that environment. A loose confederation
> of selves (each of which has a semblance of coherence that is
> ready to identify with a particular environment) cohabit the
> person....Character is constituted by the mosaic of these
> selves....[T]here is no necessary unity to the person....The
> person whose character is less than perfectly consistent is not
> a sick person. What looks like an inconsistency in *character*
> from the outside observer's view does not necessarily pose a
> conflict for any one of the selves on the inside.[11]

And then:

> The problem of life becomes how to incorporate and/or keep at
> a distance the disparate sets of standards that each have [sic]
> value in their distinct settings. When two different selves
> join together in a fashion that is more intricate than that
> which either possessed alone, we have observed what could
> be called the process of *self-inception* as the two earlier selves
> are dissolved. Life's project then becomes a matter of sur-
> passing the present with a character that reflects a more
> encompassing, co-ordinating, and satisfying integrity.[12]

In this view, we either learn to keep two enemies apart or we figure
out how to show them that they really have enough things in common
(self-inception) to warrant their focusing not on their differences but
on their similarities. This is what we do with children who dislike
one another. This is also what we do with ourselves when different
"social selves" from the "loose confederation of selves" (that *is* one's
self) are in logical conflict.

Finally, I don't think that we *are* literally a confederation of
selves. The self, as I have argued, is the complex unified act of identificatory valuation that we send off in different directions over our
lifetime—that is, we fashion any number of standards for how we see
the good life. In my terms, what Chanowitz and Langer really show
us is that these different directions are not always consistent with
one another, yet any inconsistency need not necessarily cause a sense
of struggle or self-deception for the singular self that each of us is. I
agree with them about this. However, they go too far. For one thing,

they don't seem to appreciate, even as a possibility, the crucial role that consistency plays in a person's forging his character. In fact, "valuational consistency" is part of the *meaning* of "character behavior." They seem to be blind to this. For another thing, I don't think that we are always best served by the "self-inception" maneuver. In fact, self-inception isn't always a real option. Sometimes a person's identifications are in an internal opposition for which there are no conflict-dissolving higher-order values. So there is nothing to self-incept to.

But while I disagree with Chanowitz and Langer over these points, I agree with them that, while not always the case, we do sometimes simply have conflicting identifications that, in a certain way, function and keep their distance from another. We come to realize that different kinds of practical social contexts are open to different, even otherwise conflicting, kinds of identifications. In my terms, what Chanowitz and Langer actually establish is that there are "ranges of social contexts" to which our character traits are our response. Any identification is functional within a given range but not outside that range (i.e., it is not functional in a different range). So the businessperson who regularly bluffs in order to get what he wants in business contexts might feel no strain about what he does at the office when he thinks about it in the confines of his home, relaxing with his family, living happily and honestly (i.e., where he would never even consider bluffing) in domestic tranquility.[13] Business life and domestic life simply are two separate ranges of social context. Bluffing is functional in one, honesty in the other. When an honest character fails to be honest within some of his domestic contexts, he suffers the strain that we all demand of a genuine character trait inconsistency. But when he fails to be honest in business, there is no strain, because he is outside of honesty's appropriate contextual range.

The upshot here is that character valuations require consistency *within* a given range of social contexts but not *between* ranges of social contexts. This seems right about how people behave. This point actually is a further commentary on the idea of hierarchy we discussed in the last section. Not only do valuations differ slightly in how much they matter to a person (where each relationship of difference defines the meaning that any valuation has for a person), but they are also at times in what we might call a "hierarchical obliqueness" relationship with one another. Oblique values are values that do not fit, bolster, entail, make sense of, or otherwise support one another. But they aren't logically inconsistent with one another either. They simply mean nothing to one another when one value on a character value hierarchy is being compared to another that is on the hierarchy but is realized in a different range of social contexts. There is no inconsistency within a context here but only the appearance of inconsistency across contexts. And that's really no inconsistency at all. All we have are two obliquely related character values on the hierarchy. But when the two valuations are inconsistent within a social context (or within a given range of social contexts), their relative positions on the hierarchy are quite important. The higher trumps the lower in order to put conflict to rest.

Of course, the obvious practical problem one wants to be able to settle here is how a person is to *know* when a valuational inconsistency is *within* a range of contexts and when it's simply *between* ranges of contexts. How does a person know where struggling over conflicting values is appropriate and where it isn't? Good question. I am not really prepared to say how. It will have to suffice that there are clear cases of each and that when we are immersed in them we know what to do. Having said this, let me return to looking at what happens to a person when he faces inconsistency within a given range of social contexts and struggles to resolve the conflict.

Where valuational consistency is an issue, there are psychological state accompaniments to one's expression of character that are worthy of noting. Most generally, when a person drifts from consistently acting on one of his identifications, even just momentarily, he suffers a certain amount of feelings of *lost integrity*.[14] Perhaps in the heat of emotion, he forgets himself and acts out of character. Even so innocent a lapse as this leads to at least a slight sensed loss of integrity. Normally, we refer to this as the ebb and flow of a person's sense of *dignity*. How we feel at any moment about that is a good indicator of how close or distant we are from acting on who we are as a core personal character identity. Dignity suffers in any of us when we fail ourselves. Normally this is subtle. We don't usually stray from our character all that far, nor do we usually suffer *that* much lost dignity. However, whether we stray far or not or suffer significant amounts of lost dignity or not, the point is that in responding to the unpredictable circumstances of life, most of us aren't always perfectly our ideal character selves. We go away and come back, then we go away again and come back again. And we pay the psychological price, no matter how small. None of us likes even the faintest twinges of lost dignity. So when we come back to being our ideal selves, we normally return with a bit of rededication about staying. Even so, we can count on losing that commitment on future occasions; we can depend on life and its surprising contingencies throwing us a curve that will push us off the track again. It is that difficult to be a personal identity all the time.

When a person does stray from being himself, it most often happens because his inclinations "get the best of him." He slides into acting like Professor Frankfurt's wanton. Instead of acting on some high-order character valuation, the individual allows his wanton tendencies to get the better of him. This typically means that he opts for some first-order desires without the mediation of any character valuations. He makes his decision about what to do based solely on the intensity of his wanton desires and not on character valuational standards of the good. He has momentarily forgotten about his principles and has opted instead for his (unmediated) selfish narcissistic desires. Or, more simply, he has been blinded by his selfishness. Still a character in the main, this individual eventually recognizes his transgression and experiences extreme psychic pain. He may "feel rotten about himself." Clinically, we talk about his feelings of diminished self-esteem or self-respect. Psychic pain of this sort is a person's payment for not being himself. Were one to act inconsistently with a claimed trait of character and *not* feel the slightest twinge of such pain about his self-esteem, we would suspect that, for any of the reasons just enumerated, he didn't really have the personal character identity he thought he had. He really didn't matter to himself in the way he thought he did.

Conversely, when a person acts consistently with who he thinks he is, he experiences, no matter how subtly, degrees of felt *integrity*. We say he has his dignity, his self-respect, intact. Consistency might be the hobgoblin of small minds, but it is also the singularly most important ingredient for feeling integrity. Moreover, I believe that the need to maximize a continuity in having this feeling is another one of life's biologically programmed psychological directives we are hardwired to try to follow. When things go awry, we can't help but suffer psychological pain. When we are successfully being ourselves, though, we are continually after, and succeed in getting, the integrity feeling. At least that is the norm. And we usually are in the midst of success, so much so that the felt experience of feeling integrity doesn't stand out. It is part of the relatively unnoticed everyday backdrop of successfully being our consistent personal identity selves. On the other hand, there are also familiar backdrops of inconsistency and flawed integrity in a person's life that don't particularly evoke much notice from the individual. For example, the person who identifies with being an altruist as his moral perfection and yet also identifies with an egoism that is more than likely rooted in causal biological sources is someone walking around in a constant state of dulled annoyed undercurrent feelings. He is walking around with a negative feeling that he can't quite put his finger on; it is nothing that jumps out at him and announces itself in no uncertain terms.

People usually don't appreciate what they have until they lose it. This is as true about our personal character identity selves as it is about anything else in life. When inconsistency imposes itself onto the character scene, our psyche is thrown out of kilter with the curse of lost integrity. And there's nothing enjoyable about feeling a loss of integrity. People normally will do almost anything not to lose at least their "sense" of integrity, even if they have to end up deceiving themselves into thinking they have acted in character when, in fact, they haven't. Short of self-deception, however, integrity loss can't go unnoticed by the human psyche. The everyday flow of concerns comes to a halt until we can get back on an even keel regarding our sense of integrity. Identity values must be anchored and a consistency of their appropriate behaviors must be honored. At least that is the internal dictate under which the psyche normally works.[15]

Even the individual who only momentarily strays from practicing what he preaches suffers the pangs of lost integrity. Think of the thousands of cases where we stray momentarily. We might smile at a supervisor at work just so he will believe we are thinking well of him, even though we aren't. It is just a convenience for us, or so we think. But, in fact, it is one of life's little insincerities that always comes with a price. For what this is is a straying from who we really are as a valuative being. We momentarily forsake what we really identify with. We stray so many times just to keep the world away from our private selves—sometimes we just want a breather from letting the world see who we are. Most times these little transgressions of self are nothing to bother over; we can get through the momentary twinge of integrity loss. We can live with ourselves over the long haul. But these transgressions do have a cumulative effect. Each person has his limit. And when it is reached, the normal flow of the psychological system is put on hold. In place of this normal flow, a chaotic spinning of psychological wheels occurs in the form of the individual trying desperately to get back his sense of integrity. He makes amends for his momentary character inconsistency because he doesn't want to experience it as a character loss. Each of us chooses the method of our liking for making such amends.

IV

There are problems of character inconsistency that go beyond these uneasy feelings of integrity loss, however. There are problems that cause terrible feelings of psychological imbalance and actually threaten the continued psychological existence of even a heretofore full-fledged personal identity self. These problems range from the uneasy feelings of *identity confusion* all the way to the trials and tribulations of *personal identity crisis*. I want to say a few words about these notions in this final section.

The psychological norm would have each of us develop a personality with a relatively solid personal identity. With this in mind, most of us do whatever needs to be done to anchor a reasonably solid personal identity. But sometimes the ordinary machinations seem nearly impossible because of what I'll call "identity confusion." Sometimes the introduction of a new social structure into a person's life doesn't allow her to continue being exactly the same kind of personal identity she has been to that point. She no longer can consistently live out of a particular trait she has been living out of. Who she has been all along suddenly gets suspended in the new situation.[16] And so, in the short run anyway, she feels a confusion about who she is. She wants to be her old self, but her situation isn't allowing this.

Suppose, for example, a person has been seeing herself as an entrepreneur who thrives on successful risky financial speculation. Now, however, she finds herself in the midst of a global economic depression. Life doesn't realistically afford her the luxury of practicing what she identifies with being. For a while, she might be able to handle herself in this situation. Suppose she even tries acting in ways that acknowledge her new reality—ways that affirm the character who cares about fiscal conservatism and denies the character who cares centrally about risky entrepreneurial financial success. In effect, she is playacting new behaviors that are appropriate to a different valuational standard than she is used to. Her behavior is consistent with the new reality in which she finds herself. She is trying to adapt. However, if she still identifies with being the entrepreneurial type—if she hasn't changed her identificatory valuations to go along with her new practices—she has problems. For after a while, she feels confused because she appears, even to herself, to be a personal identity other than the one she likes and, in fact, has been. This situation is a matter of wanting one identity and having taken on the behavior appropriate to another. The individual is hopelessly straddling some unhappy middleground. After some period of not being—of not "acting out"—the person she centrally identifies with being, she may begin to sense a confusion about who she actually is around financial affairs. In matters of identity, she needs an avenue to practice expressing the values with which she identifies. Otherwise, she starts to feel lost. In a very literal sense of character "I" and "me," she could honestly say, "Where am I? I don't know what's become of me." The lesson of this kind of example is that only by being able to live out one's personal identity valuations without interference can a person be said to be genuinely herself. Otherwise she is a little lost and confused.

To see how people deal with the uneasiness of identity confusion, let's go a step further with another example. I have a friend who specializes in philosophical hermeneutics. She once told me that when she was a graduate student, in order to supplement her fellowship, she took a full-time job working as a computer word processor. She learned after one false try that when people at work asked her what she was studying at school, she was better off not saying that she was a philosopher, let alone a hermeneuticist. Whatever being a philosopher is, it isn't something that the people at her workplace related to and readily would understand. Even in their imagination, they couldn't identify with that kind of life. My friend saw that her identifying with something so alien to her co-workers' very imagination and appreciation would strain the possibility of ever communicating with them about that part of herself. It would strain the rest of her social contact with them, too. So she kept quiet about that piece of who she was. She put a veil over that part of her personal identity and decided to actually lie about her "school self," all in order to have a better rapport with her co-workers. Stretching the truth, she told them that she was a Doctor of Group Behavior, technically true but in reality an equivocation. She let them fill in the meaning of this title as they chose, strongly suspecting the conclusion to which they would wrongly jump. Consistent with her guess, most of them chose to see her as studying group psychology or clinical psychology, areas of interest most of them could understand and in which the rest could at least find value. In any event, now they could all talk with my friend. They developed a friendly patter with her, and she with them. She even began acting like the psychologist self the others were seeing her as, coming up with psychological and low-level hermeneutic analyses of various company group behaviors. Of course, this was a kind of fraud on her part. But it wasn't meant to deceive for the sake of deception. I believe that it was meant to save my friend from identity confusion.

Doing what she did was probably the wisest course of action she could have taken, for the social setting she found herself in simply wouldn't allow her to be herself, the hermeneutical philosopher. In order to avoid identity confusion—something no one should have to endure—she adapted by making up something. She forged a tradeoff between psychological pain and temporarily compromising one of her character traits. While lying is normally not an admirable thing to do (especially for the person who identifies with being a truth teller), there are slices of reality where it may be called for as a reasonable tradeoff. We will assume that my friend didn't like the fact that she was lying. She didn't see herself in a special range of contexts here where lying was acceptable. As far as she was concerned, as a matter of character, lying was still impermissible. However, she lied anyway. Sometimes through a well-fashioned lie, we seek to create categories to describe ourselves because the structure of the particular social setting we find ourselves in has nothing that fits with who we really are. And we don't want to suffer the discomfort of feeling personal identity confusion over the matter. Clearly my friend had no psychological space in which to tell her co-workers that she was a hermeneutical philosopher. There simply is no built-in topic of discussion about "philosophers" or "word processors who are philosophers" that is part of the definition of that particular social context. And in general, most social contexts lack enough of this kind of interesting texture. Because of this deficit, many ways of talking about who we are fall through the social cracks. In other words, the structure of the context doesn't allow for certain talk about personal identity because it filters out many kinds of possible personal identity realities. Fellow workers would have stared at my friend in total puzzlement if she had told them she was a hermeneuticist. So she lied instead and made up a profession that wouldn't be filtered out of their understanding of personal identity possibilities. That was the price she was willing to pay for relative peace of mind.

There is more that this example suggests, however. It seems that sometimes there's no 1–1 mapping of a person's identifications onto the social structures that are her practical everyday contexts. While one's valuational commitments are normally well-fitting responses to social contexts, sometimes a good response in one context (e.g., "identifying with being a philosopher" might be a good response to the context of "leading the intellectual life") just isn't a good response in another (e.g. in the "word processor" context), even though the contexts are within the same range. Accordingly, individuals sometimes need to fine-tune their identity traits by introducing concepts that allow them a psychological space in which to be themselves. They either become reasonably comfortable in the new tradeoff identity they have created—the new identity that is appropriate to the social structure that their identity is a response to—or else they invite identity confusion. Of course, another alternative is to change the social setting to one that allows a person to be who she already is. Indeed, some people are so socially powerful or clever that instead of compromising parts of who they are, they actually create a totally new kind of setting that will allow them fully to be themselves. They don't change for the world; they make certain the world changes for them.

All this in order to stave off identity confusion and to maintain the integrity of one's personal identity. If only this were the worst kind of identity pain and challenge to integrity that a person could face. Some people have to deal with the even more severely painful experience of "identity crisis." Here one's sense of integrity seems to go on a more long-lasting vacation. Of course, some of these vacations are more long-lasting than others. Everything in degrees. But however long-lasting an identity crisis is, while a person is in one, his sense of integrity is extremely diminished. In integrity's place, life invites feelings of degrees of meaninglessness onto the scene. What does this mean?

We said some things in the last section about personal identity and meaning. I would like to extend that discussion now and see what help it can be to us. A sense of meaning*ful*ness comes from a person's valuating certain ways of living his life and putting those valuations up against one another, determining which wins the day in a conflict situation. In seeing just how important—how valued—a given valuation is by seeing where it fits on one's character hierarchy and seeing how it is chosen over whatever lower-level character values one also espouses, one is constituting the meaning that both level valuations have for him. In my view then, "meaningfulness" gets spelled out in terms of "having character values." Accordingly, the individual who wallows in existential meaning*less*ness is someone who is having problems generating character values. He is someone whose *general capacity* for identification has broken down. It's not that he needs to tinker with one of his identifications to make it fit his reality, as is the case with identity confusion. Instead, the kind of person we are talking about now is someone whose whole identificatory valuational capacity is in jeopardy. For one reason or another, this individual is having difficulty with having life projects at all to ultimately value. He is having difficulty choosing any traits as standards for an ideal good life that he can put out in front of him and stand up for regardless of what others think. In simple terms, he no longer has any mission in life. And his sense of meaninglessness portends identity crisis.

Interestingly, although sometimes an identity crisis can have a neurotic or even psychotic basis, other times it has its origins in normal life processes. The "midlife crisis" is one such normal life process. Going through this condition seems to be part of what every otherwise psychologically healthy person at one time or another experiences. Obviously, what "midlife crisis" refers to literally is the *time* in life when a certain kind of identity crisis crops up. If adolescence is the time when people are racing around looking to create a backdrop of personal identity self valuations, midlife is a time when people seriously reevaluate the whole enterprise, or at least reevaluate their most central life projects. The job usually gets done in a crisis atmosphere. It usually involves a dismissal of the center of what a person has been standing for up to that point in life. For years, an individual has had her identity in place vis-à-vis her valuations that have steered her through her course of reactions to the practical challenges of the everyday. That is, she has long ago set in place just how "she was going to be in general" in various practical contexts of life. Now she is at a point where although her ability to posit character traits still exists, many of the particular choices she has made in the past have become severely dysfunctional. The individual is thinking that her old image of the personal identity self no longer has any value to her. Her old valuational choices no longer matter as much to her. What before had been meaningful responses of her innermost self to life's everyday practical challenges are now seen by her as being trivially ritualistic and devoid of any meaning. They are devoid of meaning in the sense that she no longer is committed to putting herself on the line in defense of them. Such a person is sometimes said to be bored with her life and with herself.

This isn't always a bad thing. Some people take this dysfunction and turn it into a golden opportunity for starting anew as a person. The condition becomes a motivator for change. At this point in life, a person even more than before usually looks self-consciously at her valuational possibilities. Perhaps there is more self-consciousness now because now the individual knows what's at stake; that is, she knows what it really is to be a personal character identity. She has seen it from the accomplishment side, as it were, where before, as an adolescent, she had no idea of what becoming a personal identity actually would be like. So even though there is a level of meaninglessness about what her life has come to at this point—because many of her valuations have shut down—she is in a very unique position to appreciate her situation as a time when she can try out new self possibilities. Overpowering her sense of meaninglessness, she might actually enjoy doing things she has never done before but only fantasized doing. So, for example, she might now travel abroad for the first time, trying out being a new character with worldliness as one of her prominent traits. If she can fit such an identification into what is left of who she is, or if she can simply brutely valuate worldliness in spite of whatever else she still is, she will have taken her crisis situation and turned it into a positive opportunity for character growth. The possibilities for such growth are limitless. People read self-help books to comb the field for possibilities. Others change careers or start them for the first time. Still others get out of bad marriages. Some people become born-again in their religious belief. And so on. In many ways, meaninglessness can be overcome by pointing one's valuational capacity in new directions.

Of course, not all midlife crises are experienced as such golden opportunities. The midlife crisis that many more people experience is an extremely unsettling state of affairs, especially since people are used to being comfortable in their personal identity of old. Now that comfort is gone. The kind of person I am thinking of is valuationally dysfunctional to the point of not knowing right away how to point her valuational capacity in a new direction. She has no new character ideas to try out. No longer valuing traits in the old ways is one thing, but having no ready replacements for them is quite another. There is absolutely no valuating going on anymore. Yet the prime directive to valuate is still in force. The individual is still feeling under the basic existential directive to make herself into a distinctive personal identity. Were she to lose her connection with this directive altogether, she no doubt would either revert to being a person in the primordial object relating and narcissistic sense or invite a catatonic stupor as her stance for being or possibly even commit suicide. However, most of us maintain our connection with the prime directive. This being the case, such a person in midlife crisis isn't in a very happy situation. She needs to be valuating but she isn't. She is like a car on ice, spinning her wheels and going nowhere. Unfortunately, while she is going nowhere, she is also in the midst of unpleasant psychological accompaniments to her condition. In addition to what is a total sense of meaninglessness—meaninglessness unmediated by an awareness of possibilities for growth—there is typically also an attendant depression. This individual quite literally can only thrash about. She can't really try to break out of her depression until she is motivated once again to train her valuational capacity, which right now is dormant, on new character possibilities. Unfortunately, all this person can feel is "stuck." She has no sense of integrity and no hope for any on the horizon.

Obviously, most people in midlife crisis eventually get beyond their condition. However, what reactivates their capacity to create character again is a mystery. And why midlife crisis seems to be such a universal phenomenon in the first place is also a puzzle. These are important questions, but I won't be tackling them in this book. Whatever the reason for midlife crisis, the fact is that it does happen and it does force us to deal with meaninglessness in a way most people don't have to before this situation.

Besides midlife crisis, there are other varieties of identity crisis that offer more than a sense of meaninglessness as the unwanted psychological payoff. Losing any semblance of feeling integrity about themselves, people in more extreme identity crisis have been known to experience a more pointed sense of meaninglessness. People have been known not only to lose a general sense of integrity but also to take on a clearly defined sense of lost integrity that we call "low self-esteem." For example, people trying to "make over" others run the risk of bringing on this kind of crisis for the others. When someone is asked to change permanently a part of her character overnight, her psychological system can be thrown into chaos. A marriage in its final death throes often finds one spouse requiring the other immediately to change part of who she is. But one can't simply change a valuation with a snap of the fingers. To ask someone to be other than who she is is asking for the impossible (unless one is willing to accept mere playacting from her as the next best thing). In reality, this is asking the person to be alive in body but dead in spirit. One could be in identity crisis here in the sense that one's very psychological existence would be in jeopardy. The demand for character change can be viewed by the person asked to do this only as an attempt by another to kill off part of the self, because it is certainly understood by all but the psychologically numb that such a request can't be successfully honored by anyone other than a schizoid personality.

The truth is, people can only change identifications slowly. Demands for wholesale immediate change are not only offensive but also confused. A person can always try out new *individual behaviors* that are more consistent with values she has not identified with to that point. Everybody experiments like this once in a while. But they do this in the context of having made certain that the individual behavior change they are looking for fits in with the rest of their stable character life. In contrast, to make wholesale *massive identity* value changes is psychologically impossible. There has to be a firm untouchable base that a person can modify slowly and in pieces. As the changes are slowly made, the firm untouchable base is slightly modified. I say this for two reasons. For one thing, since, as we saw in chapter 6, character valuation is a reflexive act carried out by an already existent character with already valuated traits, then character *change* is all about the character that's already in place (in terms of the other valuated traits) reflexively changing some chosen valuation. In other words, it takes some fixed character to change some other pieces of character. There's got to be something of substance there doing the reflexive act of change. The reflexive nature of self requires that. So, there can be character evolution, but character revolution is a psychological impossibility. We need to have something to change *from* that basically remains the same. My second reason for saying this is that if the character "I" changes, there has to be most of the same basic "I" there so that I know that, indeed, it is I that has changed.[17] To allow the wholesale change would be to allow as a possibility that new psychological persons could simply pop into existence. But that isn't the style in which persons are constituted. And if one demands that an individual nevertheless try to make such a change, then the only reasonable responses on the part of the person asked is either to turn the other way, to playact what she thinks the other person wants to see, or else to experience the deep shock of identity crisis, perhaps wallowing in meaninglessness and an extreme sense of low self-esteem.

There are also kinds of identity crises that result in anxiety and depression. It happens, for example, where a person isn't aware of what she stands for anymore because standing for things at all has been crowded out of consciousness by an overriding nonidentificatory narcissistic obsession that insists on being satisfied. Due to the neurotic interference of this obsession, the individual no longer is aware of much of what she stands for. In fact, standing for many of the things she normally has stood for has been temporarily suspended in the neurotic interests of satisfying the severe obsession. Suppose, for example, an individual becomes obsessed with having a particular woman fall in love with him. All of his waking moments are aimed at this goal. He has difficulty eating and sleeping. Most importantly, he is preoccupied with thinking about her. There is enough of his character left so that he can function in the most important practical areas of his life, but all the rest of his energy goes into his obsession. If this were to happen over a long span of time, this individual would genuinely be ignorant of who he was anymore, albeit he no doubt would know himself as "the unrequited lover." But he might not be consciously aware of who he was as a full-blown personal identity. Others still might know him as his causal identity self. (He is the same person with that particular body and psychological history, for example.) But he isn't valuating things anymore. He is too busy trying to satisfy his narcissistic obsession. To others, he seems preoccupied, temporarily stalled. He isn't showing much of his old character; it has lost its vigor. To him, he feels "stopped dead in his tracks." He is certainly no longer very interesting vis-à-vis any character standards he brings to his encounters with others. He isn't much fun to be around, because he seems only to want to play the one obsessing tune in conversation.

The individual who finally realizes that he has strayed so far from his character is in a frightening position. If he has the misfortune of not at least getting his narcissistic obsession satisfied, then because he has as much as given up significant portions of how he normally lives, he really has nothing of value going on in his life. He really is a lost soul whose life has become meaningless. He may become totally depressed in the sense that he no longer has any ultimately valued life projects to be emotional about. When one no longer posits standards of value for himself, then he literally no longer experiences any value in the world. A consciousness of valuelessness is precisely a consciousness that is in depression. The world is valuatively flat. Such a person might also become anxious and filled with dread. Anxiety and dread are psychological states of fear about the self's losing itself, fear about losing the core character self as the very ground necessary for ever again becoming a being of value (valuation). Dread, anxiety, and panic are psychological accompaniments to the movement of the self imploding to nothing, the movement toward a total loss of the self's integrity, wholeness. A self with absolutely no integrity to it is fully a nonself. That is what identity crisis anticipates. Very existential. Quite terrible. It's no wonder, then, that when such hints of character dissolution make even the slightest appearance, a person does all in her power to get back on track toward a life of daily valuation of a distinctively unique personal character identity.

CHAPTER 10

Social Identity

Psychological development means people moving ever closer to becoming fully self-created personal character identities, distinctive individuals. But lest we get the wrong idea here, let me hasten to add that no adult is ever a total personal character identity package, nor does it appear that nature ever "intended" it that way. For one thing, identity activity isn't always an expression of character. We have become quite familiar in this book with the idea that there are caused properties a person possesses that she and others use for determining who she is as a causal self. These are properties that she has had no identificatory part in creating. It's noteworthy, too, that often these properties are just as distinctively unique as one's character identity properties are. So, any eventual identifications with them aside, a person's causal bodily and psychological history identities are typically unique, and elements from both arenas constitute part of how a person is recognized as being uniquely that particular individual self. For example, we certainly recognize a person to be distinctively the person she is in virtue of how she looks, what her particular body is like (e.g., her eyes, her smile, etc.). We also know her by her biologically programmed temperament, her psychologically based emotional tendencies, and so on. The point is, a person can *be* certain *distinct* ways due to the causes that act on her, but *without* her personally *identifying* with any of them. Put another way, a person has a distinct personal causal identity as well as a distinct personal character identity. Not everything one does as a recognizably unique self is a matter of character.

But there are still other factors at work on the personality that keep an individual from being totally defined by personal character identity. These factors have to do with her being a *social identity*. People not only are *distinctive personal* selves of both causal and character elements, they are also *social* selves. That is to say, in addition to being defined by how they are *distinct* from the crowd, people are also defined by how they are *part* of the crowd. People belong to groups, and sometimes that fact defines who they are. Often this social identity is a very causal affair. We all know that groups socially condition us to conform to norms. Cultural structures act as filters for how we experience life. Roles we live out of result in our acting in socially expected ways. It is difficult not to be responding to some social form or other; it is difficult to avoid being causally influenced into becoming very much like social others in various ways. Difficult, but not impossible. Certainly, personal identifying sometimes gets us past being causally stamped social actors. But so does what we will call *social identification*. People identify with being social selves and, as a result, become social *character* identities as well as the social causal identities we know them to be. They become character identities who see themselves in terms of what values they choose to share with others.

Let me put the point another way. The adult character has two basic themes organizing her valuational life. We have seen what the organization of personal character identity is about. Now we want to find out about the other kind. *Social identifications* are about a person's forging a social character self to fit into the social environment. It is about a person's valuationally choosing which ultimate ideal standards to live by in her social life with others. Instead of choosing value ideals to stand for *regardless* of what others think, she chooses ones to stand for in common with others precisely *because* of what those others think. As social identifiers, we aren't looking to make a statement about who we are as thoroughly individuated creatures; rather, we are looking to make one about who we are as beings sharing common traits with others. If as personal identities we are responding to a built-in prime directive—an existential need, as it were—to individuate from the world, then as social identities we are responding to a built-in prime directive to be like and belong with others in the world. Responding to both existential needs, we live our lives in each of two parallel discrete experiential realms. What we reflectively carve out in terms of valuational standards for living the good life in each of these realms becomes who we are as personal and social characters.

Finally, then, identity is a many-splendored thing: personal causal identity, personal character identity, social causal identity, and social character identity. In this chapter, I will investigate the two social territories. Of course, discussion of the causal side of things is nothing new; sociologists and anthropologists make knowing about this their life's work. But the identificatory field is something that hasn't received nearly as much attention. Accordingly, my central concern will be to examine some of the more salient features of social character identification.

I

Let's begin by talking about the overall self developmental picture, showing how social causal self activity eventuates in social character self activity. First, very briefly, the march of causal self development looks something like this. The relevant action starts during earliest infancy. Symbiosis is one's very first social relation, and it defines the causal social part of who one is at that time. In short order, one evolves into another kind of causal social self that's noteworthy for its extreme narcissism. As we know, the infant here is defined by her new relationship with her parents. She is someone sharing a fantasized omnipotence with her parents. As powerful as she imagines her parents to be, that's how powerful she feels herself. It is all delusion of course, but it is who she is as a rudimentary self. In taking on the "parental value *imago*," she can finally present herself to the world as a powerful value being.

This move in narcissistic development is the underpinning for the social causal identity one becomes later on. In the same way that the narcissistic infant/child connects with mother as the source of omnipotence and primitive value, the older, emerging social causal identity child places a lot of power in the developing superego as a parental stand-in source of power and value. And even further down the line, the developing social causal identity child, adolescent, and adult put that same focus on social groups and institutions as the bearers of power and value. Social groups and institutions take over the function of the narcissistic parental *imago*. However, instead of causal psychodynamic processes of object relating working exclusively on the individual here, processes of socialization join in the fun and start developing a social causal identity. What does that version of the social self look like?

There are cultural forces and both social-group and role expectations that influence how each of us fits into the world around us. They all hold causal socialization power over us. Most of us spend a good portion of our lives unreflectively acting out this social part of our causal program. For example, during latency childhood and early adolescence, *groups* are their most successful at exerting heavy "peer pressure" on us to move in a lockstep manner according to group expectations. Not only is each of us a member of a gender, a race, a religion, a political persuasion; we are also a child of our parents, a friend of our friends, a student of our teachers, a player on our teams, and so on. Social forces have it that we do what certain groups dictate. For instance, consider how group pressure affected public attitudes toward violence during the Persian Gulf war. Before that war, many Americans were ideologically dead set against violence as a way to carry out foreign policy. After being inundated with media prowar Desert Storm messages of violence, general attitudes about violence changed overnight. There was a real change in what motivations were in causal play. Television suggested that people would be more acceptable as "loyal Americans"—that is, they would be more a part of the group "loyal Americans"—if they attitudinally got behind the celebration of violence. Many people responded accordingly. "Blood thirsty" wasn't just a metaphor anymore. The promise of group membership was a powerful motive for causal social identity change.

Social *role expectations* wield a similarly impressive powerful causal stick. We unreflectively carry out the role expectations that social forces causally rain on us. So it wasn't too long ago that little boys and girls played their roles through their unreflectively chosen games of baseball and dolls. And men and women fitted unreflectively into their gender roles, chasing one another around in the name of socially defined sexual expectations. Then, too, fathers would become material providers of the family, and mothers, nurturers. And so on. These used to be some familiar stereotypical role expectations, anyway, although clearly the times are changing. The point is, when a role expectation is in force, people do, in fact, follow the social program it defines. And indeed, it seems that much of a person's early life is spent exclusively living out these sorts of causal social patterns. Where such patterns become an important part of how a person carries on the general conduct of her life, they define part of her social causal identity.

We eventually reach a place where we start to build a social character self alongside of the social causal self. Somewhere during adolescence we reach the land of serious autonomous *social identification*. For example, there are things we autonomously choose to do in order to be genuinely in moral community or in political community with our comrades. In fact, these two contexts are paradigm worlds of social identification. Hardly a soul avoids making some commitment or other to sharing values in either place. Adolescents especially are known for their strong moral and political views that bond them to likeminded thinkers. Or, to take another example, sometimes the move toward social character involves social identification with heretofore causal traits. People can transform themselves into social characters by making valuational choices about, say, their causally determined gender and race. They may involve themselves in, say, social liberation movements that are aimed at the molding of shared social character in terms of their valuational attitudes toward caused gender and race traits.

This second example is actually representative of a very large class of social character creative activity. There is a vast array of a person's heretofore causal traits that get turned into character through identification. So a person's social causal self at one time might have been defined by the religious bonds she had with people of the same faith or by shared ethnic bonds or by geographical bonds or by bonds of being sports fans together. The list is endless. All of these are traits that a person has shared as purely causal features of who she is. Merely *having* these kinds of traits in common with one another places people into a social relationship. For example, they are all Catholics, they are all Californians, they are all computer hackers. This relationship can be part of each individual's social causal identity. But it is not uncommon that, at various times, the individual reflects on any of these aspects of her causal social self and makes valuational decisions about them. She decides to take responsibility for using some of them as her value standards for judging the good life. So she might become immersed in judging what's worthwhile in her life in terms of how it feeds her ethnic pride. Or she decides to socialize only with people in her own profession. Or she decides that she will only do business with Dallas Cowboys fans. In other words, she decides to turn originally causally induced social affiliations into issues of valuation, reflective character expression. Now she is standing up for being one sort of social self rather than another. She is making herself accountable for it. Of course, instead of fully buying into one's heretofore causal self in this fashion, a person could decide that she wants to change some of her causal self. She might, for example, want to change from the old knee-jerk causal religious attitudes she has shared with some fellow believers to something new. She may decide that now that she is reflectively thinking about matters, that religious part of who she has been as a causal social self isn't to her liking. Some other social self is preferable. She now *wants* to be the social self of her own choosing.

The main point here is that a lot of social character identification is about what has been only social causal happenings before. But while I believe that the lion's share of a person's social identification in fact comes in the form of affirming, fine-tuning, embellishing, toning down, or criticizing and then changing such causal social happenings (that have been in place as parts of the individual's causal identity), that's not the social identification activity of which people are most aware. We seem to be more aware of the social character work that occurs in the arena of identification with external social models. And of particular interest in that arena is the identificatory activity that revolves around the currently fashionable idea of choosing traits of character off of social role models. We explain a great deal of social behavior these days by pointing to the activity of people and their role models. Specifically, a lot of antisocial behavior is chalked up to the absence of socially positive role models in a person's surroundings and the overabundance of negative ones. The lucky person is someone who is in close proximity of mostly positive prosocial role models. Presumably, a person socially identifies with a role model (positive or negative) when she chooses to look at what her role model has as social traits and then chooses to valuationally take on those traits as her own. She chooses to make them her standards of social goodness, standards for how she will fit into the social world around her. After all, a role model is someone who is acknowledged by the group (which the identifier wants to belong to) to be a paradigm of praiseworthy traits that all acceptable group members should aspire to have. In understanding this about the role model, the identifier naturally does whatever she can to resonate with the role model's social valuations. A person, for example, can look at the virtues of a public figure and decide that choosing those virtues as part of her own repertoire will leave her in good stead with the society-at-large, or at least with the groups to which she is concerned with belonging. So she chooses to set her sail under those social colors of the role model. Or another person might look at the "virtues" of the drug pusher and decide to self-responsibly choose those as her standards for the good life, as that life has been defined by the groups to which she wants to belong.

Role models, then, are important in the realm of social identification. They are social "character trait menus" that people can choose off of in an identificatory fashion.[1] But there's another kind of modeling that's even more relevant to our lives as social identifiers. In fact, it is what we will be focusing on for the rest of the discussion in this chapter. Not only do we find role model individuals to emulate, more often we identify with *whole groups* as models of certain valued traits. We decide that there are certain antecedently existing valued group traits that we haven't had as part of our social identity repertoire but that we would now like to take on because others in the group have them and value them. Let's try to understand this kind of social identification.

The question we will ask as a way of organizing our discussion here will be, Why do people ever come to identify with groups at all? There are plenty of occasions when a person finds groups to be to her liking. She wants to be accepted by her fellow human beings, her fellow gender members, her family, her fellow citizens, her workplace peers, her neighbors, and so on. She reflectively wants to belong to these groups. This is in contrast to groups with which she doesn't want to be identified. For example, she might not want to be part of the Ku Klux Klan, the Nazi Party, or the Mafia. Becoming acceptable to the groups of her liking places a person more safely in the world than she would otherwise be. The groups of one's liking can sometimes be counted on to lend their agency to meeting one's wants and needs. For example, were a person accosted on the street by a mugger, she would certainly like to be able to count on her fellow citizens to come to her assistance. She doesn't want to think that she has only her agency to count on. She wants to hold onto the remnants of what her primal symbiosis did for her. That kept her attached to the benefits of having an external agency at her beck and call. The logical extension of that for the character self is one's choosing to live by values that she happens to share with others in groups of her liking, the result of this value sharing being that she is able to count on their agency as well as on her own to get her wants and needs met. This becomes still another strategy for realizing those lifelong aims of maximizing satisfaction and minimizing frustration.

Of course, life as an adult is more complex than it was during infancy. What it takes to satisfy a person gets more complicated as she gets older. We adults not only need security and comfort, we also come to want strongly—if not need—things such as particular lifestyles, status, economic prosperity, and more. And we don't just seek satisfaction in these areas through our own agency; we also come to rely on social groups for assistance. We choose to try to affiliate ourselves with the groups of people whose agency we think will assist ours in doing the best job. Where we do this successfully, sharing valued traits with fellow group members grounds the kind of social empowerment we can have in the world. Specifically, as a group member, we are powerful now precisely to the degree that the group with which we are sharing valued traits influences the outcomes of any events in the world. To the extent that our group has any kind of agency power to effect real outcomes in the world, so are we entitled to feel that much more socially empowered in our lives, even if this power isn't self-generated.

But there is still more to why people socially identify. In developing as social selves, we also seek the existential psychological payoff I alluded to in the introduction to this chapter. Just as the existential psychological payoff for becoming a personal identity is one's achieving a sense of integrity and self-esteem about her unified, coherent distinctive character self, the existential psychological payoff for becoming a social identity is her achieving a sense of belonging through varied feelings of solidarity, kinship, fellowship, fellow-feeling, camaraderie, and togetherness with group members. That is, we know that a person has individual integrity in doggedly standing up for her personal valuations regardless of what others think and that the payoff for this is self-esteem. Now, what I am also suggesting is that a person has social integrity in doggedly standing up for her social valuations because of what others think, and that the payoff for this is a sense of social belonging played out through these varied feelings of solidarity and so forth. Such feelings are signposts that tell a person that she isn't in the world alone, that she isn't an isolated individuated self. The feelings of kinship and the like indicate where a person can look for agency help; but more important, they indicate where she can satisfy the existential need to experience herself as a social being.

There is even more to why people identify with groups. But before we go on to talk about this, I think we would do well to consolidate our gains so far by providing some more detail to what we have just been saying about why people identify with groups. I have two specific kinds of detail in mind. One involves the kind of sharing of values (valued traits) that is required for genuine group identification. The other is about the kind of responsibility a person takes for sharing those values. Let's talk about the required kind of sharing of values first.

At this juncture, our general position about a person's identifying with a group is that one often chooses to stand up for certain values in life because of what the groups of his choosing think. And that's because he believes that the valuations that prevail in those groups are best suited for meeting his needs and strong wants as well as the desirable existential psychological payoffs. But now let's be clear about exactly what this claim amounts to. The groups of the individual's choosing don't *causally entice* the individual to take on and share in their prevailing values. That is, the values he shares with the group aren't the causal products of his wanting admission into those groups. That kind of causality might have been true of the individual when he was still merely a social causal self, but things are different now. As a social *character* self, he wants groups to help him out with agency for meeting his wants and needs, and he wants to be filled with feelings of solidarity and the like. However, to get these things, he only *identifies* with groups that value traits that he *genuinely* does come to value. In using those groups as models of traits that he wants to take into his social character self, the individual does choose traits modeled by the groups, but he isn't simply going along with the crowd. Instead, he really is choosing to stand up for those traits as having ultimate value. In doing this, he really is constituting more parts of his self. He does, in fact, see these new parts as some of his emerging standards for how the good life is to be pursued. This totals out to quite a bit more than his simply trying to *satisfy* group entrance requirements.

Let's make a distinction here. These genuine social identifications are valuational standards, which are not to be confused with what might be called "insipid social values." The latter are social values a person does choose to stand behind because of what others think but doesn't really choose them as constitutive of his self. Rather, he simply wants to please others in certain groups that hold the values in question. He believes that doing this will go some ways toward helping him gain admittance to those groups. Part of his belief is correct. If a person really does share values with others, there is the tendency to gain admittance and to reap the rewards. However, this "insipid social valuator" misses the point that one really does have to *share* the values in question in order to obtain socially meaningful group acceptance. One really does have to identify with the shared traits. But this insipid person doesn't. And so he won't reap the rewards of group membership. At worst, the individual may playact his fondness for the value in question but not do a good job of it. Clearly, others won't welcome him to their social bosom. At best, he will skillfully playact his fondness for the value in question and convince the others that he really values life as he says he does. They may like him, but *he* won't feel the camaraderie he seeks. Rather, he will feel that he is a fraud who is hiding out in a lie. It is just a psychological fact about people that we don't feel a sense of belonging with others when we merely pretend a sharing stance with them. Of course, it is always possible that a person could effect a self-deception about his situation. So be it. The point is, that would be a deception. The normal situation is one where a failure of genuinely sharing values with others leads to a failed social belonging with others, at least from the pretender's point of view.

What I am saying is that a person can't be living by a group's values *just* to please group members. The social identifier wants to belong to the group *because* he wants to share precisely that group's values. By contrast, the "insipid social valuator" might be someone who, say, joins an antiwar movement in order to be "where the action is." He wants a kind of shared excitement in life that comes from participating with others in marches, protests, and so on. So he joins the movement that guarantees this outcome. However, he has no valuational commitment against the war. While he may finally receive some social-group agency help in a pinch, and while he may finally enjoy the trappings of social excitement that comes from "getting on the bandwagon," he will never have the full sense of social belonging that he seeks.

In general, if a person wants to gain admittance to a group, his chances of success are best if he can genuinely share in some of their more important values. Of course, this is usually not a difficult proposition. For, although it isn't always so, it is often the case that a person wants to gain admittance to those groups with which he *antecedently* shares values. He wants to join the group *because* he *already* shares their values. He would like to belong to a group that values as he does about important matters. What better place to seek camaraderie than with a group of likeminded people?

Now, not only is the successful social identifier genuine about valuing the traits he says he shares with the group, he also is genuine about his self-responsible commitment to those traits. Let me explain what this genuine commitment looks like. We saw in chapter 9 that what a person stands for as a personal identity quite often comes out in the *claims* he makes about his *rights*. There is a parallel truth we can point to now concerning one's social identity and the *claims* he makes about *obligations* (duties) to fellow group members. When a person genuinely stands up for his chosen social value standards precisely because of what people he wants to be in league with think, this often takes the form of his claiming certain social obligations to live by his shared value standards, duties he has to the group members.[2] So when I stand up for myself as a social being, I don't *just* claim certain values to be important to me and defining of me; I also define myself to be a person *committed to interacting with others* according to these values. That is, I *stand behind these values as obligations* to those people with whom I socially identify. I define myself as some-one obligated to them. For example, part of my social identification is my being a member of a family. And part of that involves my defin-ing myself as a father to my daughter. So I have certain obligations to the fraternity of fathers—obligations of behaving in certain shared fatherlike ways to my daughter. I also share certain values with my daughter that I feel obligated to uphold. These obligations are not forced upon me.[3] I decide on them for myself. That is, they are not conclusions drawn from my normative moral principles. Rather, they are expressions of my character value principles. I assert them and claim them as defining me.

A person's socially identifying with valuational groups of his choice means his embracing and defining himself in terms of how he decides he *must act toward them*.[4] Of course, sometimes a person pas-sively abides by some of what he deems obligations to others. Perhaps he is pushed or pulled by social convention to do this or that for other people. Or perhaps by Reason. Or perhaps by a coin toss. As a passive abider to obligations, a person simply lets some external mechanism decide for him what he owes others. He doesn't feel oblig-ated in his bones, as it were. He ultimately values the form of deci-sion making here more than the obligations that the form gives rise to. By contrast, the life of the self-responsible person is a life about social identificatory obligations. This kind of person has really com-mitted himself as a social identity to what he is doing. He has com-mitted himself to becoming connected to his social others. He has taken responsibility for himself as a comrade-in-valuation with them. That kind of commitment involves his wholeheartedly taking on and embracing appropriate obligations to them. Indeed, if challenged, he stands up for his obligations. (After all, we are talking about his image of the ultimate valuational life.) Indeed, he normally defends a view that these obligations are everyone's. Of course, often that's an overstatement. Nevertheless, it is clear that he embraces these obligations to others at least for himself. And these obligations are not fearfully experienced as anything that might diminish him, but rather as something that more fully empowers him as a social self. The more complex the sense of internally generated obligation he takes on, the more complex and the fuller a social self he becomes.

Perhaps all of these descriptions amount to a cumbersome way of simply saying that a self-responsible person normally goes around connecting to others through his feelings of *owing* them something. He doesn't think he is held captive by some external determiner and enforcer of what he owes. Rather, he wants to owe the others, he embraces owing them. He decides to *stand for* owing. He lays claim to it. The sum total of all this self-generated owing defines him as a social character. The more duties one genuinely feels obliged to fulfill in a self-generated way—that is, the more owed duties that stem from authentic social identity valuations he has—the fuller or larger his sense of and definition of himself as a social identity becomes.

This is all we will say about the genuine sharing of values and obligations to group members. Now we know more of the detail that goes into a person's identifying with groups and their traits. In genuinely sharing group values and in self-generating a sense of obligation to one's fellow group members, a person achieves a more full-fledged kind of social identification. One consequence of this is that he now has the group available to help get his wants and needs met. He has thus increased his social agency power. Another consequence is that he has effectively built more structure onto his social character identity. As a result of this, he is better able to meet his existential need to feel a sense of belonging in the world.

All of this constitutes a lot of motivation for why people would ever want to identify with groups. But now, there is still more to be said on the subject. There is still one other reason for identifying with groups that we haven't mentioned, a reason that I take to be the most interesting of all. And so what we will do now is proceed to an extended discussion of that reason in the next section.

II

In socially identifying with given traits, a person is intent on sharing *kinds* of traits with others. Again, the individual wants to be identified with the group of people in virtue of his shared traits with them. He wants to be seen as *similar* to the group members by virtue of their shared value kinds. That places him in the social world as that *kind* of social identity. But there is often another side to this matter. Social identification is also aimed at carving out some degree of *uniqueness* in the person, just as personal identification is. However, where personal identification is aimed at making a person "a distinctive individual," social identification is aimed at making him "a *distinctive kind* of person along with certain other people." The social identifier wants to be endowed with what we can call a "collective uniqueness." He stands up for his shared group traits *because* of what others think, but he also stands up for his *kind* of person—that is, for his group—*regardless* of what *other kinds* of persons—what other groups—think. People who identify themselves with an ethnic group, for example, know what it's like to stand up for their ethnic mates. Jews, Poles, and Italians know full well what it's like to feel "in it together" with other Jews, Poles, and Italians. Their feeling of camaraderie, especially in the face of group oppression, is difficult for an outsider either to appreciate or to destroy, let alone to fathom in the first place. Standing up for one's *distinctive* kind of person is an important feature of social identity. In this regard, when one identifies with a group, one feels *special* in virtue of being a part of that distinctive group.[5] When one has "being a part of the group" as just one more component of his social causal identity, he doesn't experience this uniqueness. But when he actually identifies with the group, he does experience it. Such a person sees his group as being better than others. Otherwise he would have chosen to belong to a different, better group. That is the force of our saying that he *identifies* with the group and its traits. He brutely chooses the shared valued traits as ultimate. And they are constitutive of him. Who he is as a social identity feels special because of this ultimate valuating. He sees his traits as being the "right" valued traits. For example, identifying with being a Democrat (not just unthinkingly causally being one) entails feeling superior to those who are Republicans. Then too, families are said to "stick together" in the sense that, insofar as their members identify with one another, they stand up for one another and their ultimate worth as family members. Other things being equal, family members are worth more to one another than anyone else. Blood is thicker than water.

The broad term that normally is used to designate this idea of group-related specialness is "in-group behavior." Being a member of an "in-group" somehow endows the individual with social specialness, uniqueness. With this in mind, what I want to do in this section is talk about the dynamics of in-group behavior and see how it bears on our understanding of social identification. I want us to appreciate especially that the pursuit of in-group specialness is often attended by social harms. What I have in mind are all the exlusionary activities practiced between groups, where one group as much as says to the others, "You can't be like us, so you aren't as ultimately good as we are." Finally, I think that although such practices are logically unnecessary elements of social identification, they nevertheless persist as central themes of in-group social identificatory behavior. And so we will examine them. It just is true that people spend a great deal of time pointing out the inferiority of other groups that don't partake of their traits, making certain that members of those other groups don't gain admittance to the special group, their group.[6] In fact, one highlights and even denigrates the differing traits in virtue of which those other groups seem unspecial to him, as though to say, "The more highlighted unspecial features the other groups have, the more special are my own group's features." The more excluded from one's favored group others appear, the more included in it one is oneself. One highlights his view of the in-group or in-crowd and carefully delineates the boundaries between that in-crowd and all others, especially the unspecial. As an in-crowder here, one devotes some of his energies to excluding others. In this exclusionary mode, he sees anyone who would disagree with his group's views as being socially trivial, dangerous, evil, or perhaps even "politically incorrect." Either a person is in the "in-crowd" or he is totally "out of it."

For example, latency children first carving out a social identity can be awfully cruel to one another. The forms are endless, but their in-group exclusionary practices stand out. We all know the routine: They mercilessly make fun of anyone who is at all different from the common crowd they have identifyingly thrown in with (i.e., the in-crowd); they make them appear to belong to some out-crowd—"Hey, four eyes," "Jimmy is a girr-lll," "Nigger!," "Sissy," "Kike." Unkind epithets are latency childhood standard fare.[7] Not solid selves yet, latency children are desperate to become so. And desperate times call for desperate measures. So they shout their excluding epithets as a way of telling all that *they*, in fact, *are* members of the in-crowd of their choice, *as opposed to* those others who are to be excluded. If there is to be a special in-crowd for them, then there must be outsiders to give that specialness clearer definition. In this manner, most latency children engage in a cutthroat competition for anchoring their special social selves. Everyone gets to be a winner or loser at one time or another. The poor unfortunate outsiders in this competition simply are seen as expendable for the greater good, that is, for the cause of "my acceptance."

To adult characters, children doing this sort of thing borders on the pathetic. *We* more fully developed social adult character selves know that, finally, behaving this way is a very weak mechanism for bolstering self-esteem, although the fact of the matter is, it does help consolidate a child's image of herself and it does attract confirmations of social acceptance from already acknowledged in-crowders. But since this childhood exclusion is at the expense of others, we adults of

moral concern frown upon it, no matter how adaptively it may actually function in social character identity formation. Of course, generally speaking, adult frowning doesn't do much good. Childhood tactics .
of exclusion seem to persist no matter how much adults complain.
And in addition to being adaptive, this behavior is "functionally deep"
in the sense that it appears to be a transtemporal and cross-cultural
sport—it is everywhere, always.

Indeed, in-group exclusion continues throughout life. Sometimes
the adulthood version of being a social self is just as coarse. Elitism,
bigotry, and individual hatreds are certainly crude ways for us to circle our own social character wagons. This is always at the terrible
expense of those discriminated against—that is, the violated others.
Moreover, adults give themselves more of a chance to exclude than
children do. For not only do adults have more groups to belong to
than children do, they also have more to distinguish themselves from.
There are more groups and group members with "other group" characteristics to sharply distinguish oneself from—the "my crowd's better than your crowd" syndrome. Furthermore, it just is clearer in
adulthood that one's excluding of an individual (or individuals) from
one's group is sharply defined by the other's belonging to some other
group, that other group being of low value—less specialness—in one's
eyes. But not only are there these group differences; it is also in
virtue of these differences that a kind of competition between groups
takes hold over which group is the "most 'in.'" If an adult is excluded
from one group, she usually can and will cast her lot with another
group. She will join in the competition if she is to be acceptable as a
social being—that is, if she is to be "in."

Adult in-group competition can be quite interesting. Part of the
activity of most groups is an unspoken competition for attaining the
status of "a publicly acknowledged in-crowd that is allowed to exclude
its competitors," something akin to competing for a "most-favored
nation" status among social groups. How this happens involves the
idea of a group trait reaching a critical mass (there's that notion
again) of popularity in a society and, in so doing, becoming a trait of
choice—becoming "the given"—for all those interested in being an in-
crowder. By virtue of attaining that status, this group and its members have the license to make other groups unspecial outsiders.
Within most societies, citizenship is a prime example of this. There
certainly are enough people in most societies who identify with
belonging to the group called "the country's citizens" to constitute this
critical mass. Being an American, for example, becomes the given for

us. Members of that group take something of a proprietary attitude toward determining who are to count as the special ones and who are to be relegated to the unspecial. It is just assumed that the general values shared by fellow citizens are the givens in any discussion.

In any case, generally speaking, when a group has reached a critical mass of acceptance in a society, no special pleas of justification for its valuational doctrines need to be made. Attaining critical mass obviates the need for the group (i.e., its members) to prove the value of its doctrines at every turn anymore. Those doctrines have become "the given" just as much as the group has. This is noteworthy because, short of reaching this status of "the given," rational debate about competing groups' doctrines is normally a "must" for people when their groups are still competing for "most-favored" group status. What I am saying is that once a particular group wins the competition, debate—rational or otherwise—takes a back seat to the reign of "the given." No justification for the doctrine is needed any longer. That is what "winning" the competition of the in-crowds *means*. The burden of debunking the winner and proving their group's disvalue now rests solely with those who would be contenders for the throne.[8]

I would like us to get more of an appreciation for the texture of these ideas about the dynamics of a person's making himself seem special through exclusion. I think it would be helpful if we could see how they come alive in a fuller example. A good arena to look for such an example is the university community. All the current debates on college campuses raging around "political correctness" are really arguments about the status of social identity definition through exclusion. In the name of giving minorities their rightful due, the politically correct sometimes, in fact, oppress other groups with their exclusionary tendencies. Where latency children try to nail down their social identity by tauntingly pointing out certain unspecial qualities that "outsider" others possess, today's politically correct individual often uses the heavy hand of liberal social criticism in order to do the same sort of excluding. It is as though he doesn't want to be left out in the cold; he doesn't want to be accused of having less-than-liberal values. Rather, he wants to ensure his liberal group acceptance. And one way of doing this is to give himself and his liberal group sharp definition. The more he can exclude others from being special—even to the point of excluding others who call themselves liberals—the more consolidated and confirmed is his liberal social identity. Now, *this* is the in-crowd. It is the *crème de la crème* of its kind. And he is more a member of that crowd if he can make others less so who would veer at all from his very special beliefs. All the more glory for him for being part of the most special group kind.[9]

Never mind the obvious moral criticism that could be leveled against such childlike behavior going on in our centers of learning and enlightenment. For our purposes, it is enough that this current university immersion in "political correctness" presents us with fertile examples for fleshing out the social identity dynamics that we are interested in. So let's look at a particular case and see what those dynamics are like.

One of the more popular venues for political correctness is the ongoing debate over what properly constitutes the socially liberal notion of *egalitarianism*. Although strong conservative voices are certainly aplenty, at this moment the American society still has a basic functioning liberal critical mass. And in our critical mass liberal society, the doctrine of egalitarianism is one of "the givens." But different sets of egalitarianism advocates within this group establishment are concerned with setting themselves up as being more special than other people within the same liberal establishment. Many people no longer feel the social distinctiveness vis-à-vis their "liberal egalitarian" designation that they might have felt a while back. And so they seek to make the distinctions of egalitarianism finer than before. They seek to define themselves and their fellow believers as the "true" liberals. They do this by defining their special brand of egalitarianism, making all other versions unspecial, even though still liberal. In this regard, today's politically correct egalitarian is ironically an excluder with a vengeance. He associates with a crowd that would oppress or turn a deaf ear to the dissent of anyone who would differ from him at all. No distinction making allowed here. No honest difference of opinion as to what counts as true egalitarianism is tolerated. Smug and of true belief, such a person would banish from the moral universe anyone whose political opinions varied in the least from his own. The irony here obviously is that this egalitarian tolerates only his in-crowd. And that kind of intolerance is precisely the kind of thing that traditional egalitarian theory of any definition is pointedly against. But today things seem to be going haywire with egalitarianism. There is a battle to see who can be of the most "in" egalitarian in-crowd. Egalitarian liberals vie for "the given."

Of course, as liberal egalitarians (as I will suppose most of us are), we start from some common assumptions. We assume that all citizens are to be treated equally; their rights should be equally respected. And we liberals are willing to put our money where our mouths are in this regard. We are all willing to make certain that all people, including minorities, are at "the starting line of life" together. No one is to have life advantages just because of some accidental circumstance of race, religion, gender, and so forth. Once at the starting line in any arena of living, of course, it is assumed that people will make their own choices about how best to proceed; and they will succeed or fail in those choices because of their own autonomous skill and some luck surrounding those choices. Let us imagine that we all feel these beliefs about egalitarianism in our identificatory bones and that abiding by them is part of who we are socially.

It is at this point that we start to go in different directions, breaking into egalitarianism subgroups who accuse one another of political incorrectness. Right now, there appear to be three such subgroups. The first one has it that people are all finally at the starting line of life together when, in the finest Aristotelian tradition, all external constraints—all externally imposed barriers—to individual autonomy have been removed. Suppose, for example, that all the gross antireligious, racist, and sexist practices—all the material mechanisms of prejudice, which in the past kept people, because of their religion or color or gender, from competing fairly in the marketplace—have been removed. No more quotas. No more special tests. No more bigoted discriminatory practices of any kind. Now people are all seen as equals. They are finally able to test their cunning and abilities in the marketplace with the rest of the citizenry.

By this concept of egalitarianism, individuals are to be evaluated as people according to how they use their autonomous powers after external constraints have been removed. If a person, once given these egalitarian benefits, succeeds in exerting his autonomous will to achieve, then he will no doubt receive the adulation he deserves from the rest of us. If he fails to exert his autonomous will to achieve, then, as far as his marketplace abilities go, he isn't worthy of the public's respect or any special concern. We are all in the same boat in this regard. We evaluate one another all the time in terms of how well the other autonomously works toward marketplace success. The other makes choices in his own special way. He brings the motivation to his success-aimed decisions that he has built up over a lifetime. He uses his intelligence, his charm, his social grace to try to effect the decisions he has aimed at acquiring success. And any onlooker will evaluate him in terms of how he fares here. Some people are admired for their particular style with these kinds of activities, some are not. And people who are admired by some are not admired by others. People are liked to varying degrees on the basis of the particular slant on these activities that they have shown, some are not. That is what normal human intercourse is about for this kind of egalitarian. We judge one another Yea or Nay, assuming that we start out as equals in terms of there being no special external constraints for any of us, and assuming that there still are reasons for evaluating one another in terms of how each of us presents herself to the world.

The second egalitarianism subgroup has it that we are all finally at the starting line of life together when, in the grandest Kantian tradition, all of the external constraints *and* all of the internal psychological constraints to individual autonomy have been removed. In this view, neutralizing external constraints alone won't do the trick. Merely lifting old discriminatory quotas, for example, won't make people equals. The oppressed will still be shackled by the systematically imposed internal constraints that make autonomous decision making virtually impossible. That's because those people who historically have had their rights of equality violated will still not know how to achieve success in this society, because they have been systematically robbed of the requisite detailed knowledge of and motivation for what to do next, after the external constraints have been removed.

In this view, the egalitarian society must provide special measures to help get the formerly violated individual motivated to achieve and to give him the knowledge that it takes to get started. The belief here is that merely to withdraw external constraints won't allow the individual to practice his autonomy. He will still be shackled by the systematically imposed internal constraints that make autonomous decision making on the road to success impossible. Accordingly, what's needed is political qua legislative action to liberate the oppressed groups from their constraining mindset. A cultural tradition of social alienation must be fought by instituting new educational programs that would free the disadvantaged of the belief that their essential selves are of less social worth than the rest of the population's. Part of that education obviously means trotting out role models of individuals and groups of worth to identify with. But this not only means having already established role models appear on TV encouraging minorities to work hard. It also involves instituting programs like affirmative action in the universities and professional schools so that their graduates go out into the minority communities to become quite live role models of success. The goal of all such programs is to eventually change the beliefs and motivation system that historically have gotten in the way of minority success. The aim is to get the disadvantaged individual to identify with being as special as the modeling group.

Right away there is a problem between the two types of egalitarians. All too often we find each group trying to capitalize on their differences, aiming at attaining a more favored in-crowd status with the public-at-large. For example, the first subgroup type defines herself in part as being respectful of people as equals. We are all moral beings entitled to the same human and political rights. And she identifies with treating people that way. However, for her this means fighting, to her last breath, the imposition of external constraints. And that is all. Listening to the second view, she becomes frustrated and sees the "internal constraint" condition as a slippery slope. She wonders how, in this view, we ever know when *enough* internal constraints have been dealt with? Perhaps only after a minority person succeeds in the marketplace? That can't be it. Egalitarianism isn't synonymous with economic utopia where everyone's life is perfect. Furthermore, she wonders what is so special about internal constraints of a minority person. Doesn't each of us have his own set of internal constraints getting in the way of one's succeeding in life? Don't we all carry along old psychological baggage whenever we make decisions about how to proceed in the marketplace? Sometimes that baggage, whether it is neurotic or something else, gets in the way of our succeeding. If we fail, we fail. That's life. Egalitarians can't guarantee success for people. All they can do is try to institute what it takes to put everyone at the starting line at the same time. If psychological baggage were to count as a factor in a person getting to the starting line, then *no one* would ever get to the starting line in the first place, let alone at the same time. In the finest *reductio* spirit, the proponent of the first view argues that the proponent of the second demands too much of egalitarianism. The second isn't *real* in-crowd egalitarianism. It is politically askew.

In pressing his own claim for living the egalitarian life, the first view's advocate complains that the second view's advocate is more obsessed with the mathematical aesthetics of "equality" than genuinely being concerned with the underlying moral motivation behind egalitarianism. The complaint is that the proponent of the second view is looking to make equal as much about people as she can. That is to happen in the context of both external circumstance and internal circumstance. The proponent of the second view would rid the world of as many differences between people as she could, differences around ethnic identifications, religious identifications, and so on. In this view, any difference is seen as a factor weighing against people really being at the starting line of life together. Total homogeneity is this view's goal. The very things that have allowed many in-crowds to define themselves (e.g., ethnic identity, etc.) are ruled out of bounds. All liberal nonproponents of this view of egalitarianism are seen as unacceptable out-crowders. They are the politically incorrect ones.

The first view's advocate sees all of this as obscene. For although the mathematical aesthetic of "equality" might be approximated better in this program, it is fascist in ruling out alternative social identities. It also completely disregards the basis of the moral issue underlying egalitarianism, that being "our respect for people as autonomous individuals." If we take care of so much about the background conditions of persons so that they are *guaranteed* success in the marketplace, we haven't allowed anything about their autonomously choosing and their taking responsibility for their choices to be factors in their succeeding. We have bypassed the importance of character for human interaction. But we shouldn't have programs that do this. We shouldn't have programs that rob people of the opportunity to fight off—to autonomously choose beyond—their internal causal constraints. That is what gives people the opportunity to build personal and social character, to allow themselves to really become—to fully take responsibility for—their images of life. Those are the factors that allow any of us to distinguish what we think are the good characters in life from what we think are the bad ones. No matter how they feel about themselves as characters, on moral grounds, not everyone is a saint. Not every minority group member is *simply* disadvantaged by internal causal constraints. Some people have characters that are, in the eyes of other people, morally offensive for reasons other than the conditions of their disadvantaged youth, just as some people in the prevailing power groups are, in the eyes of other people, morally offensive for reasons other than the conditions of their advantaged youth. Code words aside, we owe it to every person to have the opportunity to test his strength with his bootstraps. To do otherwise is to be disrespectful of the dignity of the individual. We respect a person's dignity by allowing him the psychological space in which he can try to create himself as a personal and social character self who will act as his own agency in life. With this idea in mind, egalitarianism as a moral stance is supposed to be precisely about accepting the dignity of all persons and carrying that commitment into practice.

Of course, all this kind of talk is well known. The advocate of the second view is typically a full-fledged egalitarian altruist who would deny the criticism by pointing out that complaining about the "aesthetics of 'equality'" is simply an *ad hominem* that has nothing to do with her motivation for being an egalitarian. Rather, she is just concerned with upholding the value of the individual by bringing him closer and closer to the goods of life. Whatever it takes! The advocate of this second view might then also point out that bigots always use the above sorts of objections to justify the slowing down of social liberation movements. They talk about showing respect for people by letting them flounder, when, in reality, this is just a cover for their real motives of wanting to maintain their own elitist position over minorities. Of course, the proponent of the first view need only reply that surely his criticisms aren't always a racist or sexist cover. And indeed, I am assuming in our discussion that they aren't. I am assuming that we just have two sincere egalitarians differing about important detail. We have two in-crowds doing battle for consideration as the politically correct, doing battle for "the given."

It is at this point that the proponent of the third egalitarian view comes forward. To him, people are all finally at the starting line of life together when all external constraints and *a certain class* of *internal* constraints have been eliminated. This view acknowledges many of the complaints levelled by the first view's advocate. Nevertheless, the proponent of this third view sees that there need be no slippery slope if we are careful. In this view, we have to realize that certain minorities have been systematically deprived of particular relevant knowledge and motivation for getting to the door of the workplace. The rest of us haven't been so deprived. The egalitarian who really respects the dignity of the individual will do what he can to get everyone to the marketplace door together. Then he will be happy to leave them to their own devices. Some of them—minority or otherwise—will make the best of their opportunity, some will not. Some of them will make their foolish idiosyncratic mistakes, some will not. The point is, egalitarians aren't to try to eliminate idiosyncratic constraints through social programs. That should be left up to the individual, bootstrapping and all. What egalitarians are to eliminate are the institutionally inculcated belief and attitude system that was created to keep people unequal. Once that is done, there will be enough left over to test the character of even the strongest and brightest of any group. And people will finally be able to be in the world with one another as individuals instead of as classes of people. We will be able to evaluate one another in terms of what we as individuals show one another about ourselves, not in terms of the status of the disadvantaged group to which we may belong. Until this version of egalitarianism becomes a reality, however, as moral beings, we should want to honor the special status that being disadvantaged requires, not as a celebration of the virtue of pitying disadvantage or as a celebration of the virtue of self-pitying, but rather as a celebration of the virtue of doing what it takes to guarantee equal autonomy for identificatory persons. That autonomy is the aspect of persons that is most worthy of everyone's respect; autonomous valuational choosing is the heart of what gives people dignity.

Of course, the difficult challenge for the proponent of the third view is to define and argue for the proper parameters for that "certain class" of internal constraints. I think a good case can be made for such a class. However, I am going to interrupt the debate here. I involved us in it in the first place simply to illustrate what sort of thing happens when people who share the same impulses jump on distinctions to define more sharply their in-crowd status. However this particular debate finally gets resolved, one thing that's clear is that over the years, each group of egalitarianism advocates has vied for becoming the politically correct group. They have all vied to become the in-crowd that has the power of "the given." They have vied to become the group that has attained the critical mass of popular acceptance needed to guarantee specialness, excluding from sharing this specialness anyone who would differ in the smallest detail from "the given" doctrine. I don't mean to minimize the importance of very real differences between groups of people who agree on general doctrine. Certainly the differences in our example are real enough. And, certainly, which one a government chooses to side with has a great impact on real social action. However, I do mean to emphasize that besides that fact, social identifiers use such differences to get another job done, one that has nothing to do with egalitarianism and its moral content but rather with better anchoring one's sense of social identity.

I would like to make some general observations now about how "the given" works in most social identifying contexts, especially as they pertain to groups sharing doctrinaire beliefs. These observations are reflected in the egalitarianism debate. First of all, a truth about social identification is that what doctrine a group will pursue at any point in time is always relative to what the public-at-large is *just short* of being willing to tolerate. Thirty years ago, the public-at-large was just short of a willingness to tolerate "equal opportunity" as an acceptable egalitarian group-defining doctrine. Since that doctrine was *close* to being tolerable, the egalitarian liberal ran with this doctrine in hopes of making it "the given." It finally won the day against the major nonegalitarian doctrine competitors. Many of those who had fought the good fight now rested on their laurels. Among other things, they had attained the rewards that come from a cohesive and strong social identifying group. Their sense of group kinship, which had been growing during the struggle for acceptance, had finally reached its peak. They were part of a group that was as secure as secure could be within a society. They were the specials among specials. Now they could savor their victory. They were in the process of consolidating their social identity by nailing down and immersing their sense of value kinship and shared sense of social power (narcissistic omnipotence?) by expressing and reexpressing their newly won doctrine, the newest version of "the given."

Kinship and social power have a kind of inertia to them. Once a person attains them, he will tend to go with his doctrine without thinking much more about it. Since it is "the given," there no longer is the need to work hard to defend it. The wars are over. For many people, that is acceptable. They have consolidated a kind of social identity sharing of group value and power they are satisfied with. This inertia doesn't work on everybody, however. Sometimes victors aren't satisfied. Social identity consolidation isn't enough for them. They need to reaffirm their social kinship and power. They need to go through the wars with others again and again to feel their social value and power. They need continually to find new battles to fight. That is to say, they need continually to push the boundaries of "the given" further and further along. For these people, once a doctrine has been accepted as "the given" by the public-at-large, they actually become socially insecure. So they set off on a new mission to find what new doctrine the public-at-large is now *just short* of tolerating.[10] Along with newcomers to the whole process, they expand the now given doctrine to something for which they can fight. The social identity excitement of "the old doctrine" is gone for them. Becoming "the establishment" is often at the cost of their sense of social specialness. People who were too young to participate in the battles over the old doctrine's becoming "the given" don't appreciate that doctrine's social force. They don't enjoy it as a centering activity for their sense of social identity. Neither do the constitutional social malcontents who fought the battles for "the old doctrine." None of these people enjoy "the old doctrine" as a centering activity for their sense of social identity. The doctrine is "establishment," nothing special, nothing exclusionary. To them, the doctrine is inert dogma, although perhaps still generally acceptable on moral grounds. For them, as the given, this doctrine has none of the kinship-making virtues it had for the doctrine's pioneers. So, along with the malcontents among the original battlers, the newcomers embark on expanding the old doctrine to something new. They fight to have some new version of egalitarianism, for example, become acceptable as the given by the public-at-large. Social engagement, conflict, new shared battles with comrades—all this in order to become a new special in-crowd member. In the process, one may even have to do battle with the old-timers who are stuck in the old thinking about egalitarianism. What we have here are simply two generations of egalitarian thinkers and activists, one which used to get its social identity needs met by socially identifying with one doctrine about egalitarianism, the other which currently gets its social identity needs met by identifying with a different, more expanded version of egalitarianism.

In fact, I believe that proponents of the three views of egalitarianism that we just looked at fit under this description. Moreover, I am confident that there will be still newer versions of the view to come.[11] These will involve old battlers in need of new wars to fight in order to reaffirm their sense of social identity. But, along with them, there will be newcomers looking to share in fighting for a doctrine that isn't yet "the given." They will work to make it so. Then they will enjoy the fruits of social identification. They, too, will enjoy the sense of social value, power, and specialness that comes from sharing values with comrades and excluding unspecial others. To these people, however, any virtue of the old versions of the egalitarian doctrine will seem unfathomable, except perhaps its role as a steppingstone to where things will have come by then. Short of this, however, the old doctrine seems relatively meaningless. Indeed, that doctrine *is* meaningless to them, because they *don't identify* with it. They don't identify with it because it doesn't meet the needs that motivate social identification. Only a new version of the doctrine will do. In this regard, the boundaries of any doctrine are forever being expanded, until there is nothing more to expand. The old doctrine and its variations have run their course. That is to say, the old doctrine has become so enlarged that virtually everyone accepts it and no one is socially distinct in holding it. When a doctrine no longer allows for its defenders to be special—distinct from other kinds of social identificatory groups—it has outlived its social identificatory usefulness, although it may still have moral worth. At that point, radical social change becomes a historical imperative. New social meaning arises as revolutionary doctrine. People start to make autonomous choices about wholly new forms of shared social valuation standards; that is, whole new social forms are suggested. A new cycle of evolving versions of a new doctrine vying for the status of "the given" begins. In this regard, I have no doubt but that democratic egalitarianism will eventually exhaust itself in all its many varieties. People will stop autonomously choosing it as a central defining feature of their social lives. How long this will take is anyone's guess.

I would like to close the discussion in this section by placing our focus back on the unique role that exclusion plays in social identification. Specifically, I would like to interject a moral consideration about exclusion. We have suggested that in nailing down their special social identities by exclusion of others, people sometimes point out their differences with others and also sing the praises of their own group's shared valuations. We know, too, that social identifiers also sometimes point out their differences with others, sing the praises of their group's shared valuations, and also *demean* the valuations of the excluded others. In the latter context, it is, as I pointed out earlier, as though the weaker the case for the other group's valuations, the stronger the case for one's own group's. I would like finally to comment directly on the moral shortsightedness of this view of social identifying. I would like to suggest that, as important as it is in defining in-group status, it is really an immoral distortion of the social identificatory act.

To make the point, consider what the social identificatory act might look like were there no exclusionary practice afoot, no attempt to become a member of a most-favored in-group. Clearly, this would be a context of optimal functioning social identification—maybe even something worthy of the designation "healthy social identification." Consider, for example, what can happen when people socially identify with gender, race, religion, and ethnicity. When things work optimally, it is quite proper for an African-American to take pride in his heritage. "Black is beautiful" is an affirmation of his social valuation of his race. There is nothing wrong with a person's sharing in valuing his racial group distinctiveness. We can slice the social group pie any way we like. We can join in celebration of any shared traits we wish. Indeed, white people who want to celebrate their racial heritage are perfectly within the bounds of what persons do as social character-building beings. Feminists who want to celebrate "women's

power" and "female spirituality" are expressing shared gender identifications. Men who wrap themselves in macho behavior are *just*
being a certain shared image of manhood. In and of themselves, there
is nothing wrong with these sorts of moves. I am not talking about
moral wrong here, although I can't see any moral objections here
either. What I am talking about is the way in which people function
when they are successfully acting as social identificatory beings. All
the kinds of identificatory moves I've just mentioned are precisely the
kinds of things people appropriately do when they want to carve out
and express their social selves. There are no *a priori* reasons for placing identifications with gender, race, and the like out of bounds for
the kinds of things about which people should be making social identifications. It is quite in the spirit of being a social identificatory individual that a person celebrates his valuatively special shared traits
with his social kin and tries to make clear that others are *different*
from his group. That's what people *do* as social identity beings.

If this were all people did with their social identifications, life
would be considerably more peaceful than it is. Unfortunately, matters get messy when people take their valuated social traits and proceed to use them to derogate the other's social reality. They turn their
inherent differences with other groups into more than just simply differences. These differences become a cause for moral superiority.
This happens when a person actually has as part of his character *definition* the *negation* of the other as a social entity. The individual
here defines his group as essentially *superior* to all other groups that
lack his group's defining social characteristics. So we might find
some macho men defining their social selves partly in terms of their
macho qualities being superior to all nonmacho men and women.
They believe that they are valuable social beings to the degree that
all nonmachos are of little or no value. Similarly, it isn't uncommon
to find some feminists who define themselves as valuatively special
social beings by derogating males for the feminine qualities they lack
or for the macho qualities they possess. We recognize such men and
women as "gender bashers." When Ku Klux Klan members define
themselves not only as "white" and "Christian" but also as "not black"
and "not Jewish"—where being black or Jewish is thought to encompass a nest of inferior traits of character—matters are getting beyond
the proper functioning of social identification. The difficulty I am
talking about arises where a person's being a certain kind of social
identity would make it impossible for another person to be his own
kind of social identity. "Exclusion at the cost of the other's social

identifications" is unacceptable for moral reasons. People are just being identificatory persons when they try to carve out a social identification that is special. But they aren't allowing the other to be a full-fledged person when they do it at the cost of the other's being his own social self. They show a lack of respect for the other as a person, and that is morally objectionable. Respect for persons is morally sacrosanct. Other things being equal, each individual and group of individuals is entitled to be the social self he wants or they want. By the same token, sometimes, for moral reasons, other things are *not* equal—say, there are moral objections one could raise about the value of a particular group's identifications. Here there may, indeed, be reasons to derogate the other. Of course, the problem is that most people who define themselves in terms of negating the other usually think they have morality on their side. So while I might partly define myself socially as an anti-Klan person and feel that I have morality on my side, I have no doubt but that many Klan members might define themselves as anti-Semites and feel that they have morality on their side. In such a situation, arguing ethics becomes the final arbiter.[12]

The point is, while in-group social identifying seems to require exclusionary behavior, social identification doesn't require it in principle. A person can have a full sense of a social self without focusing on exclusion. Alas, though, that isn't how most people choose to behave. We opt for behavior that is morally deficient.

III

Our focus in this chapter has been on understanding social character identification, with the major portion of that focus having been aimed at understanding what goes into identifying with external groups. I would like to make some concluding remarks now about social identification as it mixes with personal identification in the making of the full character self. What does the interplay of these two modes of organizing character look like?

For one thing, it is interesting to note that there is no character *content* that is peculiar to either personal or social character identity. The very same thing that one person identifies with as a personal identification another person might identify with as a social identification. The only factors distinguishing these two individuals are the internal existential directives—the built-in prime directives—to which their identifications are responses. So, while one person might posit ultimate valuation of the doctrine of nonviolence as an expression of her personal character identity, another person might posit ultimate valuation for the very same doctrine as an expression of her social character identity. The first individual is responding to a general existential directive to secure a sense of individuality, the second is responding to a directive for social belonging. Different concerns are determining what direction they will go in with their autonomous valuational choosing, but they end up at the same content place.

This interpersonal truth is also an intrapersonal truth. For example, while someone might be a pacifist at one point in life as an expression of personal identification, he might evolve into a pacifist at another point in life as an expression of social identification. Which existential directives one responds to at a given time is a wholly contingent matter. So, before, he didn't care if others shared his ultimate valuation. In fact, he was pleased that in holding the valuation in the way he did, he felt unique as a character. But he came to see that others held the same general kind of valuation. And he came to appreciate that in sharing the general valuation with others, he had his need for a sense of social belonging massaged. What started out as a personal identification turned into a social identification. Indeed, this identification can branch in either of two possible directions. One, the individual might *only* socially identify with pacifism now. That is, were the group to disband and disassociate itself from any concern with pacifism, his commitment to the value might disappear, too. For we have already said that he no longer has any personal identity commitment to stand up for regardless of what anyone else thinks. And now the reason for social identification with the value is gone, too. There is a second branching possibility, however. The individual might *both* socially and personally identify with pacifism. This is the more common road people generally go down with their social identifications. What starts off purely as a personal identification might evolve into a social one, too. His identifying becomes overdetermined. Ultimate valuation of pacifism meets both his concern for individuality and his concern for social belonging. Were the group to disband, he would still be committed to pacifism, but for reasons of individuality. Clearly, since a lot of social identifying arises out of valuation a person *already* is committed to for his own personal character self reasons, then the disappearance of the valuation's social function won't obliterate the valuation from his character.

Clearly, the most dramatic example of personal and social identification melding into one another revolves around the moral life. It is quite common for a person's youthful commitment to pursuing some personal vision of the moral life regardless of what anyone else thinks to evolve quickly into a social identification with morality, too. That is, as I pointed out in the first section, most people end up sharing a vision of the moral life with one another. They may differ on the fine detail, but they usually end up being in community with their comrades around some general commitment to doing the right thing. And not just a small group of comrades. People eventually discover that they belong to the group "humanity" sharing one of the many normative versions of how life should be led morally. What may have started as an anchor for the individual's sense of individuation ends up also as an anchor for his sense of belonging to humanity. And this anchor is quite weighty. The pull of being in community with humanity around the trait of "shared moral vision" may have no equal among all the kinds of social identifications.[13] For *all* people (all humanity) get to be special in their sharing of moral commitment. Indeed, the specialness they share here with the rest of humanity is played out in their feeling superior to the rest of the animal kingdom. That is where the competing excluded groups reside. It is because only people share in moral vision that they are able to feel justified in making claims about being (morally) superior to the rest of nature. In any event, the central point here is that making a personal valuational commitment to the moral life soon turns into a social identification with that same life. In the case of a person's commitment to the moral life, the directive to individuate quickly gets joined or supplanted by the directive to belong.

Another interesting feature of the mix of personal and social identification has to do with the degree to which either one tends to dominate any individual's personality repertoire. And paired against either of these identification tendencies is the contingent matter about what degree of dominance causal forces have in one's causal identity behavior. So while some people tend to be more social character identifiers than personal character identifiers, and others tend to go the other way, still others tend to be more causal selves than either kind of character identity. That is, some of us remain more causal machines than we become characters. Hedonistic wantons and social conformists are the more dramatic instances of this phenomenon. Causal tendencies aside, though, certainly some of us become more personal identities than anything else, seemingly always fighting for principle and going our own way in life. Others of us become more social identities than anything else, seemingly always fighting for one shared ideal or another, reflectively moralizing and politicizing everything about it down to the finest detail. People simply have their character tendencies, although no one but the rarest of persons is any of these possibilities exclusively. No one is a total wanton animal; no one is a total conformist; no one is a total self-enclosed individual; no one is a total social maneuverer.

Not only does each of us have his tendencies in this regard, so do whole cultures. Indeed, if we disregard any causal factors and look exclusively at personal and social character tendencies, it becomes clear that while people always have had an existential imperative to pursue each of the two senses of character identity, different historical periods have put an emphasis on one or the other for the culture as a whole. Some cultures have tended to be more deeply immersed in concerns of social identification, others more concerned with personal identity. Some cultures have seemed more concerned with people choosing individualism, others more concerned with people choosing to join together to serve some shared image of the social good. Peter Berger speculates about these ideas. However, for him, the difference in these tendencies gets expressed in the relative attention a culture pays to *dignity* or *honor*. A culture in which people are preoccupied with dignity is a culture concerned with the importance of the individual as a distinctive personal identity. A culture in which people are preoccupied with honor is a culture concerned with the importance of the individual as a social identity. Berger wants to talk about where our present-day culture fits into this schema—a culture of dignity or a culture of honor? He opts for dignity. Finally, I think he is wrong about this. Let me suggest why I think this and, in the process, flesh out the implications of his view for our discussion.

Berger says,

> The age that saw the decline of honor also saw the rise of...dignity and the rights of the individual....Dignity, as against honor, always relates to the intrinsic humanity divested of all socially imposed roles or norms. It pertains to the self as such, to the individual regardless of his position in society.[14]

The concept of honor implies that identity is essentially, or at least importantly, linked to institutional roles. The modern concept of dignity, by contrast, implies that identity is essentially independent of institutional roles.[15] I think Berger is right that the modern *concept* of dignity implies an identity centered around the individual in his nonsocial distinctiveness. But I think Berger is wrong in believing that this concept applies to who most people in our culture in fact are, for our culture has so often been characterized by social critics as one in which people pay more attention to solidifying their social identity than their personal identity. People in fact pay an inordinate amount of attention to trying to fit into the complex social structures they face. Not only do we still live in an age where people wrap themselves in their chosen ideologies, but we live in a time when social causal forces run roughshod over a lot of who we are. We are told what to say, think, and feel as social beings. The media sounds the clarion call for all of us to pay attention to our social causal selves. We are so overwhelmed both by the social structures putting these demands on us and by the media communicating the social structures' messages to us that we have lost any reasonable focus one would expect us to have on our personal selves (as well as on our social character selves too). Some social critics even claim that this media blitz is responsible for our societal angst.[16]   We are given images of social selves to follow—TV, for example, hammers away at the roles we are to live through. And all the while, most of us just don't have a clue anymore about how to be solitary individuating selves. We're out of practice. This dysfunctioning of character has become a symptom of the modern age.

Of course, not everyone is so helpless. Angst isn't the only response to the onslaught of socializing forces. Many people meet the challenge head-on and insist that social institutions had better lighten their heavy causal hand. Instead of continuing to see how one can best fit into the social world, many people are insisting more and more on being afforded their individual rights. Individual dignity takes center stage for them. I am certain that this is the image that Berger has in mind. Moreover, I take his notion of "having dignity" to be close to what I referred to in the last chapter as a person's "having integrity in being the unique individual one has chosen to be." Consequently, the current movement to have people treat one another with dignity is an acknowledgment of and respect for the individual's attempt at uniqueness of personal character identity. It is a respect for a person's standing for what he does regardless of what others think. Berger is right in thinking that securing dignity and having it both recognized and respected are now more important to us than before. However, he misses the point that this is precisely *because* there is *already* so much in our social institutions weighing against securing dignity.

The truth about the current cultural scene, therefore, is a far cry from Berger's contention that the basic character tendency of our age is distinctive personal identifying. We defensively focus as much as we do on securing human dignity because, in fact, the world has been moving so swiftly in the direction of trampling it. It only takes a casual glance at some of life's realities—assembly-line mass production, two world wars, genocide, nuclear holocaust, deafening silence to most of the world's pockets of starvation, perhaps even abortion—to see that our respect for the dignity of the individual (i.e., our respect for the importance of one's carving out a personal character identity) is fighting contrary tendencies in the social body.

Our own nation's battle to secure individual rights is certainly a response to the losses dignity has suffered. However, that observation doesn't make the point I want to make that we are more focused on securing social identity than personal identity. But *that* point is easily made by still another casual glance at the social realities. All we need to do is acknowledge how TV, advertising, economic class reality, and political institutions all conspire to make us into the image of what Herbert Marcuse called the "one-dimensional man."[17] We tend to be conformists bent on satisfying "false needs"—materialistic definitions of the social self—conditioned into us by the endless numbers of voracious social institutions that seem intent on gobbling up everything individualistic in their path. Our habits have us more concerned with the social than the individual. The rights movement is our attempt to fight these habits. So, not only are the national social liberation movements about rights that I mentioned earlier important vehicles for social identification, they are also important vehicles for fighting the objectionable intrusion into rights by social forces. These movements are reactions to our bad tendencies. The message is clear: Let people be themselves, other things being equal. Clearly, the domestic liberation movements are attempts to define and secure acceptance for minorities whose personal identities haven't in the past been popularly accepted. These movements are battles against social prejudice against the individual. But these battles are even more uphill than they would be if they just had to fight prejudice. They also have to fight the tremendous power that causal socialization processes and desires for social character identity bring to the scene. What I mean is that many of these movements get co-opted by social concern. So liberationists become popular celebrities. What starts out as a concern for promoting and respecting individualism soon gets overwhelmed by concerns for conformism. Even if one doesn't fully identify with a given liberation movement's shared values, joining the given movement still becomes the "in" thing to do. The mere notion of joining becomes another way of securing group acceptance and at least social causal identity. By joining, even without identifying, one shows himself to be an accepted member of the liberal establishment, fighting for the rights of the oppressed.

In concluding our discussion in this chapter, I want to say something about Berger's claims about honor as a sign of the importance of social character. Once again, Berger's conceptual insight is an interesting one. An age in which people are preoccupied with issues of honor *is* an age that is skewed toward people securing their sense of social character. And he is right that this isn't the profile of our age. But from the fact that he is right about this, it doesn't follow that he is right in thinking that we are centered on respecting issues of dignity. Clearly, people aren't particularly more successful with being honorable in our culture than in cultures past. But that may be because people today are more social causal identities than they are social character selves. By contrast, in a world where people are volitionally reflective about their social roles—that is, in a world where people finally make identificatory choices about how they want to fit into the groups around them—honor plays an important role. So, for any of us who make choices about how our social lives are to be good lives, acting with honor becomes an important issue. The ideal honorable person is someone who lives his social definition. He faithfully abides by his chosen social responsibilities. He is recognized by others by how well he meets this standard. In fact, when he is publicly recognized and celebrated for his excellence in consistently living through his social character identity, we speak of how he is being "publicly honored." The individual's feeling of honor to any extent is all about his feeling public acceptance. Of course, this is always a matter of degree. Most of us don't often feel fully honored or honorific. We merely feel that "we are sufficiently measuring up to shared public value standards," and so we are acceptable to our group of choice. But sometimes we do feel the full force of acceptance through the feeling of honor. The term "honor" really connotes more of a "full and complete public acceptance." This is as secure in the social world as a person can be. He fully belongs to the group of his choice; he has a total security of social character identity. He can't get any closer to being part of a group. To be paid an honor is the highest form of group recognition and acceptance a person can get.

Then too, when one is acting honorable without the frills of receiving public recognition, he is acting by the public rules even in the face of possible personal loss. Perhaps only he is aware—vis-à-vis his honorable feelings—that he has played by the socially determined values he has taken on himself. But that may be enough. He knows that he really does abide by and share important group values. His honorable feelings thus bolster his feelings of camaraderie with the group even more. He knows who he is socially, even if others don't. He feels socially confirmed to the extent that *if* others knew his commitment to group values, they *would* honor him. So, instead, he honors himself by feeling honorable.

Let me reiterate, however, that although this is how honor works as a dynamic force in social identification, people in our culture in fact aren't particularly immersed in issues of honor. Berger has that much right. But it isn't because our culture is heavily invested in the tendency to respect and foster individualism. Rather, it is because social *causal* identity forces are so overwhelming that we have neither the time nor the concern to worry about being socially honorable. Ours is a culture in which both facets of character identity suffer at the hands of causality. We've got our identificatory work cut out for us.

Conclusion

We have learned that the process of identification begins with a person's noticing various traits about either his causal identity or external models. He then chooses some of those traits to be parts of his character. He chooses to take psychological ownership of them. It is through identificatory valuation that the desired ownership starts to make any serious headway. What's needed to complete the process is self-responsibility. It is in self-responsibly standing for one's identificatory valuation that one can finally be said *to be* the character he had only before imagined being. The product of the whole process—character—branches into a personal and social self. In the case of the personal self, one's self-responsible valuations power his life as an individual distinct from all other individuals. In the case of the social self, his self-responsible valuations power his sense of social belonging.

That's the summary view of identification. Obviously, we have also come to know a great deal about the detail of the process. That has been my concern in Part II. However, the discussion can't end here. I don't want us to miss seeing the forest for the trees. So, in these concluding remarks, I would like to underscore how what we have been doing in this book addresses some basic concerns that were first expressed at the very outset of our inquiry. In the Introduction, we said that clarifying the concept of identification would be helpful with three general problem areas. One had to do with bettering our understanding of what it takes for a person to become someone he likes. Another had to do with confronting a current debate in philosophy about the fundamental nature of being a person. And a third had to do with tidying up a particular portion of the psychoanalytic conceptual map. How has what we have done with the concept of identification helped us with these issues?

Let's take the last problem area first. In Part I, I was particularly interested in reviewing the psychoanalytic accounts of self development. That was because those accounts appeared to be the major ones in the psychology literature that took seriously the importance of identification for self development. But we saw that although psychoanalysis acknowledged an important role for identification, it didn't really do enough about fully clarifying the concept. In order to understand what it *did* say about identification and self development, we needed to see what the developmental precursors to identification looked like, as they are discussed in Object Relations Theory and Narcissism Theory. We saw the gist of Object Relations Theory to be that infant persons are pre-selves that introjectively internalize the agency of others and use that introjected agency in the defensive maintenance of the individual mind/body person. Who the individual is at this stage of self development is the sum total of the mind/body's introjective processes and their other psychological defense mechanism cousins. We then saw the gist of Narcissism Theory to be that pre-self infants eventually become rudimentary selves that begin developing their own agency by copying aspects of the parent-as-agency model. Those copied qualities are distinctly grandiose, so that the first hints of an internal agency for a person are characterized by his having an unrealistic sense of internal all-powerfulness. The rest of life is about both toning down this sense of grandiosity to square better with reality and developing this glimmer of narcissistic self agency into a beacon of full-fledged internal character agency.

This last idea—the creation of an internal character agency—is part of the work of identification. But, as I have said, it is unfortunate that the psychoanalytic literature doesn't explicitly lay out the conditions for understanding this concept. It is never made clear exactly what a person must do to identify a reality-based self—a character—into existence. Identification is mostly understood as a kind of psychological "black box" process that *somehow* takes a person beyond the mere causal processes of the earlier developmental stages into the world of more rational ego reality, the end result being an adult character who has consolidated traits for living life and who can act on the world as a fully functioning internal agency. In this regard, "identification" amounts to a theoretical process construct that bridges the gap between a life where there is absolutely no internal agency and a life which has attained full adult agency. However, there is no conceptual analysis offered for this theoretical construct; there is no analysis of what actually *happens* inside the black box. And it takes such a conceptual analysis of identification to adequately fill in the psychoanalytic story.

Indeed, theoretical constructs are best not left merely dangling with other constructs in a theory. We want them eventually tied down to experience through observational language. This is as true in psychoanalysis as it is in any other theory employing constructs, for without tying psychoanalytic concepts down to something about how people actually behave, think, and feel, there is too great a chance for extravagant claims to be made through their use. Without a full airing of how a concept is tied to experience, careless assumptions might be made about the concept which lead to general misperceptions about how the world really works. This has certainly been the case with identification. It is assumed in the psychoanalytic literature, for example, that identification is a thoroughgoing unconscious object relating process along with all the others (e.g., incorporation, projection, introjection, etc.). The fact of the matter is, though, under normal circumstances, identification is not an unconscious object relating state like incorporation, introjection, and the like. Under normal circumstances, it *can't possibly* be unconscious. For if identification were inherently an unconscious act, there would be no basis for any of the claims people ever made about the process and its product, character. Character and its production are things that people praise or blame, sympathize with, control, try harder with, and so on. In short, we treat character and the process that creates it as intentional material for which a person can take responsibility. It makes no sense to speak of a thoroughgoing unconscious process or its product in these ways. But the unaired psychoanalytic assumption about identification leads to just such a position. The fact of the matter is, identification sometimes is a conscious activity. And sometimes it can be—indeed, it usually is—a preconscious activity. And in either of these contexts, responsibility-related notions *are* appropriate to talk about. Indeed, identification may even, on occasion, occur unconsciously. But that is the unusual case in need of special explanation; it's not the rule. Conceptually, identification simply can't be a *thoroughgoing unconscious* process. And so, among other things, my analysis of identification as a complex process heavily grounded in self-responsibility and various kinds of choices that identifiers make has the benefit of straightening out this wrong psychoanalytic assumption.

Another extravagant claim of psychoanalytic theory is the idea that full-fledged identification begins during infancy. As I have said before, such a claim about identification's timetable can't possibly be true. After all, full-fledged identification is all about the autonomous choosing of value standards, and infants and young children simply don't have the capacity for that sort of complex volitional/valuational activity yet. When all is said and done, I believe that the psychoanalytic mention of identification here is just inaccurate. What appears to be infancy identification is really introjection. While there may be the introjective borrowing of agency from external sources, there simply is no identificatory character self agency on the scene during infancy and early childhood. The latter is being confused with the former. My analysis enables us to bring this confusion to light.

So my work offers a critique of some of the psychoanalytic claims made about identification. However, it should be understood that what I say is in no way intended as a debunking of the central psycho-analytic thesis—viz., that identification is the developmental descendant of the unconscious object relating and narcissism processes. Indeed, part of what I have done throughout my discussion in this book has been to show the detail of how identification descends from these primitive self development states. My analysis actually has the benefit of *explaining* the connection between identification and the precursor object relating and narcissism processes. And so I hope that what I have done is taken by the psychoanalytic community in the spirit in which it is being offered—viz., as a helpful contribution to the ongoing understanding and clarification of important psycho-analytic phenomena.

Not only is my analysis intended to fill gaps in psychoanalytic theory, though; it is also intended to provide a context for dealing with the second general problem area—the philosophical debate over personhood, character. We looked at the debaters' claim that persons are essentially evaluators. This is the view that central to person-hood is one's ability to reflectively evaluate—to make value judg-ments about—which of his first-order conscious states to act on. The debate we walked in on wasn't about whether or not evaluation is central to personhood—the debaters were already in agreement about that—but rather over which variety of evaluation was the right one. The battlelines were drawn between weak evaluation and strong evaluation, the former being a nonmoral notion and the latter being a moral one. That discussion is certainly interesting. But we saw that it is beside the point. I hope that what I have shown in my analysis of identification throws some doubt into the accepted premise that *some form or other* of evaluation is the key to person-hood. What's unique about being a person isn't that one is an evalu-ator but rather that one is an identifier. A person creates his own value standards for his image of what makes life good. And in inter-nalizing those standards by the process of identification, he is being a person in the fullest sense, a character. It is only because a person has *first* done this essential character act that he is *then* able to make evaluations about first-order states. That is, *given* that a person is first a character with posited standards for what counts as the good life, he then has a basis for evaluating what he should do from moment to moment. Evaluations are only expressions of the more fundamental valuational defining feature of character.

There is another place where my analysis sheds some light on this philosophical debate. Not only is evaluation quite secondary as a criterion for personhood, but even if we were to accept the central-ity claim about evaluation, Taylor's concept of *strong* evaluation would still be lacking. I believe that what Taylor is arguing is really just a new version of the age-old philosophical idea that persons are essentially moral beings. For Taylor, strong evaluation is defined as moral (and spiritual) evaluation. So when he argues for strong eval-uation as the central criterion of personhood, he is really falling into the long tradition of arguing for humankind's moral nature. But I hope I have effectively thrown some healthy doubt into that age-old discussion. In my analysis, the moral life is simply one more kind of valuational character commitment a person may or may not make. One usually does make it, of course, especially because of the moral perspective's effectiveness in anchoring a person's sense of social com-munity and belonging. But there's nothing conceptually necessary about anchoring either sense of identity through moral commitment.

Finally, not only does my analysis fill gaps in psychoanalytic theory and offer new light to philosophical debates about the self, it also provides a very important context for understanding the most difficult of life's puzzles—how does a person ever become someone he likes? The road we have traveled in looking for an answer to this question has taken us first past the psychoanalytic theories of self development and then into our analysis of identificatory choosing. The psychoanalytic encounters allowed us to investigate and carry away what was of value for understanding the early self as a wholly causal entity. In that domain, it simply made no sense to speak of the infantile or early childhood version of the self as something that the infant or child could like. Infants and young children can't like them-selves or not like themselves as wholly causal entities. The psycho-logical prerequisites for liking or not liking oneself just have not come on the scene yet. What has come on the scene by then are a host of unconscious psychological processes, on the basis of which the per-spicacious observer can provide numerous psychological accounts of the causal nature of persons as they appear during the early stages of life. So one *can* talk about the infant as a causal identity. But *that's* not something that is worthy of being liked or not for its value by the infant. It just *is* what it is. One's causal identity is merely a set of psychological mechanisms that work efficiently or not in getting all the early life wants and needs satisfied. But in order to become a self that can justifiably like itself or not, this composite of causal mechanisms has to develop into a being of autonomous character. And we know that that takes a lot of work with identification.

Once a person starts identifying with parts of who he has already been as a causal identity or with new possibilities that he sees modeled out in the world beyond himself, he starts forming his character self. And it is in virtue of how well a person lives consistently with this character self that he can legitimately start to like himself or not. Becoming someone one likes involves one's choosing to be a character of ultimate valuation and then following through by really being that person in action, thought, and feeling. Who a person is as a character is largely defined by what he values—what he valuationally chooses—as life ideals. When we strip away everything else from life, what a person is left with as a character is what value ideals he stands for and how well he does at living up to them. I am talking about the quality of a person's life here, about what gives his life meaning, about what makes his life worthwhile. Living life by the value standards that a person thinks he ought to live his life by is the key to all of this. When one lives by his self-created standards, *he has become someone he likes*. For what has he done after all? He has made himself into a being who has chosen an image of life as he means it to be lived. And he tries to live it. He takes it upon himself to judge the worth of his life henceforth in terms of how true he is to that image. That is to say, he looks to see how well he fits his actions into his personal and social identificatory ideals.

Of course, this all becomes a very complex affair. The array of ideals is vast and they vary from individual to individual. A person may, for example, sculpt and resculpt his personal and/or social ideal images of who he would be as a husband, a father, a teacher, a friend, a colleague, a competitive ballplayer, a loyal person, a truthful person, a socially concerned person, a powerful person, an intellectually curious person, a creative person, and so on and so forth. That's the kind of picture that one person might have to consider in becoming someone he likes. He would have to see how faithful—self-responsible—he has been to his ideal valuational standards for being a husband, a father, a teacher, and so on. This is the foundation on which his whole sense of himself as a being of any worth would hinge. Indeed, each individual has his own unique foundation defining his requirements for self-worth. Each individual makes his own valuational choices about what will count as important in life. In this sense, we all get a chance to like ourselves for entirely our own reasons.

Of course, there are no guarantees here. We know what it takes to become and remain someone we like. It takes maintaining a consistency about the character traits that our identificatory acts have brought into existence. Such consistency is no easy matter. And meeting up to our character is an especially difficult proposition when we realize that there are often unforeseen consequences not always to our liking that can follow on the heels of some of our best character efforts. And perhaps most challenging is the fact that there are always people telling us that the identificatory choices we have made in life aren't as good as they might be, aren't as good as theirs. They are telling us not to be satisfied with who we are, to dislike ourselves. The challenge for us is not to listen. There are no "bests" in the universe of characters. There is only what each of us decides to create for herself. If we aren't satisfied with who we are because we listen to the choices of others, we are simply failing to appreciate the full nature of our identificatory lives. All of us, in fact, have within us the capacity to be satisfied with ourselves. Of course, it takes a certain vigilance, too (a strength of character?), to do all that's required for becoming someone we like, for being someone with whom we are satisfied. As autonomous identificatory creatures, the choice is certainly up to us. Do we always have to choose to be self-satisfied? Clearly not. Can we be characters without always doing what it takes to be people who like themselves? Of course. That's surely a large part of many people's life experience. We choose and rechoose images of the good life, but we simply don't always take our defense of those images as seriously as we might. We identify, but not fully. Nevertheless, we are still characters. In the final analysis, it is only when we take identification as seriously as we can, and so choose to be as fully self-responsible as we can about our valuational images, that we have a chance of being not just a character but a character that is someone we like. What's a person to do?

NOTES

1. In fact, that is one of my central concerns in *The Consequences of Identification*, in progress.
2. Daniel Dennett, "Why Everyone Is a Novelist," *Times Literary Supplement* 4 (459); Gerald Dworkin, "Autonomy and Behavior Control," *Hastings Center Report* (February 1976); idem, *The Theory and Practice of Autonomy* (Cambridge: Cambridge University Press, 1988); Owen Flanagan and Amelie Rorty (eds.), *Identity, Character, and Morality* (Cambridge: MIT Press, 1991); Harry Frankfurt, *The Importance of What We Care About* (Cambridge: Cambridge University Press, 1988); Jonathan Glover, *I: The Philosophy and Psychology of Personal Identity* (New York: Penguin, 1988); Thomas Nagel, *Mortal Questions* (Cambridge: Cambridge University Press, 1979); Richard Rorty, *Contingency, Irony, and Solidarity* (New York: Cambridge University Press, 1989); Charles Taylor, *Sources of the Self: The Making of Modern Identity* (Cambridge: Harvard University Press, 1989); idem, *Human Agency and Language: Philosophical Papers*, vol. 1 (Cambridge: Cambridge University Press, 1985); Bernard Williams, *Moral Luck: Philosophical Papers* (Cambridge: Cambridge University Press, 1981).
3. Dworkin, "Autonomy and Behavior Control." Actually, his view changes a bit in his later *Theory and Practice of Autonomy*, pp. 15–16. The change moves him even closer to Frankfurt and Taylor. He says that in his original *Hastings* view, to be autonomous was to identify with one's choices about first-order states; and to identify with his choices about first-order states meant that a person was endorsing those first-order states. In the later *Theory* view, to be autonomous regarding a choice meant that a person could either endorse a given first-order state *or not*. The revised view looks like the views we discuss below about Frankfurt and Taylor's notion of evaluation.
4. Frankfurt, *What We Care About*, pp. 11–25.
5. Taylor, "What Is Human Agency?", in *Human Agency and Language*, p. 16.
6. Ibid., p. 34. Let me add here the fuller text. "Shorn of these we would cease to be ourselves, by which we do not mean trivially that we would be different in the sense of having some properties other than those we now have—which would indeed be the case after any change, however minor—but that shorn of these we would lose the very possibility of being an agent who evaluates; that our existence as persons, and hence our ability to adhere as persons to certain evaluations, would be impossible outside the horizon of these essential evaluations, that we would break

down as persons, be incapable of being persons in the full sense" (pp. 34–35). His view is hard to miss.

7. Owen Flanagan, "Identity and Strong and Weak Evaluation," in Flanagan and Rorty (eds.), *Identity, Character, and Morality.*

8. There is much more than just this to the distinction. Indeed, "What Is Human Agency" is devoted to laying out the detail of the distinction. In addition to the above, Taylor makes a case that weak evaluations are quantitative while strong ones are qualitative—that weak evaluations have no accompanying contrastive vocabulary describing them while strong evaluations do (i.e., first-order desires which are "higher or lower," "noble or base," and so on), and that there is no articulacy about weak evaluations (i.e., that we don't express or describe them much through language) while there is about strong evaluations. These are all interesting distinctions, even if Flanagan casts some doubts about each of them. See Flanagan, "Identity and Strong and Weak Evaluation."

9. In "What Is Human Agency?" p. 16, Taylor says, "I agree with Frankfurt that this capacity to evaluate desires is bound up with our power of self-evaluation, which in turn is an essential feature of the mode of agency we recognize as human. But I believe we can come closer to defining what is involved in this mode of agency if we make a further distinction, between two broad kinds of evaluation of desire." Well, why? Why are we closer? He has just admitted that it is the capacity to evaluate—no distinctions necessary—that is the essential feature. What is it about "strong evaluation" that gets us even closer to the truth we are seeking?

10. Frankfurt, *What We Care About.*

11. M. Heidegger, *Being and Time* (London: SCM Press, 1962), pp. 235–41.

12. Williams, *Moral Luck*; J. J. C. Smart and Bernard Williams, *Utilitarianism: For and Against* (Cambridge: Cambridge University Press, 1973), pp. 116–117.

13. Flanagan, *Identity, Character, and Morality*, p. 55.

14. Dennett, "Why Everyone Is a Novelist,"

15. Rorty, *Contingency, Irony, and Solidarity*, p. 189.

16. Ibid., p. 73. Our final vocabularies "are the words in which we formulate praise of our friends and contempt for our enemies, our long-term projects, our deepest self-doubts and our highest hopes. They are words in which we tell...the story of our lives."

17. Ibid., p. 74.

18. See Jacques Lacan, "The Mirror Stage as Formative of the Function of the I as Revealed in Psychoanalytic Experience," in *Ecrits: A Selection*, trans. Alan Sheridan (New York: Norton, 1977), pp. 1–7. Also see John O'Neill, "The Specular Body: Merleau-Ponty and Lacan on Infant Self and Other," *Synthese* (London: Tavistock, 1980), p. 483; Maurice Merleau-Ponty, "The Child's Relations with Others," trans. William Cobb, in James Edie (ed.) *The Primacy of Perception* (Evanston, IL: Northwestern

University Press, 1964); "Henri Wallon: His World, His Work," *International Journal of Mental Health*, 1(4).

19. M. Berman, *Coming to Our Senses* (New York: Bantam, 1990).

20. See, for example, Edith Jacobson, *The Self and the Object World* (New York: International Universities Press, 1964); Margaret Mahler, F. Pine, and A. Bergman, *The Psychological Birth of the Human Infant* (New York: Basic Books, 1975); W. W. Meissner, *Internalization in Psychoanalysis* (New York: International Universities Press, 1981); D. W. Winnicott, *Playing and Reality* (New York: Basic Books, 1971); Heinz Kohut, *The Analysis of the Self* (New York: International Universities Press, 1971); Otto Kernberg, *Borderline Conditions and Pathological Narcissism* (New York: J. Aronson, 1975).

21. See, for example, John Holt's "The World of the Child" (Toronto: Canadian Broadcasting Corp., 1983).

22. Not only would analytic theory have a more powerful tool for understanding child development were it to further explore identification, but it would also have something important at its disposal for understanding self change in adults. One of the more remarkable things about our character selves is that those selves change parts in interesting ways even while maintaining their core content. It would be nice to be able to account theoretically for this. In fact, a lot of what goes on in adult character change is wrapped up in their taking on new identifications and weakening the ties of old ones. And not only is this sort of thing central to the normal process of character change, it is also some of what goes on in the change aimed at in psychoanalytic therapies as well as in other forms of therapy. So it would behoove the analytic theorists to pay closer attention to unpacking the concept of identification.

23. For the psychoanalyst, ego is that place on our mental map where all the activity aimed at the rational defeat of id impulses occurs. It is where the battle rages between reason and desiring. But that isn't what we are looking for when we are trying to get at a person's real self. It isn't what we want to learn about when we are trying to get to know who a person really is. (Of course, the psychoanalyst might have different interests here.)

The ego that the Buddhist implores us to put to rest is the Western psychological structure of reducing our self to inert images of various things. So we might see ourselves as doctors, wives, mothers, friends, scholars, and so on. These are all fixed, describable things. The Buddhist, though, believes in a self that is in motion. It has being. And being can't be pinned down as a thing. In any event, the Buddhist notion is not the psychological self we are talking about.

24. There will be brief discussion of this in chapter 2.

25. Obviously, I have just used the term "what" to talk about "who-ness." This is not inconsistent with what I have been saying. What I have

called "what" questions about persons are questions about impersonal properties of persons as members of a class. What I am calling "who-ness" questions are questions about personal properties of persons as individuals. Clearly, these are different interests.

26. For the most part, when I think that more of a technical sounding use is needed, I will say "character self." Otherwise, I will use "character."

27. Obviously, it sounds odd to say a person values being forgetful or lackadaisical. I intend to clarify this sort of claim in chapters 7 and 9.

28. Jean-Paul Sartre, *Being and Nothingness*, trans. H. Barnes (New York: Philosophical Library, 1956), pp. lxii–lxvii.

CHAPTER 2

1. I would refer the interested reader to such works as J. Piaget, *The Moral Judgment of the Child* (New York: The Free Press, 1932); J. H. Flavell, *The Developmental Psychology of Jean Piaget* (Princeton, NJ: Van Nostrand, 1963); L. Kohlberg, *The Philosophy of Moral Development* (San Francisco: Harper & Row, 1981); C. Gilligan, *In a Different Voice: Psychological Theory and Women's Development* (Cambridge: Harvard University Press, 1982).

2. The two psychoanalytic theories do not explicitly use the terms "pre-self" and "rudimentary self." Those are my terms. The two theories simply talk about "the self." In fact, though, they constantly run together different senses of "the self." So in order to avoid confusion from this practice, I am forcing my terminology on the whole discussion. As matters unfold in this chapter, the reasons for my doing this will become clear.

3. I will follow the tradition of distinguishing the metaphysical Self and the empirical self.

4. His ideas about the rational self are expressed instead as ideas about the rational soul. See Aristotle, *De Anima*, trans. J. A. Smith, in *The Basic Works of Aristotle*, ed. R. McKeon (New York: Random House, 1941).

5. R. Descartes, *Meditations*, trans. L. J. Lafleur (New York: Library of Liberal Arts, 1951).

6. G. Berkeley, *A Treatise Concerning the Principles of Human Knowledge* (Indianapolis: Bobbs-Merrill, 1970).

7. J. Locke, *An Essay Concerning Human Understanding* (New York: Dover, 1959).

8. D. Hume, *A Treatise of Human Nature*, ed. L. A. Selby-Bigge and P. H. Nidditch (Oxford: Oxford University Press, 1975).

9. I. Kant, *Critique of Practical Reason* (New York: Liberal Arts Press, 1956).

10. See, for example, W. James, *The Principles of Psychology* (New York: Dover, 1950).

11. A. Wheelis, *The Quest For Identity* (New York: Norton, 1958), p. 19.

12. Although many psychoanalytic writers disagree with this idea, Erikson and Wheelis are not totally alone in their thinking within the psycho-analytic community. See, for example, K. R. Eissler, "Notes on Problems of Technique in the Psychoanalytic Treatment of Adolescents," in *The Psychoanalytic Study of the Child*, 13:233–54 (New York: International Universities Press, 1958); or H. M. Lynd, *On Shame and the Search for Identity* (New York: Harcourt, Brace, 1958).

13. E. Erikson, *Identity and the Life Cycle; Selected Papers*, in Psychological Issues series (New York: International Universities Press, 1959).

14. Levita comments on this in *The Concept of Identity* (New York: Basic Books, 1967), p. 132

15. E. Erikson, *Identity: Youth and Crisis* (New York: Norton, 1968).

16. "Now the standard whereby conduct is judged is coming to be located in the group to which the individual adjusts." Wheelis, *The Quest for Identity*, p. 127.

17. Whether this kind of character identity is on the scene during the earli-est childhood superego Oedipal activity or during the more advanced ado-lescent superego activity (the latter appears to be Wheelis's view) is a point of contention among serious thinkers. But we won't enter that fray.

18. H. Fingarette, "Alcoholism and Self-Deception," in *Self-Deception and Self-Understanding*, ed. M. Martin (Lawrence, Kansas: University of Kansas Press, 1985), p. 54.

19. Ibid.

20. Object Relations Theory doesn't say this. I do. I believe that this is a handy conceptual device for organizing the overview developmental activity that Object Relations theorists talk about. Accordingly, I am offering the "prime directive" idea as a "friendly amendment" to the discussion.

21. The quotes are a bow to the fact that, as a pre-self, the infant really isn't a legitimate she or he yet. Nevertheless, we will use such pronouns as the easiest way to refer to the infant. Henceforth, though, I will drop the quotes.

22. Mahler, Pine, and Bergman, *Psychological Birth*, p. 111.

23. I use the quotes here and below to make the point that the infant really has no sense yet of internal and external. Those are more of our *adult perspective* conceptual distinctions. The closest the infant's version of, say, "external" comes to ours is (again in adult language) "that body over there which does things after I cry, the result of which is a relieving of my upset."

24. It's unclear exactly when the infant comes by a sense of *causality* about her cooing and so on and resulting parental behavior. Piaget investigates the matter, though. See J. Piaget, *The Origin of Intelligence in the Child* (London: Routledge & Kegan Paul, 1953); or J. Piaget, *The Child's Conception of Physical Causality*, trans. Marjorie Gabain (Totowa, NJ: Littlefield, Adams, 1965).

25. Actually, an *object representation* is an *idea* or *feeling* about either the self-object mother or a stand-in transition object associated with mother. And now that I've introduced the idea of the object representation, let me point out that Object Relations Theory has it that the infant relates both to transition objects and transition object representations. Actually, the main way object relations are categorized is in terms of relations with either real loved self-objects in the world or self-object representations which the infant internalizes as ideas about objects (e.g., the thought of mother). What we call "transition objects" can be either real objects in the world or simply ideas about real objects. But in both cases, they are proxy for some real, loved self-object that the infant "would rather" relate to if choices could effectively be made about such things. So the infant who uses her teddy bear or the pacifier or the blanket as a transition object "would rather" have her warm soft mother or her mother's nipple. She can't, so she settles for the bear or the pacifier. The infant who uses the fantasy about mother's warm breast to calm herself "would rather" have the real McCoy, but she settles for object representations that she has available.

26. According to Mahler's group, at this time there are also other self related processes going on. There are ego-*protecting* processes—processes that protect this newly unfolding ego from separation anxiety. And during that period from twenty-two to thirty-six months, there is a development not only of a self but also of a *sense* of self (one's sense of identity).

27. Mahler, Pine, and Bergman, *Psychological Birth*, p. 117.

28. Ibid., p. 99.

29. Jacobson, *The Self and the Object World*, p. 7.

30. Although the Object Relations literature is vast, I believe Meissner's *Internalization in Psychoanalysis* does a marvelous job of laying out the psychoanalytic distinctions between these process concepts. It is the inspiration for much of how I've come to think about these processes.

31. When this happens outside of the normal development of infancy, we are usually talking about symptoms of psychosis.

32. Meissner, *Internalization in Psychoanalysis*, pp. 18–19.

33. Indeed, we're all familiar with incorporative Shakespearean dialogues with the dead, in which a living character promises a dead one that he (the living) will carry out the dead one's wishes, perhaps even in the same way the dead one would have, as though the two characters were one and the same. The incorporated dead character is seen as acting *through* the living. In the literary context, we assign high drama to such behavior and sometimes high praise to the living character. In real life, however, this sort of thing borders on the crazy (seances notwithstanding).

34. Roy Schafer, *Aspects of Internalization* (New York: International Universities Press, 1968), p. 72.

35. Meissner, *Internalization in Psychoanalysis*, p. 37.

36. Why some introjects get projected out onto objects in the world while others remain wholly inside as introjects is a mystery. That is, *why* one introject would remain comfortably inside the person while another would not—but, rather, would need to be banished to another body or thing—is, as far as I know, not yet explained by psychoanalytic theory.

37. Mahler, Pine, and Bergman, *Psychological Birth*, p. 117.

38. Meissner, *Internalization in Psychoanalysis*, p. 20.

39. This usually occurs between eighteen and twenty-one months. See Mahler, Pine, and Bergman, *Psychological Birth*, p. 79.

40. An interesting thing that sometimes happens to pathologically negative introjects involves a kind of reversibility or polarization. If one introjects around feeling condemned, for example, one might also introject being the condemner. One might be the hurt and needy child *and* the powerful parent—a polar organization of introjects (Meissner, *Internalization in Psychoanalysis*, p. 32).

41. Now, although I haven't made much of it, I want to point out again that, in truth, people actually introject throughout life. None of us ever quite get to a place where we have fully stopped relating to objects. (See chapter 5 for a thoroughgoing discussion of this idea.) However, while such strands of introjection can be found blowing in the wind during virtually any part of a person's psychological development, what we've been discussing in this section should secure the idea that introjection does its most intense and important work during pre-self development.

42. Meissner repeatedly emphasizes this in *Internalization in Psychoanalysis*.

43. Meissner, *Internalization in Psychoanalysis*, p. 40. Although Meissner doesn't seem to dispute this non–object relational view of identification put forward by Modell, that doesn't keep Meissner from continuing to call identification a kind of object relation.

CHAPTER 3

1. I say "infant/child" because the Narcissism theorists claim that the central narcissistic dynamic processes unfold during the second thru sixth years.

2. Any of these situations are normal ones that, as I point out below, are required for an infant's healthful psychological development. However, on occasion, these kinds of situations become extreme and quite unhealthy, perhaps for the rest of the infant's life. In the extreme, it isn't unknown for such a person's self-esteem and sense of security to remain unfinished business. The individual has a damaged capacity for ever developing a sense of self-esteem. Indeed, the adult neuroses of narcissism occur when there are basic problems with self-acceptance in the infant or child due to a poor relationship with the self-object. See, for example, H. Kohut, *The Restoration of the Self* (New York: International Universities Press, 1977), pp. 93–94.

3. S. Freud, "On Narcissism," in *The Freud Reader*, ed. Peter Gay (New York: Norton, 1989), pp. 546–47.

4. S. Freud, "Beyond the Pleasure Principle," in *The Freud Reader*, ed. Peter Gay (New York: Norton, 1989), p. 618.

5. Of course, when Freud says that this is someone who "retains his libido in his ego," he means that the developing self qua ego is solely concerned with satisfying libidinal sexual impulses. And that supposedly goes on for the rest of self development, albeit in more and more disguised rational forms. All is sexual; all identity is of the body. My view will not mirror Freud's in this regard. I think he is right that, in the beginning, the infant/child is a body narcissist. But the infant/child's narcissism takes other forms as well. There is ego self to build beyond the body self. The idea that there is a nonbody related character self to be developed is one of the main themes we are developing in this book.

6. See, for example, O. F. Kernberg, *Borderline Conditions and Pathological Narcissism*; idem, *Object Relations Theory and Clinical Psychoanalysis* (New York: J. Aronson, 1976); H. Kohut, *Analysis of the Self*; idem, *Restoration of the Self*.

7. Kohut, *Analysis of the Self*, p. 25.

8. Consistent with what we saw in chapter 2 about Mahler's findings about infantile object relating, infants do not unfold any of this rudimentary self structure until the second year. The theme of grandiosity usually forms in the second, third, and fourth years. The other bipolar theme usually becomes ego structure in the fourth, fifth, and sixth years. (See Kohut, *Restoration of the Self*, p. 179.)

9. Kohut, *Restoration of the Self*, pp. 53–54, 242–43.

10. Actually, the philosophical literature about wanting is enormous, much too large to single out individuals for discussion. Instead, I will tailor a very general phenomenological characterization of wanting to fit the needs of our particular concerns.

11. Only later, after a full character identity has been forged, will this self be able to pick and choose for itself which of her desires are to be seriously owned. At this point, though, the rudimentary self is merely a thematic cluster of self representations about grandiosity.

12. Theorists point out that this confirmation leads to a cohesion and firmness of the developing self. Without self-object confirmation, self enfeeblement, regression, and fragmentation occur. See Kohut, *Restoration of the Self*, p. 137.

13. The immediate developmental antecedent to this state of affairs is the condition that what is desired by her isn't always desirable to the omnipotent parent. And since the narcissistic infant/child we're describing here eventually comes to introject the omnipotent-seeming parent's values (i.e., what the parent sees as desirable), she ends up having some things

become introjectively desirable to her even though these desirables conflict with some of her grandiose desires.

14. See Kohut, *Restoration of the Self*, p. 180.

15. She is, of course, once again laboring under a misconception. The idea that so long as she follows self representations of the parental ideal values, life will fall at her feet is unrealistic. In adult life, we would call such an attitude a kind of silly narcissism that is quite developmentally inappropriate (for the adult). In rudimentary infant selves, however, we understand it as being developmentally appropriate. We simply don't expect her to know any better.

16. Classical psychoanalytic theory has one way of describing this time; I have another. Classical theory is concerned with talking about ego and superego consolidation as well as a binding of libidinal impulses during latency. I have no doubt but that these tendencies are true of us then. My idea, however, is to characterize this period as the time when the individual melds a personality of introjects, narcissistic self representations, and identifications, where no one of these processes dominates the others as the central way of processing experience. There is a clear psychological movement away from being thoroughgoing object relators and narcissistic self representors, yet there is not enough of the right kinds of organization to the growing cluster of identificatory self representations to justify saying that one is significantly becoming a full character self.

CHAPTER 4

1. This last point is that while there are mixed self developmental states during latency, adolescence, and adulthood, the mixtures during latency are so plentiful and intense that the individual can't possibly be seen as a full-fledged character agency; whereas the mixtures during adolescence and adulthood are not plentiful or intense enough to detract from the fact that the individual has attained enough of a critical mass of identifications to be considered a full-fledged character.

2. I want to comment on an interesting side issue of this context. In personal correspondence, the psychoanalyst Fred Busch has expressed his belief that many of a person's adulthood identifications are what he calls "transition identifications." In this regard, Busch believes that we use people to get us over rough spots by identifying with some of their traits, these identifications constituting the appropriate kinds of self representational agency strength to get through difficult developmental transition periods. For example, a college student under extreme stress because of all the intellectual competition he faces from his classmates might identify for a while with the campus intellectual idol, copying all of his moves, mimicking all of his argumentational ploys, and so forth. A short period of identifying here might get him over the hump of competi-

tion, until his college years have ended. I think that Busch has got hold of an interesting idea. I believe he is right that adults and latency children do connect with people in order to effect transitions. However, I don't think this kind of connection is identificatory. There are no "transition identifications." There are only "transition *introjections*," pure and simple. I say this because in the kinds of transition cases Busch talks about, there is no attempt to take the other's traits and make them a part of oneself, even for a short transition period of time. Rather there is only the concern to *use*—that is, to borrow—the other's power. And that happens only with introjects that get a person through transition periods.

3. Beyond a certain age, a person's idolizing or hero worshipping seems out of place, inappropriate. We take it that by some time in a person's development, he ought to have enough character self anchored so that he needn't still be so involved in those partial infantile introjective activities or narcissistic self representing activities. He ought to be clear of being an idolizer or hero worshipper. Obviously, I'm just talking about tendencies here. Straying from the tendencies now and then doesn't normally harm anyone.

4. It's not clear that there is any grandiose mirroring component of infatuation.

5. All people have the capacity to be fans in this way. Children are especially prone to it because of their greater need to borrow agency power from those self-object substitutes (i.e., the celebrities). But adults are susceptible to being fans, too. Of course, *any* of us can *just* appreciate a celebrity for the special traits he possesses. We needn't also introject the empowered agency. But what I am saying is that, in fact, we often do. We just do feel the agency power we see (project) in the celebrity. And this experience of borrowed agency power allows us to do things we wouldn't have been able to do by ourselves as individual characters. We simply haven't yet developed an internal agency control over the kind of celebrity traits we would like to have.

6. That's not to say that *prior* to this time we might not have mirrored this perfection as grandiose self representing agency.

7. Consider an example. If I lose a beloved friend, I will probably grieve on both levels. More than likely, I had come to narcissistically introjectively need some things from my friend. Most of us do that with friendships, whether we are clear about it or not during the friendship. To that extent, the loss of my friend is a narcissistic loss for me. In my grief, I might wail and complain, "My God, what will become of me now that she's gone? Who will be strong for me? Who will make me laugh? How can I live without her?" Part of my self *was* the other person. And certainly if one *were totally* that other person, then one could *not* go on living without her. In such a case, I would have *introjected* some of her valued features. Had I gone developmentally beyond that relation with her and actually

identified with those traits and made them a part of myself while respecting them as also independent traits in her, the quality of my sense of loss would have been different. Generally speaking, it is because we most often come to identify with objects we previously had been introjectingly related to that we are finally able to survive most mourned losses.

8. See D. W. Winnicott, *The Maturational Process and the Facilitating Environment* (London: Hogarth Press, 1965); idem, *Playing and Reality*.

9. Clearly, Winnicott's concept of the "false self" could be enlarged to encompass also the workings of the narcissistically mirrored self representations that people sometimes confuse with real identificatory structure.

10. There is another way I have heard the confusion between identification and more primitive self processes take shape. It has to do with Busch's notion of "transition identification" again (see note 2). Busch suggests that while in earliest infancy we make our *lifelong* identifications (i.e., the psychoanalytic dogma again), at different points in adolescence and adulthood we form "transition identifications." Again, we supposedly form transition identifications with other people and certain of their traits that help us get through to the next stage of psychological development. As soon as we pass through the stage where we have needed the transition identification, the identification has outlived its purpose and we supposedly give it up. If identifying with father's rules helps us resolve our Oedipal conflicts, for example, then we identify with father until we no longer need to deal with the conflict. The identification then supposedly disappears from our repertoire.

While I find this idea intriguing, I think it is flawed. Not only can't I share the psychoanalytic aspect of this view, but once again I must say that what Busch calls "transition identifications" are, in fact, defensive transition introjections. The process that Busch *calls* "transition identifications" are not about what a person wants to be as a character but, instead, about how to defend losing the borrowed external agency one needs in order to get through the next stage of development.

CHAPTER 5

1. Meissner, *Internalization in Psychoanalysis*, p. 40.

2. "Identifying with buildings" aside, social critics bemoan the fact that so many of us identify with our material possessions, inanimate objects. They fear that we actually see ourselves *as* our possessions. In my view, this can't be right. For one thing, I seriously doubt that anyone thinks he literally is his TV set or stereo system. In fact, it is more likely that the *social status* that such material objects convey is what the individual identifies with, not the objects. One can perfectly well accept that an external material object has a social status attached to it and that because he possesses the object he will be associated with that status. He

will share that status with the object and all other people who own like objects. Secondly, in cases where the individual really is, in some bizarre fashion, literally seeing something such as his TV set as being part of himself and not as a distinct object of its own, I don't want to allow that the individual is really identifying with the TV. Rather, consistent with what we saw about object relations theory in chapters 2 and 4, I want to say that the individual is introjecting the TV object representation and collapsing it into part of his self representation. So when the social critic *says* of such a person that he *identifies with* his material possessions, the social critic is using "identifies" incorrectly. He should instead be talking about "'introjecting' material possessions."

3. There are yet other distinctions I should mention. Where, in the case of identificatory agency, the individual internalizes traits that she sees in the objective world and tests them against reality, in the case of narcissistic internal agency, the individual internalizes traits that are part of her grandiose fantasies and decidedly fails to test them against reality. Also, where, in the case of identificatory agency, the model for the identified-with traits is someone or something from the real world, in the case of narcissistic agency, the model is unrealistically seen as omnipotent. Clearly, the identificatory version of internal agency would tend to have a much greater survival value than the narcissistic version. And so the narcissistic version doesn't stay on the scene too long. For a while, it is a handy defensive organization of self representations—just as one begins to lose the total assistance of the all-powerful-seeming self-object agencies, one begins to believe that she has the same powers within herself— but she will soon learn that the real world simply won't bend to her grandiose self representational will. Her illusion of omnipotence lasts only until reality testing becomes functional. And then the organization of her self representations changes to the reality-based identificatory character processes.

4. A note about my terminology here. To this point in the chapter, I have been speaking about a person's "identifying with a model"—that is, identifying with a modeling object—and "identifying with that model's traits" as though they were distinct notions. I have done this as a way of emphasizing the fact that both the object model and its traits are important in appreciating the full phenomenon of identification. In fact, however, a person identifies with a model *to the extent* that he identifies with some traits of that model, that is, to the extent that he identifies with object traits. That being the case, when I talk about "identifying with object traits" in the following discussion, know that I am referring to both the model and its traits.

5. This idea might have practical implications. If a lawyer weren't able to imagine anything about what it would be like to be a criminal mind, then, among other things, we wouldn't expect that he could be sympathetic

with and identify with a criminal. Clearly, then, we wouldn't want this sort of attorney defending such a person, for although he might have the required lawyering skills, he would be lacking in the proper lawyering motivation. Of course, if one *were* able to imagine the criminal mind, that wouldn't mean that he *necessarily* then identified with it too. Criminal lawyers are at least that safe.

6. This point might also have practical implications. For if a criminal were not able to imagine what it would be like to be law abiding, then certainly he couldn't identify with being that way either. And if he couldn't identify with being that way, it would be unreasonable to expect him to make "law abidingness" part of his character. I suppose the upshot is that in such cases, a reasonable penal system needs to teach the criminal how to imagine what it would be like to be law abiding. Then, at least, there would be some hope for rehabilitation.

7. Bernard Williams, "Practical Necessity," in *Moral Luck*, p. 130.

8. Although ownership is a crucial condition of identification, I don't mean to imply that the four conditions 1, 2, 7, and 8 aren't also part of the full analysis of identification. I have already argued that they are necessary conditions. What I am arguing from this point forward is that it is the ownership aspect that is at the heart of the concept. It is the most important of the necessary conditions. This fact will come across in no uncertain terms in the remaining chapters. And, in fact, we will see that these other conditions all have something to do with ownership.

CHAPTER 6

1. Of course, if the causality of an identity network is "dense" enough, then even if a person chooses to embellish, affirm, or radically modify a caused trait, he will have a difficult time affecting things. His caused identity may succeed in holding his character down. He won't be able to become the person he wants to be.

2. Gerald Dworkin talks about this notion in his "Autonomy and Behavior Control." He distinguishes between the caused behaviors that a person identifies with and the caused behaviors that feel relatively alien to him. For Dworkin, the ones that a person reflectively chooses are the ones with which he identifies.

3. See Jerome Kagan, "The Concept of Identification," Vol. 65, No. 5 *Psychological Review* 65(5): 296–305.

4. See, for example, G. Dworkin, "Autonomy and Behavior Control"; H. Frankfurt, "Freedom of the Will and the Concept of a Person," *Journal of Philosophy* 68: 2–20; C. Taylor, *Human Agency and Language.*

5. So we hear Frankfurt say that such a person isn't simply a first-order causal "wanton"; rather, he is free because of his second-order reflective preferences. We hear Taylor say that a person isn't simply a first-order

"weak evaluator"; rather, he is free because of his second-order reflective preferences. And we hear Dworkin say that a person isn't simply a first-order "inauthentic" actor; rather, he is free because of his second-order reflective preferences. Different vocabulary, same conclusion.

6. In fact, this is part of the normal profile of a person in psychotherapy, especially psychoanalytic therapy. He is someone who has invested his introspective talents in living as much as possible on the reflective third level of consciousness, focusing his "analytic ear" inward to observe the life of his mind. This is where he feels the most free.

CHAPTER 7

1. We know now that Frankfurt, Taylor, and Dworkin are concerned only with second-order reflections about first-order states. We also know now that my notion of reflectiveness is wider than this—viz., I talk about third-order reflections as well. However, to insist on bringing this part of my notion into the discussion that we are going to have here would complicate matters beyond what is needed. So I will let the "third-order reflections" idea rest in our discussion. For purposes of uniformity and holding onto a manageable discussion—a discussion where we are all talking the same language without sacrificing anything that's crucial in principle to our respective views—I will limit myself to referring to second-order reflective states.

2. I mean this in exactly the same way that Herbert Marcuse talks about "multi-dimensional man." See his *One-Dimensional Man* (Boston: Beacon Press, 1964), chapter 1.

3. Friendship, for example, may be important to me in a certain context without my thinking at all about any moral ramifications my concerns might have, the moral critic's moralizing notwithstanding. I also often judge what to do in my daily life in terms of, say, how my decision will affect my pocketbook, without thinking about any moral ramifications. And if a moral philosopher shows that he can always raise some moral objections or other in any such practical context, that only establishes that morality is that moral philosopher's abiding everyday concern. It isn't always mine. Nor is it at every moment everyone else's either. Nor have I ever heard an argument for why anyone should think it has to be. It seems to me that Taylor is simply one of those people who has been smitten by the moral life. He and his fellow believers, in fact, always identify with the moral life. But that doesn't mean that the rest of us do or that we ought to if we want to be character selves.

4. C. Taylor, *Sources of the Self*, p. 4.

5. C. Taylor, "What Is Human Agency?", in *Human Agency and Language*, p. 35. Later he commits the same confusion: "What was said about the challengeability of evaluations applies with greatest force to our most

fundamental evaluations, those which provide the terms in which other less basic ones are made" (ibid., p. 39).

6. Ibid., p. 39.

7. C. Taylor, *Sources of the Self*, p. 27.

8. Ibid., p. 26.

9. C. Taylor, "What Is Human Agency?", in *Human Agency and Language*, pp. 41–42.

10. C. Taylor, *Sources of the Self*, p. 28.

11. Bernard Williams makes much the same point in *Moral Luck*, p. 132. In living out any of our life projects that are defined by nonmoral value standards, we are just as apt to be living a significant life as when we live out of projects of moral concern. These other projects need simply be based on images of what we see as the standard life of value, that standard sometimes being of moral import but more often of nonmoral import.

12. It might be helpful for me also to say at the outset what it does *not* mean. For one thing, "brutely chosen traits" does *not* mean a person's simple preferences that are found on a list of what his preferences are. That is, what a person prefers is not to be equated with a person's standard for the good life. That's because one can always ask about any of his preferences, "I prefer it, but is it good?" And if one can ask this, then preferences must be something different from the value standards by which we judge their goodness. So they are not the things I am saying get brutely chosen. Secondly, there's also something else that brutely chosen goods are *not*. They are *not* like what the philosopher John Rawls calls "primary goods." That is, the standards of good are not out there in the world to be accurately or inaccurately recognized by each of us if only we were fully rational about our self-interest. I don't believe that being fully rational or not has anything to do with what counts as "the good"; psychological identification does. My idea is that we create our standards of the good in an identificatory manner. We choose them; we don't recognize them for what they *already* are (or *would* appear to be, were we looking at them through the glasses of a fully rational being). See John Rawls, *Theory of Justice* (Cambridge: Harvard University Press, 1971).

13. Indeed, I believe that were one to insist that there was no such valuative positing, then whatever the fine detail of her thesis about character finally turned out to be, the general form would always have something of a homunculus lurking in the background. This homunculus would function slightly differently from the one we imagined in chapter 6. If there were no first valuative acts, then in living our life as value creatures, we would always be evaluating possible judgments and actions based on prior value commitments. That means that there would be a character there making those tough value evaluative decisions—a homunculus rationally calculating against a backdrop of prior values. We need only to ask about the origins of *that* homunculus's evaluational

value standards and we quickly see the infinite regress of homunculi that gets generated. So long as one insists that persons are always acting fundamentally as *evaluators* and never as *valuators*, she will be presupposing that there is a homunculus self doing the evaluating. And that reduces to absurdity. Evaluating can't be the value core of who a person is. Valuating must be.

14. This is the view often ascribed to Dostoevsky in *Notes from Underground*. See Walter Kaufmann, *Existentialism from Dostoevsky to Sartre* (New York: New American Library, 1965), pp. 52–82.

15. Taylor is so wildly inconsistent about his use of "evaluation" and its implications that to mention one more inconsistency here in the main body of our discussion might itself be confusing for the reader's understanding of the flow of the discussion. So let me use this footnote instead to isolate one more of his inconsistencies. After denying that people make radical choices, Taylor actually sometimes then talks about how people make "radical *re*-evaluations." These are radical choices about what will be our fundamental value standards for making subsequent evaluations. They are our inchoate evaluations. For Taylor, there still is no radical choosing that goes on *within* an evaluation. But now he acknowledges that there is radical choosing in re-evaluating the bases for our evaluations. See "What Is Human Agency?", in *Human Agency and Language*, p. 40. I agree with Taylor here. It is precisely what my thesis in this section has been about. However, it obviously doesn't square well with what Taylor has been saying elsewhere.

16. J.-P. Sartre, "Existentialism Is a Humanism," in *Existentialism from Dostoevsky to Sartre*, ed. W. Kaufmann (New York: New American Library, 1965), p. 350.

17. Milan Kundera has recently made a similar observation in his *Immortality* (New York: Grove Press, 1990), pp. 100–1. It is just a fact about how character functions that when we identify with something, we are prescribing that it should be a standard good for humankind. And because we think our value choices are good for everybody, we feel that it is our due to get those choices "acknowledged and loved" by everyone.

18. Actually, my view of autonomy is very close to Dworkin's view in his early paper "Autonomy and Behavior Control." He claims there that a person is autonomous to the extent that he makes a choice about a first-order state and that that choice is *his own*. Dworkin is quite explicit in saying that the autonomous person must identify with his choice, with his evaluation. Interestingly, Frankfurt mentions *in passing* that identification (i.e., making a first-order desire "one's own") is part of the scene for the autonomous person. However, when it comes to finally stating his *formal analysis*, he mysteriously leaves it out. So I will only claim similarity between what I am saying and what Dworkin says in his "Autonomy and Behavior Control" view. However, there are two differences between us.

One is that I would have autonomy extend to the realm of identifying with externally modeled traits as well as to first-order desires. The other is that my view requires that we understand the utter centrality of connecting the concepts of autonomy and identification—that is, that identification has to be understood quite clearly if it is to do any helpful duty in an analysis of autonomy. So my view insists on our fleshing out what it is to identify with one's choices. Having said all of this, though, I must admit that I am not certain that were Dworkin still endorsing his early view he would endorse it in the spirit of my notion of identification, because I don't really know what his notion would be about. Actually, I am more hopeful in the case of the "later Frankfurt" because of some things he says quite explicitly elsewhere ("Identification and Wholeheartedness," in *The Importance of What We Care About*) about the importance he places on identification. Be that as it may, he is all too silent about this in his early paper.

19. I can imagine someone having the view that an individual doesn't really evaluate unless, in choosing between first-order states, he chooses the one with which he most identifies. In this view, by definition, there is no such thing as a "forced" evaluation. Finally, I have no great difficulty with this idea. If someone were to insist on this understanding of the concept of evaluation, I would want only to repeat my contention that it isn't evaluating as such that is crucial to the evaluator's being autonomous. Rather, his autonomy is located in the identification condition of evaluation.

CHAPTER 8

1. And with childhood responsibility taking comes responsibility assessing from the rest of the world. When children finally turn the character corner, they are in a place where they are held more accountable for what they say and do. The playfulness associated with their being a character-in-process is gone. They have now become people to be reckoned with—people who hold themselves responsible for their character and thus now to be held fully responsible for their character by the rest of the world. Up until this point, they had been children held responsible for many things, but always with a caveat: "They are only children, so don't be too hard on them; don't expect too much of them." Now, however, this kind of excuse plea has evaporated.

2. People are inconsistent on this score. Sometimes we talk about children as though they were full identificatory beings; other times we see them as causal pretenders who still have a ways to go. This is a confusion that stems from people not having a vocabulary and a serious arena for talking about the importance of identification in a person's character life. I consider the discussion in this book a beginning toward remedying that situation.

3. Aristotle, *Nichomachean Ethics* (Oxford: Oxford University Press, 1963).
4. The person for whom it is an identified-with principle of morality obviously isn't sacrificing "being herself" by yielding to acting for the world's well-being. Rather, she sees the world's well-being as her well-being. She really does consider humanity her group of social identificatory choice, and she really identifies with a Utilitarian stance toward that group. Consistent with all of this, she wants to ruffle as few feathers as possible. In doing what it takes to let the world go around peaceably, she is simply opting to express herself through her identificatory moral concern rather than through other possible identifications. There is no sacrifice of herself here, though, for prudential reasons. She is merely being herself.
5. Understand that these character obligations are not the same as moral obligations. The sense of "ought" (and "right," "obligation," and "responsibility," too) here is morally colorless. Of course, a person might on occasion *additionally* feel a *moral* obligation to carry out a life choice she has made. But that is a secondary kind of obligation. It occurs only if a person first identifies with the moral life at all, that is, only if she first nonmorally obligates herself to pursuing a good life as defined by some image she has of morality.
6. We might refer to the latter as the "attitudinal component" of ownership and the former as the "legalistic component."
7. Irvin Yalom, *Love's Executioner* (New York: Harper Perennial, 1989), p. 85.
8. If a person *formerly* was the master of her body and has just recently *become* disabled, she probably will have some identificatory problems. She probably formerly identified herself with her bodily skills. And she probably still does. It is not easy to change identifications overnight. Such a person suffers the psychological turmoil that comes from just this sort of situation.
9. C. R. Snyder, "Collaborative Companions: The Relationship of Self-Deception and Excuse Making," in *Self-Deception and Self-Understanding*, ed. M. W. Martin (Lawrence, Kansas: University of Kansas Press, 1985).
10. Joan Didion seems to share Snyder's view. She says that self-respect encompasses knowing "the price of things...[of having] the courage of [one's] mistakes." Such a person has moral nerve, a certain toughness, character, where "character—the willingness to accept responsibility for one's own life—is the source from which self-respect springs." The point is, one can't talk about a person's taking responsibility for his life without acknowledging it as being a response to a troubled sense of self-respect. See J. Didion, "On Self-Respect," in *Vice and Virtue in Everyday Life*, ed. C. H. Sommers (New York: Harcourt Brace Jovanovich, 1985), pp. 411, 412.
11. The anthropologist Carlos Castaneda popularlized the notion of "personal power" in his "Don Juan" novels. His basic ideas are close to what I am

talking about here. However, as his vocabulary is so thoroughly different from mine, I won't try to make translations. I simply point the interested reader in the direction of Casteneda's writings.

12. Harry Frankfurt talks about this phenomenon in his "Identification and Wholeheartedness," in *The Importance of What We Care About.* Our points of focus, though, are different.

13. Again, that a person should feel these sorts of states doesn't then mean that others will agree with her values. Indeed, others may have value standards that run counter to hers. Or the social norms might deem her "wrong."

14. Of course, risk taking is commendable only within a certain range of behavior. For example, when people depend totally on luck to get them through the incalculable in life, we call them fools, even if the outcomes of what they do are often favorable. They certainly are very lucky, but also very impotent in the sense that they never have the opportunity to actively live out—control—their character. They don't get to exert the power of their character selves. They don't have the opportunity to stand up for their basic value projects. There's no sense of their having any self-responsibility to a character self. So they can never feel any self-esteem or regret about themselves. Indeed, there will be no sense of themselves in the first place to have these feelings about, other than their being "the totally lucky ones." These *total* risk takers live outside of the acceptable range of risk taking. They are without any entitlement for assessment or self-assessment as responsible characters.

CHAPTER 9

1. Recall that I alluded to this idea of "critical mass" in chapters 3 and 4.

2. This is the view of both J. Kagan, *The Nature of the Child* (New York: Basic Books, 1984); and D. Stern, The *Interpersonal World of the Infant* (New York: Basic Books, 1985).

3. There's another way of understanding my claim here. We can think of a person as being the *hero* of the personal history *stories* he lives and acts out everyday. Just as heroes are seen as people of ultimate importance, along with their stories, so, too, does each individual experience his life in terms of his being the ultimately important hero of his ultimately important story. We pay far more attention and place far more valued concern on what happens to us each moment than we place on what happens to others. That's because we see ourselves as the heroes. And so what I want to say is that when a person comes to identify with parts of what has been his personal history, he is really making them into parts of the story that defines what about his experience he considers significant. The parts of his personal history that he doesn't make into his story he simply understands as causal truths about himself.

4. For the remainder of this chapter, I will just use the expression "personal identity" to refer to "personal character identity." Remember, though, that both expressions are distinct from "personal causal identity."

5. Rorty, *Contingency, Irony, and Solidarity*, p. 73. Actually, Rorty's examples of possible final vocabulary terms don't really sound like character trait terms. He mentions terms such as "true," "good," "right," "beautiful," as well as "Christ," "England," "progressive," "rigorous," and more. Even though on the face of things such terms don't appear to be character trait terms, I believe they are. For example, the person for whom "Christ" is a final vocabulary term is a person who identifies with "having Christ in one's life" as an essential feature of the good life. The latter designates a bundle of Christian character traits (e.g., being humble, loving, devoted, and so on) that constitutes a standard of how the self functions when it is optimally being itself. A similar line of thinking can be run on the rest of Rorty's examples.

6. Ibid., pp. 73–74.

7. Rorty does, by the way, praise this way of being. It meets up to his image of what the citizen in the liberal society looks like.

8. Another way of making the point is to acknowledge that a person's final vocabulary terms are typically the terms of greatest emotional content for him.

9. I would point out here that the old existential saw that says "life is meaningless" falls apart under this analysis. Life has a plethora of meaning. Maybe not in some essentialist way—for example, that there is a God who confers purposes on us at birth or before—but there is a multitide of kinds of meaning that we make for ourselves just in the acts of being personal character identities. It happens by our deciding what degree of commitment we are going to affix to any particular character trait. When we have decided just *how* important maintaining a given ultimate valuation is, we have given our life that much more meaning.

10. Through its self-constituting valuations, character actually defines what it is "to be valuable" for a person.

11. Chanowitz and Langer, "Self-Protection and Self-Inception," *Self-Deception and Self-Understanding*, ed. M. W. Martin (Lawrence, KS: University of Kansas Press, 1985), p. 122. Of course, the general idea here is certainly not new. In fact it is quite popular among social psychologists. See, for example, O. E. Klapp, *Collective Search for Identity* (New York: Holt, Rinehart & Winston, 1969); K. J. Gergen, *The Saturated Self* (New York: Basic Books, 1991).

12. Chanowitz and Langer, "Self-Protection and Self-Inception," p. 125.

13. See Albert Carr, "Is Business Bluffing Ethical?", in *Contemporary Issues In Business Ethics*, ed. J. R. DesJardins and J. McCall (Belmont, CA: Wadsworth, 1990), pp. 21–28.

14. In chapters 7 and 8, I have already pointed out in passing that integrity is an issue in being a valuational character who takes responsibility for who he is. Now I would like to say a little more about this issue.

15. Of course, there are plenty of circumstances that vitiate the normal dictates under which people work. So, for example, sometimes people just don't seem to care about being themselves. Sometimes they deceive themselves about who they are. Sometimes they care very much about their inconsistencies but, for neurotic reasons, don't know how to get back to being themselves. And so on.

16. We will assume here that the new situation is still within the range of social contexts that require the person to try to act consistently on the relevant trait of character.

17. This is my answer to the age-old philosophical chestnut about calling a thing that changes over time (e.g., a person) "the same thing." That is, this is my way of dealing with the logical "problem of personal identity," the "problem of identification and reidentification" I mentioned in chapter 1.

CHAPTER 10

1. But while I agree that role models are useful in this way, I also want to point out that sometimes what we call "identification with role models" is really a mislabeling. It's not really identification that's going on. In fact, young people typically *introject* role models, even though we describe matters as identification. Consistent with what we saw in Part I about self development, the fact is that a young person normally internalizes the idea of what the role model does as a social player and takes it as a directive for how she herself must be in the social world. But she is really using a kind of *borrowed agency* from the model. She is acting like the model in an attempt to borrow his value standards for how her social life should proceed. She isn't creating her own standards and using them as the basis of her own social agency decisions. That's a portrait of introjective behavior. There's no self agency; there's just an internalized idea about how an external agency proceeds in various social contexts. This is just another case of running together legitimate contexts of identification with primitive self processes. Not all role modeling is about identification.

2. Regarding those people he neither feels nor wants to feel connected with in social camaraderie, either he does no calculations about how to be with them or else he just accepts what social convention dictates about appropriate behavior. In either case, he doesn't *take* responsibility for his relations with these neutral others, although we certainly might find him *acting* in a "responsible manner."

3. For some parents, parenting duties *are* forced. However, when that happens, those individuals aren't really *taking* responsibility for themselves. They are acting solely as causal social identity selves.

4. This doesn't mean that he will have no obligations to anyone who doesn't share his valuations. Surely, if he wants to get along in the world, he will figure out the obligations that overall social convention requires of him. But that is just "social forces having their causal way with him." He is certainly not defining himself in terms of the valuations inherent in these conventions. He isn't expressing the essential social him either. He is simply "getting along."

5. One can see a parallel here between what goes on during the narcissistic stage of psychological development and what goes on in social identificatory development. Social identification is, in fact, a developmental extension of narcissism in the sense that the infantile feeling of shared omnipotence with mother becomes the social identity's sense of specialness as a group member.

6. I wish to thank Sharon Feldman for helping me with the following idea. There is another parallel here between what goes on during infantile narcissism and what goes on in this social identity phenomenon. A distortion that sometimes occurs during infantile narcissism involves what is referred to as "a splitting off of the bad self," an idea we first mentioned in chapter 2. The narcissistic infant self experiences his mirrored self as two discrete kinds of self, one the omnipotent and good mirrored mother self, the other the omnipotent and bad mirrored mother self. The infant deals with experiencing himself as the bad self by projecting this bad self onto certain object relations. But he doesn't fully let go of the experience that he is bad in the same way that mother is. Unless one finally comes to terms with this sense of self-badness at some time in life—unless one comes to see it, understand it, and defeat it—one will always carry this around with him in the form of low self-esteem. It will rear its head at various points throughout life. It seems to me that social exclusion is a perverse developmental extension of this kind of narcissistic distortion. When a person tries to socially exclude others, it is as though he sees these nongroup (nongood mother-related) others as bad. That is, he may be projecting his sense of mother-mirrored badness out onto an object relation, viz., some other group. In this regard, a person's intensity at excluding people not of his own in-crowd is really the same intensity that he feels in owning a bad self.

7. The unspoken assumptions that children make in these examples are that having 20/20 vision is one of the shared value images of the social good life, that being white is another shared value image of the social good life, that being a boy is yet another of these shared value images, and so on.

8. I believe that this phenomenon is the kind of thing that Thomas Kuhn has in mind when he talks about "scientific revolutions" and the status beyond rational debate that scientific revolutions take on once they have become the scientific ground in a culture. (See T. Kuhn, *The Structure of*

Scientific Revolutions, (Chicago: University of Chicago Press, 1970).)
What I am arguing is that this isn't just true of scientific dogma, it is true
of all in-crowd behavior.

9. Of course, the situation presents all the more pain to the individual not
allowed into the in-crowd. Or, maybe worse, there is all the more pain for
the individual banished from the in-crowd. This person really has to
scurry around in order to redefine himself socially. Typically, he tries to
make some different crowd "better" than it was before and, so, worthy of
his membership. Or else he looks for an in-crowd that is acknowledged
by the popular culture to be even better than the in-crowd from which he
has just been banished. Look at what happened, for example, to many of
the political operatives who suffered public humiliation over the
Watergate scandal. They fell from their positions of political power; they
lost their in-crowd status. Fakery by some of these people aside, many of
them genuinely became religiously born again. They genuinely rekindled
their religious belief system. And this should not surprise anybody. For
what is this if not the finding of a new in-crowd that is generally acknowledged to be even more "in"—more "the given"—than the politically powerful? How can one be humiliated anymore when one is now running
with God and His crowd?

10. This should have a familiar ring. Remember that in chapter 6 I claimed
that our culture always places autonomy just beyond where the current
state of our conceptual scheme understands causes to influence our
behavior. With that idea in mind, part of what I am saying here is that
some people only feel autonomous as social beings when their social principles are just beyond what is currently acknowledged as "the given." For
them, "the *current* given" would seem to have the status of causal force.

11. In fact, I believe the newest version fighting for acceptance is the idea that
people are genuinely treated as equals only when they actually enjoy the
well-being that the rest of society enjoys. People are equals, for example,
only if they are guaranteed the same material wealth that the reigning
majority has enjoyed. And close on the heels of this view is the idea that
people are equals only if they are guaranteed the attainments of *all their
wants,* at least to the same extent that the reigning majority seems to have
its wants met.

12. We should recognize that a consequence of this variety of exclusionary
social identification is that it ends up pitting one group against the other
in the most insidious way. When the racial bigot defines himself as being
superior to black people, toleration becomes impossible. In being himself,
the bigot has to deny the value of the other.

13. The sociopath is the notable exception to feeling this pull.

14. P. Berger, "On the Obsolescence of the Concept of Honor," in *Vice and
Virtue in Everyday Life,* ed. C. H. Sommers (New York: Harcourt Brace
Jovanovich, 1985), p. 417.

15. Ibid., p. 421.
16. One might think of this angst as symptomatic of what might be called "social identity crisis."
17. Marcuse, *One-Dimensional Man*.

BIBLIOGRAPHY

Alford, C. F. 1988. *Narcissism: Socrates, the Frankfurt School, and Psychoanalytic Theory.* New Haven: Yale University Press.

Alston, W. P. 1972. "Emotion and Feeling." *In The Encyclopedia of Philosophy*, vols. 1 and 2. New York: Macmillan.

Aries, P. 1982. *The Hour of Our Death.* New York: Vintage Books.

Aristotle. 1941. *De Anima.* Trans. J. A. Smith. In *The Basic Works of Aristotle*, ed. R. McKeon, 535–603. New York: Random House.

———. 1963. *Nichomachean Ethics.* Oxford: Oxford University Press.

———. 1984. *Politics.* Revised Oxford translation. Princeton: Princeton University Press.

Axelrad, S., and L. M. Maury. 1951. "Identification as a Mechanism of Adaptation" In *Psychoanalysis and Culture: Essays in Honor of Geza Roheim*, ed. G. B. Wilbur and W. Muensterberger, 168–184. New York: International Universities Press.

Badaracco, J. 1989. *Leadership and the Quest for Integrity.* Boston: Harvard Business School Press.

Barratt, B. 1984. *Psychic Reality and Psychoanalytic Knowing.* Hillsdale, NJ: Analytic Press.

Berger, P. 1985. "On the Obsolescence of the Concept of Honor." In *Vice and Virtue in Everyday Life*, ed. C. H. Sommers, 415–426. New York: Harcourt Brace Jovanovich.

Bergmann, F. 1977. *On Being Free.* Notre Dame: Notre Dame University Press.

Berman, M. 1990. *Coming to Our Senses.* New York: Bantam.

Blum, L. 1988. "Gilligan and Kohlberg: Implications for Moral Theory." *Ethics* 98:472–91.

Brodey, W. M. 1965. "On the Dynamics of Narcissism." *Psychoanalytic Study of the Child* 20:165–93.

Brody, M. W., and V. P. Mahoney. 1964. "Introjection, Identification, and Incorporation." *International Journal of Psycho-Analysis* 45:57–63.

Busch, F. 1989. "The Compulsion to Repeat in Action: A Developmental Perspective." *International Journal of Psycho-Analysis* 70:535–44.

Butler, S. 1970. *Characters*. Cleveland: Press of Case Western Reserve University.

Carr, Albert. 1990. "Is Business Bluffing Ethical?" In *Contemporary Issues in Business Ethics*, ed. J. R. DesJardins and J. J. McCall, 21–28. 2d ed. Belmont, CA: Wadsworth.

Casteneda, C. 1972. *Journey to Ixtlan*. New York: Simon & Schuster.

Chanowitz, B., and E. J. Langer. 1985. "Self-Protection and Self-Inception." In *Self-Deception and Self-Understanding*, ed. M. W. Martin, 117–135. Lawrence, KS: University of Kansas Press.

Cooper, J. 1975. *Reason and Human Good in Aristotle*. Cambridge: Harvard University Press.

Davidson, D. 1980. *Essays on Actions and Events*. Oxford: Oxford University Press.

Dennett, D. 1984. *Elbow Room: The Varieties of Free Will Worth Wanting*. Cambridge: MIT Press.

———. 1988. "Why Everyone Is a Novelist." *Times Literary Supplement* 4(459):1016+. 459.

Dent, N. J. H. 1984. *The Moral Psychology of the Virtues.* Cambridge: Cambridge University Press.

Descartes, R. 1951. *Meditations.* Trans. L. J. Lafleur. New York: Library of Liberal Arts.

Dewey, J. 1960. *Theory of the Moral Life.* New York: Holt, Rinehart & Winston.

Didion, J. 1985. "On Self-Respect." In *Vice and Virtue in Everyday Life,* ed. C. H. Sommers, 409–414. New York: Harcourt Brace Jovanovich.

D'Souza, D. 1991. *Illiberal Education: The Politics of Race and Sex on Campus.* New York: The Free Press.

Dworkin, G. 1976. "Autonomy and Behavior Control." *Hastings Center Report* (Feb): 6:23–28.

———. 1988. *The Theory and Practice of Autonomy.* Cambridge: Cambridge University Press.

Eissler, K. R. 1958. "Notes on Problems of Technique in the Psychoanalytic Treatment of Adolescents." In *Psychoanalytic Study of the Child,* 13:223–54.

Erikson, E. H. 1959. *Identity and the Life Cycle; Selected Papers.* Psychological Issues series. New York: International Universities Press.

———. 1963. *Childhood and Society.* New York: Norton.

———. 1964. *Insight and Responsibility.* New York: Norton.

———. 1968. *Identity: Youth and Crisis.* New York: Norton.

Erwin, E. 1978. *Behavior Therapy.* New York: Cambridge University Press.

Eysenck, H. 1965. *Fact and Fiction in Psychology.* New York: Penguin.

————. 1970. *Handbook of Abnormal Psychology*. New York: Pitman & Sons.

Feinberg, J. 1970. *Doing and Deserving: Essays in the Theory of Responsibility*. Princeton: Princeton University Press.

Fenichel, O. 1926. "Identification." In *The Collected Papers of Otto Fenichel*, first series, 97–112. New York: Norton.

Festinger, L. 1965. *Theory of Cognitive Dissonance*. Stanford: Stanford University Press.

Fine, R. 1986. *Narcissism, the Self, and Society*. New York: Columbia University Press.

Fingarette, H. 1967. *On Responsibility*. New York: Basic Books.

————. 1985. "Alcoholism and Self-Deception." In *Self-Deception and Self-Understanding*, ed. M. Martin, 52–67. Lawrence, KS: University of Kansas Press.

Flanagan, O. 1991. *Varieties of Moral Personality: Ethics and Psychological Realism*. Cambridge: Harvard University Press.

Flanagan, O., and A. O. Rorty, eds. 1990. *Identity, Character, and Morality*. Cambridge: MIT Press.

Flavell, J. H. 1963. *The Developmental Psychology of Jean Piaget*. Princeton, NJ: Van Nostrand.

Fliess, R. 1953. "Countertransference and Counteridentification." *Journal of the American Psychoanalytic Association* 1:268–84.

Foot, P. 1978. *Virtues and Vices*. Berkeley: University of California Press.

Frankfurt, H. 1971. "Freedom of the Will and the Concept of a Person." *Journal of Philosophy* 68:5–20.

————. 1988. *The Importance of What We Care About*. Cambridge: Cambridge University Press.

Freud, S. 1915. "Observations On Transference-Love." In J. Strachey (Ed. and Trans.), *The Standard Edition of the Complete Psychological Works of Sigmund Freud* (Vol. 12, pp. 157–171). London: Hogarth Press.

———. 1917. "Mourning and Melancholia." In J. Strachey (Ed. and Trans.), *The Standard Edition of the Complete Psychological Works of Sigmund Freud* (Vol. 14, pp. 237–258). London: Hogarth Press.

———. 1923. "The Ego and the Id." In J. Strachey (Ed. and Trans.), *The Standard Edition of the Complete Psychological Works of Sigmund Freud* (Vol. 19, pp. 1–66). London: Hogarth Press.

———. 1924. "The Dissolution of the Oedipus Complex." In J. Strachey (Ed. and Trans.), *The Standard Edition of the Complete Psychological Works of Sigmund Freud* (Vol. 19, pp. 171–179). London: Hogarth Press.

———. 1940. "An Outline of Psycho-Analysis." In J. Strachey (Ed. and Trans.), *The Standard Edition of the Complete Psychological Works of Sigmund Freud* (Vol. 23, pp. 137–207). London: Hogarth Press.

———. 1989a. "Beyond the Pleasure Principle." In *The Freud Reader*, ed. P. Gay, 594–626. New York: Norton.

———. 1989b. "On Narcissism." In *The Freud Reader*, ed. P. Gay, 545–62. New York: Norton.

Fuchs, S. H. 1937. "On Introjection." *International Journal of Psycho-Analysis* 18:269–93.

Gaddini, E. 1969. "On Imitation." *International Journal of Psycho-Analysis* 50:475–84.

Gautier, D. 1986. *Morals by Agreement.* Oxford: Oxford University Press.

Gay, P., ed. 1989. *The Freud Reader.* New York: Norton.

Gazzaniga, M. S. 1983. "Right Hemisphere Language Following Brain Bisection: A Twenty-Year Perspective." *American Psychologist* 38:525–36.

Gergen, K. J. 1991. *The Saturated Self.* New York: Basic Books.

Gilligan, C. 1982. *In a Different Voice: Psychological Theory and Women's Development.* Cambridge: Harvard University Press.

Glover, J. 1988. *I: The Philosophy and Psychology of Personal Identity.* New York: Penguin.

Goffman, E. 1969. *Where the Action Is: Three Essays.* London: Allen Lane.

———. 1973. *The Presentation of Self in Everyday Life.* Woodstock, NY: Overlook Press.

Goldberg, A., ed. 1980. *Advances in Self Psychology.* New York: International Universities Press.

Greenson, R. R. 1954. "The Struggle against Identification." *Journal of the American Psychoanalytic Association* 2:200–17.

———. 1960. "Empathy and Its Vicissitudes." *International Journal of Psycho-Analysis* 41:418–24.

———. 1967. *The Technique and Practice of Psychoanalysis.* Vol. 1. New York: International Universities Press.

Hanly, C. M. T. 1970. *Psychoanalysis and Philosophy.* New York: International Universities Press.

———. 1992. *The Problem of Truth in Applied Psychoanalysis.* New York: Guilford Press.

Hare, R. M. 1952. *The Language of Morals.* Oxford: Clarendon Press.

———. 1963. *Freedom and Reason.* Oxford: Oxford University Press.

Harris, M. 1990. *Speed*. New York: Donald I. Fine.

Hartmann, H. 1960. *Psychoanalysis and Moral Values*. New York: International Universities Press.

―――. 1964. *Essays on Ego Psychology*. New York: International Universities Press.

Heidegger, M. 1962. *Being and Time*. London: SCM Press.

Hendrick, I. 1951. "Early Development of the Ego: Identification in Infancy." *Psychoanalytic Quarterly* 20:44–61.

"Henri Wallon: His World, His Work." 1972. Special issue. *International Journal of Mental Health* 1(4).

Hofstadter, D. R. 1982. "Prelude...Ant Fugue." In *The Mind's Eye*. New York: Bantam.

Hudson, S. 1986. *Human Character and Morality*. Boston: Routledge & Kegan Paul.

Hume, D. 1975. *Enquiries Concerning Human Understanding and Concerning the Principles of Morals*, ed. L. A. Selby-Bigge. [1777.] Oxford: Oxford University Press.

―――. 1975. *A Treatise of Human Nature*, ed. L. A. Selby-Bigge and P. H. Nidditch. Oxford: Oxford University Press.

Ibsen, H. 1961. *Little Eyolf*. In *"The Wild Duck" and Other Plays by Henrik Ibsen*. New York: Modern Library.

Jacobson, E. 1964. *The Self and the Object World*. New York: International Universities Press.

Jacoby, M. 1990. *Individuation and Narcissism: The Psychology of the Self in Jung and Kohut*. Trans. M. Gubitz and F. O'Kane. London: Routledge.

James, W. 1950. *The Principles of Psychology*. [1890]. New York: Dover.

————. 1974. *Essays on Faith and Morals*. New York: New American Library.

————. 1979. *The Will to Believe and Other Essays in Popular Philosophy*. [1897.] Cambridge: Harvard University Press.

————. 1983. *Talks to Teachers on Psychology and to Students on Some of Life's Ideals*. [1899.] Cambridge: Harvard University Press.

Jaynes, J. 1990. *The Origin of Consciousness in the Breakdown of the Bicameral Mind*. Boston: Houghton Mifflin.

Kagan, J. 1958. "The Concept of Identification." *Psychological Review* 65:296–305.

————. 1984. *The Nature of the Child*. New York: Basic Books.

Kamler, H. 1983. *Communication: Sharing Our Stories of Experience*. Seattle: Psychological Press.

————. 1984. *Character and Personal Values*. Johnson City, TN: Institute of Social Sciences and Arts.

Kant, I. 1956. *Critique of Practical Reason*. [1788.] Indianapolis: Bobbs-Merrill.

Kaufmann, W. 1965. *Existentialism from Dostoevsky to Sartre*. New York: New American Library.

Kernberg, O. F. 1970. "Factors in the Psychoanalytic Treatment of Narcissistic Personalities." *Journal of the American Psychoanalytic Association* 18:51–85.

————. 1974. "Further Contributions to the Treatment of Narcissistic Personalities." *International Journal of Psycho-Analysis* 55:215–40.

————. 1975. *Borderline Conditions and Pathological Narcissism*. New York: J. Aronson.

———. 1976. *Object Relations Theory and Clinical Psychoanalysis.* New York: J. Aronson.

Khan, M. M. R. 1972. "The Finding and Becoming of Self." *International Journal of Psychoanalytic Psychotherapy* 1(1):97–111.

Klapp, O. E. 1969. *Collective Search for Identity.* New York: Holt, Rinehart & Winston.

Klein, M. 1932. *The Psychoanalysis of Children.* New York: Grove Press.

Knight, R. P. 1940. "Introjection, Projection, and Identification." *Psychoanalytic Quarterly* 9:334–41.

Kohlberg, L. 1981. *The Philosophy of Moral Development.* San Francisco: Harper & Row.

Kohut, H. 1971. *The Analysis of the Self.* New York: International Universities Press.

———. 1977. *The Restoration of the Self.* New York: International Universities Press.

Konner, M. 1982. *The Tangled Wing.* New York: Holt, Rinehart & Winston.

Kubler-Ross, E. 1972. *On Death and Dying.* New York: Macmillan.

———. 1975. *Death: The Final Stage of Growth.* Englewood Cliffs, NJ: Prentice-Hall.

Kuhn, T. S. 1970. *The Structure of Scientific Revolutions.* 2d. ed. Chicago: University of Chicago Press.

Kundera, M. 1990. *Immortality.* New York: Grove Press.

Lacan, J. 1977. "The Mirror Stage as Formative of the Function of the I as Revealed in Psychoanalytic Experience." In *Ecrits: A Selection,* trans. A. Sheridan. 1–7. New York: Norton.

Leibniz, G. 1898. *The Monadology and Other Philosophical Writings*. Oxford: Clarendon Press.

Levin, D. C. 1969. "The Self: A Contribution to Its Place in Theory and Technique." *International Journal of Psycho-Analysis* 50:41–51.

Levita, D. J. de. 1967. *The Concept of Identity*. New York: Basic Books.

Locke, J. 1959. *An Essay Concerning Human Understanding*. New York: Dover.

Lynd, H. M. 1958. *On Shame and the Search for Identity*. New York: Harcourt, Brace.

MacIntyre, A. 1981. *After Virtue: A Study in Moral Theory*. Notre Dame: University of Notre Dame Press.

McLaughlin, B., and A. Rorty. 1988. *Perspectives on Self-Deception*. Berkeley: University of California Press.

Mahler, M. S. 1968. *On Human Symbiosis and the Vicissitudes of Individuation*. New York: International Universities Press.

Mahler, M. S., F. Pine, and A. Bergman. 1975. *The Psychological Birth of the Human Infant*. New York: Basic Books.

Marcuse, H. 1964. *One-Dimensional Man*. Boston: Beacon Press.

Martin, M. W., ed.. 1985. *Self-Deception and Self-Understanding*. Lawrence, KS: University Press of Kansas.

Massey, S. J. 1983. "Is Self-respect a Moral or a Psychological Concept?," *Ethics*. 93:246–61.

Meissner, W. W. 1981. *Internalization in Psychoanalysis*. New York: International Universities Press.

Merleau-Ponty, M. 1964. "The Child's Relations with Others." Trans. W. Cobb. In *The Primacy of Perception*, ed. J. Edie, 96–155. Evanston, IL: Northwestern University Press.

Modell, A. 1968. *Object Love and Reality*. New York: International Universities Press.

Muller, R. J. 1987. *The Marginal Self: An Existential Inquiry into Narcissism*. Atlantic Highlands, NJ: Humanities Press International.

Nagel, T. 1979a. "Moral Luck." In *Mortal Questions*, 24–38. Cambridge: Cambridge University Press.

———. 1979b. "The Fragmentation of Value." In *Mortal Questions*, 128–141.. Cambridge: Cambridge University Press.

Nietzsche, F. 1966. *Beyond Good and Evil*. Trans. W. Kaufmann. New York: Vintage Books.

Nozick, R. 1981. *Philosophical Explanations*. New York: Oxford University Press.

———. 1985. "Ethical Pull." In *Vice and Virtue in Everyday Life*, ed. C. H. Sommers, 400–408. New York: Harcourt, Brace, Jovanovich.

O'Neill, J. 1986. "The Specular Body: Merleau-Ponty and Lacan on Infant Self and Other." *Synthese* 66:201–18.

Parfit, D. 1984. *Reasons and Persons*. New York: Oxford University Press.

Perry, J. 1975. *Personal Identity*. Berkeley: University of California Press.

———. 1976. "The Importance of Being Identical." In *The Identities of Persons*, ed. A. Rorty, 67–90. Los Angeles: University of California Press.

Peters, R. S. 1966. "Moral Education and the Psychology of Character." In *Philosophy and Education: Modern Readings*, ed. I. Scheffler, 263–286. Boston: Allyn & Bacon.

Piaget, J. 1932. *The Moral Judgment of the Child*. New York: The Free Press.

————. 1953. *The Origin of Intelligence in the Child*. London: Routledge & Kegan Paul.

————. 1965. *The Child's Conception of Physical Causality*. Trans. Marjorie Gabain. Totowa, NJ: Littlefield, Adams.

Pollock, G. 1993. *Pivotal Papers on Identification*. New York: International Universities Press.

Potok, C. 1986. *Tobiasse: Artist in Exile*. New York: Rizzoli.

Quinton, A. 1985. "Character and Culture." In *Vice and Virtue in Everyday Life*, ed. C. H. Sommers, 437–48. New York: Harcourt Brace Jovanovich.

Rawls, J. 1971. *A Theory of Justice*. Cambridge: Harvard University Press.

Rey, G. 1976. "Survival." In *The Identities of Persons*, ed. A. Rorty, 41–66. Los Angeles: University of California Press.

Rorty, A. O., ed. 1976. *The Identities of Persons*. Los Angeles: University of California Press.

————. 1988. *Mind in Action: Essays in the Philosophy of Mind*. Boston: Beacon Press.

Rorty, R. 1989. *Contingency, Irony, and Solidarity*. New York: Cambridge University Press.

Sanford, N. 1955. "The Dynamics of Identification." *Psychological Review* 62:106–118.

Sartre, J.-P. 1956. *Being and Nothingness*. Trans. H. Barnes. New York: Philosophical Library.

————. 1965. "Existentialism Is a Humanism." In *Existentialism from Dostoevsky to Sartre*, ed. W. Kaufmann, 345–369. New York: New American Library.

Scarry, E. 1985. *The Body in Pain*. New York: Oxford University Press.

Schafer, R. 1959. "Generative Empathy in the Treatment Situation." *Psychoanalytic Quarterly* 28:342–73.

———. 1968. *Aspects of Internalization*. New York: International Universities Press.

———. 1976. *A New Language for Psychoanalysis*. New Haven: Yale University Press.

Scheffler, S. 1982. *The Rejection of Consequentialism*. New York: Oxford University Press.

Sherman, N. 1989. *The Fabric of Character*. Oxford: Oxford University Press.

Shoemaker, S. 1963. *Self-Knowledge and Self-Identity*. Ithaca: Cornell University Press.

Singer, I. 1992. *Meaning in Life: The Creation of Value*. New York: The Free Press.

Smart, J. J. C., and B. Williams. 1973. *Utilitarianism: For and Against*. Cambridge: Cambridge University Press.

Snyder, C. R. 1985. "Collaborative Companions: The Relationship of Self-Deception and Excuse Making." In *Self-Deception and Self-Understanding*, ed. M. W. Martin, 35–51. Lawrence, KS: University of Kansas Press.

Sommers, C. H., ed. 1985. *Vice and Virtue in Everyday Life*. New York: Harcourt Brace Jovanovich.

Southwood, H. M. 1973. "The Origin of Self-Awareness and Ego Behavior." *International Journal of Psycho-Analysis* 54: 235–239.

Stern, D. 1985. *The Interpersonal World of the Infant*. New York: Basic Books.

Sutherland, J. D. 1980. "The British Object Relations Theorists: Balint, Winnicott, Fairbairn, Guntrip." *Journal of the American Psychoanalytic Association* 28(4):829–60.

Taylor, C. 1985a. *Human Agency and Language: Philosophical Papers*. Vol. 1. Cambridge: Cambridge University Press.

———. 1985b. *Philosophy and Human Sciences: Philosophical Papers*. Vol. 2. Cambridge: Cambridge University Press.

———. 1989. *Sources of the Self: The Making of Modern Identity*. Cambridge: Harvard University Press.

Taylor, R. 1981. "The Meaning of Human Existence." In *Values in Conflict: Life, Liberty, and the Rule of Law*, ed. Burton M. Leiser, 3–27. New York: Macmillan.

———. 1984. *Good and Evil: A New Direction*. Buffalo: Prometheus.

Tenzer, A. 1984. "Piaget and Psychoanalysis: II. The Problem of Working Through." *Contemporary Psychoanalysis* 20:421–36.

Theophrastus. 1967. *Characters*. Baltimore: Penguin.

Thomas, L. 1989. *Living Morally: A Psychology of Moral Character*. Philadelphia: Temple University Press.

Watson, G., ed. 1982. *Free Will*. Oxford: Oxford University Press.

Westen, D. 1985. *Self and Society: Narcissism, Collectivism, and the Development of Morals*. Cambridge: Cambridge University Press.

Wheelis, A. 1958. *The Quest for Identity*. New York: Norton.

———. 1973. *How People Change*. New York: Harper & Row.

Wiesel, E. 1985. *A Beggar in Jerusalem*. New York: Schocken.

Wiggins, D. 1971. *Identity and Spatio-temporal Continuity*. Oxford: Blackwell.

Williams, B. 1976. *Problems of the Self*. Cambridge: Cambridge University Press.

————. 1981. *Moral Luck: Philosophical Papers*. Cambridge: Cambridge University Press.

————. 1985. *Ethics and the Limits of Philosophy*. Cambridge: Harvard University Press.

Winnicott, D. W. 1965. *The Maturational Process and the Facilitating Environment*. London: Hogarth Press.

————. 1971. *Playing and Reality*. New York: Basic Books.

Wolfe, T. 1987. *The Bonfire of the Vanities*. New York: Farrar, Straus, Giroux.

Yalom, I. 1989. *Love's Executioner*. New York: Harper Perennial.

Zetzel, E. R., and W. W. and Meissner. 1973. *Basic Concepts of Psychoanalytic Psychiatry*. New York: Basic Books.

INDEX

adultomorphism 15, 34, 61
aggressiveness 47, 149
Aristotle 29, 30, 167, 187, 199
autonomy (*see also* free will), 8, 9, 200, 285; and identification, 9, 12, 200, 285; and identificatory valuation, 185-186; and reflective consciousness, 9, 156-161, 183-186; and tests for free choice, 215-216, 280, 281; and tolerance of separateness of objects, 54, 119

Berger, Peter 293–297
Bermann, Martin 14
bipolar state 61, 62, 68
borrowing agency 46, 95, 99, 108, 118, 301
brute choosing 171, 216, 217
brute valuation 169, 175, 181, 198, 222

caprice 216
cathexis 39, 42, 56, 83, 91, 92
causal explanation 196, 197
causal identity: and automatic choices, 140-146, 149; and first-order states, 156-157; and identifications, 123-125, 168-169; and identity crisis, 260; and its traits, 106, 113-116, 135; and personal identity, 223-226, 229, 230; and reflective choosing, 136; and social identity, 263-268, 292, 296-298; vs. character identity, 106, 127-131, 134, 197, 237
causal self 20; and autonomy, 157, and choosing character, 116, 225; and firstorder states, 163, 185; and identification, 160, 285; and personal identity, 230; and

primitive processes, 106, 108, 137; and social identity, 263, 265, 266, 267, 271
celebration: introjective/identificatory states, 95-96; of the self, 212, 220
celebrity 86, 95-96, 101
Chanowitz, B. 247–249
character justice 206, 207
character structure 136, 150, 152, 153, 161
character traits 1, 87; and celebrity, 96; and conflicting identifications, 249; and inappropriate identity choices, 174-176; and meaning, 240; and obligations, 200; and ownership, 135, 160; and reflective choice, 143, 147, 151-156, 208, 215, 257; and standards of the good life, 192; and taking responsibility, 209
character valuations: always good, 187-192; as final justifications for action 198-200; change slowly, 260-261; confused for moral commitment, 167; found in hierarchies, 240–243; having ultimate valuation, 179-183; requiring consistency, 245-252; with conviction, 212; without necessity, 173-176
choice point 174
compassion 132, 134
confidence 209–213, 215
consistency: and emotions, 172, and cognitions, 172, 247; as justification for actions, 199-200; defining personal identity uniqueness, 245-252, 260; for responsible characters, 23, 198, 204–209; of our character choices, 138, 153, 168-169, 172, 183

345